Great Generals
of the Napoleonic Wars
and their Battles
1805 – 1815

GREAT GENERALS OF THE NAPOLEONIC WARS AND THEIR BATTLES

1805 – 1815

by

Andrew Uffindell

SPELLMOUNT
Staplehurst

British Library Cataloguing in Publication Data:
A catalogue record for this book is available
from the British Library

Copyright © Andrew Uffindell 2003
Maps © Spellmount Ltd 2003

ISBN 1-86227-177-1

First published in the UK in 2003 by
Spellmount Limited
The Old Rectory
Staplehurst
Kent TN12 0AZ

Tel: 01580 893730
Fax: 01580 893731
E-mail: enquiries@spellmount.com
Website: www.spellmount.com

1 3 5 7 9 8 6 4 2

Typeset in Palatino by MATS, Southend-on-Sea, Essex
Printed in Great Britain by
T. J. International Ltd, Padstow, Cornwall

Contents

Author's Note

This book re-examines the careers, personalities and battles of twelve great generals of the Napoleonic wars. My objective in comparing these extraordinary men is to provide an insight into the meaning of military greatness in that age of heroes.

The twelve soldiers I have chosen are very much a personal selection and inevitably omit many fine commanders. I have deliberately not featured Napoleon's marshals, partly because they are well known and partly because only three (Davout, Suchet and Massena) have a real claim to military greatness. In their place, I have selected two French generals, Lasalle and Eugène de Beauharnais, who deserve greater prominence.

Russia at the time used the Julian calendar, which in the eighteenth century was eleven days behind the Gregorian calendar followed by western Europe. In the nineteenth century, it was twelve days behind. All dates in this book conform with the Gregorian calendar.

Acknowledgements

I wish to record my gratitude to the many people who helped with this and my previous books, particularly Jamie Wilson and the Spellmount staff; Lucien Gerke; Lionel Leventhal; Guy and Janine Delvaux; Philip Offord; Michael Corum; Rogan Faith; Mark Le Fanu of the Society of Authors; my family; and the staff of the British, Bodleian and Berkhamsted Libraries and of the National Army Museum. I am grateful to David Grant for editing this book and to Derek Stone for drawing the thirty-one superb maps. Those illustrations that are annotated 'ASKB' are reproduced courtesy of the Anne S.K. Brown Military Collection, Brown University, Rhode Island, USA, and I am indebted to Peter Harrington for locating and supplying them.

List of Maps

Key to Maps

■	French
□	Allies
□	Infantry
◨	Cavalry
□ (I)	Company
□ (I I)	Battalion
□ (I I I)	Regiment
□ (X)	Brigade
□ (XX)	Division
□ (XXX)	Corps
□ (XXXX)	Army

Introduction

Even today, the Napoleonic wars hold an irresistible allure, largely because nowhere are the pages of military history more studded with legendary commanders.

The explanation for this extraordinary crop of generals lies partly in the sheer length and intensity of the struggle, but also in the greater scope it offered for bold, imaginative and skilful generalship. Commanders did not have to experiment with new technology, for the weapons and means of communication remained essentially the same as those used fifty years earlier. But more dynamic strategies and tactics had been developed by both theorists and commanders such as Frederick the Great. Improved roads allowed generals to wage faster and more flexible warfare, while increased cultivation of land enabled armies to rely more heavily on requisitioning and marauding. This in turn made battles more frequent, for commanders were under pressure to obtain a decisive victory before their armies had to disperse again to seek food and forage. A growth in Europe's population also made casualties more affordable and weapons and equipment became available in greater quantities.

These liberating developments were exploited ruthlessly in France following the outbreak of the Revolution and gave Napoleon and his generals such an edge over their opponents that they were able to inflict crushing defeats in the years 1805–7. Their strategy and tactics were more flexible and aggressive and he used more sophisticated methods of command and control, including permanent higher formations, namely the brigade, division and corps, which made French armies more robust and responsive to sudden developments.

This imbalance was reduced as Napoleon's enemies reformed their Armies and imitated some of his methods. They also created stronger and more comprehensive coalitions to provide the numbers necessary to meet him on favourable terms.[1] At the same time, tactics became blunter, since heavy casualties had reduced the overall quality of troops in most Armies.

Attritional battles and prolonged campaigns therefore became more common from 1809 onwards, yet even indecisive battles such as Eylau and Borodino were epic actions in which many subordinate generals added to their lustre. And it was still occasionally possible for a commander to win a battle through skill, boldness and manoeuvre, as Napoleon did at Dresden in 1813 or at Champaubert and Vauchamps a year later. Even in these later years, the sheer geographical extent of the wars created local imbalances that skilful generals were swift to exploit. In the Iberian Peninsula, for example, the often mountainous and infertile terrain gave Wellington's small but well supplied army an edge over the more numerous French forces, which repeatedly had to disperse to hold down the country and obtain supplies.

Commanders of this era also enjoyed considerable freedom in the conduct of their operations. Communications were generally limited to the speed of a ship or horse and this limited interference from governments at home. Generals in the field had to be given broad directives rather than detailed orders. The slowness of communications also enabled commanders to process the limited information that reached them either on their own or with the help of a few staff officers and thus to gain a more immediate feel for what was happening on the ground.

Armies were still small enough for a commander to exercise a highly personal command style. He could usually see most, if not all, of a battle-field from the vantage point of a windmill, a church tower, or a prominent hill and he could still intervene in the front line rather than being forced to command by remote control from several miles in the rear. Exceptions did occur, particularly in the great campaigns of 1812–13 in Russia and central Europe, where the numbers involved made for large battlefields. At Leipzig, for example, the allies fielded 360,000 men on a circular battle-front of up to twenty-two miles. But on most battlefields, the numbers of troops in an army ranged from 30,000 to 150,000 and, because of the inaccuracy of their firearms, they were packed into tight formations to fire in volleys. As a result, the front lines in a battle were rarely more than seven miles long and often only three or four.

Inaccurate weapons reduced the risk of generals being picked off by enemy marksmen, for the smoothbore flintlock muskets carried by the vast majority of infantrymen were accurate to barely seventy-five yards. Commanders still had to brave the general hail of fire between the two sides, but the risk although high was acceptable and so they could still play the hero in the style of Alexander the Great or King Henry V to inspire their men. They could still charge into battle to seek glory, without inevitably finding death. For practically the last time in history, therefore, it was possible for them personally to be involved in every level of warfare from grand strategy to minor tactics simultaneously. All this was played out against a backdrop of colourful uniforms and recorded in an unprecedented number of eyewitness accounts.

The conditions that produced so many outstanding generals in the Napoleonic wars vanished soon after Waterloo. For the Industrial

Revolution produced new technology in mass quantities, including rifled, breech-loading firearms, percussion-fuse artillery shells, barbed wire, railways and the electric telegraph, which dramatically altered the face of the battlefield and increasingly turned battles in the Western world into long and indecisive struggles of attrition.

In short, the Napoleonic wars were both a beginning and an end: they saw the last great flourish of heroic leadership and dramatically raised the curtain on an era of modern warfare, an era of massed manpower, powerful new weapons and the superiority of the defensive. Essentially, it is the turmoil between the old and the new that endows Napoleon's wars with so fascinating an insight into the problems and possibilities of command and control.

Amateurs and professionals

In the Armies of Napoleon's opponents, officers were promoted largely because of a combination of their seniority (how long they had served in a rank) and their wealth, political influence and social status. This ensured that the Army was dependable as a bulwark against internal unrest, even if it limited its effectiveness against an external foe. Promotion from the ranks did occur, but such men, however able, rarely progressed far. Instead, the highest commands usually went to relatives of the monarch or members of the aristocracy. In Britain, for example, rich and well-connected young officers could often purchase the next rank instead of awaiting promotion through seniority. This system of purchasing commissions was limited to the lower officer ranks and regulated, but enabled men like Wellington to become generals while still keen and reasonably young.

The potential drawbacks were obvious. A few men of privileged birth were given command while ridiculously young, most notoriously when Archduke John commanded the Austrian army at Hohenlinden in 1800 at the age of 18. But on the whole, the importance of seniority tended to produce old commanders. In 1809, for instance, the average age of the Austrian generals was 63, while in the Prussian Army that Napoleon smashed in 1806, half of the 142 generals were over 60, with four of them being over 80. Age did not inevitably make a general unfit to command: the Prussian Field Marshal Prince Gebhard von Blücher was 72 when he fought his last battle and was an energetic and dynamic commander. But older generals were more likely to suffer from physical ailments and to have difficulty adjusting mentally to the pace and style of Napoleon's campaigns, since most of their experience had been in eighteenth-century warfare and often against second-rate enemies such as the Ottoman Turks.

The strict seniority system in the upper officer ranks of the British Army had the added disadvantage of producing so many generals that only a proportion could gain systematic experience on active service. Wellington struggled to make do with some of the subordinates he had in the Peninsula:

> Really, when I reflect upon the characters and attainments of some of the General officers of this army . . . on whom I am to rely . . . against the French Generals . . . I tremble: and, as Lord Chesterfield said of the Generals of his day, 'I only hope that when the enemy reads the list of their names he trembles as I do.'[2]

Yet occasionally, the seniority system could be surprisingly flexible. For example, it was possible for a promising junior general effectively to command an army while officially being attached to it merely as chief-of-staff or quartermaster-general. Thus, in 1805, it was the Quartermaster-General, Karl Mack von Leiberich, who really commanded the Austrian army at Ulm, while the 24-year-old Archduke Ferdinand d'Este was only nominally in charge. In the British Army, a capable officer could be promoted to a suitable rank by simultaneously promoting all his seniors. Occasionally, seniority was ignored altogether. In 1807 Tsar Alexander appointed General Levin Bennigsen to replace the more senior Friedrich Buxhöwden in command of the Russian army in Poland, although admittedly this caused Buxhöwden to challenge Bennigsen to a duel.

The allies in fact produced a surprising number of capable commanders, including Wellington, Moore, Uxbridge, Hill, Blücher, Archduke Charles, Schwarzenberg and Barclay de Tolly. It is true that many mediocre generals were promoted above their ceiling, but the dramatically incompetent ones such as the rash young Prince of Orange and the unbalanced Major-General Sir William Erskine (two of Wellington's more notorious subordinates) have attracted a disproportionate amount of attention. Most allied generals were competent if undynamic.

In short, the manifest disadvantages of the allied methods of promotion did not prevent Napoleon's crushing victories of 1805–7 from bringing capable generals to the fore in the defeated countries. Thus in Russia, Tsar Alexander furthered Barclay de Tolly's advancement since he recognised his talents and knew that they were badly needed given the increasing threat from Napoleon. Similarly, in Prussia, Blücher's and Gneisenau's rise to prominence was boosted by the retirement of eighty-five per cent of Prussian generals either in disgrace or as part of the enforced reduction of the Army following the disaster of 1806.

In fact, the key problem that the allies faced was their limited pool of talent, rather than the flawed system that they used to exploit what they had available. The Austrian officers were notoriously routine-ridden, while their Russian counterparts were lazy, dissolute and often barely literate. Similarly, the Prussian *jünkers,* or landed aristocracy, scorned learning. As for the British, Lieutenant-General Sir Thomas Picton damningly claimed that:

> Nine French officers out of ten can command an army, whilst our fellows, though as brave as lions, are totally and utterly ignorant of their profession.[3]

Picton exaggerated, for the overall quality of British regimental officers improved during the Napoleonic wars and many were dedicated and experienced men. But senior officers needed qualities additional to those required of subalterns. This is where France held the advantage, for as the most centralised and powerful state in Europe she had superior numbers of experienced and capable military leaders. She had a larger, more homogenous and better educated population than her opponents, as well as the most advanced system of military education. In fact, so pitiful were the available institutions in Britain that Wellington, Hill, Beresford and several other prominent British generals had all attended French military academies before the Revolution.

As a result of the Revolutionary wars French generals also had an unrivalled degree of experience and self-confidence, for the allies each fought on land for limited periods and failed to form a comprehensive coalition until 1813. Furthermore, the early existence of permanent higher formations in French armies allowed French generals to exercise semi-independent command and become familiar with manoeuvring large bodies of troops before assuming responsibility for whole armies.

But the French system of selecting and promoting generals, although superior to that of the allies, was never based solely on merit even during the Revolution. The mass emigration and purging of noble officers and the perilous situation of the French Republic between 1792 and 1795 offered sudden opportunities to a generation of soldiers with talent and boldness. But although it was possible to rise from the ranks, most of those who reached the top were in fact already officers when the wars started and tended to be from the propertied and educated classes. Where they differed most from their counterparts in the allied Armies was in tending to become generals when they were middle-aged rather than very young or very old. As a result, they were still keen and active but also had maturity and experience.

Under Napoleon it was even more unlikely for men promoted from the ranks to attain senior posts, for although their prospects for advancement were better than in the allied Armies, political influence and family connections counted for much. Napoleon's inept youngest brother, Prince Jérôme Bonaparte, and erratic brother-in-law, Marshal Joachim Murat, both undeservedly benefited from his favouritism. In contrast, the career of the capable General Maximilien Foy was hindered by his staunchly held republican principles.

Even worse, Napoleon failed systematically to accustom his senior subordinates to using their initiative instead of merely obeying his orders. As a result, their performance was uneven and often deeply disappointing, particularly when they became demoralised by the defeats and disasters of 1812 onwards.

The French, in short, did not invariably have better leaders, nor was their promotion system a model of egalitarian fairness. But it is undeniable that they produced a greater number of capable division and brigade commanders and that the allied generals at this level were far less uniform in quality.

The types of commander

The position of general has always demanded a diverse range of qualities that are rarely combined in the same person. Generals of Napoleon's era tended to excel in different areas. Some were capable tacticians who repeatedly intervened in the front line and fighting generals like Marshal Ney, Napoleon's 'bravest of the brave', took this to extremes. They tended not to be the most capable commanders, but were certainly among the more memorable.

Then there were superb motivational leaders like Blücher, who had the knack of boosting morale. Others lacked the strength of character to be a commander-in-chief and shone instead at staff work, the most notable being Napoleon's Marshal Louis Berthier.

Generals like the Russian Field Marshal Prince Mikhail Kutusov excelled at the political and diplomatic aspects of high command and focused on campaign strategy rather than battlefield tactics. Indeed, some of these men, such as Marshal Jean-de-Dieu Soult, were curiously indecisive on the battlefield. They co-ordinated rather than commanded and often made good coalition commanders, such as the Austrian Field Marshal Prince Karl von Schwarzenberg, the allied supreme commander in 1813–14.

Several generals won fame primarily for their achievements as administrators. For a commander spent most of his time on routine matters rather than on fighting battles. To hold his army together, he had to be able to feed it and if he succeeded he invariably won the devotion of his men. Portuguese troops in the Peninsula were heard to cheer their British commander: 'Long live Marshal Beresford – who takes care of our stomachs.'[4] As Wellington observed:

I know of no [point] more important than closely to attend to the comfort of the soldier: let him be well clothed, sheltered and fed. How should he fight poor fellow if he has, beside risking his life, to struggle with unnecessary handicaps.[5]

Administrative skills were required not merely for logistics. Marshal Louis Davout, for example, supervised the creation of Napoleon's satellite Polish state, the Duchy of Warsaw, while Marshal Louis Suchet pacified Aragon in eastern Spain not by seeking a purely military solution, but by exploiting separatist feeling and fostering prosperity.

Some generals were closely involved in diplomatic and intelligence missions, for they not only had sufficient rank to conduct negotiations, but could also assess a situation with a trained military eye.

Men like Lieutenant-General Sir John Moore and the Prussian General Gerhard von Scharnhorst are remembered primarily as trainers of troops or military educators.

Naturally, some outstanding generals fitted into more than one of these categories, but they were exceptional. Only Wellington and Napoleon combined enough talents to join the select company of history's great captains. A few others, such as Marshal Davout, may have had the necessary combination of abilities, but were never given the chance to demonstrate their full potential in a truly independent command.

Note, too, that in the Napoleonic era generals tended to train and serve in one arm: infantry, cavalry, artillery or engineers. Some even specialised in one branch of an arm: thus in Napoleon's Army, General Etienne Nansouty made his name with the heavy cavalry and Charles Lasalle with the light. A notable exception was the French General Horace Sébastiani, who led cavalry in the campaigns of 1805 and 1812–14, but commanded infantry in the Peninsula. The Russian generals Barclay de Tolly and Kutusov also had a greater range of experience than most.

This tendency to specialise in one of the arms coloured the outlook of generals who rose to command an army. Napoleon, who had trained as a gunner, believed that 'great battles are won by artillery' and regularly massed his batteries or even personally sited or aimed guns. In contrast, Wellington regarded his infantry as the 'best of all instruments' and often assumed temporary command of a battalion at a critical spot even when he was an army commander. Conversely, Blücher, the former subaltern of hussars, loved to charge at the head of his cavalry and according to one of his staff did not like to mention any battle that was not decided by that arm.

The most demanding role was that of cavalry commander, which required the ability to seize fleeting opportunities while controlling large masses of horsemen moving at speed through the chaos of battle. A cavalry charge offered the quickest and most dramatic way of gaining glory and could have a decisive impact on the outcome of a battle, as General François Kellermann showed when he smashed an Austrian column at Marengo in 1800.

Given subordinates with such a wide range of personalities, backgrounds and skills, a commander-in-chief needed carefully to match tasks to their different capabilities and limitations. The greatest commanders of the era were superb man-managers and judges of character who knew how to get the best out of their varied team of subordinates. Their role was like that of the conductor of an orchestra, manipulating and co-ordinating the players and blending their unique talents into a powerful and yet harmonious symphony.

Men of valour

A tough head, a hard heart and an iron constitution counted for as much as genius. Napoleon thought that a commander must have both character and intellect: 'the base must equal the height.'[6] He explained:

> If courage preponderates too much, a general will undertake things above his grasp and commit errors, and on the other hand, if his character or courage is much inferior to his perception, he will not dare to execute what he has conceived.

Above all, a general needed boundless energy tightly focused by a single-minded and ruthless resolve. Grasping greed and relentless ambition were among the most powerful motivations. To one who praised Marshal Jean Lannes, Napoleon retorted:

> You are mistaken, if you picture Lannes like that. He and Ney were men who would slit your belly open if they thought it to their advantage, but on a battlefield they were priceless.[7]

Not all commanders were unpleasant. Kind-hearted and popular men like Marshal Jean-Baptiste Bessières and Wellington's Lieutenant-General Sir Rowland Hill won the affection as well as the trust of their men, so much so that veteran guardsmen wept at the Battle of Wagram when they heard a rumour that Bessières had been killed. But popularity is an unreliable guide to good generalship. Nice men do not usually make outstanding generals, for they lack the ruthlessness and egotism that aid success. Conversely, tyrants were often the most effective generals. Remember that Wellington's Light Division and the III Corps of Napoleon's Grand Army enjoyed a reputation and self-esteem of the sort that characterised such formations as Caesar's Tenth Legion and Montgomery's Eighth Army. It is no coincidence that their respective commanders were the tyrannical 'Black Bob' Craufurd and the formidable 'Iron Marshal', Louis Davout.

If the generals of this era shared just one characteristic, it was physical bravery in all its forms, from the reckless, almost suicidal rage of Marshal Ney to the nonchalant coolness of Lieutenant-General Sir William Stewart, who after a narrow escape during the Peninsular war merely remarked: 'a shell, sir, very animating.'[8]

Their courage has become legendary. At Albuera in 1811, for example, Marshal William Beresford first parried a lancer's thrust, then seized the unfortunate man by the collar and with one jerk of his arm yanked him from the saddle.

When the French General Jean Valhubert was mortally wounded at Austerlitz, he forbade his troops to carry him from the field. 'Take no notice of me,' he called, 'only of the enemy. Close your ranks! If you come back as conquerors you can pick me up after the battle. If you are overcome, I have no desire for life!'

Another Frenchman, General Louis-Pierre Montbrun, died after being wounded in the stomach at Borodino. 'A good shot!' he exclaimed as he slid from the saddle. Compare that with the impatient rebuke that General Marie-Victor de Fay, Marquis de Latour-Maubourg issued to his domestic. The general had just had a leg shot off at Leipzig in 1813 and demanded: 'what are you crying about, imbecile? You now have one less boot to polish.'[9]

Not all heroes look heroic. The bald, bespectacled Marshal Davout ought to have been a schoolteacher, whereas Sir Rowland Hill looked like the country gentleman he was in peacetime. Similarly, François Kellermann, one of Napoleon's foremost cavalry generals, was described by one who knew him as having an 'unhealthy and insignificant appearance.'[10]

But who could have forgotten the sight of the fiery, red-headed Marshal Ney at Waterloo, as he bellowed defiance and repeatedly struck his broken sword against an enemy gun barrel? Or the Russian General Peter Bagration, who had the hooked nose and piercing eyes of an eagle? Or that plain-spoken, fighting general, Pierre Cambronne of Napoleon's Imperial Guard, a man described as being literally 'tattooed with scars'? Or the towering Marshal Edouard Mortier, who was six feet six inches tall?

Who can fail to admire the Russian General Ponset for his refusal to withdraw at Craonne in 1814? 'I will die where I stand,' he insisted, 'but I will not retreat an inch.' His superior tactfully replied: 'if your Excellency wants to die here I have no objection, but I must insist that your brigade retires at once.'[11] Equally magnificent was the bearing of the Prussian General Hans von Yorck when he saw a soldier struck down beside him outside Paris on 30 March 1814. 'Why,' Yorck demanded, 'did he come so close to me?'[12]

The secret of leadership

There was something magnetic in even the most unprepossessing of these men. 'I thought,' wrote Lieutenant Johnny Kincaid of the British 95th Rifles, 'that the stranger would betray a grievous want of penetration who could not select the Duke of Wellington from amid five hundred in the same uniform.'[13]

What was the secret that lay behind their leadership? Soldiers willingly followed generals like Wellington, who won battles without wasting lives. But trust was not the full answer, for commanders like Napoleon and Blücher retained the devotion of their men even after the most crushing of defeats. They did so by sheer force of personality, by providing hope, spreading confidence and sharing faith in ultimate victory. In short, they were charismatic leaders: up-beat, undismayed and ready to accept both risks and responsibility.

Field Marshal Sir Archibald Wavell, himself a distinguished British commander during World War Two, pointed out that:

> To learn that Napoleon won the campaign of 1796 by manoeuvre on interior lines or some such phrase is of little value. If you can discover how a young unknown man inspired a ragged, mutinous, half-starved army and made it fight, how he gave it the energy and momentum to march and fight as it did, how he dominated and controlled generals older and more experienced than himself, then you will have learnt something. Napoleon did not gain the position he did so much by a study of rules and strategy as by a profound knowledge of human nature in war.[14]

Good commanders were seen as mascots and father-figures and were duly dubbed 'Papa Blücher,' or 'Daddy Hill'. Alternatively, they were given such nicknames as might be used for comrades, including 'Nosey' or 'Arty' for Wellington; *le Tondu* for Napoleon[15]; *le Rougeaud* for the red-faced Marshal Ney; or *der alte Isegrim* for the Prussian General Yorck.[16]

A commander could strengthen this bond by surrounding himself with representatives of his army, men whom the troops knew and trusted to defend their interests. When Napoleon appointed his marshals, he deliberately selected them from a range of backgrounds. Some of them had served under him in the Army of Italy, but others had fought in the Armies of the Rhine or Pyrenees. Their political sympathies covered the spectrum from republicans to monarchists and they came from aristocratic, professional and humble families. His choice of marshals thus helped to unite the French Army and nation behind him. In contrast, one of the reasons why the Russian General Barclay de Tolly was so unpopular in the 1812 campaign was the presence in his staff of foreigners whom the xenophobic Russians distrusted intensely.

Generals relied on their staff and subordinates to provide moral support and a buffer against needless interruptions. Napoleon, during his expedition to Egypt in 1798, felt himself able to discuss the reported infidelity of his wife only with his ADC and stepson, Eugène de Beauharnais. But the insulation of a general within his staff could easily become isolation, particularly if he listened to sycophantic staff officers, as Kutusov did at Borodino. A general therefore needed to reconnoitre and see the situation at first hand and had to be able personally to motivate his men. Different generals had remarkably different styles in addressing their troops. Wellington gave orders that were crisp, simple and crystal clear, in contrast to the bitter sarcasm of his subordinate, Major-General Robert 'Black Bob' Craufurd, or the foul language that peppered the thunderous commands of that rough Welshman, Sir Thomas Picton: 'Come on, ye rascals! – Come on, ye fighting villains!'

Marshal Ney relied on vigorous exhortation. 'Death touches only those who hesitate,' he roared at Montmirail in 1814. 'See! It does not touch me.' At Quatre Bras a year later, it was:

> General, the salvation of France is at stake. A supreme effort is required. Take your cavalry, throw yourself into the middle of the English. Crush them! Trample them underfoot!

But more important than driving one's troops on to greater deeds of valour was simply to reassure them, sometimes by a few calm words, often by merely being at the critical spot in person. 'Whore's ar Arthur?' demanded a British redcoat at Albuera as he anxiously looked around for Wellington. 'Aw wish he wor here.' The Russian General Mikhail Miloradovich made his men smile at his wit even under the heaviest fire, while taking care not to let his presence hinder or undermine his subordinates. 'Act as you think best,' he used to tell them, 'and look on me solely as your guest.'[17]

To provide reassurance, generals at all times had to project an image of imperturbability under pressure. Those who failed to do so quickly undermined their own position, as Barclay de Tolly demonstrated when he let his despair communicate itself to his army during Napoleon's invasion of Russia in 1812. In contrast, Napoleon described in his memoirs the height of the Battle of Waterloo:

> To know whether we were victorious or in danger the soldiers, even the officers, sought to divine the answer from the expression on my face; but it radiated only confidence. It was the fiftieth pitched battle that I had conducted in twenty years.[18]

Indeed, any leader had to be something of an actor. Wellington had acted in amateur productions in India[19], while the Prussian General August von Gneisenau as a young officer directed an amateur theatre when stationed in a peacetime garrison town. The antics of some of Napoleon's marshals were pure theatre and Murat, the most ostentatious of them all, was even nicknamed 'King Franconi' after the director of a theatre in Paris. Napoleon himself is said to have taken lessons from the great tragedian François Joseph Talma in how to act the Emperor.

Generals tended to assume a public persona that they had created to meet the expectations of those under their command. That included fostering an image of toughness, authority and unflappability. One of Marshal Ney's staff officers noted that he 'kept us at a great distance from him. On the march, he was on his own out in front and he never spoke to us unless he had to . . . He ate alone, without ever inviting any of his ADCs.' Ney's attitude seemed to stem from his recent elevation to the marshalate: 'he thought that he was able to command respect only through aloofness and sometimes he went too far in this respect.'[20]

But when generals put on a show, it was usually to inspire their men by acting the hero. These were surely the most memorable moments in their careers: moments when, ironically, they descended from high command, assumed the role of a subaltern and by their personal intervention at the critical point snatched victory from the jaws of defeat. Archduke Charles reputedly seized a flag to rally his Austrians at Aspern–Essling in 1809, while Napoleon did the same on the bridge of Arcole in 1796. Such incidents did not always involve a flag. Marshal Lannes grabbed a ladder and threatened to lead the assault on the city of Ratisbon in 1809, while General David Chassé took a drum at Arcis-sur-Aube in 1814 and beat the charge when the enemy threatened a vital bridge. Marshal William Beresford even grasped a timid Spanish colonel by the epaulettes at the height of the Battle of Albuera and hauled him out in front of his battalion.

For sheer moral force, nothing could beat leadership by example. Marshal Mortier scorned the chance to abandon his men at Dürenstein in 1805 and escape across the Danube river in a boat. 'No!' he exclaimed, 'we must not separate from these brave fellows; we must be saved or perish together.' But leadership by example could be taken too far, as Marshal Ney proved at Waterloo when he immersed himself so much in the front-line fighting that he lost touch with the battle as a whole. Wellington took a more sensible line. 'I never expose myself except when it is necessary,' he told a lady friend. 'It is very wrong in a commander to expose himself unnecessarily.'[21] Bravery, in short, was not enough: there was nothing, Wellington said, so stupid as a gallant officer. What he looked for in officers was:

A cool discriminating judgement in action, which will enable them to decide with promptitude how far they can, and ought to go, with propriety; and to convey their orders, and act with such vigour and decision, that the soldiers will look up to them with confidence, in the moment of action, and obey them with alacrity.[22]

Generals had to have a degree of detachment, even aloofness, from the fighting. As Wellington once retorted, 'I prefer to appoint an Officer to an independent command, who keeps out "of the thick of it".'[23] Napoleon agreed:

The foremost quality of a commander is to have a cool head, receiving accurate impressions of what is happening without ever getting excited, or dazzled, or intoxicated by good or bad news.[24]

It was when operations failed to go according to plan that the true worth of a general became clear. Wellington declared that the best test of a general was 'to know when to retreat; and to dare to do it,'[25] while Napoleon claimed that as to moral courage, he had rarely come across 'two o'clock in the morning courage, that is to say instantaneous courage'. But without this inner fortitude, it was difficult for a general to stand up to the strain of his unremitting responsibility. 'The commander-in-chief's role is a truly big one,' observed Napoleon. 'The least fault can cost the lives of thousands of men.'[26]

It is small wonder that the supreme challenge of independent command felled many a hitherto promising general. Beresford temporarily lost his nerve after his narrow victory at Albuera and, according to Wellington:

He wrote to me to the effect that he was delighted I was coming; that he could not stand the slaughter about him nor the vast responsibility. His letter was quite in a desponding tone. It was brought to me next day . . . and I said directly, 'This won't do; write me down a victory.' The dispatch was altered accordingly.[27]

It sometimes helped to be a little unbalanced. For example, Blücher's obsessive determination to topple Napoleon helped him to bounce back from defeats with confidence intact.

Note, too, how many successful generals were outsiders: Napoleon was more Corsican than French, while Barclay de Tolly was a Livonian rather than a pure Russian and Wellington came from the minority caste of the Anglo-Irish aristocracy. As for the two foremost Prussian military reformers, Scharnhorst was born in Hanover and Gneisenau in Saxony and they served respectively with the artillery and the light infantry, both of which were shunned by the nobles who constituted the bulk of the officer corps.

War, although destructive, calls for an abundance of creativity, initiative and imaginative leadership and this was why the best generals were often mavericks and outsiders, those who cut across the grain, who had the moral courage and independence of outlook to defy tradition and regulations and even direct orders in their determination to seize opportunities. A good example of such enlightened disobedience occurred at Aspern–Essling in 1809, when Generals Georges Mouton and Jean Rapp ignored Napoleon's instructions and held on to the village of Essling in order to secure the vulnerable eastern flank of the French bridgehead on the north bank of the Danube.

Such disobedience could backfire. Sir Thomas Picton repeatedly exceeded his orders, successfully at Badajoz in 1812 and Vitoria a year later, but unsuccessfully and at heavy cost at Toulouse in 1814. It was therefore understandable, if ironic, that independent-minded men like Wellington demanded unquestioning obedience from most of their subordinates.

Perils and penalties

For the most famous generals, triumph in war could be a springboard to the highest political power: Wellington rose to be Prime Minister, while even Jean-Baptiste Bernadotte, one of the less dynamic of Napoleon's marshals, became Crown Prince of Sweden in 1810, and subsequently King and founder of the royal dynasty that still rules the country today.

But the risks were as great as the rewards and many of those who sought high rank paid for glory with their lives. Among the most famous, Bessières, Lasalle, Auguste de Caulaincourt and Picton all met a hero's death on the battlefield. Craufurd, Moore, Lannes, d'Hautpoul, Bagration and Scharnhorst lingered on for a while in the agony of a mortal wound. Hundreds more were injured at some stage in their careers, with Marshals Nicolas Oudinot and Emmanuel de Grouchy and General Jean Rapp each being wounded at least twenty-two times.

Napoleon lost fourteen generals killed or wounded at Austerlitz, forty-seven at Borodino, sixty-six at Leipzig and thirty-six at Waterloo. According to a survey by Georges Six, of the 2,248 French general officers of the period 1792–1815, 230 were killed and another 1,005 wounded in action, so that fifty-five per cent became casualties. Others fell victim to murder, accident, duelling or suicide.[28]

In fact, the proportion of casualties among Napoleonic-era generals was often higher than among the units they commanded, as the statistics for Waterloo show. In the French III and IV Cavalry Corps, which took part in Marshal Ney's massed charges, ten out of the fourteen corps, division and brigade commanders became casualties: a total of seventy-one per cent. The figure for the regimental officers who charged with them was but forty-nine per cent.

Again at Waterloo, two of Wellington's corps commanders (Uxbridge and the Prince of Orange) were wounded, while the third (Hill) was concussed; of his seven divisional commanders present on the battlefield, one (Picton) was killed, another (Collaert of the Netherlands cavalry) mortally wounded and two (Cooke and Alten) injured. This was seventy per cent, in contrast to the casualty ratio of twenty-two per cent for Wellington's army as a whole.

High-ranking officers naturally fared better during the routine rigours of the retreat from Moscow or of the guerrilla warfare in the Iberian Peninsula, protected as they were by privileges and escorts. But in battle they led for the most part by example and paid the price all too often. Small wonder that when Napoleon promised a decoration to one of his cavalry generals, Auguste de Colbert, he received the reply: 'make haste, sire, I feel that I am already growing old.' Colbert died soon afterwards, aged 32, picked off by a British rifleman in Spain in January 1809.[29]

Wellington and Napoleon both suffered minor wounds and had several lucky escapes from death, injury or capture. Unsurprisingly, many generals dressed plainly to avoid attracting enemy fire. In fact, vanity could work both ways: in the Russian campaign of 1812, the Cossacks were so filled with admiration for the flamboyant Marshal Murat that they wanted to capture rather than kill him. But in an age that bestowed colourful uniforms on even the lowest rank and file, it was difficult for generals to outdress their troops and many did not try. Wellington adopted a largely civilian outfit, while Kutusov at Borodino wore an undistinguished grey tunic with a green greatcoat. Most famously of all, Napoleon used the simple combination of a grey greatcoat and black cocked hat to emphasise his uniqueness and present a familiar image, just as Frederick the Great of Prussia had clung to his shabby uniform during the Seven Years' War.

The ultimate peril faced by commanders was not death but the disgrace of a shameful defeat. The Austrian General Karl Mack von Leiberich was court-martialled and imprisoned for surrendering his army to Napoleon at Ulm in 1805. A worse fate overtook the Spanish General Benito San Juan in 1808, when after being defeated at the Somosierra pass north of Madrid he was murdered by his own troops.

For some battle-weary generals, being obliged continually to run such risks eventually dulled the allure of fame and riches. By 1814, many of Napoleon's marshals wanted to settle down and enjoy the rewards of their long and arduous service in peace. Physical problems also arose. Rheumatic gout afflicted Marshal Jacques Macdonald so severely in 1814 that he could hardly mount his horse. In vain did the Minister of War write to Marshal Pierre Augereau that same year: 'the Emperor bids you forget that you are fifty-six years old, and remember only the glorious days of Castiglione.'[30] Several generals had to command at some stage from a carriage rather than a saddle: Blücher through illness, Marshal André Massena as a result of a fall from his horse, Marshal Laurent Gouvion Saint-Cyr because of a wound and Kutusov and the Spanish General Don Gregorio de la Cuesta from a combination of old age and poor health.

Illness could strike at awkward moments, such as the sciatica that incapacitated Marshal Mortier on the eve of the 1815 campaign. Even Wellington, who kept himself fit and active, suffered from lumbago in December 1812. Kutusov actually died on campaign from natural causes, while the strain of high command contributed to Marshal Davout's premature death in 1823 at the age of 53. Another of Napoleon's generals, Georges Mouton, Count of Lobau, died in 1838 from the re-opening of a critical wound that he had received nearly four decades earlier.

Short-sightedness was another handicap. Major-General Eberhardt von Bock had to be shown where the enemy was when he led a cavalry charge at Garcia Hernandez in 1812,[31] while Lieutenant-General Sir Edward Paget's short-sightedness contributed to his capture by French dragoons later that year. Deafness, too, was a problem: at the Battle of Malojaroslavets in 1812, the Russian General Ivan Dorokhov could not hear the whistle of passing projectiles and so did not move to a safer place, being seriously wounded as a result.[32]

But usually, generals had to be in good physical condition and a staff officer recorded seeing Marshal Bernadotte on the eve of Austerlitz, stripped to the waist despite the cold December air and doing gymnastic exercises.[33] Horsemanship was also important: Wellington only escaped capture at Quatre Bras in 1815 by leaping his charger over the bayonets of the 92nd Highlanders who were lying on the ground. The fittest generals often survived to reach a grand old age. Sir Thomas Graham, a keen sportsman, lived to be 95; Sir Stapleton Cotton to 91; the Earl of Uxbridge to 85; Wellington to 83; Marshal Soult to 82 and Marshals Oudinot, Grouchy and Bernadotte to 80.

The political dimension

Napoleon's dual position as both Emperor and Commander-in-Chief enabled him to bring the full weight of both military and diplomatic pressure against an enemy. He also had supreme power, whereas many of his opponents such as Wellington or Archduke Charles had limited authority and were often unable to dismiss or appoint subordinates on their own initiative.

Allied rulers did sometimes accompany their armies to war, but even though they did not assume command, they undermined the position of their generals. Tsar Alexander notoriously usurped Kutusov's authority at Austerlitz in 1805 and intermittently hindered Schwarzenberg, the allied Supreme Commander, in 1813–14. On the other hand, Alexander played a pivotal role on 24 March 1814 when he used his authority to persuade the allies to march on Paris and topple Napoleon rather than tamely retreat once more to counter a threat to their rear.

There was the obvious risk that a ruler might fall into enemy hands, ending a campaign as disastrously as the loss of a king in a game of chess. This never actually happened in the Napoleonic wars, although Napoleon narrowly escaped death or capture at Eylau in 1807 and Malojaroslavets in Russia, while Alexander came under heavy artillery fire at La Fère-Champenoise in 1814 and was sufficiently endangered at Leipzig a year earlier to oblige his escort to charge the enemy.

Political skills were vital for a general to justify his actions and win advancement. One reason why this was so important was that the upheaval caused by the French Revolution and the subsequent wars made this an age of military intervention in politics. The collapse of the French King's authority after 1789 led to power struggles involving generals and culminating in Napoleon's coup d'état of November 1799. Napoleon himself was targeted by imitators: General Claude de Malet escaped from a mental institution and vainly attempted to overthrow the empire in 1812. Furthermore, it was a revolt of Napoleon's marshals that forced him to abdicate in 1814 after the fall of Paris and primarily the support of the Army which briefly restored him to power the following year. Elsewhere, generals were heavily involved in the murder of the Russian Tsar Paul I in 1801, the abdication of the Spanish King Charles IV in 1808 and the subsequent power struggles there and the deposition of King Gustavus IV of Sweden in 1809. The most notable exception to this trend was Britain, which was spared enemy occupation and where the spectre of Oliver Cromwell's military dictatorship in the seventeenth century kept the Army firmly under political control.

The most acute political dilemmas were faced by French generals during Napoleon's abdication in 1814 and return from exile the following year: should their allegiance be to him or to the Bourbon monarchy? The stakes were high. Marshal Auguste Marmont destroyed a reputation won in over twenty years of battles by his fateful decision in April 1814 to betray Napoleon and surrender his corps to the allies. He ended his days in lonely exile and heard his once proud title, Duke of Ragusa, enter the French language as *ragusade:* treason. Many other French generals who fought for Napoleon in the 1815 campaign had to go temporarily into exile after his defeat at Waterloo while others, most famously Marshal Ney, were shot by the restored Bourbon monarchy.

Similarly, the collapse of Napoleon's empire in 1813–14 caused former allies and satellites to defect and join his enemies and this produced some remarkable twists in the careers of generals from these states. Take, for example, a Dutch general, David Chassé, who earned the nickname

'General Bayonet' while serving with the French and then fought against them as the commander of one of Wellington's Dutch-Belgian divisions at Waterloo. In fact, at Waterloo Chassé found himself in the II Corps under Lieutenant-General Sir Rowland Hill, whom he had fought at the Battle of St Pierre in the Peninsula two years before.

It was not unusual for generals to serve in foreign Armies, for in the eighteenth century limited manpower had forced states to seek mercenaries from abroad. In Napoleon's era, the Spanish and Russian Armies in particular continued to entrust a large number of senior commands to foreigners, since they had few capable native-born officers. Of the most famous Russian generals of the era, Levin Bennigsen was a native Hanoverian; Friedrich Buxhöwden an Estonian German; Barclay de Tolly a Livonian with Scottish ancestry; and Louis de Langeron a Frenchman who had emigrated and offered his services to the Empress Catherine the Great. Such men had often served loyally for years, but their presence rankled with the notoriously xenophobic Russians.

Indeed, internal feuds and personality clashes could have a remarkably destructive impact on military operations. Lack of co-operation between the Russian generals Barclay de Tolly and Bagration nearly handed Napoleon a crushing victory at the outset of his invasion of Russia in 1812, while Marshal Grouchy found it impossible to control his unruly subordinates during the Waterloo campaign when Napoleon detached him to pursue the Prussians.

The balance sheet

No one can rate precisely the impact that the great generals had on Napoleonic battlefields. Some actions were soldiers' battles, in which generalship played little part. Marshal Soult reportedly said of the British at Albuera:

> There is no beating these fellows, in spite of their Generals. I always thought them bad soldiers, and now I am sure of it; for I turned their right flank, penetrated their centre; they were completely beat and the day mine, but yet they would not run.[34]

Napoleon himself in an uncharacteristically modest remark claimed that his own contribution counted for only fifty per cent in his victories and that it was a bit much for the general to be given the credit, for 'it is the army that wins the battle.'[35] Similarly, when Wellington was asked to account for his repeated victories over French marshals, he replied: 'well, the fact is their soldiers got them into scrapes: mine always got me out.'[36]

Numerical strength often counted for more than inspired generalship. Of the most decisive battles of the age, Austerlitz, Jena, Friedland, Vitoria,

Leipzig and Waterloo were all won by the commanders with the most troops. Conversely, as Napoleon found while defending France in 1814, genius could not stave off defeat indefinitely at the hands of superior odds. Generals could only achieve so much with the instruments at their disposal. Some had the bad luck to be given impossible missions: the Peninsula was a notorious graveyard for the reputations of hitherto promising French commanders. Others, like Marshal Grouchy in the Waterloo campaign, were saddled with disputed authority or a confused chain of command and were made scapegoats for inevitable failures.

Indeed, incompetence was often perceived more than real and the Spanish Army is a case in point. None of its generals were outstanding, but neither were they all hopeless. They had the misfortune to face a host of problems, including a lack of resources, inexperienced troops, insufficient cavalry and intense political pressure to take action even when it was militarily unwise. Nor, until 1812, did they have a commander-in chief to co-ordinate their various armies.

Yet it is easy to underrate the potential impact of a good general. According to Wellington, Napoleon's presence on the field of battle made the difference of 40,000 men. After learning of the death of Scharnhorst, his Chief-of-Staff, in 1813, Blücher lamented that a lost battle would not have been a bigger loss.[37] Who, moreover, would not echo Napoleon's exclamation during the retreat from Moscow:

> I have three hundred millions in francs at the Tuileries. I'd give up the lot to save Ney. What a soldier! The army of France is full of brave men, but Michel Ney is truly the bravest of the brave.[38]

Consider, too, what happened when a commander-in-chief became a casualty. Wellington won so stunning a victory at Salamanca in 1812 partly because of the dislocation of the French high command: the two most senior officers, Marshal Auguste Marmont and General Jean-Pierre Bonnet, were seriously wounded one after the other and only because the third, Bertrand Clausel, was a dynamic general did the French eventually manage to counter-attack. Similarly, when Marshal Bessières was unhorsed and knocked unconscious at Wagram in 1809, the Imperial Guard cavalry was paralysed when it should have supported Marshal Macdonald's attack. Likewise, at Orthez in 1814, the troops of the veteran French General Maximilien Foy began to give way when he was carried wounded from the field. No wonder that Napoleon rode through his army at Ratisbon in 1809 to dispel rumours that he had been seriously injured.

But what of the legacy? What had changed in the art of generalship since 1792? There was one key trend, which was indicated partly by the unprecedented influence of Antoine-Henri Jomini and Carl von Clausewitz, the two great military theorists produced by the Napoleonic wars. It was indicated, too, by the increased emphasis on military education, as revealed by the establishment of now-famous military schools in France (Ecole Spéciale Militaire); Britain (the Royal Military College); and Prussia (the Military School for Officers in Berlin, later the Kriegsakademie). These changes indicated that method was becoming more important than style in command. This was recognised, more so than anywhere else, in Prussia. Her Quartermaster-General Staff had been reorganised as early as 1803, but it was the reforms following her disastrous defeat at Napoleon's hands in 1806 that accelerated the process. Since Prussia lacked a great captain of the stature of Wellington or Napoleon, she evolved a permanent General Staff of professional staff officers trained in a common doctrine and directed to share responsibility for command decisions with the generals to whom they were attached. In short, the Prussians tried to replace the highly personal, and occasionally amateur, command of one general with a more systematic and robust command system that could cope better with the increased scale of campaigns and continue to function even if the commander-in-chief became a casualty (as indeed happened when Blücher was unhorsed and temporarily mislaid after the Battle of Ligny in 1815).

It was the Prussians, therefore, who best encapsulated the legacy of Napoleon's wars. Napoleon himself was a refiner of existing methods rather than an innovator and he left behind little that was original in the military sphere except glorious memories and an inspirational legend. He and Wellington represented the end of an era in which one genius could direct an army with the obedience rather than partnership of his subordinates. They were essentially one-man bands: they neither systematically trained potential successors nor shared responsibility with a second-in-command or chief-of-staff in any meaningful sense. Wellington told one of his subordinates that:

> I did not know what the words *'second in command'* meant, any more than third, fourth, or fifth in command; that I alone commanded the army ... that ... I would treat ... him ... with the most entire confidence, and would leave none of my views or intentions unexplained; but that I would have no *second in command* in the sense of anything like ... superintending control; and that, finally and above all, I would not only take but insist upon the whole and undivided responsibility of all that should happen while the army was under my command.[39]

Yet this reluctance to delegate often stifled initiative and created problems when an army became too large or over-extended. In contrast, the Prussians managed by creating their General Staff to institutionalise genius and thus avoided some of these problems. Britain and France naturally looked back with pride and nostalgia to their great campaigns under Wellington and Napoleon. But in fact, it was the Prussians with their more robust and systematic command system who would be best placed to handle the increased scale and scope of future warfare in Europe.

When the sun set on the evening of Waterloo, it therefore marked not simply the final defeat of Napoleon and the resolution of twenty-three years of war, but also the end of a golden age of generalship.

NOTES

1 See G. Craig, 'Problems of coalition warfare: the military alliance against Napoleon, 1813–14,' in *War, politics and diplomacy: selected essays* (1966).
2 Second Duke of Wellington, ed., *Supplementary despatches, correspondence, and memoranda of Field Marshal Arthur Duke of Wellington, K.G.* (1858–64), v.6, p.582
3 R. Gronow, *The reminiscences and recollections of Captain Gronow* (1984), v.1, p.325
4 C. Oman, *A history of the Peninsular war* (1902–30), v.2, p.216
5 M. Glover, *Wellington as military commander* (1968), p.231
6 J. Herold, *The mind of Napoleon* (1961), p.220
7 G. Gourgaud, *Sainte-Hélène: journal inédit de 1815 à 1818* (nd), v.2, p.83
8 Glover, *op. cit.*, p.199
9 J. Elting, *Swords around a throne: Napoleon's Grande Armée* (1988), p.162
10 C. Yonge, ed., *Recollections of Colonel de Gonneville* (1875), v.1, p.250
11 H. Houssaye, *Napoleon and the campaign of 1814* (1914), trans. R. McClintock, p.156
12 *Ibid*, p.408
13 J. Kincaid, *Adventures in the Rifle Brigade* (1929), p.10
14 A. Wavell, *Generals and generalship* (1941), p.18
15 'The shorn one,' a reference to Napoleon's short hair cut.
16 'The old man in the iron helmet,' a reference to the wolf in German folklore.
17 A. Brett-James, *1812: eyewitness accounts of Napoleon's defeat in Russia* (1967), pp.160–1
18 S. de Chair, ed., *Napoleon's memoirs* (1985), p.531
19 P. Guedalla, *The Duke* (1931), p.104
20 R. de Fézensac, *Souvenirs militaires* (1863), p.116
21 R. Edgcumbe, ed., *The diary of Frances Lady Shelley, 1787–1817* (1912), v.1, pp.106–7
22 J. Gurwood, ed., *The dispatches of Field Marshal the Duke of Wellington* (1834–8), v.7, p.560
23 W. Fraser, *Words on Wellington* (nd), p.44
24 N. Bonaparte, *La correspondance de Napoléon 1er* (1858–70), v.32, pp.182–3
25 Fraser, *op. cit.*, p.28
26 Gourgaud, *op. cit.*, v.1, p.586
27 P. Haythornthwaite, *The armies of Wellington* (1994), pp.244–5
28 G. Six, *Les généraux de la Révolution et de l'Empire* (1947), p.236
29 A. Macdonell, *Napoleon and his marshals* (1934), p.175
30 Houssaye, *op. cit.*, p.193. The Battle of Castiglione in northern Italy in 1796 had been Augereau's finest hour.
31 N. Beamish, *History of the King's German Legion* (1837), v.2, p.82

32 M. Weil, ed., *Mémoires du général-major russe Baron de Löwenstern* (1903), v.1, p.308
33 L. Lejeune, *Mémoires du général Lejeune* (1895), v.1, pp.32–3
34 W. Tomkinson, *The diary of a cavalry officer in the Peninsular and Waterloo campaigns 1809–1815* (1894), pp.108–9
35 Gourgaud, *op. cit.*, v.2, p.425
36 Fraser, *op. cit.*, p.174
37 H. Delbrück, *Das Leben des Feldmarschalls Grafen Neithardt von Gneisenau* (1882), v.1, p.281
38 R. Horricks, *Marshal Ney: the romance and the real* (1982), p.139
39 J. Croker, *The Croker papers* (1885), v.1, p.343

CHAPTER I
Napoleon

Napoleon is known to millions around the world as one of the greatest soldiers of history, but he began life in humble circumstances. He was born in 1769 at Ajaccio in Corsica, which had been acquired by the French less than two years before. In fact, his father, Carlo Bonaparte, initially followed the Corsican freedom fighter, Pasquale Paoli, before settling down to collaborate with the French. Carlo, an impoverished lawyer from the minor nobility, had married Letizia Ramolino, a formidable but affectionate young woman who imbued Napoleon with a strict code of honour and the importance of courage. From Corsica itself, Napoleon acquired a strong clan loyalty, superstition, a habit of intrigue and an occasional vindictiveness.

Of Napoleon's twelve brothers and sisters, eight survived to adulthood, but not all shared his burning ambition and the eldest surviving brother, Joseph, was particularly easy-going. Napoleon was indebted for his start in life to a close family friend and admirer of his mother, Count Louis de Marbeuf. In fact, it has been suggested that Napoleon was Marbeuf's illegitimate son and that he was born in February 1770 rather than on the official date of 15 August 1769.[1] At any rate, it was Marbeuf, the influential French Governor of Corsica, who ensured that Napoleon was educated at some of the best schools in pre-Revolutionary France. After four months learning French in the college at Autun, Napoleon in 1779 joined the royal military school at Brienne, an institution founded for the sons of the nobility and to which he gained entry on a scholarship thanks to the Bonapartes' noble lineage.

The five years that Napoleon spent at Brienne were crucial to his development. His Corsican accent made him conscious of being an outsider and his fierce independence was intensified by the scorn of some of his haughtier fellows. He worked hard and proved good at history and geography, but above all at mathematics and he would later calculate distances and numbers of troops with a cold and ruthless brilliance.

In October 1784 he entered the Ecole Militaire, the famous military school in Paris, for a year of more specialised military education that was paid for by the King. Meanwhile, Carlo Bonaparte's premature death in

1

February 1785 left his family in a precarious financial situation and Napoleon increasingly took the lead in managing its affairs. After graduating from the Ecole Militaire, he joined the La Fère Artillery Regiment at Valence and began training as a gunner. He took a long period of leave in Corsica and then studied for a year at the Auxonne Artillery School from 1788. Here, he found a mentor in the Commandant, General Jean-Pierre du Teil, one of the foremost gunners of the time, who recognised his potential and lent him a wide range of books. Napoleon read them avidly, later urging would-be commanders to study again and again the campaigns of Alexander, Hannibal, Caesar, Gustavus Adolphus, Turenne, Eugène and Frederick the Great and to take these great captains as models.

Then, in 1789, the Revolution threw France into turmoil and offered glittering opportunities to the bold and ambitious. Napoleon initially saw his chances as a politician in Corsica and took extensive periods of leave to advance himself there. But he was in Paris in the summer of 1792 and on 10 August witnessed the massacre of King Louis XVI's Swiss Guards at the Tuileries Palace, an episode that contributed to his fear and loathing of mobs.

Apart from subduing food riots, Napoleon first saw action in February 1793, when he served in a subordinate role in a raid on the Sardinian island of La Maddalena. He handled his battery well, but the operation as a whole was a fiasco because of the incompetence of the expedition's commander. His unscrupulous Corsican political ventures also ended in failure and in June 1793 he and his family were forced to flee to France.

The French Republic at this time was beset with both invasion and civil war. The southern provinces had rebelled against Paris and Revolutionary forces were besieging the key naval base of Toulon, which had been occupied at the end of August by a British, Spanish, Sardinian and Neapolitan force. Napoleon, still only a 24-year-old captain, used influential patrons to secure command of the artillery of the besieging force after the original incumbent was wounded. His leadership and expertise as a gunner were crucial in forcing the enemy to evacuate Toulon.

Napoleon thus established a reputation and won promotion to *général de brigade*. Toulon marked the start of his rise to power but in the short term was followed by a coup d'état in Paris in July 1794, which resulted in him being imprisoned for two weeks because of his links with supporters of the toppled Jacobin regime. He then spent a year of frustration and insecurity until in October 1795 he was called on by Paul Barras, an influential member of the Directory that now governed France, to crush an insurrection in Paris. His artillery training once again served him well and he smashed the revolt with 'a whiff of grapeshot', a ruthless action that won him command of the Army of the Interior and promotion to *général de division.* He also fell passionately in love with Josephine de Beauharnais, a widowed beauty whom he shortly married.

In March 1796 he was appointed by the Directory to command the French Army of Italy and took the offensive against the Austrians and Piedmontese in the north of the Italian peninsula. He swiftly knocked Piedmont out of the war and pursued the Austrians eastwards into Lombardy. He failed to trap them, despite violating neutral territory and storming the bridge at Lodi in a legendary if futile action in May. Laying siege to the city of Mantua, he defeated four relief attempts in a series of battles, including Castiglione, Arcole and Rivoli, and used the practical experience he gained in these operations to refine the concepts that he had already developed in studying the art of war.

It was not until February 1797, after a siege of eight months, that Mantua finally fell, enabling Napoleon to thrust north-eastwards into the Alps. By early April he was seventy-five miles from Vienna, but having outrun his supplies he secured an armistice and that October negotiated the Peace of Campo Formio to set the seal on his conquests. He had become a popular hero, not only through his victories but also as a result of the art treasures and financial contributions that he had extorted from the Italian cities and sent back to Paris. This allowed him to act with an independence that increasingly worried the Directory.

Now only Britain remained at war. Napoleon realised the impracticalities of attempting a direct invasion and instead advocated threatening British trade and possessions in India with an expedition to Egypt. The Directors approved, doubtless being keen to see him at a safe distance from France. He sailed from Toulon and after capturing Malta and narrowly evading a British fleet under Rear-Admiral Horatio Nelson, landed in Egypt in July 1798. He won some glamorous if undemanding victories against the Mamelukes, but suffered a disaster when nearly all his ships were destroyed by Nelson in Aboukir Bay on 1 August, leaving him cut off from home and faced by a holy war.

Napoleon, knowing that the Sultan of Turkey was preparing to reconquer Egypt, struck a pre-emptive blow in February 1799 by invading Palestine (then known as Syria). He brutally massacred 2,500 prisoners after storming the town of Jaffa in March and crushed a Turkish army at the battle of Mount Tabor a month later, but failed to conquer the city of Saint-Jean-d'Acre. He then beat a demoralising retreat back to Egypt, but subsequently drove a Turkish army into the sea when it landed at Aboukir in July.

At this time, France was again fighting for her life in Europe following the creation of an allied Second Coalition led by Britain, Austria and Russia. The Egyptian expedition had therefore not only failed to achieve its objectives but had also over-extended French resources. Nonetheless, Napoleon had created an illusion of success through his battlefield victories, which added to his fame and contrasted with the setbacks and political instability at home. His expedition had captured the popular imagination in France and his accompanying team of civilian experts had made important discoveries about Egyptian history and culture.

Napoleon himself had developed his skills as a soldier–statesman administering his conquered territories. Now, seeing opportunities in the volatile situation in Paris, he handed his army over to General Jean-Baptiste Kléber and slipped back to France by sea with a few trusted companions. Back in Paris, he found that plotters were seeking to use a military hero as a figurehead for a coup d'état against the corrupt and unpopular Directory. Their initial choice, General Barthélemy Joubert, had fallen at the Battle of Novi in August and Napoleon took his place. The actual coup, on 10 November 1799, blundered to success after Napoleon lost his nerve, made a lacklustre speech and had to be rescued from the furious deputies of the Council of the Five Hundred by guardsmen. Hence his coup succeeded through military force rather than by legitimate political means as had been hoped, but by the end of the year he had established himself as First Consul with effectively dictatorial powers.

He then sought to consolidate his position and pose as the saviour of his country by securing a victorious peace. The military situation had already begun to improve following successes by Generals André Massena in Switzerland and Guillaume Brune in Holland and in May 1800 Napoleon in a brilliant encircling move crossed the Alps into northern Italy, which had been lost to the Austrians the previous year. He narrowly avoided defeat at the Battle of Marengo on 14 June after seriously misjudging the situation, but cynically portrayed the victory in the official accounts as one of the most brilliant of his career. The Austrians then sued for an armistice and evacuated Lombardy, but renewed hostilities in November. They finally signed peace only in February 1801 after being decisively beaten at Hohenlinden in southern Germany by the Army of the Rhine under General Jean-Victor Moreau, who relentlessly pursued to within fifty miles of Vienna.

Peace also followed with Britain in March 1802, allowing Napoleon to rebuild France and unite the nation behind him. He restored the economy, centralised the administration, remodelled French law and signed a Concordat with the Pope. In addition, he reformed the educational system and encouraged the return of royalists who had emigrated during the Revolution. But his regime also became more authoritarian and on 2 December 1804 he crowned himself Emperor of the French at the age of 35.

During these years, and particularly following the resumption of war with Britain in May 1803, Napoleon reformed the armed forces, which under the Directory had deteriorated in both numbers and morale. In particular, the Army was organised into permanent corps for greater flexibility and cohesion. For over two years, these corps were trained intensively in both tactics and large-scale manoeuvres in six camps established along the Channel coast ready for an invasion of England. Napoleon also established the Imperial Guard as an exclusive formation of veterans that both inspired the rest of the Army and formed a powerful reserve under his direct control. Napoleon's Grand Army[2] when it took the field in 1805 was the most formidable military machine of its time, although it later declined in quality under the cumulative impact of heavy casualties and the increasing use of raw conscripts.

Napoleon's rise to political power had gone hand-in-hand with his success as a soldier. Now he was Emperor, he was answerable as a commander only to himself and could co-ordinate the full weight of political and diplomatic measures to isolate enemies before destroying them in the field. But equally, he could not be absent from Paris for long and was prevented from giving his full attention to military matters.

Napoleon unwisely provoked the European powers into forming a Third Coalition at the very moment when he planned to invade England. One of his blunders was his brutal kidnap and execution of an exiled Bourbon prince, the Duke of Enghien, as a response to a spate of royalist assassination plots against his own life. His coronation as Emperor of the French in 1804 and King of Italy the following May antagonised the old European monarchies, who were also alarmed by his occupation of Hanover and expansionist ambitions in the Mediterranean. Russia and Austria duly prepared for hostilities, although Prussia remained un-committed.

Postponing his plans to invade England, Napoleon seized the initiative and in the autumn of 1805 swept across the Rhine and down to the Danube. There, he encircled and captured an Austrian army at Ulm and occupied Vienna, before thrusting northwards and destroying the main Austro-Russian army at Austerlitz on 2 December. This decisive victory smashed the allied coalition: Austria immediately sought an armistice and suffered severe territorial losses at the Peace of Pressburg, while the Russians retired to their frontiers.

Napoleon thereby shattered the balance of power in Europe and in July 1806 formed his German satellite states into a Confederation of the Rhine to act as a buffer on the eastern frontiers of France. As a result, he replaced Austria as the dominant power in both Italy and Germany. Prussia, now increasingly alarmed, belatedly formed a Fourth Coalition with Britain and Russia. On 1 October she rashly sent Napoleon an ultimatum without waiting for the arrival of Russian support and within a fortnight was overtaken by catastrophe as Napoleon launched a powerful offensive. The Prussian Army was crushed at Jena–Auerstädt and there followed one of the greatest pursuits of history, with Berlin, a host of fortresses and 140,000 troops falling into Napoleon's hands with minimal resistance.

Apart from some garrisons, all that remained of the Prussian Army were some 15,000 soldiers. But two Russian armies were now in the field, forcing Napoleon to fight a tough winter campaign in East Prussia and Poland, between Warsaw and the Baltic coast. He won an empty and notoriously bloody victory at Eylau in February 1807, but decisively won Friedland in June. The following month, he secured at the Peace of Tilsit the Franco-Russian alliance that seemed to make him master of the continent. He again redrew the map as he humiliated Prussia and created two more satellites, Westphalia in northern Germany and the Grand Duchy of Warsaw, a revived Polish state.

Tilsit marked the highpoint of Napoleon's fortunes, for the years of victory were almost over. Britain, his most inveterate enemy, remained unsubdued, so he tried to undermine her with a European trade embargo and by securing the fleets of neutral Sweden, Denmark and Portugal so as to outnumber the Royal Navy. Napoleon's Continental System could have obliged Britain to seek a negotiated peace, but proved difficult to enforce. Britain, moreover, ruthlessly seized the Danish fleet in September 1807 in a pre-emptive strike that encouraged Sweden to defy France and Russia. Furthermore, Napoleon was drawn into a disastrous involvement in the Iberian Peninsula when he sent troops through Spain to enforce Portugal's compliance with his trade restrictions. For good measure, he then impatiently ordered Spain to be taken over even though that country was an ally. He appointed his brother Joseph as the new Spanish King, but subsequent revolts led to a humiliating French defeat at Bailen and by converting Spain into an enemy of France dramatically relieved the pressure on the Royal Navy and opened to the British important new markets in the Spanish colonies of Central and South America. The débâcle also enabled a British expeditionary force to liberate Portugal and secure a foothold there on the continent of Europe.

Napoleon intervened personally in the Peninsula in November 1808. He quickly smashed the Spanish regular armies and re-captured Madrid before being diverted on a fruitless pursuit of the British expeditionary force under Lieutenant-General Sir John Moore, which was evacuated by sea from Coruña on the north-eastern coast of Spain. In January 1809 he returned to Paris believing that he had cured the problems of the Iberian Peninsula, whereas in fact they had only just begun. He was obliged to leave thousands of troops to contend with both guerrillas and the revived Spanish regular armies. Furthermore, the British reinforced the 10,000 men they still retained in Portugal and over the next five years their small but highly professional army under Wellington inflicted repeated defeats on the French.

Napoleon could not cut his losses and evacuate the Peninsula without suffering a disastrous blow to his prestige and so the debilitating war dragged on. Yet he never personally returned to Spain, nor did he impose a unified command structure on the marshals he left behind. His own attempts to direct the war by remote control from Paris merely made matters worse, for he undermined the authority of King Joseph and often ignored the realities of the situation on the ground.

Conflict also broke out at the opposite end of his Empire in April 1809. Austria was set on avenging her defeat of 1805 and joined Britain in the Fifth Coalition. Although Austria enjoyed neither Russian nor Prussian support, the demands of the Peninsular war had seriously weakened Napoleon's forces in central Europe. The Austrian army invaded Bavaria, Napoleon's ally in southern Germany, and initially held the advantage. But once Napoleon arrived in the area, he quickly restored the situation and in a series of blows defeated the Austrian army, although he failed to destroy it or prevent its escape eastwards. He then advanced along the southern bank of the Danube and after seizing Vienna boldly crossed the river. To his surprise, he was immediately attacked by the rallied Austrian army in the Battle of Aspern–Essling on 21–2 May. After failing to break out, he was forced to evacuate his bridgehead. This had been a serious check, but Napoleon resolved to avenge it as soon as possible and again crossed the Danube six weeks later after making thorough preparations. This time, he beat the Austrians at Wagram on 5–6 July. An armistice followed later that month, but marked the last time that Napoleon would end a campaign victoriously. In 1810 he cemented a new alliance with Austria by divorcing Josephine and marrying the Austrian Emperor's daughter, Marie-Louise, who bore him a son and heir the following year.

Napoleon's relations with Russia now began to deteriorate dramatically, largely because of the harm done to Russia's commercial interests by the Continental System, from which she withdrew at the end of 1810. In June 1812 Napoleon invaded Russia with a massive army of over half-a-million men, drawn not only from France but throughout his Empire. He won indecisive battles at Smolensk and Borodino in which he failed to destroy the Russian army and in September had the hollow triumph of occupying Moscow. This failed to bring the Russians to the peace-table and he had to leave the devastated city in October with the approach of winter. At first, he hoped to break through to fertile provinces in southern Russia, but after an indecisive action at Malojaroslavets he lost his nerve and instead retreated along his ravaged line of advance. The collapse of his logistics and, from November, the onset of bitter cold all but destroyed his army. Barely 93,000 of his troops returned. They left behind a staggering 570,000 comrades, 200,000 horses and 1,050 guns.[3]

The retreat from Moscow was the most famous military disaster in history and marked the beginning of the end for Napoleon. In December he returned to Paris, where in his absence there had been an unsuccessful attempt to overthrow him. He cobbled together a new, largely conscript army and in the spring of 1813 brought it back to central Europe to join the

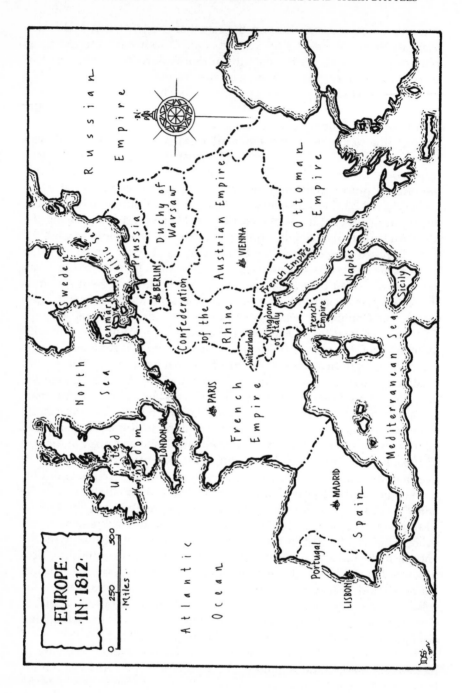

·EUROPE·
IN·1812·

·Miles·
0   250   500

N

Russian Empire

Sweden

Baltic Sea

Denmark

Prussia

Duchy of
Warsaw

Austrian Empire

VIENNA

Ottoman
Empire

BERLIN

Confederation

of the

Rhine

French Empire

Kingdom
of Italy

Switzerland

French
Empire

Naples

Sicily

North
Sea

United
Kingdom

LONDON

PARIS

French
Empire

Mediterranean Sea

Atlantic
Ocean

MADRID

Spain

Portugal

LISBON

remnants of the army that had perished in Russia. Ranged against him now was the powerful Sixth Coalition of Britain, Russia, Prussia and Sweden while Austria was neutral. Napoleon boldly counter-attacked and beat the advancing Russian and Prussian forces at the Battles of Lützen and Bautzen in May, but was unable to exploit these victories, crippled as he was by his shortage of cavalry following the losses of 1812. He subsequently agreed to an armistice in order to raise and organise more troops, but in the event it was the allies who benefited even more from this two-month truce. Austria now joined the coalition, so that when hostilities resumed in August superior numbers of Austrian, Russian, Prussian and Swedish troops confronted Napoleon in central Europe, while Wellington had driven the French from Spain and was poised to cross the Pyrenees into south-western France.

Never before had Napoleon been pitted simultaneously against Austria, Prussia and Russia, his big three continental enemies. The allies had also learnt how to counter his art of war: they fielded three (later four) armies and avoided battle with him in person unless they had overwhelming numerical superiority. They instead attacked his more vulnerable detached forces under less capable subordinates. Although Napoleon won the Battle of Dresden in late August, he could not be everywhere in person and found that his marshals tended to be beaten in his absence, while his German allies had begun to desert him. The end came in October when he fought and lost the massive, three-day Battle of Leipzig against the converging allied armies. The defeat cost him central Europe and the cycle of imperial expansion had now gone into reverse, for as his Empire shrank, so too did his sources of manpower, finance and supplies. From Leipzig, he retreated westwards, beating his former Bavarian allies at Hanau on the way, and crossing the Rhine into France in November.

By the beginning of 1814, enemy armies had already penetrated on to French soil. In the south, Wellington had reached the city of Bayonne on the Atlantic coast, while in the north-east the two main allied armies under Field Marshal Gebhard von Blücher and Prince Karl von Schwarzenberg had crossed the Rhine and were marching on Paris. Further allied forces reduced French-held fortresses in the rear and operated in the subsidiary theatres of Belgium and northern Italy.

Napoleon seized the initiative, struck at Blücher and beat him at Brienne, the scene of his schooldays, only to be checked the following day at La Rothière. The campaign had begun badly, but Napoleon skilfully retrieved the situation. In February he beat elements of Blücher's army four times in five days, before turning on Schwarzenberg and defeating him at Montereau. He scornfully rejected peace offers, but proved unable to repeat such victories indefinitely. As a result, the allies eventually fumbled their way to success through weight of numbers. When Napoleon returned north at the beginning of March to deal once again with Blücher, he was checked at Laon and forced to retreat. Then, after being repulsed by Schwarzenberg at Arcis-sur-Aube, he took a gamble and, leaving just 17,000 men to cover Paris, struck eastwards at Schwarzenberg's lines of communication in the hope of intimidating him into retreat and of collecting troops from fortresses left isolated by the allied advance. But the allies discovered Napoleon's plan through an intercepted letter and jointly advanced on Paris, ignoring the threat to their rear. Realising that his bluff had been called, Napoleon hastened back to save his capital, but was too late. Marshal Auguste Marmont after stiff fighting had surrendered the city to the allies, who occupied it on 31 March.

Napoleon wanted to fight on, but on 4 April was forced by his war-weary marshals to abdicate in favour of his son and this became an unconditional abdication two days later. After an unsuccessful attempt to kill himself with poison, he was exiled to the Mediterranean island of Elba. He ruled his new domain as King, but was financially insecure and had indications that he might be removed to a remoter location. He was encouraged to try and regain power in France by the unpopularity of the restored Bourbon monarchy, so he slipped away in February 1815 and landed on the southern coast of France with fewer than 1,000 Imperial Guardsmen. His boldness tipped the balance in his favour, for it paralysed his opponents with fear and royalist troops sent to stop him simply went over to his side.

He triumphantly entered Paris on 20 March, but the European powers had declared him an outlaw and formed the Seventh Coalition to end for good the threat he posed. Napoleon knew that vast Russian and Austrian armies would be ready to cross the eastern frontiers of France at the beginning of July and therefore struck a pre-emptive blow in the north, against the two allied armies of Wellington and Blücher, who were guarding the Low Countries. He invaded on 15 June, defeated Blücher's Prussians at Ligny the next day and on the 18th attacked Wellington at Waterloo, twelve miles south of Brussels. But he was unable to break through Wellington's strong position and was surprised to discover that the Prussians had rallied and were now descending on his eastern flank. By dusk, he had gone down to his final and most famous defeat and four days later he abdicated for the second time.

Exiled once more, this time to the barren South Atlantic island of St Helena where he was kept a prisoner by the British, Napoleon died on 5 May 1821. He was 51 years old.

The little corporal

'Fear nothing, my friends,' declared Napoleon at Montereau, 'the cannonball that is to kill me has not yet been made.' It was this sense of destiny that sustained him through his tumultuous career. In fact, it was one of his three greatest assets, the others being a relentless energy and phenomenal mind. Equally, it was over-confidence that led to his downfall, for as a Minister of the Empire observed, 'it is strange that though Napoleon's common sense amounted to genius, he never could see where the possible left off.'

As a leader, Napoleon was unparalleled. His eyes had a magnetism that intimidated even hardened soldiers and forced an Imperial Guardsman, Jean-Roch Coignet, to admit: 'I could not look at him: he would have frightened me; I only saw his horse.'[4] But Napoleon's blistering rebukes and fits of temper were only one side of the coin, for he praised and rewarded the deserving on a grand scale. He appointed twenty-six of his generals as Marshals of the Empire and gave many other men titles and lavish financial rewards. He inspired the rank and file by creating a cult of glory, by introducing awards for bravery such as the coveted medal of the Legion of Honour, and by fostering the notion, however illusory, that advancement was open to talent and bravery rather than being reserved for a privileged élite.

Napoleon instinctively knew how to extract the maximum effort from his men. During the siege of Toulon, for example, he had a sign erected at a particularly dangerous post. It read 'battery of men without fear' and ensured that there was no shortage of volunteers to serve the guns. Napoleon also knew that men will fight better if they know why they are fighting and one of his soldiers, Captain Elzéar Blaze, noted:

> In general, after a battle, an order of the day acquainted us with what we had done; for we often achieved great things without knowing it. In his proclamations to the army . . . he told us that he was satisfied with us, that we had surpassed his expectations, that we had flown with the rapidity of the eagle; he then detailed our exploits, the number of soldiers, cannon, and carriages that we had taken; it was exaggerated, but it was high-sounding and had an excellent effect.[5]

Napoleon regularly showed himself to his troops, recognised old soldiers and talked and joked with them man-to-man. At the Battle of Brienne, he rode in front of his men: 'Soldiers, I am your colonel; I shall lead you. Brienne must be taken.' The troops roared out 'Long live the Emperor!' and then swiftly expelled the foe.[6] He regularly shared dangers and discomforts and in Egypt bravely visited some of his men who were stricken with bubonic plague. Yet the degree to which he genuinely cared for the lives of his soldiers is debatable. In Egypt, he readily abandoned an army that he had led to disaster and especially in later years he tended to use brutal frontal assaults regardless of heavy casualties.

It was to his Grand Army, and not just to his own talents, that Napoleon owed his success. Moreover, he created this remarkable army from the often outstanding men, material and methods that he had inherited from the Ancien Régime and the Revolutionary wars. For the sheer numbers of troops he needed, he was able to use both conscription and contingents from satellite states. In fact, no other general of this era had such resources at his disposal, although few, if any, could have matched his genius for organising them.

Napoleon in his art of war made little impact on minor tactics, which he left largely to his subordinates and which had evolved successfully during the Revolutionary wars. As a trained gunner, however, he took a personal interest in the handling of artillery and followed the theories of the writer General Jean du Teil (brother of the Commandant of the Auxonne Artillery School) in massing his guns against key points as a powerful offensive weapon in their own right.

It was in the higher art of war that Napoleon made his greatest contribution, but here, too, he drew heavily on the concepts of others, especially the great military theorists of the late eighteenth century, Generals Pierre de Bourcet and Jacques de Guibert. His genius lay in fusing existing ideas, doctrines and resources and exploiting them to the limit.

His headquarters, the *Grand Quartier-Général*, was centred around his *Maison*, or personal staff, which included Marshal Louis Berthier, his indispensable Chief-of-Staff, and General Louis Bacler d'Albe, the head of the topographical department. At its height, in 1812, the *Grand Quartier-Général* contained some 14,000 personnel and its sophistication enabled Napoleon to centralise authority to an astonishing degree, despite several notorious cases of inefficiency in the delivery of messages. It was unparalleled until the development of the Prussian General Staff after 1806, but whereas the Prussian staff officers made operational decisions in conjunction with their commanders, Napoleon's *Grand Quartier-Général* merely served his genius. In fact, Napoleon rarely consulted even his marshals and when he did so, it was often, as on the morning of Waterloo, simply to win them over to his views or boost their morale rather than genuinely to seek advice. This centralisation of authority usually proved an advantage in the early years, but posed serious problems in 1809–13 when Napoleon tried to command large armies operating over a wide area.

The key to Napoleon's strategy was the corps, a concept that he perfected rather than invented. This flexible and self-reliant formation usually had between 15,000 and 30,000 men and included infantry, cavalry and artillery, plus supporting services such as engineers and a staff. Its combination of all three arms enabled it to hold its own against superior numbers for a day without being destroyed. As a result, Napoleon's army could march dispersed, with each corps within a day's march of its neighbours. This dispersal eased congestion and made it possible for the army to march fast and live to a large extent off the country. In 1806, for example, Napoleon advanced with his corps arrayed in a vast diamond formation, the so-called *bataillon carré*, which could change direction as soon as the enemy was located. The corps at the tip of the diamond would make contact with and tie down the enemy while the others converged on the area. The corps organisation also increased the army's flexibility and speed of reaction in battle, whereas opposing armies initially lacked such permanent higher formations and subsequently introduced them imperfectly.

Napoleon was quick to seize opportunities, but also planned ahead and left as little as possible to chance. 'If,' he explained, 'I seem always ready to meet any difficulty, to face any emergency, it is because before undertaking any enterprise I have spent a long time thinking it out, and seeing what might happen.' Napoleon wanted short, sharp and decisive campaigns. He nearly always seized the initiative at the outset and repeatedly surprised his opponents by the timing, speed and direction of his onslaughts. He rarely fought on the defensive as he held that a passive defence inevitably ended in defeat: even in 1814, during the invasion of France, he repeatedly took the initiative and attacked the allied armies. He was usually single-minded in pursuit of his objective, although he did sometimes allow the lure of an enemy capital to distract him from the more important aim of destroying the hostile army. Madrid in 1808 and Moscow four years later are good examples.

One of Napoleon's favourite campaign strategies, particularly when he enjoyed numerical superiority, was to outflank an opponent and threaten his lines of communication. This was the *manoeuvre sur les derrières* and he employed it on numerous occasions, most notably to surround the unfortunate Austrian General Karl Mack von Leiberich at Ulm in 1805. But Napoleon sometimes had to contend with more than one enemy army in the same theatre of war, for example when he tackled both Wellington and Blücher in 1815. In such cases, he usually occupied a central position and sought to divide his opponents and concentrate the bulk of his army to overwhelm each of them in turn. However, this strategy was less likely to produce a truly decisive victory as he could not fully pursue one enemy until he had also defeated the other.

Just as Napoleon preferred aggressive campaigns, he nearly always fought offensive battles. Although he started on the defensive at both Rivoli and Austerlitz, he soon switched to the offensive. In battles such as Leipzig and Arcis-sur-Aube, he fought on the defensive only after the failure of his initial assault. Usually, he attacked from the start and maintained the initiative to the end. He often began with a succession of attacks to tie down the enemy and make him commit his reserves; he might also try to turn a flank. He would then concentrate a deadly artillery crossfire against a vulnerable spot in the enemy's now beleaguered battle line, before breaking through with his Imperial Guard and other reserve units and, ideally, exploiting the victory with a relentless pursuit. The key lay in the timing, which he judged to perfection.

But in later years, as his army grew larger and the quality of his troops declined, Napoleon relied increasingly on brutal attritional tactics devoid of skilful manoeuvres, most notably at Eylau, Wagram, Borodino and Waterloo. Such battles were usually costly and indecisive.

When necessary, Napoleon generally exercised personal command in battle. He received a bayonet wound at Toulon, personally sited the guns at Lodi, led an attack on the bridge at Arcole and rallied his men at Marengo. At Lützen he was repeatedly exposed to enemy fire and at Arcis-sur-Aube rode his horse over a live shell to steady his young soldiers by his example: the explosion disembowelled his horse, but left him unharmed. Yet his ability to control a battle depended on the size of the battlefield. Borodino, for example, was too big for him to be everywhere and partly for this reason he commanded from the rear through his staff and senior subordinates. The problem was greater when he had to divide his army into two wings to tackle two enemy forces simultaneously, for example in the 1815 campaign when he commanded at Ligny but could not simultaneously supervise Marshal Ney six miles away at Quatre Bras.

It is difficult to summarise Napoleon's art of war, but he himself stressed the essential elements:

> These three things you must always keep in mind: concentration of strength, activity, and a firm resolve to perish gloriously. They are the three principles of the military art which have disposed luck in my favour.[7]

Yet Napoleon despite his long catalogue of victories was not infallible. Over-confidence and vague communications were primarily responsible for his worst defeats. He also failed to ensure that his plans could be underpinned logistically, most notoriously when he invaded Russia in 1812. His methods of war became increasingly predictable and this allowed opponents to devise counter-measures. In later years he faced some more capable enemy commanders: the mistakes that undid him in 1815 were the same errors of judgement and over-confidence as those that he had made at Marengo, Aspern–Essling and Smolensk, but never before had he faced a combination of two such formidable opponents as Wellington and Blücher.

Napoleon continues to awe posterity. He was one of the great captains of history, a commander who helped transform the art of war and whose concepts of strategy and leadership still have relevance today. He was extraordinary, but at the same time beset with flaws that were all too human. As a general, he has a secure place in the halls of fame, but went down to several defeats on the battlefield and lost his final four campaigns, those of 1812–15. As a statesman, he gave France glory, but denied her liberty and failed to secure a just and lasting peace. His Empire lasted less than a decade and his most enduring legacies were the *Code Napoléon*, ironically a civil achievement, and a propaganda legend that even today exercises a powerful influence on French national consciousness. His life serves mankind as both example and warning.

The Battle of Austerlitz: 2 December 1805

Fought precisely a year after Napoleon's coronation as Emperor, the Battle of Austerlitz established him as the foremost commander of his age and baptised his Empire in martial glory.

On 23 August 1805, faced by imminent hostilities in central Europe, Napoleon postponed his planned invasion of England. His intelligence indicated that a coalition led by Austria, Russia and Britain was preparing to field an array of armies to crush his Empire. He therefore intended to knock Austria out of the war before the Russians could intervene. He ordered his forces, now dubbed the Grand Army, to leave the Channel camps and cross northern France to the Rhine.

Luckily for Napoleon, the allies did not co-ordinate their offensive. On 10 September an Austrian army under General Karl Mack von Leiberich invaded Bavaria, Napoleon's ally in southern Germany, and occupied the city of Ulm but then halted to await the Russians. The Austrians fielded another army under Archduke Charles in northern Italy and a third under Archduke John in the Alps.

Napoleon decided to surround Mack, who in his position at Ulm could block an advance from the west through the Black Forest but was exposed to a descent on his northern flank. On 25 September the Grand Army began to cross the Rhine. Its corps swept forward on a front of 160 miles and converged as they wheeled southwards until they crossed the Danube to the east of Mack's army on a front of seventy miles. Unfortunately, the advance had crossed an enclave of Prussian territory called Ansbach. Prussia as a result signed a convention with Russia on 3 November but did not actually declare war, for she instead hoped to extract maximum advantage from the two sides by offering armed mediation.

Mack was soon encircled, although some Austrian detachments managed to evade the trap while Archduke Ferdinand broke out with 6,000 cavalry. Mack surrendered with his remaining 23,000 men on 20 October, while subsequent mopping-up operations boosted the tally of Austrian prisoners since the start of the campaign to 60,000.

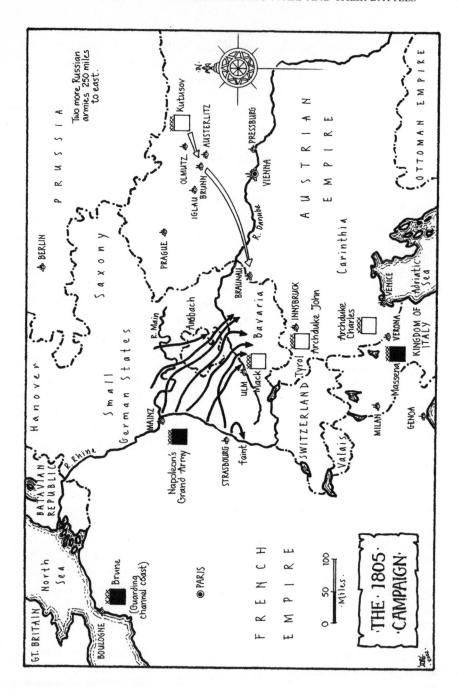

Napoleon had achieved all this without a major battle and with barely 2,000 casualties. Within a week, he was advancing eastwards down the Danube on Vienna. The leading Russian army, 27,000 men under General Mikhail Kutusov, had belatedly reached Braunau, 135 miles east of Ulm, but now hurriedly retreated. Napoleon captured Vienna on 12 November, but failed to trap Kutusov, who withdrew north-eastwards, picking up surviving Austrian units and uniting with the main Russian army under General Friedrich Buxhöwden. These combined forces then fell back to Olmütz, over 100 miles north-east of Vienna, where they were joined by the Russian Imperial Guard from St Petersburg. They now numbered about 73,000 men and were accompanied by both the Russian and Austrian Emperors.

On 20 November Napoleon arrived before the town of Brünn, an important depot and road junction forty miles south-west of Olmütz. He halted, for he was now 500 miles from France and had been forced to detach units to guard his lines of communication all the way back to Vienna and along the Danube. His troops were demoralised and badly needed rest; there were many stragglers. He had only four corps, a total of 53,000 men, in the immediate vicinity of Brünn. Marshal Bernadotte with the I Corps and 15,000 Bavarians was at Iglau, fifty-five miles to the north-west. Another four corps were over sixty miles to the south around Vienna or blocking the Alpine passes to prevent Archdukes Charles and John from coming due north from Italy to join the main allied army around Olmütz.

Napoleon's problem was that he needed a quick and decisive victory, for he faced not only a daunting strategic and logistical situation, but also the onset of winter and a financial and economic crisis in Paris. He would soon exhaust the available supplies around Brünn, while his opponents would be reinforced. Furthermore, the Prussians were slowly mobilising 200,000 men within their frontiers, just fifty miles north of Olmütz.

Rather than retreat, Napoleon decided to use the dispersal of his forces to lure the main allied army into a rash offensive. He could then rapidly concentrate for battle and smash the allies with a powerful and totally unexpected counter-attack. He had already identified a suitable battleground seven miles east of Brünn. It was crossed in the north by a road that ran eastwards to Olmütz past two hills, the Zuran and the Santon. In the centre were the Pratzen heights, which extended diagonally for nearly five miles from the north-east to the south-west. These heights, although modest, were the key feature of the battlefield and their easiest slopes were those on the west, facing the French. Farther south lay the villages of Sokolnitz and Telnitz and the frozen ponds of Satschan and Menitz. A marshy brook, the Goldbach, ran from north to south a mile west of the Pratzen, while the village of Austerlitz, which would give its name to the battle, stood four miles to the east.

Napoleon inspected this ground on 21 November. 'Slowly and silently,

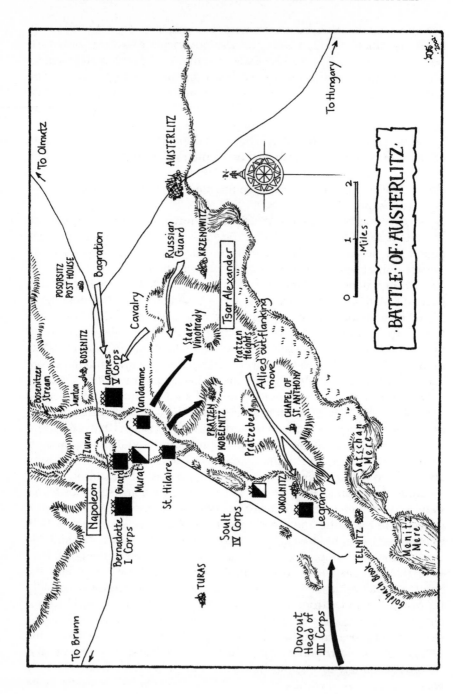

·BATTLE·OF·AUSTERLITZ·

the Emperor went over this exposed plain,' recalled one of his staff, Philippe de Ségur:

> He often halted on the highest points, especially towards Pratzen. He closely examined all its undulations. Several times during this reconnaissance he turned to us and said: 'Gentlemen, examine this ground well, it will be a battlefield. You will have a part to play on it.'[8]

The allies held a council-of-war on the 24th. They had practically exhausted the Olmütz region of supplies and could not remain there. Unless they wanted to retreat, they therefore had to advance and win a decisive victory and they duly attacked Napoleon's outposts on the 28th. Once convinced that this offensive was for real, Napoleon began to concentrate his forces. He instructed his most advanced corps to fall back westwards behind the Goldbach brook and summoned additional units from either wing of his dispersed army, namely Bernadotte's I Corps from Iglau in the west and Marshal Louis Davout's III Corps from Vienna in the south. These moves, hidden by a cavalry screen, still left sizeable detachments to watch the outlying allied forces.

The allies over the next three days continued their advance and began to shift southwards across the battlefield that Napoleon had selected, for they intended to cut him off from Vienna. Napoleon was pleased to see this move as it accorded with his plans. To discourage the allies from attacking in the north, he had previously strengthened the Santon hill by escarping its eastern slopes. He now deliberately abandoned the Pratzen to draw the allies westwards into striking distance. Napoleon also had an interview with an arrogant young Russian envoy, Prince Dolgoruky, at which he pretended to be anxious in order to boost allied over-confidence.

Napoleon deliberately kept his dispositions unbalanced to encourage the allies to attack him in the centre or south. They would thus expose themselves to a counter-stroke by his powerful northern wing, which would be seconded at the other end of the battlefield by the arrival of Marshal Davout's III Corps from Vienna. The northern wing consisted of the V Corps under Marshal Jean Lannes and Murat's Reserve Cavalry, a total of 21,000 men, plus another 22,000 (the Imperial Guard, General Nicolas Oudinot's grenadiers and Bernadotte's newly arrived I Corps) hidden behind the Zuran in reserve. The rest of the battlefront was held only by Marshal Soult's IV Corps of 27,000 troops. The bulk of it stood in the centre opposite the Pratzen, leaving just the 7,000 men of General Claude Legrand's division holding the line of the Goldbach farther south. Napoleon would be able to field almost 75,000 men and 157 guns, including those of Davout's units that would arrive in time for the battle.[9] The allied army numbered 73,000 men, seventy per cent of them Russian, and 318 guns.[10]

Towards 8.30 pm on 1 December, Napoleon altered the emphasis of his plan, mainly because he realised that only Davout's two leading divisions would be within range to intervene the following day. His original plan had been to trap the allied offensive in a vice between Davout and his northern wing. Davout's role was now limited to containing the allied thrust while Napoleon decided the battle with the counter-attack in the north.

Napoleon had an Order of the Day read to his troops around their bivouac fires. They were told that the honour of the French infantry and of the whole nation was at stake and that they could not afford to let victory slip through their hands. No one was to leave the ranks under the pretext of helping the wounded, for it was vital to beat the Russians. Victory would end the campaign, obtain rest in winter quarters and enable Napoleon to make a worthy peace. According to General Paul Thiébault:

> One sentence in particular really electrified the troops, that is the one where the Emperor announced that if they justified his hopes, he would limit himself to directing the moves, but otherwise he would expose himself to the greatest dangers.[11]

At 9.00 pm Napoleon retired to a hut that his engineers had built, but was woken barely an hour later with the news that heavy musketry could be heard in the south, near Telnitz. This in fact was only a minor, local clash, but Napoleon mounted a horse and rode off with a small party for another personal reconnaissance. He actually went beyond his outposts to watch for enemy moves and had to gallop to safety when he nearly blundered into some Cossacks in the darkness. What he had seen and heard convinced him that the allied offensive would fall in the extreme south, near Telnitz and Sokolnitz, and he slightly altered his dispositions to take account of this.

As Napoleon walked back to his headquarters through the French encampments, he was recognised by some soldiers and soon the camp was lit by thousands of torches in spontaneous celebration of his coronation as Emperor. Napoleon was initially angry at this breach of security, but soon softened and called the evening the most beautiful of his life. One of Marshal Soult's ADCs recalled how Napoleon:

> stopped at each step and talked kindly to these brave men who were as surprised as they were delighted at the unexpected visit of the emperor. The enthusiasm was at its height.[12]

Ironically, the allies took the sudden blaze of light to be a decoy to cover a retreat.[13] The rest of the night passed reasonably peacefully and at 4.00 am on 2 December Napoleon's troops moved silently into their battle positions under the cover of darkness and the early morning mist.

The allies renewed their advance towards 6.30 am, as the sky began to lighten. They were formed into five columns, besides the Advanced Guard under General Peter Bagration and the Imperial Guard. The first four columns, a total of 46,000 men, were to make the outflanking move in the south under General Buxhöwden, while the remaining 27,000 remained in the north. Confusion quickly set in, largely as the result of poor staff work and the delays caused by having to translate orders from German into Russian. Then shots came from the southern sector as allied skirmishers ran into Legrand's division near Telnitz. Legrand had orders to fall back and draw the allies on, but found that his soldiers, not wanting to retreat, fought with more success than expected.

Napoleon ate breakfast on the Zuran hill and then, towards 7.30 am, held a final briefing, to which he summoned all his corps commanders except Marshal Davout, who was too distant. Philippe de Ségur never forgot the sight of the gilded subordinates assembled around the Emperor. It was, he thought,

> the most incredible gathering you can imagine. A wonderful sight! What assembled celebrities were in this fearsome circle! What warlords, justly and variously famed, surrounding the greatest warrior of ancient and modern times![14]

After the briefing Napoleon dismissed his marshals to rejoin their corps, except for Soult who remained for the time being. Each marshal left an ADC behind to carry any additional orders that Napoleon might deem necessary.

It was 8.00 am and the rising sun shone through the mist as a spectacular red orb. Napoleon intended to open his counter-stroke with two infantry divisions of Soult's corps seizing the Pratzen. He therefore waited while more allied formations ponderously left these heights to reinforce the assault on his southern wing. At 8.45 am he turned to Soult and asked how long his divisions needed to reach the top of the Pratzen. 'Less than twenty minutes, Sire,' came the crisp reply, 'for my troops are hidden at the foot of the valley, hidden by fog and campfire smoke.'

'In that case,' Napoleon decided, 'we will wait a further quarter of an hour.'[15]

The minutes ticked past. Then Napoleon turned to Soult and sent him on his way with the words: 'one sharp blow and the war is over.'

Soult harangued his men before unleashing the attack. Commanded by Generals Louis Saint-Hilaire and Dominique Vandamme, his two divisions stormed up the western slopes of the Pratzen on a front of about two miles. These 16,000 infantrymen emerged into bright, uplifting sunlight, gained the plateau and then halted to consolidate.

As a result of this totally unexpected attack, the allied high command lost control of the battle and was reduced to reacting as best it could to developments. But the outcome was far from decided. The allies had been advancing southwards so sluggishly that contrary to Napoleon's calculations their Fourth Column was still descending from the Pratzen. This formation hurriedly counter-attacked, while the rear of the Second Column was also recalled from the southern sector. As a result, Saint-Hilaire came under such pressure that he held a council of war and considered withdrawing his division. He was dissuaded by Colonel Pouzet, the commander of the 10th Light infantry, who advocated a desperate bayonet charge and this, together with the timely arrival of six 12-pounder cannon, saved the situation.

Napoleon kept track of the battle from the Zuran by both mounted messengers and semaphore telegraph stations established along the rear of his army. He issued orders after consulting a log that was kept up-to-date by his staff with details of the condition of all his divisions and brigades.

In the north, Bagration was held in check by Lannes's V Corps and Murat's cavalry. Likewise, the main allied thrust in the south had been blunted. Davout's leading brigade had arrived at Telnitz just in time to save Legrand from being overwhelmed. After a further two hours, the allies finally took Telnitz and Sokolnitz, but by 10.00 am their 25,000 troops here had been checked by approximately 10,000 Frenchmen.

In the centre, the fighting had moved eastwards with the advance of Soult's two divisions. Towards noon, Napoleon therefore transferred his command post to Staré Vinohrady, the second highest point on the Pratzen, to be in a better position to see and direct the battle. At the same time, he ordered forward his reserves: the Imperial Guard, Bernadotte's I Corps and Oudinot's division of grenadiers.

Napoleon arrived on Staré Vinohrady in time to witness the climax of the battle, the counter-attack of the 8,000-strong Russian Imperial Guard. Crashing into the northern flank of Soult's infantry, these formidable troops routed the 4th Line infantry and smashed the 24th Light, thus tearing open a gaping hole in the French positions atop the Pratzen.

Napoleon ordered his staff not to try and stop the mob of fugitives that came streaming back. He would later harangue the 4th Line mercilessly, but for the moment had more pressing matters to settle. He ordered Marshal Jean-Baptiste Bessières to charge with elements of the Imperial Guard cavalry and thus won time for part of Bernadotte's I Corps to arrive and bolster the French position. Napoleon then sent an ADC, General Jean Rapp, to join the fray with some more Guard cavalry. Rapp galloped off and towards 2.00 pm the Russian Imperial Guard finally broke, leaving the allied centre irreparably shattered. The scores of Russian corpses that now littered the ground caused Napoleon to remark drily that many fine ladies of St Petersburg would lament that day. To a captured Russian officer who had lost his guns and was in despair, he added: 'calm yourself, young man; you have nothing to be ashamed of in being beaten by Frenchmen.'[16]

It was time to turn the allied defeat into a disaster. Napoleon had originally intended to wheel the whole of his army southwards, using Legrand and Davout as a pivot, but was foiled by Bagration's unexpectedly tough resistance in the north. He therefore settled for a reduced version of the wheeling movement, involving only the centre of his army. Lannes and Murat would continue to drive back Bagration in the north, while Bernadotte's I Corps covered the now-undisputed Pratzen. Napoleon gave the orders for the wheeling move directly to Soult's two divisional commanders, Vandamme and Saint-Hilaire[17], and then followed their advance up to the Chapel of St Anthony on the southern slopes of the Pratzen, which became his third command post. Below him, in the southern sector, a mass of allied units under General Buxhöwden lay exposed to catastrophe, for once their escape route eastwards was cut, they would be pinned against the frozen Satschan and Menitz ponds.

Buxhöwden's units were already under attack from the west, where the admirable Davout and Legrand were counter-attacking in the Telnitz–Sokolnitz sector, and Soult's infantry now descended from the Pratzen to cut him off to the east. Yet even at this stage, Napoleon's decisive victory seemed for a moment to be slipping from his grasp. Fierce resistance allowed many of Buxhöwden's men to escape before the trap closed. Napoleon vented his frustration on his subordinates, accusing the luckless commander of a dragoon division which was repelled by allied cavalry of being no good and replacing him with one of his ADCs, General Matthieu de Gardane. But the wretched allied troops were hemmed in at last against the frozen meres and began to make off across the ice under artillery fire from the heights.

A French gunner, Captain Théodore Seruzier, remembered how Napoleon galloped up and shouted: 'you are wasting your time in striking these masses – you must engulf them. Fire on the ice!'[18] Soon, the frozen surface of the meres broke under both the impact of red-hot cannonballs and the weight of fugitives and their guns. Napoleon dismounted and watched the resulting turmoil through his eye-glass. According to one account, he remarked: 'it is Aboukir,' a reference to the battle in Egypt six years previously when he had driven the Turks into the sea.[19] Only about 200 men drowned in the shallow ponds and just thirty-eight guns were recovered from them later, but Napoleon exaggerated the incident in his subsequent bulletin to reinforce the image of a great victory and it readily entered the mythology of the First Empire.

The allied southern wing had now disintegrated, but what of developments on the rest of the battlefield? In fact, once Napoleon had gone southwards to envelop Buxhöwden, a curious paralysis had fallen on his forces elsewhere. In the north, Lannes and Murat had failed to encircle Bagration or inflict significant casualties on him as he left the field, while in the centre Bernadotte had halted tamely on the Pratzen rather than push on eastwards to the village of Austerlitz and cut the road to Hungary. Napoleon, being absorbed in the task of destroying Buxhöwden, apparently neglected to send orders to Lannes and Murat and the loss of impetus allowed many fugitives to escape.

Night fell and so did the cold rain that finished off many of the injured. Austerlitz cost Napoleon nearly 9,000 men, or twelve per cent of his army. Of his generals, one died from injuries and another thirteen were wounded. Allied losses amounted to 29,000, or forty per cent, plus 183 guns. As Napoleon rode northwards across the stricken battlefield, he ordered his suite to be silent so that they could hear the groans of the wounded and bring them help. He himself gave several of them a glass of brandy and ordered prisoners to be treated well. Finally, at 10.00 pm, he entered the Posorsitz Post House on the Brünn road for some much-needed sleep.

'Soldiers, I am pleased with you.' Thus began the exuberant Order of the Day that Napoleon completed on the morning after the battle. He told his men what they had achieved, how many prisoners and guns they had taken and promised to lead them back to France as soon as he had obtained a good and lasting peace. On their return, they would be greeted with joy and would only have to say 'I was at the Battle of Austerlitz' to hear the reply, 'there is one of the brave.' Four days later, Napoleon awarded 200 francs to each soldier, with even more for officers. Widows of the slain would receive a pension while orphaned children would be adopted by the Emperor and allowed to add 'Napoleon' to their names.

It remained for Napoleon to tie up diplomatic loose ends. He met the Austrian Emperor Francis on 4 December and granted him an armistice, while the Russians retreated homewards. Napoleon had smashed the Third Coalition and saved his Empire from a premature end. Yet he failed to secure a durable peace, partly because he won so decisive a victory at Austerlitz that he lost touch with the need for moderation. The Treaty of Pressburg, concluded three weeks after the battle, led to renewed war with Austria in 1809 and by drastically altering the balance of power provoked Prussia to take the field in 1806.

Austerlitz remained unsurpassed as Napoleon's finest battlefield achievement. His Grand Army, superbly trained and motivated and as yet unsapped by the massive casualties of subsequent years, had proven its prowess. 'At Austerlitz,' he later declared, 'the army was the most solid that I ever had.'[20] His corps commanders were almost all reliable and some, notably Davout, were brilliant. Their ages ranged from 35 to 42 and they were more than a match for the lacklustre allied leaders, who included not only the aged Kutusov and Buxhöwden at 60 and 55, but also the inexperienced Tsar Alexander and his brother Constantine at 28 and 26.

Yet despite the battle's celebrated place in Napoleonic mythology, it was not an easy victory, nor had it proved as complete as he had hoped. The outcome had hung in the balance even after the morning's fighting and the French had not dared to take prisoners until the closing stages. It had not gone entirely as Napoleon expected, but he knew that he could plan only the opening moves in detail and that he would have to seize opportunities as they developed. In contrast to the allies, he had a flexible plan and exercised continuously effective battle control by moving to the front to keep pace with the advance of his troops and react promptly to developments.

Austerlitz, in fact, shows Napoleon at his very best as a battlefield commander. After other important battles, he often recognised the valour of one of his chief subordinates by giving him the name of the action as a title. But he never created a Duke of Austerlitz, for he saw it as his personal triumph and one of his greatest claims to fame.

NOTES

1 B. Weider and É. Guegen, *Napoleon: The Man who Shaped Europe* (2000)
2 The Grande Armée was Napoleon's main army, under his personal command. Secondary armies would be operating in other theatres, for instance Italy or Spain.
3 D. Chandler, *The campaigns of Napoleon* (1966), pp.852–3
4 J. Coignet, *The notebooks of Captain Coignet* (1986), p.202
5 E. Blaze, *Life in Napoleon's army: the memoirs of Captain Elzéar Blaze* (1995), p.132
6 Coignet, *op cit.*, p.261
7 J. Herold, ed., *The mind of Napoleon* (1955), p.220
8 P. de Ségur, *Histoire et mémoires* (1873), v.2, p.445
9 Of Davout's corps, an infantry division and a cavalry division, 4,300 men in all, arrived on 2 December in time to fight. Another of Davout's infantry divisions, under General François-Marie-Auguste Caffarelli, also saw action, but having arrived on 29 November was attached to V Corps under Lannes's command.
10 S. Bowden, *Napoleon and Austerlitz* (1997), p.505, demonstrates that the usual figures given for the allies (85,000) reflect only their theoretical strength, rather than the numbers actually present on the battlefield.
11 F. Calmettes, ed., *Mémoires du général baron Thiébault* (1894), v.1, pp.453–4. Doubts have been raised about the authenticity of the order of the day. The versions published in the official accounts were probably edited after the battle in the light of what actually happened. See Chandler, *op. cit.*, p.422.
12 A. Pétiet, *Souvenirs militaires* (1844), p.26
13 A. Mikhailovsky-Danilevsky, *Relation de la campagne de 1805 (Austerlitz)* (1846), p.231
14 Ségur, *op. cit.*, v.2, p.463
15 Chandler, *op. cit.*, p.425

16 Ségur, *op. cit.*, v.2, p.471
17 The whereabouts of Soult himself is shrouded in controversy, with one of his brigade commanders, General Paul Thiébault, claiming that Soult was not personally present on the Pratzen for more than three hours despite the crisis there. Although a capable organiser, Soult was not a great battlefield commander and after serious wounds early in his career tended to avoid being too close to the fighting. See Calmettes, *op. cit.*, v.3, p.506.
18 T. Seruzier, *Mémoires militaires du Baron Seruzier, colonel d'artillerie légère* (nd), p.28
19 Ségur, *op. cit.*, v.2, p.473
20 G. Gourgaud, *Sainte-Hélène: journal inédit de 1815 à 1818* (nd), v.2, p.111

CHAPTER II
Eugène de Beauharnais

It took just a whiff of grapeshot on 5 October 1795 to crush a royalist revolt in Paris, but the sense of alarm lingered on and led to an edict that all unauthorised weapons in the city be handed in. The story goes that a young lad came to see General Bonaparte, the man who had smashed the insurrection and who now commanded the Army of the Interior. The youth's name was Eugène de Beauharnais and he had come to ask for the return of his late father's sword. Touched by the request, Bonaparte gave him the weapon and Eugène burst into tears.[1]

Eugène, although only 14, was already formed in character and throughout his life would live up to his motto, Honour and Fidelity. He was the son of Viscount Alexandre de Beauharnais and a Créole beauty called Rose Tascher de la Pagerie, later known as Josephine. They had married in 1779, but were unhappy in their arranged union and separated six years later. But they did produce two remarkable children, who were each destined to play a prominent role in world affairs. Eugène, born on 3 September 1781, would be a viceroy, a prince and army commander; Hortense, who followed in April 1783, would become a queen and the mother of an emperor. Brother and sister would remain devoted to each other through a host of troubles for the rest of their lives.

Eugène had an unsettled childhood. He lived in twelve different homes before he was 13 and inevitably suffered from a haphazard education as a result. Further upheaval resulted from the Revolution in 1789. Eugène's father became a member of the Constituent Assembly as an enlightened aristocrat. Following the outbreak of war with Austria in 1792, Alexandre rejoined the Army (in which he had previously made a career) and took command of the Army of the Rhine in May 1793. Eugène attended a college at Strasbourg and frequently visited his father's headquarters at nearby Weissenburg.

But as the Revolution became more extreme, General Alexandre de Beauharnais was forced to retire to his estates and was arrested in March 1794 and accused of treason in having failed to relieve the city of Mainz. The following month Josephine, too, was imprisoned. Alexandre died gallantly at the guillotine and Josephine nearly shared his fate, but was saved by the fall of the ruthless Maximilien de Robespierre of the Committee of Public Safety, which signalled an end to the Terror. She returned to her children in August 1794 and Hortense recorded that Eugène now:

> considered himself as the natural protector not only of myself but also of my mother. Despite his youth he already showed that decision of character and calmness in the face of danger which he has displayed since.[2]

Two father figures took Eugène under their wing. The first was General Lazare Hoche, one of Josephine's admirers who had served under Eugène's father. Hoche as commander of the Army of the West was fighting in the Vendée against royalist rebels and an *émigré* landing at Quiberon. Eugène served with him as an orderly from September 1794 for almost a year, came under fire and learnt much about the military profession. But this could not fully compensate for lack of a formal and systematic education and when Josephine could afford to do so, she recalled him to finish his schooling.

Then, in October 1795, royalists attempted a counter-Revolution in Paris, only to be crushed by Bonaparte's famous 'whiff of grapeshot'. It was the subsequent edict that all unauthorised weapons be handed in that brought the 14-year-old Eugène to ask Bonaparte for the return of his father's sword.

Josephine called on Napoleon the next day to thank him for his kindness towards Eugène. This was not, apparently, the first time that she had met Napoleon, but it led to a whirlwind romance. Neither Eugène nor Hortense viewed the marriage in March 1796 with enthusiasm and subsequent events would prove them right. But the move was crucial for Eugène's career, for it made him Napoleon's stepson.

Eugène now settled down to a full twenty months of boarding school. Then, in July 1797, he left France to join his stepfather, who had won a dazzling string of victories over the Austrians in northern Italy. Eugène, in fact, was in an enviable situation, being 15, a Second-Lieutenant in the 1st Hussars and ADC to Napoleon. His privileged years of service on Napoleon's staff certainly compensated in part for the deficiencies in his education. Although the fighting in Italy had ended in April, Eugène was kept busy, being sent by Napoleon to reconnoitre in the mountains of the north-east, an area where he would subsequently command an army in both 1809 and 1813. He also went on a tour of inspection to the island of Corfu, which had been newly acquired by France. While returning through Italy that December, he was caught up in unrest in Rome, when fighting between a republican crowd and papal troops spilled over into the grounds of the French embassy. Eugène kept his cool and helped calm the situation.

In May 1798 he sailed from Toulon as part of Napoleon's expedition to Egypt. The fleet stopped first at the island of Malta, which Napoleon soon captured from the Knights of St John. Eugène saw action during a sortie by the garrison of Valletta and even seized a flag. By sheer luck, the French fleet evaded Rear-Admiral Horatio Nelson's British warships and at the beginning of July appeared off the coast of Egypt. After taking Alexandria, Napoleon made an epic march across the desert and then advanced up the Nile on Cairo.

The Battle of the Pyramids followed on 21 July 1798. Eugène heard Napoleon's famous exhortation, 'Soldiers, consider that from the top of these monuments forty centuries look down on you.'[3] The French formed into huge defensive squares, which the mameluke horsemen were unable to penetrate. But Eugène as one of Napoleon's ADCs had to ride around the battlefield and constantly ran the risk of being accidentally shot by his own side or killed by a mameluke.

During the occupation of Cairo, Eugène was repeatedly sent to reconnoitre in the desert, where he often encountered parties of the enemy. He also led the advanced guard of a detachment sent to occupy the port of Suez and after a gruelling march across the desert was the first Frenchman to enter the town, which had been abandoned by the enemy.

The news that two Ottoman armies were about to attack caused Napoleon to launch a pre-emptive invasion of Syria in February 1799. Eugène nearly died in April during the siege of Saint-Jean-d'Acre, when the explosion of a shell left him badly wounded in the head and trapped under the rubble of a ruined bastion. The siege failed and Napoleon retreated to Egypt, where in July he beat an Ottoman army that landed at Aboukir.

Meanwhile the situation in Europe had gone badly for France, beset as she was by military reverses and political instability. Napoleon resolved to return and seize supreme power in Paris. That August, he abandoned his army, taking with him only Eugène and a few other trusted companions. By this stage, Josephine's marriage was already a sham, despite Eugène's tact and diplomacy in trying to mediate. Both she and Napoleon had been blatantly unfaithful during their long separation and it took all Josephine's charm and the pleas of both Eugène and Hortense to win Napoleon's forgiveness on his return.

Napoleon seized power by a coup d'état on 9 November 1799 as one of three consuls and swiftly consolidated his position so he was effectively a dictator. But Eugène became bored with his palace duties as Napoleon's ADC and longed for a return to soldiering. Heeding his pleas, Napoleon gave him command of the company (later squadron) of Chasseurs à Cheval in the newly created Consular Guard.[4] He also appointed General Jean-Baptiste Bessières, who was Second-in-Command of the Guard, to act as Eugène's tutor. Eugène, by now a captain, was keen to learn as much as he could, but also enjoyed himself with his friends in Paris and delighted in practical jokes.

The spring of 1800 saw him march with Napoleon over the Alps and into northern Italy to take the field against the Austrians. He commanded his chasseurs at the Battle of Marengo that June, the first time that he had commanded a unit in action. He would not do so again for nine years and on that occasion would be in charge of an army. Marengo induced the Austrians to sue for an armistice in northern Italy and allowed Napoleon to return home in triumph. Eugène, now a major, had the honour of bringing back to Paris the flags captured in the battle.

It took another seven months before Austria finally concluded peace in February 1801. Hostilities continued with Britain, except for an interval of fourteen months, but France enjoyed four years of peace on the continent. Eugène, stationed with his chasseurs in the vicinity of Paris, strove to fill the gaps in his education and training and swiftly gained promotion and honours, being appointed colonel in 1802; Colonel-General of the Chasseurs à Cheval of the Guard and *général de brigade* in 1804; and Prince and Arch-Chancellor of State in 1805.

Then came the turning point. Napoleon, who had crowned himself Emperor of the French on 2 December 1804, went to Milan and in May 1805 crowned himself King of Italy. The kingdom consisted of the central part of northern Italy, but would later be extended to include the north-east of the peninsula and a strip of territory down the eastern coast as far as the Kingdom of Naples in the south. (The western side of northern Italy was directly annexed to France.) Napoleon needed a trustworthy subordinate to administer the kingdom and chose Eugène, who became Viceroy on 7 June at the age of 23.

Napoleon believed that Eugène's loyalty and conscientiousness would outweigh his youth, inexperience and patchy education. He left detailed instructions and a team of administrators to help him in his task. He advised him to be prudent, to punish any dishonesty ruthlessly, keep his subjects happy and personally inspect the kingdom and familiarise himself with the terrain in case he should need to fight there in future years. Eugène would receive many more letters on a whole range of topics, from the quartering of troops to the planting of trees outside the city of Mantua, and while he inevitably made mistakes, he settled into his new role and helped make the Kingdom of Italy the most successful of Napoleon's satellite states.

The prospect of a full-scale war grew during 1805. Eugène was kept busy preparing his kingdom, but would not be given command of its Army in the field, for Napoleon sent the experienced Marshal André Massena to this theatre. Hostilities finally broke out in September. The crucial region was north of the Alps, where Napoleon was personally engaged against the Austrians and Russians. But the Austrians fielded another army in north-eastern Italy, under their best general, Archduke Charles. Massena failed to defeat Charles at Caldiero, six miles east of Verona, but found that Charles then retreated anyway, because of allied reverses at Napoleon's hands in the Danube valley.

Eugène, meanwhile, had been preparing to defend the Kingdom of Italy's southern frontier with a reserve corps of second-line troops against an Anglo-Russian force that had landed in the Kingdom of Naples. But news of Napoleon's decisive victory over the main allied army at Austerlitz that December caused the allies in southern Italy to re-embark without attacking. In December Eugène was appointed *général de division* and at the beginning of January 1806 took over as Commander-in-Chief of the Army of Italy, although by now the fighting was over. As a result of the peace terms, Austria ceded several tracts of land to the Kingdom of Italy, including Venetia and Istria in the north-east of the peninsula and Dalmatia, an isolated province on the eastern coast of the Adriatic sea. (Dalmatia after 1809 would be administered directly by France as part of the Illyrian provinces.)

Napoleon now sought to tie Bavaria, his important ally in southern Germany, more closely to his interests and arranged a marriage for Eugène to Princess Auguste Amélie, the eldest daughter of Maximilian Joseph, the Elector of Bavaria, whom he elevated to the status of King. Eugène went to meet his bride in January 1806 and found that she was remarkably beautiful. He apparently offered that, if she did not want to marry him, he would take the responsibility for calling it off. But the wedding took place on 14 January and although Auguste had initially been horrified at the prospect of marrying Napoleon's stepson, she was soon informing her brother that:

> I am wonderfully fortunate. Eugène is so good and kind. Forgive me for saying this, but I do not believe you could be so indulgent to a wife as he is.[5]

On 16 February Napoleon formally adopted Eugène as his son and subsequently appointed him to be his successor as King of Italy, unless he himself produced a legitimate male heir, as he would in fact do in 1811. Eugène hence took the title of Eugène Napoleon and became Prince of Venice, although he still itched to be a successful soldier. He asked to be allowed to participate in the campaigns against the Prussians in 1806 and the Spaniards two years later, but was refused, since his duty as Viceroy was to run the Kingdom of Italy. But in 1809 war came to the Italian peninsula and, with so many French marshals tied down in Spain, Napoleon could no longer afford to dispense with Eugène's services.

Never before had Eugène commanded more than a squadron on the battlefield, but he now found himself entrusted with the whole Army of

Italy and, because Napoleon's orders took about five days to reach him, he would have to act on his own initiative as a semi-independent commander. For a year now, Napoleon had been writing him letters outlining suitable responses to an Austrian invasion of the Kingdom of Italy, but no amount of theoretical study could fully compensate for the lack of practical experience.

In April 1809 an Austrian army under Archduke Charles attacked along the Danube into Bavaria. Another army under Charles's less able brother, Archduke John, meanwhile crossed into the mountainous north-eastern region of the Kingdom of Italy. After detaching troops to support an insurrection in the Tyrol and to attack the province of Dalmatia on the eastern coast of the Adriatic, John had 44,000 men with his main body.

About a third of Eugène's Army of Italy consisted of Italian units, the rest being French. Napoleon had ordered him to fall right back to the Adige river and concentrate before offering battle. Eugène was not to take the offensive, but simply contain John so as to guard Napoleon's southern flank. Eugène steadily withdrew before John's superior numbers for three days, but then disobeyed his instructions and on 14 April turned at bay at the forward position of Sacile, thirty-eight miles north of Venice. This would prove the greatest blunder of his career. He was too keen to prove himself and disliked exposing the people of the Kingdom of Italy to invasion; he was also over-alarmed by the insurrection in the Tyrol and hoped to keep the situation there under control by defeating John.

Sacile was Eugène's first battle as an independent commander. His advanced guard was seriously mauled in a preliminary action at Pordenone, seven miles east of Sacile, on 15 April. He expected that more of his troops would arrive in time for the battle that ensued on the 16th, but reckoned without the heavy rains and flooding that prevented a division of infantry and another of dragoons from reaching him in time. As a result, while he could match John's 35,000 infantry, he had only 2,000 cavalrymen against John's 4,000.

Eugène planned to remain on the defensive in the open terrain in the north of the battlefield, where John's superiority in cavalry made an advance dangerous, while he attacked over the more broken ground in the south. Eugène had carefully reconnoitred the battlefield and initially made progress, but found that the difficult terrain in the south slowed his advance. Furthermore, he had over-extended his army and when the Austrians counter-attacked his exposed northern wing, he had to withdraw. He lost 6,500 men and fifteen guns and more men besides during the subsequent retreat. Fortunately, John failed to launch an immediate or vigorous pursuit.

Eugène re-organised his army behind the Adige and Alpone rivers, seventy miles south-west of Sacile. John had to detach more troops to guard his communications as he advanced and was numerically inferior to Eugène by the time he arrived before the Adige. Furthermore, Napoleon's dramatic repulse of Archduke Charles on the Danube in mid-April lifted the pressure on Eugène in Italy and caused John on 1 May to begin retreating north-eastwards after some minor clashes with Eugène on 29 and 30 April. Eugène followed and on the 7th reached the Piave river, one of a series that flowed across his line of advance.

The next day, Eugène feinted in the west and boldly attacked across the Piave in the centre and east. Taken by surprise, the Austrians counter-attacked, but had kept the bulk of their troops too far back from the river bank. Eugène won a clear-cut victory that compensated for Sacile and established his dominance over John. One of Eugène's subordinates, General François-Marie-Auguste Caffarelli, wrote:

> The Prince behaved like a worthy son of the Emperor. I admired his coolness and presence of mind; the only fault I could find with him was that he was too brave.[6]

Eugène continued to pursue John, first over the Tagliamento river and then into difficult, mountainous terrain near the frontier, fighting minor actions on the way and further reducing John's strength. Eugène's right flank was covered by a detached corps under General Jacques Macdonald and, farther to the south-east, by General Auguste Marmont's IX Corps advancing northwards from Dalmatia. (Macdonald had arrived after Sacile but, contrary to his deceitful memoirs, had not been sent to take over from Eugène following that defeat. His appointment had already been made at the beginning of April and he served in a subordinate position.)

On 17 May Eugène stormed the fort of Malborghetto and a day later took that of Predil, thus opening the two main routes through the mountains into the Austrian Empire. He also defeated an Austrian force holding a fortified position at the nearby town of Tarvis by falling on its flank. He rested temporarily at Klagenfurt, 150 miles south-west of Vienna, before resuming his advance on the 23rd on Napoleon's orders. Two days later, he smashed and vigorously pursued a detached Austrian division of 7,000 men under General Franz von Jellacic after it blundered into him at the village of St Michael near Leoben. Then, on the 26th, his light cavalry linked up with Napoleon's at the Semmering pass, forty-five miles south of Vienna. Eugène's vigorous pursuit of John had taken 20,000 prisoners and 140 guns.

Eugène went to Vienna to meet Napoleon and was then sent with his troops into Hungary, while Napoleon remained near Vienna opposite the main Austrian army under Archduke Charles. Eugène's task was to seek out and destroy John's army, which had been reinforced by both regulars and 10,000 men of the Hungarian *Insurrectio* under Archduke Joseph, the Prince Palatine of Hungary.

After several minor clashes, Eugène arrived before the fortress city of Raab, eighty miles south-east of Vienna, and on 14 June fought a major battle against Archdukes John and Joseph outside that city. He enjoyed a slight numerical superiority and had better quality troops, since half of John's men were from the *Landwehr* or the hastily mobilised Hungarian *Insurrectio*.[7] Nonetheless, John held a tough position on top of a plateau, with a brook, a village and a fortified farm out in front to anchor his line. It took Eugène's troops four hours to conquer the battlefield. He personally rallied some of his Italian soldiers after his advance was checked and kept up the pressure until, by 5.00 pm, his men had gained the battlefield. Part of John's army withdrew into the city of Raab, while the rest retreated from the field.

'I congratulate you on the battle of Raab,' Napoleon informed Eugène, 'it is a grand-daughter of Marengo and of Friedland.'[8] But in fact, Eugène had damaged rather than destroyed John's army and was unable to mount an effective pursuit, though in the event, this would not matter, as John would fail to unite with Charles.

Following the capitulation of the city of Raab on 23 June, Eugène was summoned with the bulk of his strength to reinforce Napoleon at Vienna. The Army of Italy hence became part of the Emperor's main army and took part in the crossing of the Danube and the subsequent two-day Battle of Wagram on 5–6 July between Napoleon and Archduke Charles. Eugène on the 6th personally led several cavalry charges, while Macdonald at the crisis of the battle assaulted the Austrian centre with a massive hollow formation of 8,000 of Eugène's troops. Macdonald suffered appalling casualties and failed to break through, but helped induce the Austrians to retreat and won his marshal's baton.

After Wagram, Eugène was again detached and sent to pursue John into Hungary, this time with German troops from Saxony and Württemberg attached to his command. An armistice on 12 July ended hostilities; peace was formally signed in October.

Before Eugène could return to Auguste in Italy, he had to pacify the mountainous Tyrol, where an innkeeper called Andreas Hofer was leading an insurrection. Eugène issued a proclamation in an attempt to persuade the insurgents to give up the struggle. Andreas Hofer initially responded favourably, but later changed his mind, while the King of Bavaria was annoyed at Eugène's leniency. Eugène as a result of Napoleon's orders reluctantly issued another proclamation, this time threatening that any inhabitant found with a firearm would be shot. The campaign ended in bitter fighting. Hofer was captured in January 1810, taken to Italy and shot, despite Eugène's efforts to have him spared.

Eugène returned to his family at Milan in November 1809, but was summoned to Paris just two weeks later, for Napoleon in pursuit of his dynastic ambitions had decided to divorce Josephine and remarry.

Eugène stoutly supported his mother, arguing that if Josephine were no longer Empress, he could not remain as Viceroy. He found the divorce such an ordeal that he later spoke of this time as the most terrible of his life and at one point fainted from the emotional strain.

Napoleon's subsequent marriage in February 1810 to Marie-Louise, the daughter of the Austrian Emperor, had a major impact on Eugène's prospects. Napoleon named the son he hoped to father 'the King of Rome' and decreed that Eugène was to remain as Viceroy for twenty years, until Napoleon's son could take over the kingdom. By way of compensation, Eugène was named heir to the Grand Duchy of Frankfurt.

The thunderclouds of war again gathered on the horizon, for Napoleon's relations with Russia were on the verge of collapse. He assembled a mighty army of over half-a-million men with which to invade Russia in June 1812 and drew contingents from the various states of occupied Europe. The IV Corps was formed from Italian and French troops from the Kingdom of Italy and Eugène himself took the field at its head.

Eugène commanded 95,000 men, namely his own IV Corps plus the VI (Bavarian) Corps and III Cavalry Corps. He formed part of Napoleon's main body, but connected it with Jérôme Bonaparte's detached command operating against the Russian 2nd Army under General Peter Bagration in the south. Initially, Eugène was involved only in minor clashes, but had enough problems with logistics. Some of his Italians complained that they were deprived of supplies captured from the Russians, since the French tended to appropriate them all. But Eugène could do little and under the strain of command burst out:

Eh! __, gentlemen. What you want is impossible. If you are not happy, be aware that I fear your swords no more than your stilettos.[9]

He never fully wiped out the effect of these sarcastic words, which alienated many of his hitherto devoted Italians. Napoleon's contempt for the Italian people seems to have rubbed off on Eugène during their correspondence. Note, for instance, Eugène's jibe in a letter to the Emperor about what he saw as the Archbishop of Udine's cowardice: 'this was doubtless his way – that is to say, an Italian's way – of getting out of a tight corner.'[10]

Eugène saw no real action until the Russians under General Mikhail Kutusov finally halted at Borodino, eighty miles west of Moscow, to offer the great battle that Napoleon had desired for so long.[11] It was 7 September. Eugène took the village of Borodino and then twice attacked the Great Redoubt, but with only temporary success. Towards noon he was preparing to throw in a third assault when Russian cavalry and Cossacks descended on his rear from the north and obliged him to pull back to deal with the threat. In fact, the Russian horsemen were easily checked, but their appearance had alarmed and distracted Napoleon. After this two-hour lull Eugène finally captured the Great Redoubt with the help of a massive cavalry onslaught and according to an Imperial Guard captain, 'among a host of generals who added to their fame that day, Eugène and Ney were hailed by all.'[12] But the bloody and fruitless battle petered out in mutual exhaustion and that night the Russians resumed their retreat.

On 14 September Napoleon finally reached Moscow, but found that his occupation of the city did not bring the Russians to the peace table. After five weeks, he ordered his army to retreat south-westwards through more fertile southerly land. Eugène's IV Corps led the way, but after seventy miles found the road blocked by Russian forces at Malojaroslavets. Eugène attacked at dawn on 24 October and took and lost the village several times. One of his divisional commanders, General Alexis Delzons, was among the slain. An assault by the Italian Royal Guard and the Italian infantry division of General Dominique Pino finally drove back the Russians. It had been Eugène's battle. As he wrote to his wife:

> Yesterday was a superb day for my corps. I fought from dawn to dusk against eight enemy divisions and I ended by maintaining my position. French and Italians covered themselves with glory.[13]

But it was a costly and indecisive success and Napoleon did not dare to press on. He could not afford another murderous battle like Borodino and was unnerved when almost captured by Cossacks while reconnoitring on the 25th. Abandoning the idea of a southerly line of retreat, he ordered his army to retire north-westwards to reach its devastated line of advance.

Napoleon's army as it retired became over-extended and prey to harassment from the Russians. On 3 November Eugène had to turn back to prevent Marshal Davout's I Corps, at the time serving as the army's rearguard, from being cut off. The situation rapidly worsened the next day when winter set in with a vengeance. Following Napoleon's orders, Eugène took a side-road to the north of the main line of retreat, only to find that the bridges over the Vop river had been destroyed, thus blocking his advance. The Italian Royal Guard duly marched in formation through the river, breaking the ice on the surface with their chests and then clearing the west bank of Cossacks. Eugène's remaining troops followed, but inevitably suffered heavily.

Eugène found supplies at the town of Dukhovschina, but since he was dangerously exposed, he sensibly rejoined the bulk of the Grand Army farther south at the city of Smolensk. A series of clashes ensued as the Russians again attacked Napoleon's strung-out corps as they retreated from Smolensk. On 16 November Eugène was intercepted by the Russian advanced guard at the defile of Krasnoe, thirty miles south-west of Smolensk. He failed to break through by frontal assault, but escaped after dark by slipping round the Russians' northern flank. Three days later, he marched back eastwards to bring in the rearguard under the heroic Marshal Ney.

After crossing the Beresina river at the end of November, Eugène brought his handful of survivors out of Russia the following month. Utterly disillusioned, he wrote:

> The Italians are dying like flies ... How happy should we be to see our homes one day. It is my sole ambition now. I search no more for glory. It costs too dear.[14]

Napoleon had departed for Paris on 5 December to raise another army, leaving Marshal Joachim Murat, the King of Naples, in command of the remnants of the units that had invaded Russia. But Murat departed on 18 January 1813 on the pretext of illness for the warmer climate of Italy. Eugène reluctantly replaced him after persuasion from Marshal Berthier, Napoleon's chief-of-staff. The marshals were too proud to serve willingly under one of their own number, but Eugène's status as Napoleon's adopted son gave him added authority. Marshal Macdonald thought it a pity that Napoleon had not given Eugène the command in the first place.[15]

Eugène established his headquarters at Posen and strove to re-organise the army. He had fewer than 20,000 men in hand, but did his best in the Duchy of Warsaw to restore their shattered morale and took care to have provisions distributed regularly. 'He looked after everything,' wrote a French veteran, Jean-Roch Coignet, 'and never allowed three days to pass without going to the out-posts to reconnoitre the enemy.'[16]

Eugène saw that if he remained in his exposed easterly positions, he risked being outflanked and cut off by the Russians, who were advancing on a broad front. He was already being harassed by Cossacks and on 12 February pulled back westwards, first to the Oder river and then, abandoning Berlin and picking up more troops, to the Elbe. Napoleon unrealistically expected him to hold out farther east, ignoring the fact that the frozen rivers were useless as lines of defence. The main disadvantage of his retreat was that Prussia, now largely free from occupation, was able to enter the war in March alongside Russia. Eugène's conduct was steady and sensible, but he wrote to his wife that he disliked such defensive actions as he was not used to them and he also suffered from rheumatism and exhaustion.

Pelted with orders from Napoleon, Eugène concentrated most of his units around Magdeburg on the Elbe. Some of his forces were engaged in limited actions with allied units around Möckern on 3–5 April, during which Eugène personally rescued his orderly by charging a group of

Cossacks and firing a pistol. When the allies menaced his southern wing, Eugène simply withdrew it to a stronger position behind the Saale river.

At the end of April Napoleon arrived with a new army of 121,000 men that had been assembling on the Main river under the cover provided by Eugène's Army of the Elbe, which now numbered 58,000. Napoleon linked up with Eugène, advanced and on 2 May defeated the allies in the pitched Battle of Lützen. Eugène took part in the subsequent pursuit, drubbing the Russian General Mikhail Miloradovich, who tried to make a rearguard stand at Colditz on the 5th. A week later, Napoleon, having decided to amalgamate the Armies of the Elbe and the Main, ordered Eugène to return to the Kingdom of Italy in order to prepare its defences in case Austria should enter the war.

Eugène never saw Napoleon again, although he continued to be bombarded with instructions. Arriving in Milan on 18 May, he began to raise a new army following the loss of so many Italian veterans in Russia. But the quality and equipment of the troops were poor. As Eugène's Chief-of-Staff, General Martin de Vignolle, recalled:

> When the army began the campaign, we saw recruits, mostly in jackets and forage caps, led by other recruits, carrying their cartridges in their pockets, fighting bravely and upholding the reputation of the units to which they belonged and of which they had inherited only the name.[17]

Another eyewitness recorded that Eugène 'held frequent reviews and encouraged officers and soldiers by awarding them, or giving them hope for, favours or advancement.'[18] But desertion would be a serious problem. In September Eugène would ask Napoleon to return two divisions of Italian veterans currently serving with the French occupation forces in Spain, but these would not arrive until the end of the year.

Austria declared war on 12 August 1813. Although she channelled most of her energies into the struggle with Napoleon in central Europe, she fielded an army under General Johann von Hiller to recover her former possessions in northern Italy. Eugène faced a repetition of the 1809 campaign, but by now had matured as a commander. He had his army in position on the Saura river in the north-east. Hiller first detached a corps into the French province of Illyria on the eastern side of the Adriatic: aided by local insurrections and British naval support, this corps made good progress by the end of September, although some towns held out until at least December. Meanwhile, Hiller with the bulk of his troops advanced through the mountains into the Kingdom of Italy.

Eugène resisted with some success, but without risking a decisive battle against the odds. Then, on 8 October, his father-in-law, the King of

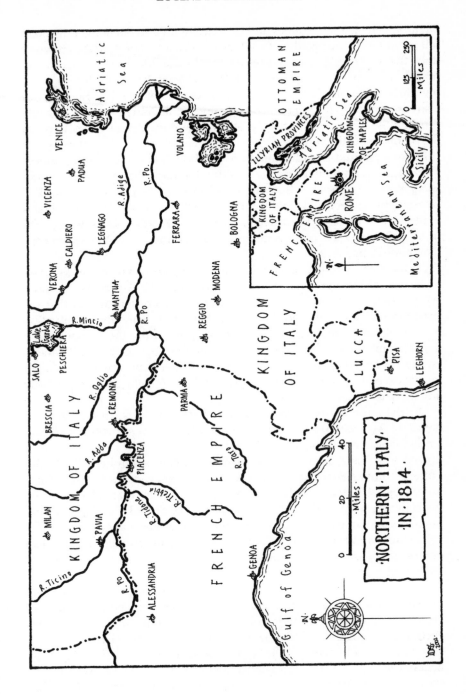

NORTHERN·ITALY·IN·1814·

Bavaria, defected to the allies and repeatedly tried to persuade Eugène to follow suit. Eugène loyally refused, despite an allied offer of the crown of Italy; the Austrian statesman Prince Clemens von Metternich remarked in disappointment that Eugène had a lofty character. Bavaria's defection not only released more Austrian troops to take the field against Eugène, but also compromised his left flank by opening a potential new invasion route through the mountains of the Tyrol and down the Adige valley to reach the plains of northern Italy.

Eugène realised that the situation was hopeless if the war continued, but sought to hold on as best he could in the hope that Napoleon would soon conclude peace. But in mid-October, Napoleon suffered a catastrophic defeat at Leipzig and was obliged to fall back to defend France itself. Eugène, meanwhile, retreated 120 miles south-westwards until in the first days of November he reached the city of Verona and the line of the Adige river.

On the 15th Eugène won an important rearguard action at Caldiero, six miles east of Verona, when he counter-attacked the Austrians, captured 900 prisoners and two guns and destroyed the entrenchments that the Austrians were making on the heights here. But generally the situation was quiet, with only minor engagements puncturing the winter lull. In mid-December a new Austrian commander, the 57-year-old Field Marshal Heinrich von Bellegarde, replaced General Hiller, who was reprimanded for his excessive caution. Fortunately for Eugène, Bellegarde was hardly any more dynamic.

But the situation elsewhere was less promising. On 15 November a detached Austrian division under General Laval Nugent von Westmeath landed from British ships at Volano, ten miles south of the Po river as it flowed into the Adriatic sea, to threaten Eugène's southern flank. But Eugène counter-attacked and forced Nugent to evacuate Ferrara, thirty miles west of Volano, on the 26th. Next day Eugène received a bruise on the right leg from a spent ball while driving back Hiller's outposts from Legnago, a town twenty-four miles south-east of Verona.

Joachim Murat, the King of Naples in the southern half of the Italian peninsula, posed another threat, as he was negotiating with the allies to switch sides and was beginning to send troops northwards towards Rome and Ancona under the pretext that they were making their way to help Eugène. Murat, less honourable than Eugène, nursed ambitions of becoming king of a united and independent Italy and was actively encouraged by his wife Caroline Bonaparte, Napoleon's sister.

For the first few weeks of 1814, all was quiet on the Adige. Although Bellegarde had 70,000 troops against Eugène's 50,000, he was awaiting co-operation from Murat before attacking, particularly as many of his own forces were detached or tied down in blockading important points in the rear, including Venice and the town of Dalmatia on the eastern side of the

Adriatic. In fact, these commitments left him with an active army of not much over half his total strength.[19]

Murat signed a secret treaty with the Austrians on 11 January and an armistice with Lieutenant-General Lord William Bentinck, the British Commander-in-Chief and representative in the Mediterranean, on 3 February. His troops openly took control of Rome, Ancona, Florence and Bologna, but then halted. He hesitated actually to declare war against Eugène, although his occupation of territory belonging to France and the Kingdom of Italy south of the Po was tantamount to such. His treaties with the allies had yet to be ratified and he was naturally more interested in his political ambitions than in military co-operation with the Austrians.

To counter Austrian proclamations encouraging the Italian people to rise against his rule, Eugène issued his own addresses to his people and his soldiers. He showed how well he had learnt from Napoleon's rhetoric:

> Frenchmen! Italians! I have confidence in you; count on me, too! You will always find in me your benefit and glory. Soldiers! My motto is *Honour and Fidelity!* Let it also be yours; with it and the help of God we will triumph at last over our enemies.[20]

But such addresses failed to have the intended effect. A Frenchman explained that:

> The time when such language could have made some impression on the morale of Italian troops had passed. All [their] illusions were dispelled. Our Italians saw no more, in the rest of this war, than endless dangers.[21]

On the other hand, the Austrians had little success in trying to instigate insurrections.

The potential threat posed by Murat's 30,000 Neapolitans and the detached Austrian division of 8,000 men under General Nugent on the south bank of the Po induced Eugène to abandon the Adige on 3–4 February. He withdrew without hindrance, except for a minor rearguard action at Villafranca, and crossed the Mincio, which he adopted as his new defence line, anchored as it was by the fortresses of Peschiera in the north and Mantua in the south. His southern flank rested on the Po river, which would form a good east–west defence line against any advance by Murat and Nugent. To guard his right rear, Eugène ordered a division of reserve troops to go to the town of Piacenza, which lay on the south bank of the Po fifty miles west of Mantua.

Eugène also wrote a personal letter to Bellegarde, asking him to look after his wife and children should he be forced to resume his retreat and leave them behind, which was a distinct possibility given that Auguste was heavily pregnant. (In the event, she safely gave birth to her fifth child on 13 April.) Bellegarde chivalrously agreed to Eugène's request.

The first major clash of the campaign occurred on 8 February, when Bellegarde attacked over the Mincio but was forced to retire back on to the east bank. Having checked Bellegarde, Eugène found his left rear under threat from an Austrian detachment of about 4,000 men under General Aaron von Stanissavljevich which was operating on the western side of Lake Garda. He sent his Royal Guard west and personally followed, leaving his army on the Mincio. Local forces drove back a strong party of Austrian troops that threatened the town of Brescia on 15 February. Next day Eugène himself repelled an Austrian force at Salò on the shores of Lake Garda, inflicting heavy losses and neutralising the threat in this sector. He then rejoined his army on the Mincio.

Napoleon, meanwhile, faced with an allied invasion of eastern France, had written to Eugène in the middle of January, ordering him to abandon Italy as soon as Murat declared war and bring his army over the Alps to help defend France. On 16 February Eugène received another despatch, ordering him to march all his French units immediately over the Alps to Lyons. Letters from Josephine and Hortense arrived two days later, urging him to lose no time in obeying Napoleon's orders.

Eugène in reply calmly pointed out that a third of his army was Italian and that even in regiments that were officially French, more than half of the soldiers were actually native Italians. If he abandoned Italy, large numbers of these men would desert. 'I am therefore convinced,' he wrote, 'that the retrograde movement ordered by Your Majesty would have been very fatal to your arms and it is very fortunate that up to now I have not had to make it.'[22] Partly because of Eugène's success on the Mincio and his own victories in eastern France, Napoleon changed his mind. Eugène was ordered to hold on to Italy as long as possible.

Eugène re-organised his army, placing most of his Italian units inside Peschiera and Mantua to try and reduce their desertion rate. He also positioned more troops on the Po, including a weak division of Italian veterans that had just returned from Spain.

Although Murat finally declared war on 15 February, he was reluctant actually to attack Eugène's troops. Nugent's Austrian division led the Neapolitan advance north-westwards from Reggio towards Piacenza, but encountered stiff resistance and fell back. But after Eugène recalled some of his troops from this flank to rejoin him on the Mincio, the remainder under General Filippo Severoli were counter-attacked outside Reggio on 7 March. Severoli himself had a leg smashed by a cannonball and his men were forced to retreat into Reggio, where they were in danger of being cut off. But to Nugent's fury, Murat offered a ceasefire and allowed them to evacuate the town. Considerable numbers of Frenchmen in the Neapolitan Army had meanwhile left and joined Eugène.

After his repulse on the Mincio, Bellegarde lapsed into inactivity, even though Eugène had been forced to detach troops to strengthen his southern flank on the Po. Eugène even launched an offensive on the Mincio on 10 March, but was repulsed with considerable loss. However, this aggressive move further discouraged Bellegarde from attacking, especially as his attention was diverted by a quarrel between Murat and Lord William Bentinck, the British commander in the Mediterranean. On 7 March Bentinck landed with 6,000 British and Sicilian troops at Leghorn on the western coast of Tuscany and a week later called on all Italians to rise against Napoleon and form a free and independent nation. Murat, who had his own ambitions as King of Italy, naturally was more interested in keeping troops in Tuscany to prevent Bentinck having a free hand than in marching them north against Eugène. Bentinck, in contrast, wanted to use Tuscany as a base for his operations against the port of Genoa ninety miles farther to the north-west and demanded that Murat evacuate it.

The situation deteriorated to such an extent that Bentinck threatened to march on Naples and overthrow Murat. After an intervention by Bellegarde and a rebuke for Bentinck from the British Foreign Secretary, Lord Castlereagh, the deadlock was broken. Bentinck agreed to leave Tuscany and occupy Genoa, while Murat undertook to capture Piacenza on the Po river and co-operate with Bellegarde on the north bank of the river in driving Eugène from Lombardy.

Only now did a co-ordinated allied effort emerge. Ironically, the war was all but over. Murat finally attacked Eugène's forces on the Taro river south of Piacenza on 13 April and occupied the town itself two days later. Bellegarde meanwhile prepared to resume the offensive on the Mincio and Bentinck occupied Genoa on the 18th. Meanwhile, Napoleon had abdicated on 6 April and on the 11th signed the Treaty of Fontainebleau in which he abandoned his claims to the thrones of France and Italy. This meant that Eugène was no longer Viceroy and was free to agree to the Convention of Schiarino-Rizzino on the 16th. According to its terms, his French troops were to return immediately to France, while the allies would decide the fate of the Kingdom of Italy.

Eugène hoped to retain the kingdom and be given its crown. But his opponents, supported by the Austrians, stirred up unrest in the capital, Milan, where the Minister of Finance, Giuseppe Prina, was brutally murdered by a mob on the 20th. Bellegarde demanded that Eugène hand over the Kingdom of Italy to enable the Austrians to restore order. Eugène had no choice but to accept another convention on the 23rd and to leave for Bavaria three days later to avoid further bloodshed. His farewell proclamation was superb:

> And you, brave Italian Army! Soldiers, I shall always carry engraved on my heart all your faces, all the wounds that I have seen you

receive, all the heroic deeds for which I have been able to obtain fitting rewards. It is possible that never again will you see me at your head and in your ranks; it is possible that I will never again hear your cheering. But if your country ever calls you back to the colours, I am sure, brave soldiers, that in the thick of danger you will still fondly recall the name of Eugène.[23]

On 4 May he and his family reached Munich, the capital of Bavaria. He then set off for Paris, where his mother, Josephine, had fallen ill; he was at her bedside when she died on 29 May. While in the city, he visited the allied monarchs and the French king, Louis XVIII, to press his claim to have a suitable domain outside France, as had been laid down in the Treaty of Fontainebleau that Napoleon had signed on 11 April. He followed the allied rulers to the Congress of Vienna in September, but to no avail.

In the spring of 1815 Napoleon escaped from exile and regained power in France. Eugène was no longer bound to him and remained aloof, but an indiscreet letter written by his sister Hortense led to some distrust of him among the allies following Napoleon's defeat at Waterloo and this did nothing to help settle his claims. In the meantime, he resided in Bavaria and did what he could to help old friends and members of Napoleon's family fleeing the royalist backlash in France.

At last, in November 1817, Eugène was made His Royal Highness the Duke of Leuchtenberg, Prince of Eichstätt by the Bavarian king. But the accumulated strain of the past years had been too much and after two strokes, he passed away at Munich on 21 February 1824. He had lived a full life, yet one cut tragically short at the age of 43. Nonetheless, the good that he did lived on after him and his descendants include the monarchs of Belgium, Denmark, Norway and Sweden.

Honour and Fidelity

Napoleon was born and bred a Corsican and in character remained one even after he became Emperor of the French. He took it for granted that he could count on absolute loyalty from the members of the Bonaparte clan and so placed them on thrones throughout Europe. In this, he was rapidly disillusioned, for his family were simply incapable or disloyal. The experiment worked only in the Kingdom of Italy and as he himself admitted in 1814, 'Eugène is the only one of my family who never has given me a single cause for dissatisfaction.'[24]

The reason for Eugène's reliability is simple: he lacked the ruthless, driving ambition that characterised unscrupulous men like Marshal Murat. 'I was never ambitious,' he confessed in 1807:

My present position sometimes seems to me like a dream. In the midst of all my splendours I sometimes long to return to my independence in Paris – the days when I was with my regiment. But, as regards the Emperor, I have only one course – obedience.[25]

What is surprising about Eugène is not his intense loyalty, but his competence. He had not only divorced parents, but an intermittent and incomplete education. A different man would have developed an inferiority complex and an arrogance to match, whereas Eugène had the humility to accept advice. He was fortunate to have as his tutors in the military profession two such able men as Generals Hoche and Bonaparte.

As we have seen, Eugène regularly received detailed instructions from Napoleon. He held him in awe, yet was not so subservient as to obey orders that he knew to be wrong. In 1814, for example, he rightly refused to abandon northern Italy and withdraw into France.

Some would deny Eugène a place among the great generals of the era. Napoleon in one of his less charitable moods claimed:

Eugène is a real square head; by that, I mean that he has judgement and skills, but not this genius, this confident character which sets apart the great men.[26]

Eugène was certainly not a born commander and was denied the opportunity to accumulate experience in a logical progression up through the ranks. In 1809 he commanded an army without having commanded so much as a regiment in action. He lost his first battle, Sacile, but learned from his mistakes. In fact, his conduct of the 1809 campaign was better than is often realised, for Marshal Jacques Macdonald in his memoirs deceitfully exaggerated Eugène's caution and mistakes in order to portray himself as having saved the situation.

Although often kept under Napoleon's immediate command, for instance at Wagram and Borodino, Eugène did enjoy opportunities to show his ability as an independent army commander and it was as such that he must ultimately be judged. But for his defeat at Sacile, he acquitted himself well, largely because he was a conscientious man who made a point of examining the ground and seeing the situation for himself. He was always at the critical spot during a battle and inspired his men by his personal example. Like Napoleon, Eugène preferred to attack, but rather than launch a purely frontal assault, tended to favour a flank attack or a strong push by one of his wings, for example at Sacile, the Piave and Tarvis in 1809 and the Mincio in 1814.

Had Eugène been a mere general and not also Viceroy of Italy, his military reputation would have been even higher, for he would have been permitted to take an active part in the campaigns of 1805–8 and would have gained valuable experience. Even those who question his skill recognise that his loyalty made him more valuable than such capable but untrustworthy generals as Marshals Joachim Murat and Auguste Marmont.

But those who knew Eugène remembered him for his humanity more than anything else. He was one of those rare heroes whose moral courage matches their physical bravery.

The Battle of the Mincio: 8 February 1814

The Mincio was one of the more unusual battles of military history. Each commander attacked and did not expect his opponent to do the same. Although Eugène ended up with his army split into two and at odds with both northern and southern flanks of the Austrians, he successfully retrieved the situation.

At the beginning of February 1814 Eugène had fallen back westwards to the Mincio. The river flowed southwards all along his twenty-mile front, from the fortress of Peschiera at the south-eastern tip of Lake Garda to the city of Mantua, which was protected by lakes and marshes on three sides. From Mantua, the Mincio flowed another ten miles south-eastwards into the Po, the broad river that runs from west to east right across the flat plains of northern Italy.[27]

Eugène intended to use the Mincio as a defence line against an offensive by the Austrian army of Field Marshal Heinrich von Bellegarde from the east and the Po against a possible attack by King Joachim Murat and his Neapolitans from the south. For although Murat had not yet formally declared war, he had joined the allied coalition and occupied southern parts of the Kingdom of Italy. Eugène's only reassurance from this side was a letter that he received from Murat on 4 February, promising not to attack without prior warning.

Eugène intended to launch an attack southwards across the Po against the treacherous Murat, but first needed to strike a preliminary blow against the Austrians to put them out of action at least temporarily. On 5 and 6 February he inspected his troops and prepared for the coming clash. On the evening of the 7th, he wrote to his wife:

> I don't have much time to myself, my dear Auguste, for I have many orders to give for a movement that I am going to make, not backwards as everyone fears, but forwards. I hope that fortune will favour me and that in the next few days I will be able to take my revenge on the Neapolitans.[28]

Eugène left just 7,000 troops to guard his southern flank on the Po and managed to concentrate about 34,000 men on the Mincio without the knowledge of his opponents. These forces consisted of the Italian Royal

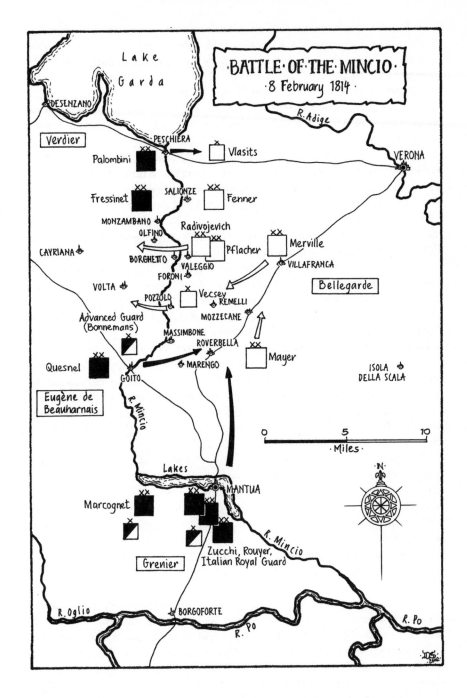

BATTLE·OF·THE·MINCIO·
·8 February 1814·

Lake Garda

DESENZANO

R. Adige

VERONA

Verdier

PESCHIERA

Palombini

Vlasits

Fressinet

SALIONZE

Fenner

MONZAMBANO

OLFINO

Radivojevich

CAVRIANA

BORGHETTO

Pflacher

Merville

VILLAFRANCA

Bellegarde

VALEGGIO

FORONI

VOLTA

POZZOLO

Vecsey

REMELLI

MOZZECANE

Advanced Guard
(Bonnemans)

MASSIMBONE

ROVERBELLA

Quesnel

GOITO

MARENGO

Mayer

ISOLA
DELLA SCALA

Eugène de
Beauharnais

R. Mincio

Lakes

0   5   10

·Miles·

·N·

MANTUA

Marcognet

R. Mincio

Zucchi, Rouyer,
Italian Royal Guard

Grenier

R. Oglio

BORGOFORTE

R. Po

R. Po

47

Guard, a cavalry division and two lieutenancies (these approximated to corps) under Generals Paul Grenier and Jean-Antoine Verdier. Eugène, typically, eschewed a mere frontal attack and instead decided on a two-pronged advance, with the main attack in the south and a secondary thrust in the north, in order to catch the Austrians in a vice.

The southern prong, consisting of 20,000 men and forty-eight guns, would cross the Mincio at two points, Mantua and Goito. Eugène himself would accompany the troops advancing eastwards from Goito, namely an advanced guard under General Pierre Bonnemains and a division of French infantry. From Mantua, General Grenier would push due north along the main road towards Villafranca and Verona with the Italian Royal Guard, two French infantry divisions and a cavalry brigade. Eugène and Grenier were to unite near the village of Roverbella and then fall on the Austrian army, which Eugène hoped to surprise in the plains near Villafranca, fourteen miles north of Mantua.

Eugène's northern prong, under General Verdier, consisted of 5,000 men and eight guns, namely General Philibert Fressinet's French infantry division and the Italian 4th Chasseurs à Cheval. It had orders to cross the Mincio at Monzambano and advance eastwards to descend on the Austrian northern wing near Villafranca.

Eugène allocated his two Italian infantry divisions to the secondary task of guarding his flanks. In the north, General Giuseppe Palombini's division would leave Peschiera and push eastwards to contain those Austrian units that were covering this fortress. In the south, meanwhile, General Carlo Zucchi's division, aided by a cavalry brigade, would leave Mantua and advance to the north and north-east to tie down the Austrian division blockading that city.

This plan looked fine on paper, but did not take into account the possibility of an Austrian attack, perhaps because Bellegarde's pursuit from the Adige had been noticeably cautious. Yet an offensive was exactly what Bellegarde intended, as he was convinced that Eugène, having fallen back from the Adige, was now abandoning the Mincio and continuing to retreat westwards.

Bellegarde, after detaching troops to contain isolated garrisons in his rear, concentrated about 35,000 men on the Mincio. On either flank, he had units in position to cover the two fortresses: the brigade of General Franz von Vlasits in the north, drawn up in an arc to the east of Peschiera and a division under General Anton Mayer von Heldenfeld in the south to watch Mantua.[29] Of his remaining forces, Bellegarde had a division in the north under General Franz Fenner von Fennerberg.[30] In the centre were the two divisions of Generals Paul von Radivojevich and Franz von Pflacher, which were concentrated around Valeggio, six miles south of Peschiera, apart from a brigade under General August von Vecsey which was posted three-and-a-half miles farther south at Pozzolo. In reserve, near Bellegarde's headquarters at Villafranca, stood the division of General Franz von Merville.

Bellegarde's plan involved a triple breach of the line of the Mincio, with his main thrust at Borghetto (near Valeggio) in the centre, supported by secondary attacks at Pozzolo in the south and Monzambano to the north. His two wings would remain on the east bank to cover Peschiera and Mantua, while the centre pressed on deep into the fertile region of Lombardy.

That evening Austrian patrols saw that French troops were still on the Mincio. This seemed to indicate a strong rearguard to cover Eugène's retreat. As a result, Bellegarde ordered his reserve division under General Merville not to follow across the river at Borghetto as originally planned, but instead to remain on the east bank on a small height near the village of Pozzolo, where it could be called on as became necessary. But for this last-minute adjustment, Bellegarde might have suffered a disaster.

The night of 7–8 February passed quietly. But, without the knowledge of either Eugène or his senior subordinates, a gap opened in his centre. The bulk of his troops were massed on the two wings, for that was where the fortresses of Peschiera and Mantua stood and from where his two prongs would depart. Outposts had been guarding the centre between Monzambano and Pozzolo, but were withdrawn during the night as units called in their advanced posts ready to take the offensive at dawn. A subordinate later recorded:

> [Eugène] with his noble bearing always deeply regretted this fault, which his men had committed before dawn and which had uncovered the Mincio, and the boldness of the enemy in instantly profiting from it.[31]

Fog shrouded the Mincio at dawn on the 8th. Austrian advanced guards crossed at both Borghetto and Pozzolo to cover the establishment of bridges (the French had blown up the stone bridge at Borghetto three nights earlier). They met no opposition and the disappearance of Eugène's outposts during the night seemed to confirm that he was in retreat. At 8.00 am, without a shot being fired, two brigades of General Radivojevich's division began to pour across the Mincio on a pontoon bridge and a trestle bridge at Borghetto.

Shortly afterwards, as the fog lifted, Austrian troops clashed with an outlying detachment of Eugène's northern wing at Olfino, two miles north-west of Borghetto. General Verdier personally went to Olfino to assess the situation and, alarmed at the turn of events, abandoned the offensive. He was cut off and unable to tell what had befallen Eugène and the southern prong. He therefore ordered Palombini's Italian division to return to Peschiera and placed Fressinet's division behind a stream, so that it faced south and rested its left flank on the Mincio, ready to contain an attack from Borghetto.[32]

Meanwhile, at 9.00 am, the remaining brigade of Radivojevich's division, under Vecsey, crossed the Mincio three-and-a-half miles to the south of Borghetto over a hastily built pontoon bridge at Pozzolo and established itself unopposed on the heights of the west bank. Three squadrons of Austrian uhlans spread out into the plain to the south-west and seized some unescorted baggage. Fugitives brought the news of this capture to the troops that Eugène had left to guard Goito and nearly caused panic there.

On the Austrian northern wing, Fenner's division meanwhile remained on the east bank and exchanged a few shots with the French outposts. In the centre, one of the two brigades of General Pflacher's division now followed Radivojevich over the river at Borghetto; the other brigade, under General Karl von Quosdanovich, remained on the east bank. The reserve division under Merville arrived at Pozzolo after marching from Villafranca and in accordance with Bellegarde's instructions likewise remained on the east bank pending further orders.

Only in the south had Eugène's offensive gone as planned. Grenier had left Mantua at 8.00 am and advanced northwards along the road to Roverbella. Eugène himself had crossed the Mincio at Goito and pushed eastwards. Spearheading his move was the advanced guard under General Bonnemains, consisting of the 31st Chasseurs à Cheval, two light infantry battalions and four guns. The heavily outnumbered and over-extended outposts of General Mayer's division covering Mantua were cut up around Roverbella and lost over 500 men as prisoners. Grenier and Eugène linked up as planned near Roverbella.

Mayer was now in danger of being cut off, with his eastern flank being threatened by Zucchi's outlying Italian division. Mayer hence retired three-and-a-half miles north-eastwards to the village of Mozzecane to cover Villafranca, where Bellegarde's army had its artillery reserve and the caissons of its park, as well as its baggage and magazines.

Eugène advanced north-eastwards, expecting to meet the bulk of the Austrians near Villafranca. But towards 10.00 am, he heard gunfire from the north, on the opposite bank of the Mincio, and personally hurried to a height near the village of Massimbone, one-and-a-half miles south of Pozzolo. From this vantage point, he was astonished to see smoke and Austrian columns on the other side of the river, advancing from Borghetto on Monzambano about seven miles from where he stood.

Eugène immediately grasped what had happened. He took the crucial decision not to abandon his own offensive, but to press boldly on, in the hope that the sound of his guns would cause alarm and distract the Austrian forces on the west bank. He did, however, send the Italian Royal Guard back to Goito to secure the bridge there. Also, to protect his eastern wing against Mayer's division, he detached General Pierre-Louis Binet de Marcognet's division, which pushed towards Villafranca. Farther to the right, Zucchi's Italian division was already dispersed on a wide front north and north-east of Mantua, where it skirmished with some of Mayer's men amidst the network of canals and ricefields.

That left Eugène with fewer than 13,000 men and about thirty guns in the centre, namely the cavalry brigade of General André-Thomas Perreymond, the advanced guard under Bonnemains and two infantry divisions under Generals François-Jean-Baptiste Quesnel du Torpit and Marie-François Rouyer. With these formations, he now thrust due north, parallel to the Mincio and towards Valeggio in a bid to cut the line of retreat of the Austrian units on the west bank. Eugène himself accompanied the advance guard.

The Austrians still had Merville's division on the east bank of the Mincio near Pozzolo, three-and-three-quarter miles north-west of Roverbella, and Quosdanovich's brigade farther north at Borghetto. Alerted to Eugène's approach, Merville ordered his division (a brigade of grenadiers and another of dragoons) to change front and form up between Pozzolo and the farm of Remelli to meet his advance from the south.

As Perreymond's cavalry brigade came up, it was vigorously counter-attacked by a regiment of Merville's dragoons. Perreymond's leading unit, the French 1st Hussars, made the mistake of halting to deploy rather than advancing to meet the charge. The hussars, badly equipped and poorly mounted young men, broke and carried off the rest of Perreymond's brigade as they fled. The Austrian dragoons seized the brigade's battery and forced Eugène to shelter within an infantry square. The dragoons were repelled with infantry fire and were then counter-attacked by Perreymond's cavalry, who had rallied and who now retook five of their six lost guns.

Eugène had run into unexpectedly tough opposition. In front of him, Merville formed his division into three lines. The front two consisted of General Josef von Stutterheim's crack brigade of about 2,000 grenadiers, while the third was formed by the brigade of dragoons, which also had the task of covering the division's eastern flank. The grenadiers had formed up in eleven masses, or solid rectangular clumps, which were a good defence against cavalry but vulnerable to artillery fire.

A lull ensued while Eugène waited until all his troops were ready. To replace Perreymond's shattered brigade, he ordered the cavalry of the Royal Guard to rejoin him from Goito. In the centre of his line stood Quesnel's infantry division, with Rouyer's drawn up behind in support. The Guard cavalry would occupy the western wing, while in the east the advanced guard under Bonnemains was striving to outflank Merville, with little success and considerable loss.

After three-quarters-of-an-hour, Eugène advanced with strong artillery support. Though dangerously outnumbered, Merville gallantly opposed Eugène's advance and even counter-attacked. Nothing that day surpassed the magnificent conduct of the brigade of grenadiers under Stutterheim, which retired in superb order, despite losing thirty-two officers and 758 men by the end of the day, or forty per cent of its initial strength.[33] But Merville had to abandon Pozzolo and, covered by cavalry, fell back to a new position about a mile to the north.

Eugène detached General Gaspard-François Forestier's brigade from Quesnel's division and sent it to occupy Pozzolo. But Bellegarde still had the bridges at Borghetto three-and-a-half miles farther north. Eugène assaulted Merville's new position towards 3.00 pm, after Rouyer's division had advanced from the second line and passed through Quesnel's division to spearhead the attack. Heavy artillery fire knocked out all four of Merville's guns and inflicted serious losses. Bellegarde had been slow to react to Eugène's advance, but belatedly sent Merville sufficient reinforcements to stem the tide. General Karl von Quosdanovich, whose brigade had been left on the east bank near Borghetto, joined Merville with some of his battalions and three batteries towards 3.30 pm.[34] Merville was able to counter-attack, but was checked after recapturing the farms of Mazzi and Pasini when Eugène personally rallied his men.

Towards 5.00 pm, in a final effort, Eugène's troops resumed their general advance and seized the contested farms of Pasini and Mazzi. According to a captain on his staff, Eugène during the battle:

> continually went down the line from one end to the other, ordering and himself leading the moves in the midst of the most murderous fire. Several officers of his staff were wounded or had horses killed around him.[35]

General Quosdanovich was seriously wounded in the head as he tried to inspire his Austrians and had to leave the field. His men, having suffered heavy losses, hurriedly fell back to the hamlet of Foroni, where reinforcements helped to check the French advance at nightfall. Eugène's push northwards had taken him to within a mile of Valeggio and the crucial bridge at Borghetto, but despite all his efforts, he was too late.

Eight miles to the north-west, meanwhile, General Verdier had finally checked the Austrians on the west bank of the Mincio after hard fighting. The Austrians had sought to tie down Fressinet's division along the Olfino stream west of Monzambano, outflank it in the west and drive it into the Mincio. The outnumbered French troops exhausted their ammunition early in the afternoon, but were resupplied in the nick of time. The situation remained critical until the sound of gunfire from Eugène's forces on the other side of the Mincio restored morale and induced Bellegarde to order Radivojevich to break off the action and fall back towards Borghetto. This enabled Verdier to switch to the offensive, although his attack was beaten off. Dusk put an end to the fighting.

Bellegarde, alarmed at Eugène's advance on the east bank, assumed that he would resume the offensive the following morning and therefore withdrew his own forces from the west bank during the night. Only one infantry brigade remained on the far bank, in a bridgehead covering the bridge at Borghetto.

Eugène likewise needed to withdraw, in order to re-establish contact with his northern wing. He therefore pulled his southern prong back across the Mincio at Goito and Mantua on the morning of the 9th. As the day dawned, Eugène himself was at Goito and was joined there by a messenger from Verdier. The messenger recorded that he arrived:

at the moment when, surrounded by his staff, [Eugène] was seeking through the half-light ... to make out the enemy's position at Volta and to open up for himself a road to free Verdier, if he was not already too late, as he feared. His doubts were relieved very much at the right moment (he told me) by my arrival and the re-establishment of the army in its former position on the west bank of the Mincio was immediately decided on, and executed by him this very day and the following one.[36]

Eugène's units took up positions along the west bank of the river. Fortunately, the Austrians were too exhausted after their own withdrawal during the night to intervene. Eugène was pleased at the outcome of the battle and wrote to his wife:

Another victory, my good and dear Auguste. The action was hot and lasted until 8.00 pm; at the same time as I crossed the Mincio to attack the enemy, he himself crossed at another point. Nonetheless, I beat him and made nearly 2,500 prisoners. Our troops behaved well, especially the infantry. My health is good, I am only very tired.[37]

Eugène also sent one of his ADCs, his cousin, Colonel Louis Tascher de la Pagerie, to Napoleon with both a written report and instructions to give the Emperor verbal details of the battle. Eugène wrote:

I regret, however, that the results have not been decisive enough for the future. If I had been able to push the Austrians back to beyond Verona, my plan would have been to fall immediately by Borgoforte [over the Po river] on your new enemy [Murat].[38]

The Austrians had put up a tough fight and lost about 4,000 men; Eugène's casualties numbered around 3,500. The Chief-of-Staff of the Army of Italy, General Martin de Vignolle, recorded that its infantry, cavalry and artillery 'all vied with each other in glory and co-operated perfectly.'[39] But another French eyewitness thought that, with more numerous and better-mounted cavalry, Eugène would have been even more successful.[40]

Further fighting flared up on 10 February when Eugène attempted to crush the Austrian bridgehead at Borghetto by attacking it from three sides. He drove the Austrians back and seized the outlying houses of Borghetto village before calling a halt towards dusk in order to limit casualties, for he believed that the Austrians would evacuate the remainder of the bridgehead of their own accord. Losses were light: apparently about 500 Austrians and less than half that number of Eugène's troops.[41]

Few battles have been more unusual than that of the Mincio, in that each side gained a bridgehead on the opposite bank of a river. The outcome was a modest victory for Eugène, but he had lost heavily on the 8th and might not have been able to contain a renewed Austrian onslaught. Fortunately for him, his opponents were too cautious and disunited to mount an immediate, co-ordinated offensive on all fronts. Bellegarde, who had been shaken by Eugène's unexpected resistance, informed the Austrian Emperor:

> I am now going to attend to the completion of the blockade of Mantua and Peschiera and I will await the moves of the King of Naples before resuming active operations towards the Po.

It was, in fact, the moral effect on Bellegarde that constituted the most substantial benefit of Eugène's victory. An officer who reached the Austrian headquarters a week later recorded:

> I noticed that the marshal's mind was deeply agitated. The battle that the Viceroy had just fought against him had acted strongly on his spirit . . . I arrived, then, at the headquarters at a time when they were very disconcerted.[42]

NOTES

1   The fact of Eugène's visit seems well-established, although the details of the story are in some doubt: see Musée national des châteaux de Malmaison et Bois-Préau, *Eugène de Beauharnais: honneur et fidélité* (1999), pp.10–11, 56.

2   C. Oman, *Napoleon's Viceroy: Eugène de Beauharnais* (1966), pp.44–5

3   A. du Casse, ed., *Mémoires et correspondance politique et militaire du Prince Eugène* (1858–60), v.1, p.41

4   The Chasseurs à Cheval were designated a regiment in November 1801 and

the Consular Guard was renamed the Imperial Guard following the creation of the Empire in 1804.

5   Oman, *op. cit.*, p.215
6   V. Montagu, *Eugène de Beauharnais: the adopted son of Napoleon* (1913), p.209
7   Macdonald, despite his fraudulent claims, did not arrive in time to take part in the battle.
8   Casse, *op. cit.*, v.5, pp.385–6; both Marengo (1800) and Friedland (1807), like Raab, were fought on 14 June.
9   Anon, *Mémoires sur la cour du Prince Eugène et sur le Royaume d'Italie . . . par un français attaché à la cour du vice-roi d'Italie* (1826), p.241
10 Montagu, *op. cit.*, p.212
11 Eugène had not come up in time to take part in the Battle of Smolensk on 17 August.
12 L. Fantin des Odoards, *Journal du général Fantin des Odoards* (1895), p.327
13 Casse, *op. cit.*, v.8, p.71
14 Oman, *op. cit.*, p.351
15 C. Rousset, ed., *Recollections of Marshal Macdonald* (1893), p.205
16 J. Coignet, *The notebooks of Captain Coignet* (1986), pp.243–4
17 M. Vignolle, *Précis historique des opérations militaires de l'armée d'Italie en 1813 et 1814* (1817), p.9
18 *Mémoires sur la cour du Prince Eugène*, p.252
19 G. vom Holtz, *Die innerösterreichische Armee 1813 und 1814* (1912), p.145
20 Casse, *op. cit.*, v.10, pp.7–9
21 *Mémoires sur la cour du Prince Eugène*, p.245
22 Casse, *op. cit.*, v.10, p.94
23 *Ibid*, v.10, pp.177–9
24 Oman, *op. cit.*, p.392
25 *Ibid*, p.230
26 G. Gourgaud, *Sainte-Hélène: journal inédit de 1815 à 1818* (nd), v.1, pp.95–6
27 Eugène knew the area well, since it lay within the Kingdom of Italy and he had campaigned here before; the Austrian commander, Field Marshal Heinrich von Bellegarde, had also served here during the French Revolutionary wars.
28 Casse, *op. cit.*, v.10, p.76
29 The actual commander of this Austrian division was General Franz Marziani von Sacile, while Mayer was his superior. But since the rest of Mayer's units were elsewhere, Mayer for the moment had only Marziani's division under his direct command.
30 The overall command of Bellegarde's northern wing lay with General Hannibal, Marquis Sommariva.
31 C. Vacani, *Bataille du Mincio du 8 février 1814 entre l'armée du Prince Eugène et celle du maréchal comte de Bellegarde* (1857), p.36
32 Some writers have unjustly criticised Verdier. In fact, he made the right initial decision to abandon the offensive and subsequently held out stubbornly against heavy odds.
33 Holtz, *op. cit.*, p.140
34 Another two of Quosdanovich's battalions were sent to support Mayer at Mozzecane, but arrived too late to take part in the fighting there.
35 L.D****, *Journal historique sur la campagne du Prince Eugène, en Italie, pendant les années 1813 et 1814. Par L. D****, capitaine attaché à l'état major du prince* (1817), pp.65–6
36 Vacani, *op. cit.*, p.35

37 M. Planat de Faye, *Le Prince Eugène en 1814* (1857), p.38
38 Casse, *op. cit.*, pp.77–8
39 Vignolle, *op. cit.*, p.127
40 L. D****, *op. cit.*, p.65
41 M. Weil, *Le Prince Eugène et Murat 1813–1814* (1902), v.4, p.114
42 *Ibid*, v.4, pp.89–90

CHAPTER III

Lasalle

According to Antoine-Charles-Louis de Lasalle, any French hussar who was not dead by the age of 30 was a blackguard.[1] He himself fell at the Battle of Wagram aged 34, yet managed in his short lifetime to make his name a legend. He was the epitome of Napoleon's dashing cavalry generals: a man who lived life to the full, addicted as he was to the perils and excitement of the battlefield.

Born into a noble family on 10 May 1775, Lasalle grew up in the city of Metz in north-eastern France. Fooling around with a gang of local children in the city's maze of streets developed his talent for leadership, but the greatest formative influence on his life was that of his adored mother, who once fought a duel, using swords, with a woman who had stolen one of her many lovers. It was from her that Lasalle inherited his fiery spirit.

In common with other sons of the nobility, he began his military career at an early stage and in 1786 entered an infantry regiment in Strasbourg as an officer cadet aged only 11. At a young age, therefore, discipline tempered his natural ebullience. Five years later, he became a second lieutenant in the 24th Regiment of Cavalry at the age of 16. But in 1792, as the French Revolution became more extreme, Lasalle's father was arrested as a noble and accused of treason; although the charge did not stick, the family had to flee to Paris. At the end of 1793, with France threatened by invasion, Lasalle joined the Army of the North as an infantry volunteer. He came under fire, gained valuable experience and in February 1794 entered the 23rd Chasseurs à Cheval. That he was popular is clear from his unanimous election to the rank of sergeant just one month after he joined the regiment. He saw bitter fighting, captured a battery in an action near the town of Landrecies, fifty-eight miles south-west of Brussels, and in 1795 both sought and obtained promotion to lieutenant.

At this time, General François-Christophe Kellermann, the victor of the Battle of Valmy in 1792 and a future marshal of Napoleon, was in command of the Army of the Alps. He knew Lasalle's mother well as he had previously been stationed in Metz and duly appointed him as one of his ADCs. Lasalle set out in August 1795 to take up his new appointment and found that his duties included writing scores of letters. As he later admitted, 'the marshal gave me my first understanding of my profession. I began by being his ADC; it is to him that I owe what I am.' Beginning a career was always the hardest part, he added, and without Kellermann's patronage he would not have succeeded.[2]

Kellermann's own son was also on his staff as an ADC, but both Lasalle and Kellermann junior longed to be with Napoleon Bonaparte's Army of Italy, which was currently beating the Austrians in the plains of the Po valley. When young Kellermann was appointed to the staff of the cavalry division of Napoleon's army, he took Lasalle with him and arrived in May 1796, just after Napoleon had taken the bridge of Lodi.

Lasalle almost immediately had an uncharacteristic stroke of bad luck when he was captured by the Austrians at the town of Brescia, fifty miles east of Milan. The Austrian Field Marshal Dagobert Wurmser reputedly asked him how old Napoleon was, to which Lasalle insolently replied, 'as old as Scipio when he defeated Hannibal.'[3] In any case, Lasalle was soon exchanged and then attached to the staff of General André Massena's division.

It was in December 1796 that he undertook one of his most famous escapades. He was by now a captain and had fallen violently in love with one of the inhabitants of the city of Vicenza, the Marquise de Sali. But after the French were forced to abandon the city to the Austrians, he so longed to see the marquise again that he hand-picked an escort of about twenty élite cavalrymen and went through the Austrian lines after dark. He reached Vicenza, hid his men and was soon blissfully engaged with the marquise. Later that night, he was alerted by sudden firing and hurriedly rejoined his men to ride back to the French positions. On the way, he broke through one hundred Austrian hussars guarding a bridge, while on other occasions he had to bluff his way through with his excellent German. Yet he returned with the loss of only four of his men, who had been captured, and to round off the adventure he appeared abruptly at a review that morning, unkempt and mounted on an Austrian horse. Asked by Napoleon for an explanation, he was able to supply the information about Austrian dispositions that the marquise had given him. He was promoted to major and, more importantly, had come to Napoleon's notice.

He won further renown in January 1797 when, charging at the head of just twenty-six chasseurs à cheval, he threw back an Austrian infantry column at the height of the Battle of Rivoli. Later, he skilfully reconnoitred in the mountains of north-eastern Italy during Napoleon's offensive against the Austrians under Archduke Charles before hostilities ended in April 1797.

Lasalle then went to Rome with the 7th *bis* Hussars[4], as part of the French force sent to occupy the Papal States early in 1798. After leading a mutiny over lack of pay, he took as his mistress the wife of Léopold Berthier, the brother of Napoleon's Chief-of-Staff, not perhaps the wisest career move.

More adventures followed with Napoleon's expedition to Egypt. Lasalle, who was still with the 7th *bis* Hussars, landed eight miles south-west of Alexandria on 1 July 1798 and accompanied General Louis Desaix's division, which formed Napoleon's advanced guard. After an epic, forty-five-mile march across the desert, the French defeated the mamelukes of Murad Bey at the Battle of Shubra Kit on 13 July and a week later fought the famous Battle of the Pyramids outside Cairo. Lasalle's role in this action was to take sixty hussars to help cut the escape route of the defenders of the village of Embabeh, which was being attacked by French infantry, and to drive them into the Nile river.

Napoleon rewarded Lasalle with promotion to the provisional rank of colonel and placed him in command of both the 7th *bis* Hussars and the 22nd Chasseurs à Cheval. Cairo was now in French hands but the campaign was far from over, for Ibrahim Bey, one of the mameluke rulers of Egypt, was retiring north-eastwards on Syria. Lasalle took part in the pursuit and at the oasis of Salahieh charged a mass of mamelukes with only 150 horsemen. At one point, he had to dismount to retrieve his sword and then fought for a while on foot until he could get back in the saddle. A fellow hussar officer later remarked of this episode that 'one must have seen a cavalry combat to appreciate the courage, coolness and dexterity which such a deed requires, especially in the presence of horsemen like the Mamelukes.'[5]

Napoleon subsequently invaded Syria, but Lasalle did not share in this campaign, instead being sent from Cairo southwards up the Nile as part of General Desaix's brilliant campaign to pacify Upper Egypt. He was often in action against insurgents, notably in February 1799, when he charged to save General Louis Davout, a future marshal who had fallen into a mameluke ambush at Redecieh. The region gradually settled down, but Napoleon left for France in August, leaving his army with a sense of abandonment. Lasalle's luck had temporarily deserted him and although he left for France early in 1800 after the Convention of El-Arisch, he arrived too late to share in Napoleon's victory over the Austrians at Marengo in northern Italy that June. Nonetheless, the expedition to Egypt, however militarily fruitless for France, had added another glittering chapter to Lasalle's reputation. He also added something to his dash and style, for he would adopt the colourful, baggy trousers of the mamelukes and perhaps also try to imitate some of their wild bravery.

In August 1800, still only 25 years old, he was appointed Colonel of the 10th Hussars. He went to Italy, but saw no immediate fighting as a shaky armistice had been in force with the Austrians since July. Even after hostilities broke out again in late November, he fought only in minor engagements before the conclusion of peace in February 1801. There followed four years of inactivity. First, he went to Spain in 1801 as part of a French corps under General Charles Leclerc, sent to aid the Spaniards against the Portuguese, and after returning to France spent his time in riotous living in garrison towns. On one occasion, a ball was held in the prefecture of Agen in south-western France, to which neither he nor his officers were invited. Taking this as an insult, he led his officers into the salons. An argument developed; he struck the prefect with his whip and then had his hussars throw the supper out of the windows. The prefect duly complained to the Emperor, who cynically remarked that it took a signature to make a prefect, but at least twenty years to make a Lasalle.[6] Lasalle was merely placed under arrest for thirty days, while the prefect was transferred.

In December 1803 Lasalle married Josephine Berthier, who by now had been divorced from her previous husband. Promotion to *général de brigade* followed in February 1805, as war clouds began to gather once more over Europe. Lasalle unaccountably was given a brigade of dragoons for the 1805 campaign against the Austro-Russians, rather than the élite hussars at whose head he truly flourished. Hostilities opened dramatically in October, with Napoleon swiftly surrounding the Austrian army of General Karl Mack at Ulm in Bavaria and forcing it to surrender. But a sizeable Austrian detachment under Archduke Ferdinand d'Este broke out of the trap and Lasalle took part in the pursuit, harrying Ferdinand's forces until they broke up in late October. Since Lasalle was then posted to Vienna, he missed the decisive Battle of Austerlitz, which brought the campaign to a victorious close.

In December 1805 he was reassigned to the light cavalry and at the end of the year given the command of the 5th and 7th Hussars. It was at the head of this crack brigade that Lasalle was destined shortly to win fame as one of the great cavalrymen of history. For Prussia, after failing to join Austria and Russia in the field for the Austerlitz campaign, belatedly prepared for war, only to be taken aback early in October 1806 when Napoleon seized the initiative and advanced north-eastwards on Berlin. Lasalle's 1,200 hussars, scouting out in front, seized five hundred caissons of equipment and gold at Gera, twenty miles east of Jena, on 11 October. The French then swept round to the west and defeated the Prussians in the twin Battles of Jena and Auerstädt on the 14th. Lasalle was not present at either action, being ordered south-westwards towards Jena when he might otherwise have been able to help the outnumbered Marshal Davout at Auerstädt.

But he truly came into his own during the whirlwind pursuit that followed, beginning on the 15th. His hussars were to the fore and rapidly acquired renown as the so-called Infernal Brigade. For Lasalle, though, an unpleasant incident initially threatened to wreck everything. Prussian troops under General Gebhard von Blücher, retreating after the defeats of the 14th, reached Weissensee, twenty-five miles north-west of Auerstädt, on the 16th and bluffed their way past a dragoon division under General

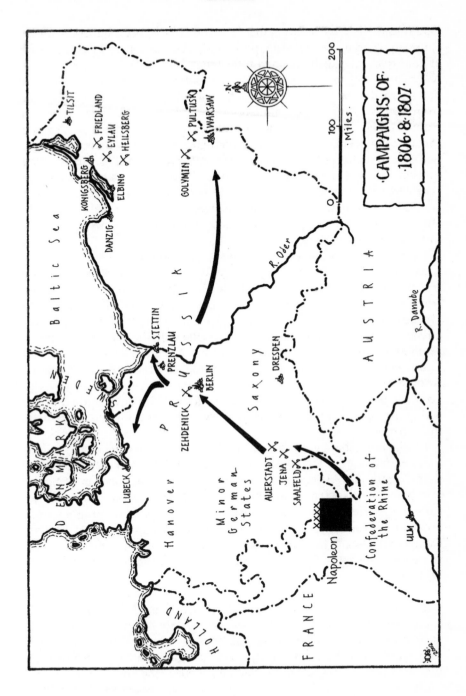

Dominique Klein by claiming that an armistice had been signed. Another Prussian column tried a similar ploy to pass Lasalle ten miles farther west at Tennstädt. Lasalle in fact had little choice but to allow it through as he had by now only eight hundred hussars and would have been wiped out had he tried to stop the column. But, misled by a self-justificatory report from Marshal Murat, the commander of the Reserve Cavalry, Napoleon blamed Klein and Lasalle in his Order of the Day of 19 October, sarcastically asking in reference to the fictitious armistice since when he had passed on his orders through the enemy. Stung, Lasalle wanted to kill himself, but was persuaded to go and remonstrate instead. Napoleon accepted that he had been misled and reassured Lasalle: 'be calm and continue to serve me as you have done up to now.' In any case, he would shortly wipe clean his record with a deed as audacious as any seen before in the history of warfare.

He continued north-eastwards, past Berlin and towards the Oder river, sometimes covering over thirty-five miles a day. About 40,000 Prussian troops under Prince Friedrich von Hohenlohe-Ingelfingen were retreating from Jena–Auerstädt north-eastwards on Stettin, apparently seeking to escape into what is now Poland and link up with Russian forces who were advancing westwards. On 26 October Lasalle with the support of General Emmanuel de Grouchy's dragoons smashed some Prussian cavalry at Zehdenick, an action that forced Hohenlohe to veer to the north before turning north-east again towards Prenzlau and Stettin. Two days later Lasalle attacked Hohenlohe at Prenzlau and tied him down until Marshal Murat arrived with more French cavalry and Murat bluffed Hohenlohe into surrender.

Lasalle immediately pressed on and late on the 29th reached the heights that overlooked the fortress town of Stettin. By this stage, he had fewer than eight hundred hussars remaining, whereas the garrison of Stettin numbered over 5,000 men and 281 guns. He placed his men under shelter from the guns of the fortress and had his one caisson of cartridges moved about on the hills to trick the Prussians into thinking that he had artillery. Colonel Schwarz of the 5th Hussars then went to summon the garrison to surrender, but returned with a refusal. Lasalle promptly sent him back with the message that if the garrison did not capitulate by 8.00 o'clock the following morning, Stettin would be bombarded, stormed and sacked. This threat, combined with pressure from the terrified citizens, forced the aged governor, General von Romberg, to agree to capitulate.

Next morning Lasalle's hussars assembled to receive the surrender of the garrison, which filed out to lay down its arms. Suddenly, the Prussians realised how few troops Lasalle had and some rushed towards the pile of muskets, only to be charged immediately by the hussars and driven back; French infantry then arrived to consolidate the stunning success. The unfortunate General von Romberg generously presented Lasalle with a

Turkish pipe enriched with precious stones. A fine tribute also came from Napoleon, who wrote to Marshal Murat: 'if your hussars are taking fortified towns, I may as well melt down my siege artillery and dismiss my engineers.'[7]

By now, only one detachment of survivors from Jena–Auerstädt was left intact, under Blücher. Lasalle marched westwards to join the French units pursuing this force towards the Baltic coast and took part in a series of actions, which culminated in Blücher being forced to surrender near Lübeck in early November.

Lasalle then returned eastwards to East Prussia and what is now Poland, where two Russian armies had finally arrived. Conditions were harsh, for the region was cold, muddy and impoverished, while the battles were usually bloody, bitter and fruitless. Napoleon occupied Warsaw on 28 November and the following month clashed with the Russians north of the city. Lasalle located Russian forces at Golymin on 26 December, was reinforced and in the ensuing battle held the far left flank. According to Second-Lieutenant Jean-Nicolas Curély of the 7th Hussars, Lasalle's men unaccountably panicked and fled before they even came under fire. Apparently, Lasalle then rallied his brigade, led it forward under the enemy guns and as a punishment kept it there under a murderous fire. 'Men and horses fell all the time, no one budged and not even a murmur was heard.'[8] Lasalle himself had two horses killed under him. Other accounts suggest that the brigade broke not of its own accord but because it was charged and overthrown. Nor is it possible to prove that Lasalle then placed the brigade under heavy fire specifically as a punishment: it was simply inevitable that the brigade would take heavy losses in such a murderous battle.[9]

After Golymin, Napoleon's army went into winter quarters to rest. Lasalle was promoted to *général de division* and given command of a division of three brigades of light cavalry, including his infernal brigade. The campaign flared up again in January 1807 when the Russians launched an offensive. Napoleon reacted strongly and forced them to retreat, but fought another bloody and indecisive battle at Eylau on 8 February. Lasalle had gone with two of his brigades on a separate mission with Marshal Ney, but hastened with Ney to Eylau and arrived there late in the day as the battle ended.

A four-month lull ensued, for the harsh conditions forced both sides back into winter quarters. Lasalle set up his headquarters at Elbing near the Baltic coast, thirty miles south-east of Danzig. Here, he relieved the tedium by holding dinner parties, to which he invited his officers simply by having his valet put a table-napkin on a stick on the balcony of his lodgings and leaving it there until all twenty places at his table were occupied.[10]

On 8 May Napoleon held a grand cavalry review at Elbing, where he lavished medals and promotions on his men to reward them and provide a powerful incentive for further deeds of valour. Lasalle himself was dissatisfied and dared to ask Napoleon for command of the Chasseurs à Cheval of the Imperial Guard, but was too wild and headstrong to be entrusted with such a precious regiment. 'When General Lasalle drinks no more, swears no more and smokes no more,' the Emperor retorted, 'not only will I put him at the head of a cavalry regiment of my Guard, but I will make him one of my chamberlains.'[11] Bitterly disappointed, Lasalle then asked for command of a frigate, but of course was refused, since his unique talents would be wasted on a naval command, particularly after Trafalgar.

Fighting resumed once more at the beginning of June. Lasalle now had four brigades in his division and saw action at Guttstadt, from where the Russians then fell back to a formidable entrenched position at Heilsberg. On 10 June Napoleon attacked the Russians here, only to win another costly and empty victory. Lasalle was in the thick of the fighting and at one stage actually had to shelter inside an infantry square. He rescued Marshal Murat from some Russian horsemen and is said in turn to have been saved by Murat later in the day.

From Heilsberg, Lasalle was sent north towards the city of Königsberg and so missed the Battle of Friedland on 14 June, the decisive victory that Napoleon had sought for so long. The Peace of Tilsit in July at last ended the war with Prussia and Russia. The consequences for Lasalle were dramatic. His division was quickly reduced to a quarter of its strength, but he himself had to stay in Poland until he managed to obtain leave in the autumn. On the other hand, he received the title Count of the Empire and two generous endowments.[12]

Lasalle never returned to Poland, for while on leave he received a summons to organise at Poitiers in western France a reserve cavalry division. This contained four so-called *régiments de marche*, units formed from a variety of small detachments temporarily cobbled together so that they could be marched to where they were needed and then allocated to their permanent regiments. Such units naturally lacked both equipment and cohesive spirit.

In 1807 Napoleon had sent a corps under General Andoche Junot through Spain in order to crush Portugal. Now, early in 1808, he sought to supplant the Spanish king and take over the country, despite the fact that Spain was nominally an ally. He already had two corps in Spain under General Pierre Dupont and Marshal Moncey and he ordered Marshal Murat to advance with them on Madrid. A third corps occupied north-eastern Spain, while Marshal Jean-Baptiste Bessières took command of the Corps of Observation of the Western Pyrenees and occupied northern Spain in order to guard the vital road that linked Madrid with the French city of Bayonne on the Atlantic coast. The four cavalry regiments that

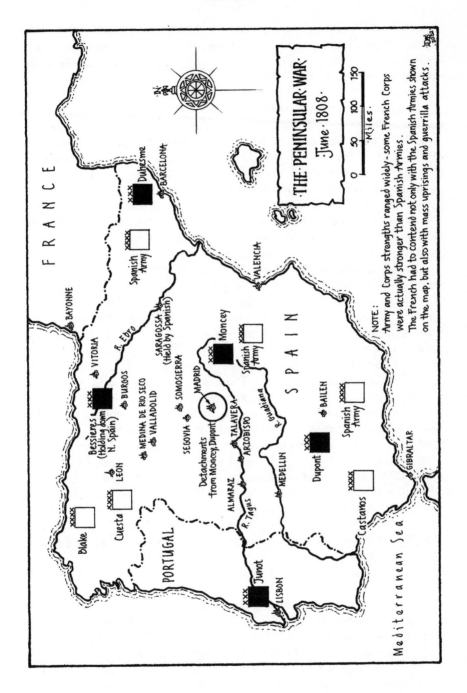

Lasalle had organised entered Spain in March; he himself followed in April, having been appointed to command the light cavalry division in Bessières' corps. Since several of his units were yet to arrive, Lasalle for the moment had only a small mixed detachment of cavalry, infantry and artillery.

Napoleon's plan soon backfired. The removal of the Spanish royal family to France provoked a revolt in Madrid on 2 May, followed later that month by uprisings all over Spain. Bessières had 20,000 men, but they were scattered between Madrid and the French frontier. The other French corps in Spain were tied down in the south and east of the country.

Bessières promptly detached troops to crush the main local centres of revolt. On 5 June he sent Lasalle from Burgos with just over 2,500 men to crush an insurrection in the city of Valladolid, a strategic road junction seventy miles to the south-west. Lasalle had a composite division, containing a brigade of provisional infantry units, six guns and just over six hundred men of the 10th and 22nd Chasseurs à Cheval. He first encountered resistance on the evening of the 6th at the village of Torquemada, thirty-seven miles south-west of Burgos. His leading units quickly smashed a force of insurgents, sacked and burnt the town.

This ruthless example had an immediate effect, with the town of Palencia eleven miles to the west submitting on his approach. He waited here for four days to allow a supporting column of 4,500 men under General Pierre Merle to catch up. Then, on the 12th, he found the Spanish General Don Gregorio de la Cuesta with about 7,000 men, most of them barely trained volunteers, blocking his advance at Cabezon, twenty miles south-west of Palencia and seven miles outside Valladolid. But Cuesta had taken up suicidal positions, with a line of troops out in front with a river at their backs to impede any retreat. Lasalle opened fire with his guns, then charged and immediately routed the raw Spaniards. Cuesta abandoned Valladolid and escaped north-westwards. Lasalle at once occupied Valladolid and extracted both hostages and a heavy financial contribution before falling back to Palencia. Joined here by his wife and daughter, he kept up patrols to gather information from the surrounding area.

Cuesta meanwhile formed a new army of volunteers, united with General Joachim Blake's army of Spanish regulars and returned to menace French communications between Burgos and Madrid. Bessières hurriedly concentrated what troops he could spare, including some veteran infantry reinforcements, and joined Lasalle at Palencia. He then advanced and on 14 July clashed with Cuesta and Blake at Medina de Rio Seco, twenty-eight miles to the south-west. The Spaniards had about 50,000 men, but their two armies had a gap between them and some of their troops were guarding their rear. Bessières had 12,000 troops. On the southern wing, Blake managed to check a French infantry assault until his left flank was suddenly assailed by Lasalle and his cavalry. As Blake was routed, Cuesta belatedly attacked in the north. When Bessières hesitated, Lasalle on his own initiative charged at the head of some Imperial Guard cavalry and routed a body of Spanish horsemen who were cutting up a company of French skirmishers. The French infantry advanced; Lasalle charged again and the Spaniards fled.

Lasalle's wife and daughter were present at the battle and became terrified by cannonballs raining down around them. Lasalle later explained how up to then, his wife had been reasonable, but after caring for the wounded at Medina de Rio Seco, she returned to France and no longer accompanied him to war: 'she has totally changed.' To a friend who told him he should have been concerned for her safety, Lasalle replied simply that he had not given it a moment's thought, since he did not know fear himself.[13]

Unfortunately, Bessières pursued too cautiously after Medina de Rio Seco to finish off his opponents. He established his base at Leon, fifty-five miles to the north-west, and was joined by reinforcements. Lasalle's division now temporarily included the Polish light horse of the Guard (later to become the famed Polish Lancers) and he instructed them in outpost and advanced guard duties.

Despite the victory of Medina de Rio Seco, the situation had deteriorated for the French elsewhere in the Peninsula, particularly when General Dupont surrendered his 18,000 troops to the Spanish General Francisco Castaños at Bailen on 22 July. The French thereupon abandoned Madrid and pulled right back behind the Ebro river in north-eastern Spain.

Napoleon resolved personally to go with reinforcements and restore the situation. He reorganised his army and launched an offensive in early November. Lasalle, who now had 2,000 horsemen, saw action near Burgos and advanced along the Madrid road in the advanced guard. On 21 November he reached the village of Boceguillas, which lay in front of the Somosierra pass through the Guadarrama mountain range fifty miles north of Madrid.

Napoleon stormed the Somosierra pass on 30 November and four days later seized Madrid. Lasalle, meanwhile, had been detached in pursuit of some retreating Spanish forces. Instead of going through Somosierra, his division was sent south-westwards through the town of Segovia and then across the Guadarrama mountains to circle round to the west of Madrid. He then headed to the south-west and reached Talavera on the Tagus river on 11 December.

Napoleon planned to march from Madrid on Lisbon to drive the British army of Sir John Moore into the sea and he intended Lasalle to form part of his advanced guard for this advance. When Napoleon realised that Moore was not retreating on Lisbon but instead striking at French communications in north-western Spain, he abandoned his initial plan and instead returned northwards to pursue Moore.

Reinforcements had meanwhile arrived at Talavera and Lasalle came under the orders of Marshal François Lefebvre, the commander of IV Corps. Lefebvre advanced thirty miles westwards down the Tagus to the bridge of Almaraz, a key crossing point on the main road from Madrid to Portugal. He failed to trap a Spanish force under General Galluzzo here, but seized the bridge intact after the Spaniards had tried in vain to destroy it.

Lefebvre drove back Galluzzo on the south bank of the Tagus, but then blundered, misunderstanding his orders and heading north-eastwards, until he was rebuked and told to return to Madrid, which he reached in January 1809. Napoleon, who had meanwhile forced Moore to evacuate his army from Spain by sea, now left for Paris. Although he left behind sizeable forces, he had failed completely to subdue the Peninsula. Southern Spain and Portugal remained unconquered and could not be occupied until the French had enough troops available for this task. In the meantime, their forces in the area sought merely to hold on to the bridges over the Tagus at Talavera and nearby Arzobispo as launchpads for future operations, while Lasalle was sent back to repair the damaged bridge at Almaraz and establish a bridgehead on the southern bank. He fought his way through, but, as he had foreseen, was unable to maintain his exposed position in such mountainous terrain with a heavily outnumbered cavalry force and duly fell back at the end of January. The Spaniards then finally managed to break the bridge.

In March 1809 the French finally took the offensive in southern Spain, as part of Napoleon's plan for a pincer advance into Portugal, with Marshal Soult's II Corps attacking from the north and Marshal Claude Victor's I Corps from the east. Victor first had to defeat the Spanish Army of Estremadura under General Cuesta and hence advanced southwards across the Tagus. Cuesta withdrew fifty miles southwards on Medellin to collect reinforcements before giving battle. Lasalle's cavalry division led Victor's advance and pursued the Spanish rearguard. But on 21 March the leading unit, the 10th Chasseurs à Cheval, fell into an ambush and suffered heavily before Lasalle could arrive with reinforcements. Second-Lieutenant Albert de Rocca of the 2nd Hussars arrived to find 'the colonel of the 10th . . . endeavouring to rally his chasseurs, and tearing his hair at the sight of the wounded strewed here and there over a pretty considerable space of ground.'[14] The episode enraged the whole of Lasalle's division, particularly as some of the chasseurs had apparently been murdered after being taken prisoner and their bodies mutilated. Victor pressed on southwards, crossed the Guadiana river and on 28 March defeated Cuesta at the Battle of Medellin, in which Lasalle was heavily engaged.

The stormclouds of war were meanwhile gathering over central Europe. Determined to avenge the disasters of 1805, Austria was preparing for hostilities. At Napoleon's command, Lasalle was sent back to France and hastened across Spain so as not to miss the new campaign and its opportunities for fresh glory. On the way, he passed through Torquemada, which he had sacked the year before. But he had given money to enable the posthouse to be rebuilt and the inhabitants actually welcomed him.

In the early hours of 28 April, Lasalle reached Burgos, where he woke an old friend stationed in the city, General Paul Thiébault. A clatter and shouts of 'I'm tired; I'm thirsty; I'm hungry,' announced the arrival of the 'amiable madman', as Thiébault described him. That evening, they dined with Pierre-Louis Roederer, a prominent politician and economist, who was on his way to Madrid on a mission entrusted to him by Napoleon. Roederer, who came from Lasalle's birthplace, the city of Metz, was so impressed by his wit and personality that he recorded their conversation for posterity. He also admitted to Thiébault that although he had known Lasalle was the most brilliant of their light cavalry generals, he had been miles from realising how deep and able a man he was.[15]

Lasalle explained how he was desperate to reach the theatre of war on the Danube and how he feared that he would arrive after the start of hostilities:

> The Emperor has given me a superb division: eight light cavalry regiments and eight guns. It is more than I need. I will be in despair if it begins without me.

In fact, the first battles had already been fought, since the Austrians had invaded Bavaria, Napoleon's ally in southern Germany, on 10 April. Nonetheless, Lasalle would arrive in time to take part in the subsequent fighting. He intended to go via Paris:

> I will arrive at 5.00 am, I will order myself a pair of boots, make my wife pregnant and leave.

He declined Thiébault's offer of an escort, despite the danger from guerrillas, as it would slow him down and he was loath to miss the war in Germany. When Roederer remonstrated that he should not risk his life when it could be useful, he retorted:

> I have had a full life. What is the point of living? To win renown, gain advancement, make a fortune. Well! I am thirty-three, I am a *général de division*. Do you know that the Emperor gave me an income of 50,000 francs last year? It is immense! . . .

Roederer protested that Lasalle's career was far from finished and that he should avoid pointless perils in order to enjoy his fame and riches. Lasalle would have none of it: he had enjoyment enough, he said, in acquiring those things, in waging war, in being in the noise, smoke and excitement of battle:

> And then, when we have made our name, well, we have had the pleasure of making it. When we have made our fortune, we are sure that our wives and children will lack for nothing. All that is enough. I am ready to die tomorrow.[16]

Had he been able to see into the future, he might have added that he was returning from Spain with his reputation not only intact but enhanced, in contrast to many French commanders who over the next five years would cover themselves with defeat and dishonour.

He arrived on the Danube just in time for the Battle of Aspern–Essling. Napoleon had captured Vienna, but now needed to cross the river to finish off the Austrian army under Archduke Charles on the north bank and secure peace. Lasalle commanded a light cavalry division in the Reserve Cavalry under Marshal Bessières.

Napoleon did not realise that the Austrian army was so close to the river and on 20 May pushed an infantry division and Lasalle's light cavalry on to the north bank. Lasalle reconnoitred, but was unable to penetrate the strong Austrian cavalry screen and thus did not discover that the Austrians were present in strength. More of Napoleon's troops arrived in the bridgehead on the 21st and were attacked that afternoon by the Austrian army. Lasalle was heavily engaged in the centre, between the villages of Aspern and Essling, and at one point personally rescued Marshal Bessières from some cavalry. When the battle resumed on the 22nd, Lasalle again charged repeatedly. But the Austrians successfully contained the bridgehead and obliged Napoleon to evacuate it that night.

In the six-week lull that followed, Lasalle was placed under Marshal Louis Davout and ordered to watch the line of the Danube from Vienna eastwards to Pressburg. Davout sent Lasalle farther east to aid Napoleon's stepson, Eugène de Beauharnais, whose Army of Italy was operating against a detached Austrian force under Archduke John. Lasalle helped besiege the city of Raab in the middle of June, ably placing his batteries of siege artillery and winning praise even from the exacting Davout. After the surrender of Raab on 22 June, Lasalle returned westwards to rejoin Napoleon, who was preparing for another attempt to cross the Danube near Vienna. This bid to avenge the setback of Aspern–Essling was destined to lead to the two-day Battle of Wagram.

Lasalle, whose division was attached to Marshal André Massena's corps[17], duly crossed over the Danube in the early hours of 5 July. He was depressed, having been disturbed by some odd mishaps. His orderly had fallen into Austrian hands while taking his horse to drink at a stream. He also found that his porcelain pipe and a brandy bottle had broken in his baggage, while the glass covering a portrait of his wife had cracked in his sabretache. He turned to an ADC and bluntly said: 'I will not survive this day.'[18] He handed his will to a young officer and told him to give it to the Emperor in the event of his death.

The smell of powder swept away these gloomy premonitions and he helped to drive back the Austrian advanced troops retreating across the extensive plain on the north bank of the Danube. He did not die. But next day, 6 July, the battle resumed in earnest. He was heavily engaged, and when Massena had to shift his corps southwards to help plug a gap in Napoleon's line, he covered the movement. He also recaptured two French guns near the village of Aspern. The fighting gradually swung in Napoleon's favour and culminated in a massive infantry assault in the centre. Archduke Charles ordered a retreat to avoid the destruction of his army. On Napoleon's left wing, Lasalle charged the Austrian infantry of General Johann Klenau near the village of Léopoldau. Beaten off at first, he renewed the charge with elements of the 1st Cuirassiers. Then, as he rallied his men, he was fired on by an infantryman at a range of fifteen paces, was hit between the eyes and killed on the spot. He could not have wished for a better end.

Lasalle

There were two General Lasalles. One was a brutal, legendary warrior; the other was a sensitive man, deeply in love with his wife and devoted to his children. When the smoke of battle clears temporarily from his life, we catch glimpses of that second Lasalle and see a man prey to fits of depression and self-doubt. The general who bluffed the garrison of Stettin into surrender put on no less a bluster to hide his inner self.

It was when he was deprived of action that he succumbed to melancholy, particularly in Egypt and later in Poland. He had a moody, self-destructive streak, like Marshal Ney. What else would have made him apply for a post in the navy simply because he was refused command of the Chasseurs à Cheval of the Imperial Guard?

It is hard to like him. He was an utterly ruthless warrior who responded to brutality in kind and won the reputation of being a man 'who feared nothing and made the whole of Spain afraid.'[19] He and his troopers were élite soldiers and they swaggered through life with the arrogant indiscipline unique to hussars.

What redeemed him was his outstanding talent. Great cavalry generals were rare and this is what made him so remarkable. He was a thorough professional who knew as much about horses as he did about how to manoeuvre formations of cavalry. Marshal Auguste Marmont claimed that in the twenty-five years of the Revolutionary and Napoleonic wars, only Generals François Kellermann, Louis Montbrun and Charles Lasalle knew how to handle massed cavalry. (Marshal Joachim Murat, though more famous, was too erratic and careless of the welfare of the horses.) For this, Napoleon was prepared to tolerate Lasalle's foibles, to the extent, according to a fellow hussar officer, Jean-Baptiste de Marbot, of 'laughing at all his freaks, and never [letting] him pay his own debts.'[20]

Lasalle was unique. Although only five foot eight inches tall, he stood out with his alert eyes and manner and had as many conquests in the bed as on the battlefield. His flamboyant moustaches, his pelisse liberally decorated with buttons and glittering lace and his extraordinary, baggy red breeches commanded attention, even in an age which bestowed colourful uniforms on the rank and file. Much of all this panache was, of course, mere bluff. As Marbot explained:

> He was a handsome man, and of a bright wit, but, although well-educated, he had adopted the fashion of posing as a swashbuckler. He might always be seen drinking, swearing, singing, smashing everything, and possessed by a passion for play.[21]

No one ever forgot the time when Lasalle rode into a ballroom and made his horse dance in time to the music. It was a revealing incident, for it combined his reckless eccentricity with his superb horsemanship. The key to understanding Lasalle lay in his mixture of extreme wildness and tight control. From his mother, he inherited the inner fire of the born leader and his unruly childhood in the streets of Metz developed the quick wits and aggressive spirit that flourished at the head of his hussars. But he also had ruthless self-discipline and this was often overlooked. As Marbot pointed out:

> [Lasalle's] death left a great gap in our light cavalry, which he had trained to a high degree of perfection. In other respects, however, he had done it much harm. The eccentricities of a popular and successful leader are always imitated, and his example was long mischievous to the light cavalry. A man did not think himself a chasseur, still less a hussar, if he did not model himself on Lasalle, and become, like him, a reckless, drinking, swearing rowdy. Many officers copied the faults of this famous outpost leader, but none of them attained to the merits which in him atoned for the faults.[22]

Lasalle truly excelled when acting as the advance guard, in reconnoitring aggressively, collecting intelligence and sending back model reports. He failed only once in this respect, on the eve of Aspern–Essling, when the strength of the Austrian cavalry screen prevented him from discovering the proximity of the Austrian army. According to Marbot:

> [Lasalle] was the best light cavalry officer for outpost duty, and had the surest eye. He could take in a whole district in a moment, and seldom made a mistake, so that his reports on the enemy's position were clear and precise.[23]

He was equally good in pursuit and in charge of the rearguard of a retreat. In an actual battle, he was a master of timing and of the beautifully controlled charge. His trademark was a pipe clenched in his fist and held in the air to signal the switch from the trot to the gallop. His skill lay in judging the precise moment when he should begin to gallop so as to achieve maximum momentum just as he struck the foe. Usually, his opponents would have begun to gallop too early and would arrive disordered, with blown horses and in no state to resist his hussars.

For all his flaws, Lasalle was a truly great general. He was terrifyingly professional, energetic, quick to seize opportunities and ruthless in getting his way. Above all, he was lucky. He never lost a battle and, except for sabre cuts received while crossing the Tagliamento river in 1797, was hit only once, by the shot that killed him. Even in death he was fortunate, for he fell in Napoleon's last successful campaign and was thus spared the disasters, disillusionment and disgrace that subsequently befell so many of his glittering colleagues. Remember, too, that the quality of the French cavalry, both men and horses, declined dramatically after the losses in the Russian campaign of 1812 and reduced the opportunities for Napoleon's surviving cavalry generals to win further glory.

It was in 1806, at the head of a brigade of crack hussars, that Lasalle achieved his greatest feats. He later showed that he was able to handle a division and would probably have been a success in command of the Reserve Cavalry, although he never had a chance to prove it.

Lasalle had no time for politics or intrigue. He was one of the finest examples of the fighting general. In his last letter to his wife, he wrote: 'my heart is for you, my blood for the Emperor and my life for honour.'[24]

The Battle of Medellin: 28 March 1809

Neither of the two opposing commanders at the Battle of Medellin could be called outstanding, but they were both brave and stubborn men. General Don Gregorio Garcia de la Cuesta, at the head of the Spanish Army of Estremadura, was 69 years old and a veteran soldier who had fought the French during the Revolutionary wars and more recently had been badly beaten by them at Medina de Rio Seco in July 1808. In contrast, the French commander, Marshal Claude Victor, was 44 and had distinguished himself two years earlier against the Russians at the Battle of Friedland, where he had won his marshal's baton. He was a capable tactician and tenacious in defending a position.

In March 1809 Victor launched an offensive into southern Spain, which had yet to be occupied by the French. Cuesta fell back before the French advance until, after being reinforced on the 27th by 7,000 men, he immediately began to retrace his steps. Victor, meanwhile, had been obliged to leave behind detachments to guard his communications as he pushed southwards, but through cavalry reconnaissances located Cuesta's army and discovered that there were no other Spanish forces in the region. He therefore concentrated his available troops by the early morning of the 28th near the town of Medellin.

Once alerted by his cavalry that Cuesta was approaching, Victor prepared for battle in the extensive and open plain outside Medellin. Along the northern edge of the battlefield ran the Guadiana river, which was crossed at Medellin in the north-west by a long, narrow bridge. The western edge of the battleground was marked by the steep-sided valley of the Hortiga river, which ruled out any sweeping outflanking moves.

The overall odds marginally favoured Cuesta, who had about 23,000 men to Victor's 17,500. But it was Victor who had more guns (fifty to thirty) and, crucially, more cavalry (4,500 to 3,000). He placed his army one-and-a-half miles south-east of Medellin, blocking the road that crossed the plain. His left flank rested on the high-flowing Guadiana in the north-east and his right on the ravine of the Hortiga in the south-west. This was conventional enough, but the arrangement of his troops was unusual, for the centre, consisting of an infantry division under General Eugène Villatte, was held back while the two wings were placed farther forward. Each wing contained a cavalry division and two battalions of Napoleon's German troops from the Confederation of the Rhine. Finally, well to the rear and near the town of Medellin, stood the reserve, which was not destined to be engaged. This contained an infantry division under General François Ruffin, a regiment of cavalry and an artillery reserve. Thus Victor's army formed an arc, with the two ends nearest the foe and the centre considerably farther back, indicating that he planned to fight a flexible battle, using a considerable depth of ground.

Cuesta's arrangements were equally unorthodox, but less rational. He, too, extended his army in an arc between the Hortiga and Guadiana, with each flank resting on a river and secure from being outflanked. But, unlike Victor, he kept no reserve. He had just one line of troops, four ranks deep, extending a full four miles across the battlefield, with three regiments of cavalry at either end. As he advanced between the two converging rivers, his front would become progressively narrower, but he would be defeated before this released enough troops to form a second line. He simply did not have enough men to warrant attacking and would have done better to

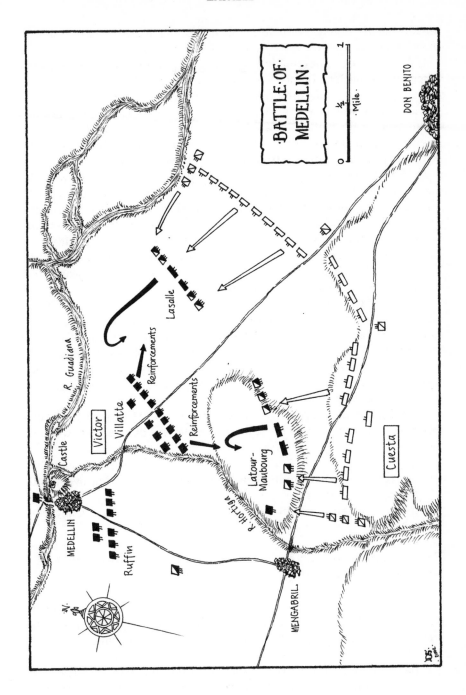

remain on the defensive or to avoid battle, but unfortunately political pressures precluded these two alternatives.

The preliminary cannonade began at 1.00 pm and grew in intensity. After three-quarters of an hour, Cuesta ordered an advance. Victor delegated considerable authority to his two wing commanders, Lasalle on the left and General Marie-Victor-Nicolas de Fay, Viscount de Latour-Maubourg on the right. He told them to charge when they had a good opportunity to do so, but not to risk a major counter-attack until the advancing ranks of Spanish troops had lost their cohesion.

The battle initially went in favour of the Spaniards. Over on the western flank, Latour-Maubourg ordered a brigade of his dragoons to charge, but misjudged his moment. Shattered by musketry and artillery fire, his dragoons broke and fled, thus uncovering the flank of the two German battalions on this wing. On Victor's orders, Latour-Maubourg withdrew step by step, under fire from the Spanish skirmishers who were surging boldly forward. The curved nature of the Spanish line meant that musketry poured destructively inwards into Victor's units.

The retreat of Victor's right wing forced Lasalle on the left to conform. He had two good infantry battalions from the German state of Baden and four cavalry regiments: the 2nd Hussars, a regiment of dragoons and the 5th and 10th Chasseurs à Cheval[25], or a total of 2,000 cavalry and 2,500 infantry. His situation was particularly tricky, for if he had to retreat more than a mile, he would find his left flank being forced increasingly against the Guadiana river.

Second-Lieutenant Albert de Rocca of the 2nd Hussars left an unforgettable account of how his squadron withdrew during these difficult moments:[26]

> We retired for two hours slowly and silently, stopping every fifty paces to face about and present our front to the enemy, in order to dispute our ground with him before we abandoned it, whenever he attempted to drive us from it.

The men were silent; only the voices of the officers were heard above the whizzing of passing shot. Out in front, individual horses from both sides were galloping about, many of them trying to dislodge the burden of their slain riders, whom they were dragging along by a stirrup. Cannonballs ploughed up the earth all around, but as the enemy pressed closer, the French officers merely gave their orders more coolly and collectedly:

> As we retired, the cries of the Spaniards redoubled; their skirmishers were so numerous and so bold, that they frequently forced ours back to their ranks. They shouted to us from afar, in their own tongue, that they would give no quarter, and that the plains of Medellin should be

the grave of the French. Had our squadron been broken and dispersed, the Spanish horse of the right would have burst through the opening, on the rear of our army, and surrounded it.

The Spaniards were ready to exploit any sign of panic and three of their cavalry regiments pressed forward along the bank of the Guadiana to try and turn this flank. Lasalle's imperturbable air did much to reassure his men. Rocca wrote how he 'rode proudly and calmly backwards and forwards in front of his division.'

Victor thus pulled his entire line back towards Medellin in a long, but steady retreat. He had apparently planned from the start deliberately to retire like this, so as to draw the Spaniards on, thus disturbing the cohesion of their ranks as they advanced and leaving them ripe for a decisive counter-attack. He probably based the battle on that of Marengo in northern Italy nine years earlier, where he had been forced to beat a fighting retreat with his outnumbered corps for four hours so as to gain time for the arrival of the reinforcements whose counter-attack decided the day in Napoleon's favour. Nonetheless, Victor was taking a risk because if anything went wrong, he could be forced right back to the town of Medellin, trapped against the Guadiana river and there destroyed.

His two wings withdrew until they were within supporting distance from Villatte's infantry division, which formed the centre of his army. The western wing under Latour-Maubourg now stood on the crest of some high ground, which offered a good position on which to fight it out. Victor duly reinforced him with both the 94th Line infantry and a battalion of grenadiers from Villatte's division. Latour-Maubourg's ten guns also helped to stabilise the situation. Lieutenant-Colonel Benjamin d'Urban, a British observer with Cuesta's army, recorded that the fire of the more numerous and better-served French guns was severely felt.[27] But the Spanish infantry pressed on regardless and attacked Latour-Maubourg's infantry battalions, which were handicapped by having to stand in hollow square formations to face the threat of the Spanish cavalry and as a result had limited firepower.

Then, just as the foremost Spaniards were about to capture his guns, Latour-Maubourg ordered his dragoons to counter-attack once more. This time, the charge succeeded. Cuesta tried in vain to have the three regiments of cavalry present at this end of his line to charge the dragoons in the flank and was himself knocked down as they broke and fled the field. Deserted by their cavalry, the courageous Spanish infantry lost their nerve and disintegrated. The disaster rapidly unfolded, for once Cuesta's thin battle line had been pierced, he could do nothing to contain the breach as he had no reserves.

An equally sudden reversal of fortune had occurred on the eastern wing, where Lasalle had likewise received reinforcements from Villatte's division in the centre, namely a brigade of French infantry and a battalion of Germans from the Duchy of Nassau, seven fresh battalions in all.[28] When Lasalle saw Latour-Maubourg's charge in the west, he immediately stopped retreating. His horsemen were eager to be unleashed after bearing for so long the bottled-up tension of their retreat. The 2nd Hussars, supported by a regiment of chasseurs à cheval, quickly smashed the Spanish cavalry next to the Guadiana. Second-Lieutenant Albert de Rocca recalled how:

> Our hussars, who in the midst of the threats and abuse of the enemy had preserved the strictest silence, then drowned the sound of the trumpet as they moved onwards, by a single and terrible shout of joy and fury. The Spanish lancers stopped; seized with terror, they turned their horses at the distance of half [a] pistol-shot, and overthrew their own cavalry, which was behind them.

This uncovered the eastern flank of the line of Spanish infantry, which Lasalle promptly charged after reforming his men. At the same time, his infantry, including the fresh reinforcements that he had received from Villatte, engaged the Spanish battalions frontally. The final collapse of Cuesta's army came as some of Latour-Maubourg's victorious dragoons charged the flank and rear of a Spanish infantry division in the centre of the battlefield. The action quickly became a massacre. As Albert de Rocca noted:

> In an instant the army that was before us disappeared, like clouds driven by the wind. The Spaniards threw down their arms and fled; the cannonade ceased, and the whole of our cavalry went off in pursuit of the enemy.

Lasalle's men ferociously slaughtered the fleeing Spaniards to avenge the brutal massacre of some of their comrades in the 10th Chasseurs à Cheval in an ambush several days before the battle. 'Our men,' admitted Albert de Rocca, 'who had seen themselves threatened with certain death, had they sunk under the number of their foes, and irritated by five hours' resistance, gave no quarter at first.' Fortunately, a thunderstorm in the late afternoon brought the bloody pursuit to an end.

Perhaps 8,000 Spaniards were killed or wounded and another 2,000 captured. Seven standards and up to twenty of the thirty Spanish guns were also taken. Cuesta's army had been smashed; he himself had been pulled from the hooves of his fleeing cavalry and, bruised and nearly unconscious, put on a horse to be escorted to safety.

But it had not been an easy victory and it had probably cost Victor over 1,000 casualties. Shortly before dusk, Albert de Rocca returned across the battlefield to the town of Medellin:

Silence and quiet had succeeded to the activity of battle, and the shouts of victory. In the plain, the only audible sounds were the groans of the wounded, and the confused murmurs of the dying, as they raised their hands in prayer to God and the blessed Virgin.

NOTES

1 F. Hourtoulle, *Le général comte Charles Lasalle, 1775–1809* (1979), p.68
2 C. Sainte-Beuve, *Causeries du lundi* (1856), v.8, p.542
3 The Roman general Publius Cornelius Scipio beat Hannibal at Zama in 202 BC at the age of 35.
4 The distinction *bis* meant that there were two 7th regiments of hussars, of which this was the junior one.
5 A. Butler, trans., *The memoirs of Baron de Marbot* (1892), v.2, p.25
6 C. Thoumas, *Les grands cavaliers du premier empire* (1890), v.1, p.19
7 *Ibid*, v.1, p.26
8 J. Curély, *Le général Curély: itinéraire d'un cavalier léger de la Grande Armée, 1793–1815* (1887), p.203
9 Dr F. Hourtoulle re-examines the entire question of the panic at Golymin. It is impossible either to confirm or to disprove Curély's account.
10 C. Parquin, *Souvenirs et campagnes d'un vieux soldat de l'empire* (1892), pp.142–3
11 *Ibid*, p.143
12 The title was made official in March 1808.
13 Sainte-Beuve, *op. cit.*, v.8, pp.534–40
14 A. de Rocca, *In the Peninsula with a French hussar* (1990), pp.76–7
15 F. Calmettes, ed., *Mémoires du général Baron Thiébault* (1894), v.4, p.332–3
16 Sainte-Beuve, *op. cit.*, v.8, pp.534–40
17 Besides his own division, Lasalle therefore also commanded the light cavalry brigade of General Jacob Marulaz, which was a part of Massena's corps.
18 M. Dupont, *Le général Lasalle* (1929), p.236
19 Sainte-Beuve, *op. cit.*, v.8, p.535
20 Butler, *op. cit.*, v.2, p.25
21 *Ibid*, v.2, p.24
22 *Ibid*, v.2, p.26
23 *Ibid*, v.2, p.24
24 Thoumas, *op. cit.*, v.1, p.20
25 Hourtoulle, *op. cit.*, p.218
26 Rocca, *op. cit.*, pp.76–82
27 I. Rousseau, ed., *The Peninsular journal of Major-General Sir Benjamin d'Urban 1808–1817* (1930), p.48
28 The Nassau battalion came from General Jean-François Leval's division of German troops, which had been split up, with two of its battalions being attached to each wing and the fifth – the Nassau battalion – to Villatte's division in the centre.

CHAPTER IV

Moore

Few commanders have won the affection of their men with the ease of Lieutenant-General Sir John Moore. He was one of those inspirational leaders who become legends in their own lifetime. One colleague called him 'the most perfect soldier and gentleman I ever knew', while another remembered him as 'a most extraordinary man. The nearer you saw him, the more he was admired. He was superior by many degrees to everyone I have seen.'[1]

Yet this brilliant commander was also one of the most controversial of his age. His final campaign, that of Coruña in the winter of 1808–9, sparked such bitter recriminations that it has only recently been possible to re-assess his record. Only now can we obtain a more balanced picture, avoiding both the wild criticism of his detractors and the hero-worship of admirers. He was, in truth, an outstanding soldier, but his sensitive and over-emotional nature proved a fatal flaw.

Sir John Moore was born at Glasgow on 13 November 1761. He was the son of Dr John Moore, a Scottish physician and author who had married the daughter of a professor at the University of Glasgow. Dr Moore won the friendship of an influential patron, the Duchess of Hamilton (later the Duchess of Argyll) and in February 1772 was invited to escort her son, Douglas, Eighth Duke of Hamilton, on a four-year Grand Tour of Europe. Dr Moore accepted and set out in April with both his pupil and John, his eldest surviving son.

During their four years of travelling, John was educated under his father's guidance and became increasingly keen on a military career. 'He is often operating in the fields,' Dr Moore wrote, 'and informs me how he would attack Geneva,'[2] while in Prussia he met Frederick the Great and saw field manoeuvres involving 40,000 troops. At Vienna in 1775 Dr Moore declined an offer from the Emperor Joseph II to take John into the Austrian Army. The Duke of Argyll instead obtained for him an ensigncy in the 51st Foot.

John did not immediately join his regiment, but continued on the Grand Tour and narrowly escaped death after going too close to the crater of Vesuvius at the moment of a minor eruption. At last he returned to

England and early in 1777 joined the 51st on the Mediterranean island of Minorca. He hated garrison life, but it was to dog him throughout his career. He longed instead for active service and knew that heavy fighting was in progress across the Atlantic, where the American colonies were in full-scale rebellion. His father's influence smoothed the wheels of bureaucracy and he sailed across the Atlantic with some of the 82nd Foot, a new unit raised by the Duke of Hamilton.

He came under fire for the first time at the end of July 1779, when an American fleet landed troops at Penobscot Bay, 150 miles north-east of Boston. As a lieutenant, he commanded a picket of twenty soldiers and had to rally them under fire. 'Will the Hamilton men leave me?' he shouted. 'Come back, and behave like soldiers.'[3] They obeyed and kept up a heavy fire until relieved; a fortnight later, British warships appeared on the scene and the Americans fled, losing all their ships. Moore was only 17 and had acquitted himself well, but later admitted to his father that he had been devilishly frightened. He had also shown his horror of killing, when he had aimed but not fired at an American officer. Moore saw no further fighting in America, but went with the 82nd into quarters at Halifax, where an obliging general let him study his numerous books on military science. After enduring a long period of inactivity, Moore went to New York in August 1781 and sailed home early the following year. His regiment, the 82nd, was now disbanded as the war in America came to an end, so he went on half-pay, won a seat in Parliament in the 1784 election and held it until 1790, when he decided not to seek re-election. Contrary to popular belief, he was not a Whig: he disliked party politics and made it clear to his patron, the Duke of Hamilton, that he would follow his conscience on all matters rather than commit himself to any party. Indeed, as it happened, he generally supported the Tory Prime Minister, William Pitt the Younger.[4]

His military career picked up again in 1787 when he was promoted major and given the task of training a new battalion of the 60th Foot. The following year, he transferred back to the 51st, which was now stationed in Ireland. By the end of 1790, he had pressurised its incompetent commander to retire and purchased the Lieutenant-Colonelcy. He then set about restoring the regiment to good shape with training and the replacement of unsatisfactory officers.

In March 1792 Moore was sent with the 51st to help garrison Gibraltar. Following the outbreak of war with Revolutionary France in February 1793, he embarked in December with the 51st to reinforce the allied troops holding the southern French naval base of Toulon, but arrived after it was evacuated. The British then turned their attention to the nearby island of Corsica, where freedom fighters under General Pasquale Paoli sought independence from French occupation. In January 1794 Moore was sent on a military and diplomatic mission to see if the British could wrest the island from French control and use it as a base in the Mediterranean. He landed in the north of the island with both a fellow officer and a diplomat, Sir Gilbert Elliott. After meeting Paoli and inspecting the terrain, he produced a plan for a landing in the Gulf of San Fiorenzo in the north of the island.

On 7 February Moore led the first British units ashore under the overall command of Major-General David Dundas. He then helped subdue a fortified tower that had been erected to guard the bay of Mortella. The British were so impressed by its effectiveness that they later built similar structures, the famous Martello towers, to guard their own shores against potential invasion.

Following the surrender of the tower on 10 February, the British moved against the remaining defences of the bay. During this fighting, Moore led a night assault on the Convention Redoubt and personally slew a Frenchman who tried to bayonet him. He never forgot the horrid sensation he felt when he withdrew his sword from the corpse. The French then evacuated their remaining positions in the neighbourhood.

The British, having thus secured their bridgehead, moved against the fortress of Bastia seven miles to the east. After it was starved into surrender in May, they went by sea to the north-western coast and besieged Calvi, the other major fortress in the area. Relations between the army and Royal Navy were strained during these operations and this was exemplified by Captain Horatio Nelson's belief that Moore was over-cautious in demanding so thorough a bombardment of the fortifications. It was during the fighting for one of the forts at Calvi that Nelson lost the sight of his right eye; Moore himself suffered his first wound when hit in the head by a shell-splinter but fortunately was not seriously hurt. Calvi finally surrendered in August and Corsica remained in British hands until it had to be abandoned in 1796 when the Royal Navy temporarily withdrew from the Mediterranean to concentrate on the security of the British Isles.

Moore had established his reputation as a fighting soldier, but during the months that followed he revealed a lack of judgement that might have wrecked his career. In October 1795 he quarrelled furiously with Sir Gilbert Elliott, who had been appointed British viceroy of Corsica a year earlier. Moore felt that Elliott had been invested with too much power, resented his high-handedness and even feared that he was unnecessarily antagonising the inhabitants to such an extent that revolt might break out at any moment. He unwisely shared his views with Paoli, was challenged by Elliott for undermining his position and promptly ordered to return to England.

Despite this humiliating experience, Moore had an interview in London with Prime Minister William Pitt, was promoted to brigadier-general and sent to the West Indies. These Caribbean islands were a crucial source of cotton, coffee and sugar, which generated much of the money that Britain needed to maintain the struggle and subsidise her continental allies. But the war was going badly for the British in this theatre and so 33,000 troops, including Moore, were sent under Major-General Sir Ralph Abercromby to mount a counter-offensive against the French.

The West Indies were deadly. Yellow fever and malaria carried off thousands of troops every year and Moore himself would barely survive a bout of illness. After capturing St Lucia in May 1796, Abercromby left Moore as its governor while he and the bulk of his troops attacked other French-held islands. Moore's task was essentially counter-insurgency against escaped slaves and negro soldiers armed and trained by the French. He found himself tested to the limit by the mountains, jungle and unhealthy climate, but learned the value of light infantry in such conditions. He also realised that 'it is not the climate alone that kills the troops in this country; it is bad management.'[5]

Abercromby restored the situation in the Caribbean by the middle of 1797. Moore returned to England that July and the following year saw action as a major-general during the unsuccessful Irish rebellion. He was restless and frustrated and wrote to his father:

> I cannot reconcile myself to remain here, and be troubled with the continued broils of this distracted people, when active and distinguished service is going on elsewhere. I consider myself yet as in my apprenticeship; I wish to serve it under the best masters, and where there is most business, that at some future day I may be able to direct and instruct in my turn. Our business, like every other, is to be learned only by constant practice and experience; and our experience is to be had in war, not at reviews.[6]

His chance came with the Duke of York's expedition of 1799 against the French in the Batavian Republic, present-day Holland. Entrusted with a brigade command, Moore landed in August with an initial force under Abercromby. After some fighting in the bridgehead, the French withdrew to the south and a squadron of the Dutch fleet surrendered. The Duke of York then arrived to take overall command of both the British troops and a Russian contingent. But the Franco-Batavian forces used ditches and dykes to prepare strong defensive positions and on 19 September beat off an attack at Bergen near the coast.

The Duke of York attacked again on 2 October, but lost heavily. Moore was among the casualties, being struck in the head while leading an advance along the beach towards the village of Egmond-aan-Zee in a bid to outflank the foe. He recovered with care from his father and brother James, who were both doctors. But in his absence, the expedition ended with a convention and the evacuation of the Duke of York's army.

Moore's immediate fate was another fiasco. In May 1800 he sailed from England as part of reinforcements bound for the island of Minorca, where they came under Abercromby, the newly appointed Commander-in-Chief in the Mediterranean. Abercromby had instructions to assist the Austrians in northern Italy and duly embarked the 5,000 troops he could spare, but arrived off the port of Genoa on 30 June too late to intervene following Napoleon's victory over the Austrians at Marengo a fortnight earlier. The expedition returned to the island of Minorca, until ordered to sail to Gibraltar. Then, after being reinforced, Abercromby was instructed to attack the arsenal and warships at Cadiz in Spain, which at the time was a French ally. Moore considered the operation to be excessively risky, particularly as the weather could easily turn bad at such a late season and prevent the re-embarkation of the army. As it happened, insufficient boats and the fact that the fleet was anchored too far offshore forced the landing to be aborted and adverse winds prevented another attempt from being made the following morning from closer in.

Moore's next experience of active service was an altogether happier one. Napoleon had led an expedition to Egypt in 1798, only to be marooned by the destruction of his fleet at the hands of Rear-Admiral Horatio Nelson. Napoleon himself had slipped back to France in the autumn of 1799, but had been forced to leave his army behind. The British Government was keen to expel these troops in order to remove the French threat to India and ordered Abercromby to sail from Gibraltar with 15,000 men to the eastern end of the Mediterranean.

Abercromby hoped for co-operation from an Ottoman Turkish army based at Jaffa. In January 1801 he disembarked his troops in Marmorice Bay, forty miles north of the island of Rhodes, so they could train for an assault landing in Egypt. Moore met the Turkish Vizier at Jaffa, but failed to secure the desired support from the inefficient and plague-ridden Turkish forces.

Abercromby sailed for Egypt on 22 February and prepared to land at Aboukir Bay, fifteen miles north-east of the city of Alexandria, at dawn on 4 March. Bad weather postponed the operation to the 8th and resulted in all loss of surprise. But as far as Moore and Abercromby could see when they personally reconnoitred the coast from offshore, the French failed to take any additional defensive measures.

Responsibility for the assault rested with Moore and Captain Alexander Cochrane of the Royal Navy. Moore commanded the British Reserve, which led the initial assault. The troops were rowed to the coast in three waves of boats, but having been delayed by several hours had to land in broad daylight rather than at dawn. Nonetheless, 6,000 men were landed in the first hour in one of the most successful examples of combined operations in this era. Moore distinguished himself by leading an attack against a large sand dune that formed the key French position and capturing four cannon. As a midshipman observed, 'the flower of the British Army was in action . . . I saw General John Moore in front, waving his men onward with his hat.'[7]

After securing their bridgehead, the British advanced and fought a sharp action on 13 March. The famous Battle of Alexandria followed a week later when the French attacked before dawn on the 21st. The brunt of their offensive fell on Moore's troops on the northern wing and, despite desperate fighting, was eventually defeated. But Moore suffered a bad flesh wound in the left leg, which kept him out of action for three months, while Abercromby was mortally wounded.

Major-General John Hely-Hutchinson now took over command and after some hesitation advanced on Cairo, over one hundred miles to the south-east. Some of his subordinates, unhappy with his leadership, apparently sought to have him replaced until they were rebuked by the invalid Moore. In any case, the 13,000-strong French garrison of Cairo was so demoralised that it capitulated on 28 June, on condition that it would be shipped back to France. After Hutchinson temporarily fell ill, Moore commanded the army as it escorted the French troops to the coast.

The British, once again under Hutchinson, turned their attention back to Alexandria, which surrendered without a fight on 2 September. The French were repatriated on British ships and the reconquest of Egypt was complete. It had been a rewarding experience for Moore, marking as it did the regeneration of the British Army following its uneven performance during the early years of the Revolutionary wars. He was earmarked for command of 6,000 men to remain in Egypt while the rest of the army departed, but managed to be excused this tedious duty by pleading illness and concern to see his sick father, who in fact would die in November soon after Moore's return to England.

As a result of the Peace of Amiens in March 1802, Britain enjoyed a brief respite until the resumption of the war with France in May 1803. She now faced the threat of invasion and Moore, who had been appointed commander of the Southern Military District, was responsible for the most vulnerable sector of Britain's coast, between Deal and Dungeness in the south-east. It was at this time that he became involved in the formation of Britain's first permanent light infantry regiments. The Revolutionary wars had shown that the British badly needed skilled light infantry to counter the large numbers of skirmishers employed by the French, for those light infantry regiments that had been raised in the American War of Independence (1775–83) had since either reverted to ordinary line infantry or been disbanded. The Duke of York had been Commander-in-Chief of the British Army since 1795 and had gained personal experience of fighting the French in the Low Countries. Since then, he had been seeking ways to redress the balance, including the creation of the rifle-armed 5th battalion, 60th Regiment from German mercenaries and the formation in

1800 of an Experimental Corps of Riflemen (soon to become the famous 95th Rifles). The invasion threat now added to the demand for more light infantry who would be able to fight effectively both in dispersed order as skirmishers and in the close order formations of ordinary units. Attempts to convert militia into light infantry had failed, so the experiment was now tried with regular line infantry and Moore suggested the 52nd, of which he was Colonel, to try out the idea.

Early in 1803 the 52nd went to a camp at Shorncliffe, near Sandgate, for retraining in its new role. The success of the venture depended on the regimental officers and Moore chose them well, particularly the principal trainer, Colonel Kenneth Mackenzie. He also made the 52nd an élite unit by replacing its less suitable soldiers with better men from its second battalion (which became the 96th Foot). But the drill for the 52nd was in fact devised by Colonel Kenneth Mackenzie and taught by him and the regimental officers rather than by Moore himself. Mackenzie drew inspiration from the work of Colonels William Stewart and Coote Manningham in establishing the 95th Rifles and from the light infantry manuals written by General Francis Jarry and Lieutenant-Colonel Francis de Rottenburg. Furthermore, it was the Duke of York who chose the lighter fusil which was issued to the light infantry in place of the ordinary musket. In short, the methods implemented at Shorncliffe did not originate with Moore, nor did he introduce them single-handed. He was more of a supervisor than executor: he had the authority to foster the implementation of the new training and he did so because he had seen at first hand the value of light infantry, particularly in America, the West Indies and Egypt. The success of the Shorncliffe experiment led to the 43rd being converted to light infantry using the 52nd as a model, while the 51st, 68th, 71st and 85th would follow in 1808–9.

Moore and Mackenzie in their work at Shorncliffe also advocated an enlightened concept of motivating the rank and file to use their initiative instead of simply following orders. For this to work, the regimental officers had to be keen, intelligent and highly professional and Moore took a close interest in their welfare. Again, this philosophy of command was not an original one, but Moore was influential in putting it into effect at Shorncliffe. His premature death at Coruña cut short his advocacy of these forward-looking notions and allowed the more authoritarian attitudes of Wellington to prevail. But Moore's impact was curtailed rather than lost. Wellington's Light Division in the Peninsula was built around the 43rd, 52nd and 95th and while Brigadier-General Robert Craufurd's iron discipline perfected the division, his methods supplemented rather than supplanted Moore's notions of individual initiative. In addition, Moore either in person or by repute made a deep impression on many junior officers, who ensured through their later service that his legacy lasted years after the end of the Napoleonic wars.[8]

While stationed in southern England, Moore became attached to Lady Hester Stanhope, whose uncle William Pitt returned to office as Prime Minister in 1804. After being knighted that November, Moore went on a secret mission the following month to reconnoitre the port of Ferrol on the north-western coast of Spain. He landed near the town with a couple of naval officers including his brother, Commodore Graham Moore, and since they were unaware that Spain had just declared war on Britain, they narrowly escaped capture. Moore had seen enough to know that the defences of Ferrol were being strengthened and his report caused Pitt to abandon the idea of an expedition against it. In October 1805 he went on another reconnaissance, this time to examine the French port of Boulogne from offshore. His reports were pessimistic on the feasibility of an amphibious assault to destroy the invasion flotilla assembled there and the idea was dropped.

By 1806 the invasion scare was over and Moore, by now a lieutenant-general, was appointed to be Second-in-Command in the Mediterranean under Lieutenant-General Henry Fox. He had his headquarters on the island of Sicily, a vital base for the Royal Navy as well as a launch pad for expeditions in the Mediterranean and a depot for smuggling British goods into Europe in defiance of Napoleon's trade embargo, the so-called Continental System. Moore spent a wretched year in Sicily enmeshed in arguments over strategy and although he fell in love with Caroline Fox, his superior's 17-year-old younger daughter, he felt that he could not reveal his feelings to her in view of their age gap. General Fox was amiable but so feeble in health and character that Moore acted as the effective commander and took over when Fox returned home in the summer of 1807. Moore vainly argued against detaching 6,000 troops from Sicily on an expedition under Major-General Alexander Mackenzie Fraser to secure the city of Alexandria in Egypt and thus guard against the possibility of a French expedition returning to this region and threatening India.

On the other hand, Moore successfully resisted pressure to land troops on the Italian mainland to try and drive the French from the Kingdom of Naples. He rightly argued that he had too few troops to spare from the force needed to hold Sicily and that little support would be forthcoming from the local inhabitants. The issue was complicated by the corruption and ineptitude of the Neapolitan Court based at Palermo, by the intrigues of Queen Maria Carolina and by the presence of both Rear-Admiral William Sidney Smith, the eccentric local naval commander, and Sir William Drummond, the indiscreet British envoy. Moore favoured annexing Sicily altogether to exploit its resources more effectively and avoid the damage being done by Britain's association with the unpopular Court. He quarrelled furiously with Drummond, who had fallen under Maria Carolina's influence.

In October 1807, as a result of Britain's isolation following the Peace of

Tilsit between Napoleon and Tsar Alexander of Russia, Moore was ordered to embark 7,000 of the British troops based in Sicily. The Government's intention was for these 7,000 men to form a strategic reserve based at Gibraltar from where it could be used in response to Napoleon's moves. Napoleon had sent 25,000 soldiers to occupy Lisbon and seize the Portuguese fleet, but although the French had marched into Lisbon by the time Moore reached Gibraltar at the beginning of December, the Portuguese fleet was sent away to safety just in time.

Moore then sailed for England and early in 1808 took command of a total of 11,000 men to help the beleaguered Swedes in their war with Napoleon's new allies, Russia and Denmark. At last, Moore had an independent command, although since the situation in Sweden was unclear, he could not be given a precise objective for his mission. He was, however, directed to remain near the coast in contact with the fleet and on the defensive. In the event, he arrived at Gothenburg in May but achieved nothing owing to the intransigence and impossible demands of the mad Swedish king, Gustavus IV. Moore realised that it was impossible to co-operate with him and, when forbidden to leave Stockholm, slipped away, disguised as a peasant, back to the fleet.

Moore angrily returned to England in July and at the end of the month set sail again with his units to help reinforce 15,000 troops who had been sent under Sir Arthur Wellesley to tackle the French in Portugal. Although senior to Wellesley, Moore would not assume command, for two more senior if less experienced generals were also being sent, namely Lieutenant-Generals Sir Hugh Dalrymple and Sir Harry Burrard. Moore wrongly believed that the Government had appointed them specifically to deprive him of the command and protested to Lord Castlereagh, the Secretary of State for War. In fact, the Government had wanted Wellesley to retain command, but King George III and the Duke of York had demanded the appointment of a more senior general. The Government certainly did not favour Moore, but was even more concerned to prevent the command going to the Duke of York. Moore might have been treated more sensitively given that he was being placed in a subordinate position after returning from an independent command in Sweden, but equally, he over-reacted.

After becoming becalmed, it was not until 25 August that he reached the headquarters of the British army in Portugal. By then, Wellesley had already beaten the French at Vimeiro on the 21st, but had immediately been superceded by the arrival of both Burrard and Dalrymple and prevented from pursuing the French to Lisbon. Moore wrote Wellesley a letter of congratulations and received a reply in which Wellesley regretted that Moore had not been able to arrive sooner and use his influence to prevail over Burrard and Dalrymple.

Moore sensibly declined to be involved in the negotiations that led to the Convention of Cintra, by which it was agreed that the French troops in Portugal, cut off as a result of uprisings in Spain, would be repatriated on British ships. The convention regained Portugal in a most cost-effective way now that all hope of a quick and decisive military campaign had been lost, but it proved extremely controversial, particularly as the French tried to take their loot with them. Wellesley by this stage was keen to return home. On 18 September he met Moore and offered to use his influence with the Government to press for Moore's appointment as commander in the Peninsula. Moore shared Wellesley's views of Dalrymple's incompetence but refused to enter into any intrigue. In the event, Wellesley's help would not be needed as the commanders were changed before he reached England as a result of the popular outcry against the Convention of Cintra. The Government recalled Dalrymple and Burrard to face a court of enquiry and on 6 October Moore received news of his appointment as the new commander, since neither the King nor the Government had dared cause further upheaval by insisting on a more senior general.

The revolts in Spain had obliged the French forces in that country to abandon Madrid and pull back north-eastwards to the Ebro river. Stories of the epic defence of the city of Saragossa by Spanish patriots and the capitulation of a French corps at Bailen in July stirred British hearts and created dangerous illusions about Spanish strength and capabilities. It seemed that the Spaniards, with British support, might inflict a devastating blow to Napoleon's empire.

Moore was instructed to leave 10,000 troops to defend the Portuguese capital, Lisbon, and to take his remaining 20,000 with him into Spain. A subordinate force of over 10,000 under Lieutenant-General Sir David Baird would meanwhile sail from England and land at Coruña on the north-western tip of Spain. Castlereagh envisaged a campaign in northern Spain, with Moore going mostly by sea to link up with Baird. Moore's combined forces would thus be concentrated in safety near the coast and able subsequently to co-operate with the Spanish regular armies farther east on the Ebro river. However, Moore decided to march to northern Spain rather than face the disruption of being transported there by sea. This would oblige him to link up with Baird in the interior of Spain far from British naval support, but he counted on being able to unite his forces in safety behind the Spanish armies.

Moore's advance began in October, but soon encountered problems. The Spaniards had promised to supply him, but had neither the resources nor the competence to do so. He was also handicapped by poor maps and an untried staff. Advice from the Portuguese that artillery could not cope with the routes he was using for his advance had caused him to detach his guns and cavalry under Lieutenant-General Sir John Hope and send them separately along the main road from Badajoz to Madrid. This further

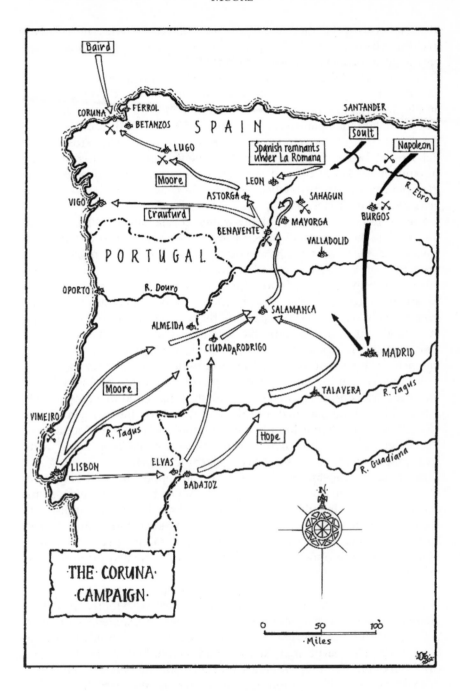

THE·CORUNA·
CAMPAIGN·

divided his army. Furthermore, Baird was delayed, for when he sailed up to Coruña he was not allowed to land for nearly a fortnight thanks to the obstinacy of the local Spanish authorities.

Moore reached the city of Salamanca inside Spain on 13 November and halted for three weeks for his other columns to join him. But time was not on his side. Reports began to reach him of a succession of disasters that had overtaken the Spanish regular armies 150 miles to the north-east. At the beginning of November, Napoleon had personally crossed the Pyrenees at the head of massive reinforcements, determined to restore the situation in the Peninsula and crush all resistance. He was soon smashing the Spanish armies, bedevilled as they were by rivalry between their generals and their lack of a supreme commander.

Matters rapidly worsened. Moore waited at Salamanca until he learnt of the defeat of the last intact Spanish army in the north-east. Then, late on 28 November, he bowed to the inevitable and ordered a retreat, despite pressure not to do so, especially from the intemperate British Pleni-potentiary to the Spanish Central Junta, John Hookham Frere. 'I wish it to be apparent to the whole world,' Moore wrote, 'that we have done everything in our power in support of the Spanish cause, and that we do not abandon it until long after the Spaniards had abandoned it.'[9] Baird, who was still 100 miles away to the north of Salamanca, was to retire independently to Coruña, while Moore himself would fall back on Lisbon.

But then something unexpected happened. Napoleon, having defeated the Spaniards, simply ignored the British as he assumed that they were in retreat. Instead, he marched directly southwards on the Spanish capital, Madrid. Meanwhile, Sir John Hope's column reunited with Moore on 4 December and the following day came news that the people of Madrid were preparing to defend their city against the French.

In these circumstances, Moore saw an opportunity to strike at Napoleon's rear and by the evening of the 5th he had boldly reversed his original decision to retreat. He would first march north to unite with Baird's column and then strike eastwards against Napoleon's line of communications. His small army could do nothing directly to defend Madrid, but could punch above its weight if it threatened the vulnerable French rear. But the risks were great. 'If the bubble bursts, and Madrid falls,' Moore noted, 'we shall have to run for it.'[10] In fact, Madrid had already fallen on the 4th. To make matters worse, Moore, misled by Spanish intelligence, was seriously underestimating Napoleon's numbers.

On 10 December the first of Moore's troops began to advance from Salamanca. He learnt that Madrid had fallen, but pressed on and discovered on the 13th from a captured copy of one of Napoleon's despatches that his position was unknown to the French Emperor. Furthermore, the despatch ordered a corps under Marshal Jean-de-Dieu Soult currently operating in northern Spain to advance with just 18,000 men westwards against a Spanish force under General Pedro, Marquis of La Romana. This would leave Soult dangerously isolated 120 miles north-east of Salamanca. Moore duly united with Baird at Mayorga on 20 December and pressed on north-eastwards to attack Soult.

On the 21st his horsemen brilliantly defeated some of Soult's advanced cavalry at Sahagun. Then, late on the 23rd, he learnt that large numbers of Napoleon's troops were advancing northwards from Madrid to the passes over the Guadarrama mountain range. He had clearly stirred up a hornet's nest and could no longer proceed with his aim of smashing Soult before slipping away. He therefore ordered an immediate retreat westwards, towards Astorga.

Napoleon himself was on the way, having declared that 'Moore is the only General now worthy to contend with me. I shall now move against him in person.'[11] A storm hindered, but did not prevent, his crossing of the Guadarramas. But Napoleon, believing that Moore was farther south than he in fact was, failed to trap him in the open plains of Leon and Old Castille. Moore fell back to the important road junction of Benavente, which he reached ahead of his pursuers. His cavalry fought a successful rearguard action here on 29 December and captured the hot-headed General Charles Lefebvre-Desnouëttes of the Imperial Guard Chasseurs à Cheval. Moore himself washed the general's head wound and gave him a sword to replace the one that he had lost.

The bulk of Moore's army reached Astorga and the relative safety of the Cantabrian mountains on the same day as the action at Benavente. Moore then continued his retreat north-westwards on Coruña, intending to evacuate his army by sea. Napoleon personally advanced no farther than Astorga and on 1 January 1809 handed the pursuit over to Marshal Soult before leaving for France five days later. But Moore had escaped only at the cost of relentless marching, which took its toll on discipline and contributed to scenes of drunkenness, looting and vandalism. Some units were worse than others, for much depended on the character of their generals, junior officers and NCOs. Brigadier-General Robert Craufurd, for instance, enforced ferocious discipline in his Light Brigade and held it together when other formations all but fell apart. Throughout the retreat, Moore remained with the Reserve, which formed the rearguard, to set his army an example. But Captain Alexander Gordon of the 15th Hussars blamed him for much of what happened. He thought that Moore:

appeared to labour under a depression of spirits, so different from his usual serene and cheerful disposition as to give a mournful expression to his countenance, indicative of the greatest anxiety of mind.[12]

Part of the morale problem stemmed from the number of times that Moore had changed his mind earlier in the campaign, when he had agonised over whether to retreat or advance. The cause of this apparent indecision had been the swiftly changing situation and the arrival of incomplete or incorrect information at Moore's headquarters. It gave a misleading impression of a weak and confused commander.

Many of the difficulties experienced during the retreat were beyond Moore's control. He had done what he could to have supplies assembled on the route to Coruña, but it was impossible to collect enough for so many men in the middle of winter, particularly as Spanish units under La Romana had been thrown back into the same area. This was one reason why Moore did not stand and fight a pitched battle during the retreat: even if he had managed to beat the French, he would have had to continue his retreat, from either shortage of supplies or fear of being outflanked.

In order to ease the difficulties of finding supplies and guard his southern flank, Moore detached Craufurd's Light Brigade and a King's German Legion brigade and sent them westwards to embark separately at Vigo. He continued north-westwards with the rest of his army on the cold, barren road to Coruña, briefly turning at bay at Lugo on 6 January. Heavy skirmishing flared up on the next day and Moore was his old self again, exulting in the thrill of danger, waving his hat in the thick of the fight and inspiring his men by example. But he resumed the retreat two days later as he could not risk remaining at Lugo any longer. He finally reached Coruña on the 11th, but was unable to embark his army before Soult arrived and therefore fought a major battle on the hills outside the port on the 16th. He himself was struck down, but his troops defeated the French attacks and then embarked in safety.

The unlucky general

Few described Moore objectively, for as one of his officers explained:

> Everything in Moore was real, solid, and unbending . . . His manner was singularly agreeable to those whom he liked, but to those he did not esteem his bearing was severe.[13]

He was totally dedicated to his profession and never married, yet he was a likeable man and had a good sense of humour. His Military Secretary, Major John Colborne, later remarked:

> I recollect poor Sir John Moore getting into a scrape once for saying, when asked if the hussars were to wear their pelisses, 'Oh, yes, and their muffs, too.'[14]

He was also a chivalrous foe and even admitted, as a professional soldier, to a certain regard for Napoleon: 'he has done many acts which are unpardonable, yet I cannot help having admiration and respect for him.'[15]

Moore was exceptional in being not merely a distinguished commander in the field, but also a reformer, trainer, administrator and agent on secret reconnaissance missions. He played a key role in developing Britain's unequalled light infantry arm, even though his personal contribution has been over-estimated and it is an exaggeration to call him 'the father of modern British infantry'.

Moore had few regrets when cut down at the moment of victory at Coruña, for it was a hero's death. In the West Indies, he had written, 'if I fall, it shall be by a good round cannon or musket shot, not by an ignominious fever.'[16] He led from the front by heroic example, as his numerous wounds testify. 'I note that the place for a Commander-in-chief is his advanced post,' he wrote in 1796. 'If he is not there numberless opportunities are lost.'[17] By treating his soldiers with consideration, he won their love as well as their respect. Robert Blakeney of the 28th Foot noted:

> Moore's constant habit of speaking to every officer of his army whom he met, whatever his rank, asking such questions as tended to elicit useful information, and in the most good-humoured and courteous manner making such remarks as indirectly called forth the most strenuous endeavours of all to a full discharge of their duties.[18]

But the sensitivity that made Moore such an inspirational leader also detracted from the iron morale required of a commander in adversity. It was a serious flaw and one that grew in significance the higher he climbed in rank. We have seen how he felt revulsion early in his career at having to take an enemy's life and how he became over-emotional in his quarrels with Sir Gilbert Elliott in Corsica and Sir William Drummond in Sicily. He was too mercurial and tended to veer erratically between furious impatience and black despair. For example, when the situation in Spain began to deteriorate at the end of 1808, he advised Castlereagh that Portugal was indefensible should the French occupy Spain, an assessment that Wellington would later prove to be over-pessimistic.

Moore was often unlucky, particularly in the way that his controversial Coruña campaign eclipsed his earlier service. His mission was doomed from the start: he simply had too little time and not enough men to help the Spanish regular armies before they were overwhelmed by Napoleon's onslaught. Only later did the long-term benefits of his actions become clear. He disrupted Napoleon's hitherto successful offensive and thus delayed the French occupation of southern Spain until 1810; he evacuated his army, in poor condition but intact; he gave the Spaniards courage, for he struck a blow rather than retire tamely without firing a shot. Had he simply withdrawn to Lisbon, the French could have followed him there and forced him to embark. As it was, after Coruña the French did not have enough troops to move immediately on Lisbon and this enabled Wellington to use Portugal as a base and source of manpower for the rest of the Peninsular War.

As Wellington himself commented later to his Military Secretary, 'you know, Fitzroy, we'd not have won, I think, without him.'[19]

The Battle of Coruña: 16 January 1809

A commander who is slain at the moment of victory almost invariably becomes a legendary figure. When Sir John Moore fell at Coruña in 1809, he joined in popular memory Vice-Admiral Horatio Nelson and Major-General James Wolfe, the hero of Quebec in 1759.

But when he reached Coruña late on 11 January, he was not even sure that he would fight a battle there. Unfortunately, his fleet of transports had yet to arrive from Vigo farther down the coast and he was obliged to remain ashore for several days. But the French had suffered during the pursuit and needed to collect their strung-out units before they could attack. To impose further delay, Moore had destroyed the main bridge over the Mero river at El Burgo, four miles south-east of Coruña.

Shortly after dawn on the 12th, Moore left his headquarters in Coruña to see where he could cover the town while he waited for his fleet. Essentially, he had a choice of three positions, but the more southerly two were too distant and extensive. That left the third, a ridge called Monte Mero just two miles outside Coruña. It was 2,500 yards long, short enough to be held firmly, and its eastern end rested securely on the Mero estuary. But it had two serious defects in the west, where it was both open to envelopment and dominated by the heights of Peñasquedo to the south.

Moore was out on horseback again for the whole of the 13th and resolutely dismissed suggestions that he negotiate with the French to secure an unmolested withdrawal. On the morning of the 14th, he again rode out of Coruña to see his army on the hills to the south. As he did so, he told his ADC, Captain George Napier:

> I have often been thought an unlucky man by my friends, in consequence of my being generally wounded in action – and some other events in my life. But I have never thought myself so till now. And if the transports do not arrive this day, I shall certainly be convinced I am an unlucky fellow, and that Fate has so decreed.[20]

But that afternoon, the fleet began to sail into Coruña harbour, allowing Moore to evacuate his cavalrymen and most of his artillery. Lieutenant Charles Boothby of the Royal Engineers arrived with the ships and later described how:

I went immediately to Sir John Moore, who received me most kindly, and notwithstanding the cruel anxiety he must have suffered, still supported that most engaging exterior so endearing to his friends and so prepossessing to strangers on whom he did not think proper to frown.[21]

Moore realised that the late arrival of the ships had made it increasingly likely that the French would be able to interfere with his embarkation. They had already located an intact bridge over the Mero seven miles upriver and had also repaired the main bridge at El Burgo. On the morning of the 15th they drove the British outposts off the heights of Peñasquedo, one mile south of Monte Mero, during which each side lost about 100 men. Lieutenant Boothby recorded that:

Sir John Moore was out all day, and I followed in his suite over our whole position. He spoke to all officers as he went along, giving cautions, orders, and instructions, and looked wistfully at the enemy, apparently wishing with painful eagerness for a battle.[22]

Two of Moore's divisions, under Lieutenant-Generals Sir John Hope and Sir David Baird, were actually on the Monte Mero. The other two, under Lieutenant-General Alexander Mackenzie Fraser and Major-General Edward Paget, stood a mile or two to the north-west around the town of Coruña, from where they would be able to counter any attempt to outflank the vulnerable western flank of the Monte Mero.

Dawn on 16 January found the British still at Coruña. Moore went out to see if anything was happening, decided that Soult was not going to attack and returned to Coruña for something to eat. In fact, the difficult terrain was simply delaying the French deployments. Moore ordered Paget's division to withdraw into Coruña to embark and planned to follow with the rest of the army after dusk. 'Now, if there is no bungling, I hope we shall get away in a few hours,' he remarked.

Minutes afterwards, towards 2.00 pm, word came that powerful French forces had begun to advance. A terrific bombardment opened on the British line and Moore's anxieties slipped from his shoulders. He shouted to one of his staff, Colonel Thomas Graham, that he was very happy and indeed the change in him was remarkable. 'It was,' remembered Graham, 'a transition from fixed gloom, bordering almost on despair, to a state of exultation.'[23] Moore knew that a victory would not only check the French and prevent them from harassing his army as it embarked, but also end the campaign on a bright note after the horrific retreat.

Moore had already embarked his cavalry, since the broken and rocky ground was covered with gorse and stone walls. Although Soult had 4,500 cavalry, the battle would be decided almost exclusively by the infantry

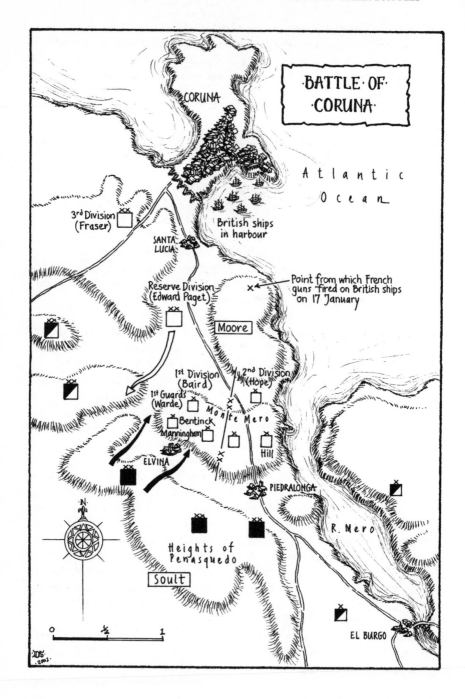

BATTLE·OF· CORUNA·

CORUNA

Atlantic Ocean

3rd Division (Fraser)

British ships in harbour

SANTA LUCIA

Reserve Division (Edward Paget)

Point from which French guns fired on British ships on 17 January

Moore

1st Division (Baird)

2nd Division (Hope)

1st Guards (Warde)

Monte Mero

Bentinck
Manningham

Hill

ELVINA

PIEDRALONGA

R. Mero

N

Heights of Penasquedo

Soult

0   ½   1

EL BURGO

and artillery and in numbers of infantrymen the odds were nearly equal, for the British could pit almost 15,000 against Soult's 15,500. But they were seriously outgunned with only nine six-pounder cannon against Soult's forty guns (twenty of which would come into action).

Soult attacked all along the Monte Mero but landed his first and heaviest punch at the western end, in an attempt to cut Moore off from the town and harbour of Coruña. In fact, the fighting farther east would be little more than heavy skirmishing. The crucial western sector was held by Baird's division, with two of its brigades in the front line and the third (two strong battalions of the 1st Guards) about a quarter of a mile to the rear, while at the foot of the ridge some outposts held the village of Elvina.

Preceded by a heavy swarm of skirmishers, thousands of French infantrymen advanced on Baird's division in a seemingly irresistible array of battalion columns. It was a terrifying sight. They scented blood and were shouting savagely now: 'Forwards, kill, kill!' Moore's men looked instinctively to him for reassurance and a murmur rippled through the tense British ranks: 'where is the general?' Nor did he disappoint them. Major Charles Napier of the 50th Foot heard a thunder of hooves and turned to see him gallop up. 'He came at speed,' Napier recalled, 'and pulled up so sharp and close he seemed to have alighted from the air.' Moore and his horse stared intently at the French advance. Napier never forgot the electrifying moment:

> The sudden stop of the animal, a cream-coloured one with black tail and mane, had cast the latter streaming forward; its ears were pushed out like horns, while its eyes flashed fire, and it snorted loudly with expanded nostrils, expressing terror, astonishment and muscular exertion. My first thought was, it will be away like the wind! but then I looked at the rider, and the horse was forgotten. Thrown on its haunches the animal came, sliding and dashing the dirt up with its fore feet, thus bending the general forward almost to its neck. But his head was thrown back and his look more keenly piercing than I ever saw it. He glanced to the right and left, and then fixed his eyes intently on the enemy's advancing column, at the same time grasping the reins with both his hands, and pressing the horse firmly with his knees: his body thus seemed to deal with the animal while his mind was intent on the enemy, and his aspect was one of searching intenseness beyond the power of words to describe. For a while he looked, and then galloped to the left without uttering a word.[24]

The situation rapidly worsened and Moore soon returned to Napier's position. The French artillery, especially ten guns posted at the western end of the heights of Peñasquedo, were raking the British lines diagonally across their front. A cannon-ball fell near Moore's horse, making it whisk round in terror. But Moore's gaze remained fixed on the foe. Only when a dreadfully wounded Highlander screamed in pain did he look round. The screams had unsettled the man's comrades and Moore knew that he had to reassure them. 'This is nothing, my lads,' he told them. 'Keep your ranks, take that man away.' Then he added kindly to the injured soldier: 'My good fellow, don't make such a noise, we must bear these things better.'[25]

The French skirmishers soon drove the British advanced posts from the village of Elvina and on to Lord William Bentinck's brigade, whose battalions, the 4th and 50th Foot and the 42nd Highlanders, occupied the western end of Monte Mero. Two French infantry regiments now thrust directly at Bentinck's brigade while a third, supported by a division of cavalry, sought to turn its western flank. Moore had already ordered Paget's division in reserve to counter the outflanking move with the support of Fraser's division and he now also told the 4th Foot to throw back its right wing to be able to fire to the west. So steadily did the 4th execute the manoeuvre that Moore shouted: 'that is exactly how it should be done.'[26]

The 50th and 42nd meanwhile counter-attacked the two French columns that had advanced from Elvina up the forward slopes of the Monte Mero. The 50th triumphantly chased the French back through the streets of Elvina and some of its men even thrust their way out the other side before being checked by the French reserves and either captured or driven back.

Moore ordered up the 1st Guards from the second line to fill the positions just vacated by the 50th and 42nd. Because of the smoke and failing light, he could not see what was happening to the west and as yet had no news from Paget's division as to the outcome of the French outflanking move. He therefore decided to distract Soult's attention with a counter-attack in the centre of his line and ordered one of the Guards battalions to advance. Unfortunately, the battalion moved too slowly and as a result of subsequent events never attacked. But on seeing it march forward, the 42nd Highlanders fell back in the mistaken belief that they were to be relieved. Moore was instantly on the spot. 'My brave 42nd,' he called, 'if you've fired your ammunition, you've still your bayonets. Remember Egypt! Think [of] Scotland! Come on, my gallant countrymen!'[27]

Moore realised that he was needed with Bentinck's brigade, where the fighting was heaviest. As a result, he rode around in a small area and continually returned to a crossroads immediately north-west of Elvina. So did many of his senior officers and their movements were noticed by French gunners. Suddenly, Moore was struck by a cannonball and thrown from his saddle. The shot had smashed his shoulder and lacerated his chest, yet his expression was unchanged. A shocked cluster of men moved him to the protection of a bank and then lifted him into a blanket to carry him from the field. His sword became entangled with its straps but he refused to have it removed: 'it is as well as it is; I had rather it should go out off the field with me.'

He was carried slowly to Coruña, with frequent halts so that he could see how the battle fared. The news of his fall had immediately spread through the right wing of his army. 'It added fresh vigour to the troops,' noted Lieutenant Charles Cadell of the 28th Foot, 'they were determined to be revenged.'[28]

Moore was taken to his headquarters to die and laid on a mattress in one of the rooms. He turned to an old friend, Colonel Paul Anderson. 'You know,' he said, 'I have always wished to die this way.' Major John Colborne, his Military Secretary, returned to Coruña after the end of the battle. Moore asked, 'Colborne, have we beaten the French?' and was assured that they had been repulsed at every point. 'Well,' he said, 'that is a satisfaction. I hope my country will do me justice.'

Colborne recalled how Moore begged to be remembered to his friends and requested promotion for his deserving officers. He also wanted to know if all his ADCs were safe and was told that they were, to spare him the pain of knowing that one of them had been mortally wounded. At one point, he murmured that he was in great pain and that he feared he would be a long time dying, but his suffering at last drew to an end. His face was so serene that, but for the ghastly wound, he might have been sleeping.

After Moore's fall, the French had mounted a second attack on Elvina, only to be repelled once more. Paget's division had advanced southwards and completely checked the French attempt to outflank the Monte Mero to the west. The British had lost about 700 men and the French about double that figure; neither side had won or lost much ground. Soult, indeed, was so disheartened by the result that he reported untruthfully that he had intended only a strong reconnaissance.

Had Moore not fallen, he might have been able to ensure an even more favourable outcome by assailing the western end of the heights of Peñasquedo and silencing the destructive guns posted there. As it was, Paget had only refrained from attacking the heights because he lacked the necessary authorisation. The problem was that the French artillery fire had disrupted the British high command. Moore's senior subordinate, Sir David Baird, had also fallen grievously wounded. Sir John Hope, like his two seniors a Scot, took control but since daylight was now beginning to fade, he wisely called a halt and turned his attention to evacuating the army. The troops marched into the town and embarked during the night despite some confusion. Pickets alone stayed on the Monte Mero to watch the French and keep campfires burning.

Another day dawned. At 8.00 am a chaplain, four officers and a party of the 9th Foot went along the ramparts of the landward bastion of Coruña's citadel. There, they buried Sir John Moore:

Not a drum was heard, not a funeral note,
As his corpse to the rampart we hurried;
Not a soldier discharged his farewell shot
O'er the grave where our hero we buried.
Slowly and sadly we laid him down,
From the field of his fame fresh and gory;
We carved not a line, and we raised not a stone,
But we left him alone with his glory.[29]

The brigades of Major-Generals William Beresford and Rowland Hill had yet to be embarked, but the French interfered only in the afternoon, when six of their guns opened fire on the transport ships from the heights overlooking the bay. Some of the naval officers momentarily panicked and four vessels ran aground, but the sailors recovered their nerve, the guns of the warships blazed in reply and all was well. The last troops left Coruña that night. 'It was evening,' wrote Commissary August Schaumann:

[Coruña] lay hidden by a thick mist, through which the gleams of the lighthouse and the flames of a burning suburb projected a faint glow. The bombardment had ceased; only now and again could we hear the report of one of the great French mortars. At last the blackness of night fell upon the coast and the sea, and the past lay behind me like a nightmare.[30]

NOTES

1   *Journal of the Society for Army Historical Research* (1933), p.185; G. Moore Smith, *The life of John Colborne* (1903), p.109
2   Carola Oman, *Sir John Moore* (1953), p.23
3   *Ibid*, p.47
4   It was primarily the bitter political passions aroused by the outcome of the Coruña campaign that caused Moore to be labelled a Whig, for it was the Whigs who defended his conduct in order to attack the Government's handling of the campaign.
5   Carola Oman, *op. cit.*, p.157
6   J. Maurice, ed., *The diary of Sir John Moore* (1904), v.1, p.360
7   Carola Oman *op. cit.*, p.259
8   For details of Moore's role in the training of light infantry, see the important re-assessment by D. Gates, *The British light infantry arm c.1790–1815* (1987).
9   A. Bryant, *Years of victory 1802–1812* (1944), p.273
10 J. Moore, *Narrative of the campaign of the British Army in Spain* (1809), pp.92–3
11 Carola Oman, *op. cit.*, p. 567
12 A. Gordon, *A cavalry officer in the Corunna campaign 1808–1809* (1913), p.169
13 H. Bunbury, *Narratives of some passages in the war with France, from 1799 to 1810* (nd), p.271
14 Moore Smith, *op. cit.*, p.219

15 Carola Oman, *op. cit.*, p.307
16 *Ibid*, p.155
17 Maurice, *op. cit.*, v.1, pp.209–10
18 R. Blakeney, *A boy in the Peninsular war: the services, adventures and experiences of Robert Blakeney* (1899), p.25
19 C. Hibbert, *Corunna* (1961), p.199
20 G. Napier, *The early military life of General Sir George T. Napier* (1886), p.61
21 C. Boothby, *Under England's flag from 1804 to 1809* (1900), p.214
22 *Ibid*, p.217
23 A. Delavoye, *Life of Thomas Graham* (1880), p.801
24 W. Napier, *The life and opinions of General Sir Charles James Napier* (1857), v.1, p.95; see also A. Leith Hay, *Narrative of the Peninsular war* (1879), v.1, pp.123–4
25 W. Napier, *op. cit.*, v.1, p.96
26 Charles Oman, *A history of the Peninsular war* (1902–30), v.1, p.588
27 Blakeney, *op. cit.*, p.121
28 C. Cadell, *Narrative of the campaigns of the Twenty-Eighth Regiment* (1835), p.71
29 Charles Wolfe, 'The burial of Sir John Moore at Corunna,' published in 1817. The first and the last verses are quoted here; the rest of the poem is magnificent, but inaccurate.
30 A. Schaumann, *On the road with Wellington* (1923), p.146

CHAPTER V
Wellington

Wellington, like so many of Britain's greatest soldiers, came from the Anglo-Irish Protestant ascendancy, the minority caste that dominated Ireland. Men bred in such a background have a natural authority and it is not surprising that all four of Wellington's surviving brothers had distinguished careers in the public service. As the biographer Philip Guedalla pointed out, 'generations of secluded life amongst an alien and subject population breeds aristocrats ... Anglo-Irish magnates knew themselves observed by long, resentful rows of Irish eyes; and what conqueror would condescend before such an audience?' He added that 'castes mark their children deeply' and drew the parallel with the slave-owning southern states of America, another noted breeding ground of great warriors.[1]

The future Duke of Wellington was born in 1769 as Arthur Wesley (later Wellesley), the third surviving son of Garret Wesley, 1st Earl of Mornington. He was a late developer and gave little evidence of any ability except in mathematics. He was lazy, aloof and often unwell and was totally overshadowed by his oldest brother, the ambitious and academically brilliant Richard. But his loneliness fostered a fiercely independent streak and he admitted in later years that he liked 'to walk alone'.[2]

Following his father's death in May 1781, Arthur was removed from Eton to ease the strain on the family's finances. He instead received private tuition from a barrister in Brussels and according to a friend who knew him there, he

> was extremely fond of music, and played well upon the fiddle, but he never gave indication of any other species of talent. As far as my memory serves, there was no intention then of sending him into the army; his own wishes, if he had any, were in favour of a civilian life.[3]

He joined the Army simply because he was unfit in his mother's eyes for anything else: he was 'food for powder and nothing more'.[4] In 1786 he duly went to the military academy at Angers in France, where he

105

mastered French and horsemanship, completed his education and acquired some social polish. A year later his brother Richard bought him an ensign's commission in the 73rd Foot, for it was Richard who shouldered his late father's debts, rescued the family's fortunes and ensured that his siblings were educated and launched on suitable careers. Similarly, in 1787 it was family influence that secured Arthur's appointment as ADC to the Lord Lieutenant of Ireland; he also won election three years later to the Irish House of Commons.

In spring 1793 Arthur offered to marry Kitty Pakenham, only to have his proposal rejected by her brother, the 3rd Baron Longford, because of his lack of prospects as a penniless captain. The rebuff made him abandon his more frivolous pursuits, burn his violin and dedicate himself to his career. By now he had passed through a variety of regiments, though it is doubtful if he actually did much regimental duty. Following the outbreak of war with Revolutionary France in February 1793, he used a loan from Richard to purchase a major's commission in the 33rd Foot (later The Duke of Wellington's Regiment) and in September purchased the Lieutenant-Colonelcy at the age of 24.

The following year he took the 33rd to Flanders and joined the British army of the Duke of York, who in conjunction with the Austrians was unsuccessfully fighting the French Revolutionaries. The Duke was obliged to withdraw into what is now Holland and Arthur saw action for the first time at Boxtel on 15 September when the 33rd checked some French cavalry while covering a retreat. The remainder of the campaign saw the British make a dismal succession of retreats, while beset by inadequate logistics, French harassment and appalling winter conditions. Thoroughly disillusioned, Arthur returned home on leave at the end of February 1795, while his regiment was evacuated with the rest of the army two months later. He later remarked that at least he had discovered what not to do: 'I learned more by seeing our own faults, and the defects of our system in the campaign of Holland, than anywhere else'.[5] He considered selling his commission, but returned to the 33rd in July 1795 after failing to find alternative employment.

In 1796 he sailed for India as the commander of his regiment, taking with him an extensive library of books and forming the habit of studying for several hours each day. On his arrival in February 1797, he found the subcontinent divided between rival native rulers. British influence had grown steadily since the East India Company had started trading there in the 1600s. The Company had bases at Madras, Bombay and Bengal and had established indirect rule over larger areas by deploying troops to protect native states, in return for a subsidy and effective control of their foreign policy.

In 1798 Arthur's brother Richard arrived in India as Governor-General, the supreme British executive. Richard had great ambitions and knew that

India could be a springboard to both riches and the highest political power in England.

Richard was pre-eminent among the Wellesley brothers until 1812, but relied heavily on Arthur as a trusted adviser and subordinate. Arthur in turn benefited from Richard's patronage and soon saw action in the Fourth Mysore War (1799), which broke out when the British launched a pre-emptive attack on a troublesome native ruler, Tipoo Sahib of Mysore. Arthur served in a subordinate role, but was then appointed governor of Tipoo's captured capital, Seringapatam, and pacified Mysore in his first independent command.

Bitter disappointment followed in 1801 when he was superseded as commander of a force destined to help attack a French army in Egypt. He resigned himself to going as Second-in-Command, but fell ill with the Malabar Itch, a nasty form of ringworm, and stayed in India, while the ship on which he would have sailed sank with no survivors.

The Second Mahratta War broke out in 1803 and conclusively demonstrated Arthur's greatness as a general. While General Gerard Lake took the offensive in Hindustan in the far north, Arthur led another advance in the Deccan in central India, where he boldly attacked and smashed huge Mahratta armies at the Battles of Assaye in September and Argaum in November 1803. He then stormed the fortress of Gawilghur, before negotiating treaties.

Arthur was knighted in 1804 and had collected enough prize money to make him financially independent. He had played a key role in helping Richard extend British control, direct and indirect, right down the eastern coast and across the entire southern part of India. His military triumphs were firmly based on painstaking attention to logistics, a thorough understanding of the situation, self-confidence and successful diplomacy.

Arthur returned to England in September 1805, in time for a chance meeting with Vice-Admiral Horatio Nelson shortly before Trafalgar. He had reached the rank of major-general in 1802, but needed to see active service in Europe, for 'sepoy generals' who had won reputations solely in India were not highly regarded. But Lord Cathcart's expedition to Hanover, in which Arthur led a brigade, had to be withdrawn early in 1806 without seeing action. Arthur then commanded a brigade at Hastings on the south-eastern coast of England and resumed his political career to help defend Richard against his detractors. He entered Parliament in April 1806 and became Chief Secretary to the Lord Lieutenant of Ireland the following year. He also finally married Kitty Pakenham, only to find that they were a woefully mismatched couple; yet their union, though unhappy, bore two sons and lasted until Kitty's death in 1831.

In 1807 Arthur again saw active service, this time as a brigade commander in Lord Cathcart's expedition to prevent the neutral Danish fleet from falling into Napoleon's hands. Following the investment of Copenhagen, Arthur quickly routed a Danish relieving force at the village of Kiøge on 29 August and was then sent to negotiate the city's capitulation on 7 September. The expedition returned home following the surrender of the Danish ships.

Meanwhile, Napoleon occupied Portugal to enforce his continental trade embargo on British goods and then, in the spring of 1808, he also ordered his troops to take control of Spain, his nominal ally. Widespread Spanish revolts obliged his forces to evacuate most of the country, leaving 25,000 troops cut off in Portugal and opening the way for British military intervention. Arthur was given command of 9,000 men at Cork initially intended for an expedition to the Americas, but now redirected to the Peninsula. He landed on the Portuguese coast on 1 August and was reinforced by another 5,000 troops, but learnt that he would shortly be joined by further units under more senior generals, Sir Harry Burrard and Sir Hew Dalrymple. For Arthur had been promoted to lieutenant-general only in April that year and despite his experience and political connections could not reasonably command such an augmented force.

After landing, Arthur advanced southwards on Lisbon and rapidly won two victories over the French: a bold frontal assault at Roliça and a defensive battle at Vimeiro. He was then superseded by the arrival of the lacklustre Burrard and Dalrymple and prevented from pursuing the French. Dalrymple concluded the controversial Convention of Cintra, by which the French troops in Portugal were repatriated in British ships, with both arms and baggage and left free to fight again. Arthur sailed home frustrated by the situation and was soon followed by Burrard and Dalrymple, who were recalled to face an enquiry following popular outcry against the convention.

As a result, Lieutenant-General Sir John Moore took command of the British army in the Peninsula and after leaving 10,000 troops in Portugal, advanced with the rest into Spain to support the Spaniards. But Napoleon personally intervened with massive reinforcements, smashed the Spanish armies and forced Moore to retreat in the middle of winter to Coruña on the north-western coast. Here, Moore was slain as he checked the French outside the town and his army was then evacuated by sea.

Napoleon returned to France, but left behind sizeable forces to complete the conquest of Spain and Portugal. Nonetheless, the British Cabinet decided to maintain its commitment to the Peninsula. Vindicated by a Court of Enquiry over the Cintra affair, Arthur returned to Portugal in April 1809 to take command of the 10,000 British troops left there, plus reinforcements from home, and secure Portugal as a base. He duly advanced against a French corps under Marshal Jean-de-Dieu Soult that had invaded northern Portugal and drove it from the country after audaciously crossing the Douro river at Oporto on 12 May.

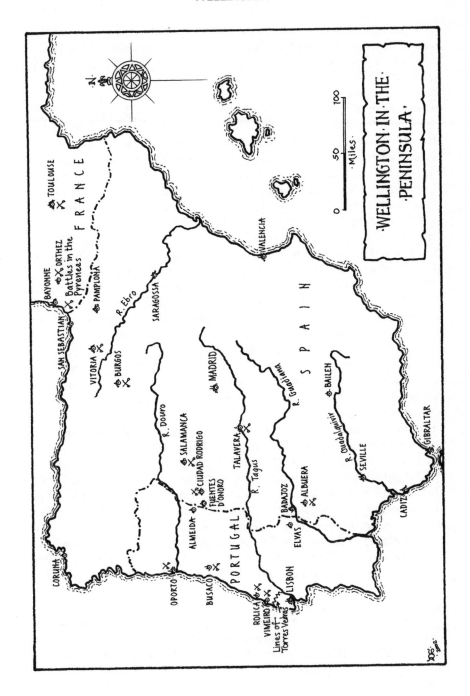

He returned south and advanced eastwards after receiving money and permission from the British Government to operate in Spain. He intended to link up with a Spanish army under General Don Gregorio de la Cuesta, defeat an exposed French corps under Marshal Claude Victor and liberate Madrid. But his plan was over-ambitious and his Spanish allies were unable to supply him as they had promised. At the end of July he fought a bloody defensive battle at Talavera, seventy miles south-west of Madrid, after the French unexpectedly managed to concentrate an almost equal number of troops against his and Cuesta's combined armies. Although he won the action, Arthur lost a quarter of his men and had almost exhausted his provisions. His line of retreat was also under threat, for Soult had rallied and was marching south with three corps. Arthur withdrew in the nick of time to the Portuguese border, but despite the failure of his intervention in Spain, he had boosted morale in Britain with his battlefield victories and was raised to the peerage as Baron Douro of Wellesley and Viscount Wellington of Talavera (he would be made Duke in 1814).

Napoleon, having crushed Austria at the Battle of Wagram that summer, began to send reinforcements into Spain to subdue the Peninsula once and for all. Wellington ordered the construction of fortifications, the lines of Torres Vedras, to seal off Lisbon in case the rest of Portugal was overrun. He had effective control of Portugal's Council of Regency and tried to mobilise the country's resources more efficiently. One of his generals, Marshal William Carr Beresford, was already reorganising the Portuguese Army, which Wellington carefully integrated with his British units to boost his numbers.

The French now had 325,000 troops in Spain, but had to contend with both the ubiquitous guerrillas and the Spanish regular armies and could spare only 65,000 men under Marshal André Massena to invade Portugal in autumn 1810. Wellington occupied the ridge of Busaco across Massena's line of advance and checked his frontal assaults, but was then outflanked to the north and had to fall right back to Lisbon. He had already mobilised the semi-irregular Portuguese *ordenança* (a form of Home Guard) to harass the French and deny them the use of supplies, transport and important roads, which were destroyed as far as possible. Massena wisely declined to attack the formidable lines of Torres Vedras and finally retreated from Portugal in the spring of 1811 when his army could starve no more.

Wellington now sought to liberate Spain up to the Pyrenees. His immediate objective was to capture the fortresses that guarded the two main invasion routes into Spain. He occupied Almeida in the north after narrowly defeating a relief attempt at Fuentes de Oñoro on 3–5 May 1811, but later had to abandon the sieges of Badajoz in the south and Ciudad Rodrigo in the north when the French concentrated against him each time. Hence 1811 was indecisive: although the French were too strong for

Wellington to defeat them offensively, they were now too cautious to attack him unless given a favourable opportunity.

This stalemate was broken when Napoleon made two fatal mistakes. First, he took 27,000 soldiers from the Peninsula to join his impending invasion of Russia and second, he ordered his forces to conquer Valencia in the east of Spain. Both these moves reduced the numbers of troops directly opposed to Wellington under a new commander, Marshal Auguste Marmont, and enabled him to take the offensive. In the first half of 1812, he stormed both Ciudad Rodrigo and Badajoz. He then advanced into Spain and after much manoeuvring fell on Marmont's army and smashed it at Salamanca on 22 July. The battle shattered French assumptions that he was merely a master of the defensive and as one of their generals recorded:

> Hitherto we had been aware of his prudence, his eye for choosing a position, and his skill in utilizing it. At Salamanca he has shown himself a great and able master of manoeuvres.[6]

Wellington triumphantly entered into Madrid and then, in a fit of over-confidence, thrust north and tried to take the fortress of Burgos in a costly and mismanaged siege. He hoped that Burgos would anchor his position deep inside Spain, but was forced to abort the siege and fall back to Portugal when the French concentrated their armies against him. His retreat was marred by indiscipline and unnecessary losses after the temporary breakdown of his supply system and the onset of heavy rain.

Despite the disappointing end to the campaign, the whole balance in the Peninsula had drastically altered. The French had abandoned southern Spain; the Spanish guerrillas were bolder than ever; and Napoleon's disaster in Russia had undermined French morale and ruled out any reinforcements. The keys to Spain – Ciudad Rodrigo and Badajoz – were still firmly in Wellington's hands. Meanwhile, he used the winter to bring his army to a peak of efficiency and in January 1813 accepted his appointment as Commander-in-Chief of the Spanish armies. In previous years, he had benefited from varying degrees of co-operation from Spanish regular and irregular forces, including both direct assistance on the battlefield and indirect help in the form of diversionary and guerrilla operations elsewhere in Spain. He now had more authority and around 20,000 Spanish troops served as part of his army for the rest of the war, although their discipline was poor and the Spanish *Cortes,* or Parliament, often proved obstructive.

In the spring of 1813 Wellington again took the offensive. Taking the 80,000 French troops in central Spain by surprise, he stormed round their northern wing and forced them to retreat over 200 miles by relentlessly outflanking all their positions. The culmination came on 21 June, when he swept round and dealt them a decisive defeat at Vitoria, a victory that won him promotion to Field Marshal and reinvigorated Napoleon's opponents in central Europe.

Wellington now sought to consolidate his gains by taking San Sebastian and Pamplona in north-eastern Spain. The French field armies opposed to him had been driven back into the western Pyrenees and were being re-organised by Marshal Soult. Towards the end of July, Soult tried to relieve Pamplona, but his offensive was repelled at Sorauren, four miles north of the city, when Wellington arrived to take personal command. San Sebastian and Pamplona both now fell, the former by assault, the latter by starvation.

The last months of 1813 saw Wellington cross the Bidassoa river into France. He drove Soult out of his fortified lines above the Nivelle river in November and arrived south of the city of Bayonne near the Atlantic coast, where in December he repelled a series of counter-attacks in the four-day Battle of the Nive. A lull followed and then, in February 1814, he outflanked Soult and forced him to retire eastwards, inland and away from Bayonne, which was promptly invested by a detachment of his army. A major action at Orthez on 27 February and minor ones farther east preceded a final battle at Toulouse on 10 April.

Napoleon had now abdicated following the occupation of Paris at the end of March by the continental allies led by Austria, Prussia and Russia. Wellington had played a crucial, though indirect, role in toppling him, firstly by tying down large numbers of French troops in the Peninsula but secondly by invigorating the allies through his victories and sustaining Britain's Tory Government, which resolutely prosecuted the war.

Wellington, who was created Duke in May, returned to England and then took up a post as Ambassador to France – not the most sensible of appointments, as an assassination attempt made clear. In February 1815 he left Paris to replace Lord Castlereagh at the Congress of Vienna and the following month, news came of Napoleon's escape from exile. Tsar Alexander I of Russia turned to Wellington and said: 'it is for you to save the world again.'[7]

Wellington reached Brussels and prepared in conjunction with a Prussian army under Field Marshal Prince Gebhard von Blücher to defend the United Netherlands. This consisted of an amalgamated Belgium and Holland under Dutch rule and was a crucially important region strategically. The allies, including the powerful Austrian and Russian armies, would not be ready to invade France until July and that gave Napoleon a chance to strike a pre-emptive blow against Wellington and Blücher. Unfortunately, Wellington had an army inferior to the one that had been broken up a year earlier at the end of the Peninsular War. Fewer than a third of his soldiers were British, the remainder being less reliable troops from the Netherlands and some minor German states.[8]

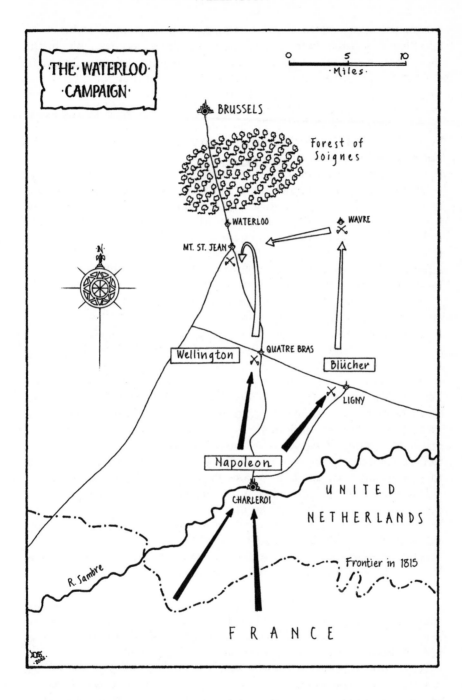

THE·WATERLOO CAMPAIGN·

Miles

BRUSSELS

Forest of Soignes

WAVRE

WATERLOO

MT. ST. JEAN

·N·

QUATRE BRAS

Wellington

Blücher

LIGNY

Napoleon

CHARLEROI

UNITED

NETHERLANDS

Frontier in 1815

R. Sambre

FRANCE

Napoleon invaded on 15 June, striking at the junction of Wellington's and Blücher's armies in the hope of defeating them piecemeal. Blücher, in the east, concentrated reasonably quickly to meet the onslaught, but in the west Wellington reacted more slowly, in the belief that Napoleon's real thrust would come farther west and that it was better to move late than to make the wrong move. (He had, similarly, reacted sluggishly to Marshal Soult's offensive in the Pyrenees in July 1813.) Napoleon consequently beat Blücher at Ligny on 16 June and forced him to retreat eleven miles northwards to the town of Wavre.

Wellington, who had survived a desperate battle at Quatre Bras against a detached wing of the French army, also fell back and occupied a position near the village of Waterloo, twelve miles south of Brussels. He resolved to fight Napoleon here on the 18th, in the knowledge that Blücher had rallied his Prussians and was marching to his support. The battle that ensued ended in a decisive defeat for Napoleon, but as Wellington admitted afterwards, 'I never took so much trouble about any Battle . . . [and] never was so near being beat.'[9]

Wellington and Blücher triumphantly advanced on Paris and secured an end to hostilities. Wellington then served for three years as Commander-in-Chief of the 150,000 strong allied Army of Occupation in north-eastern France and his moderation contributed to the general European peace that lasted into the 1850s.

On his return to England at the end of 1818, Wellington was a national hero and he resumed his political career as Master-General of the Ordnance, which entitled him to membership of the Cabinet. His immediate tasks were diplomatic as much as political and he also served briefly as Commander-in-Chief of the British Army. A bitter dispute with George Canning led him to resign from the Cabinet in April 1827, but following Canning's death he became Prime Minister in January 1828.

His term in office coincided with turbulent times. Unemployment, economic distress and an unpopular monarchy increased pressure for change. Despite being instinctively conservative, he pragmatically forced through the liberal measure of Catholic Emancipation so as to avoid revolution in Ireland, though in doing so he felt obliged to fight a duel in 1829. Less successful was his handling of the other great issue of his day, namely reform of the right to vote, which split the Tory party and led to the fall of his Government in November 1830. His opposition in the next couple of years to the Reform Bill made him temporarily unpopular, to the extent that he had to have iron shutters fitted to protect the windows of his London home, Apsley House, from stone-throwing mobs.

Wellington's fears that reform would lead to a repeat of the French Revolution were eventually proven wrong. He acted as Prime Minister for three weeks in 1834 and then served as Foreign Secretary under Robert Peel for four months. He advised the young Queen Victoria and from 1841 to 1846 had a Cabinet seat without office. He returned to his old post of Commander-in-Chief of the Army in 1844, but financial constraints and to a lesser extent his own conservatism deadened chances of much-needed reform and the consequences became fully apparent during the Crimean war (1854–6).

Wellington was beset in old age by increasing deafness and failing health, but as late as 1848 he skilfully organised the defence of London against the possibility of riots during Chartist unrest. Resounding cheers at the Great Exhibition of 1851 confirmed his restored popularity and he died, aged 83, on 14 September 1852.

The Duke

Wellington was a remarkably complete commander who excelled at every level of warfare from minor tactics to campaign strategy. In British military history, he is rivalled in significance only by Oliver Cromwell and the Duke of Marlborough and is unsurpassed in fame.

Wellington was not an innovator, but by sheer force of personality made the existing methods and tools work with unprecedented efficiency. He explained:

> There is but one way; – to do as I did – to have A HAND OF IRON. The moment there was the slightest neglect in any department I was down on them.[10]

Wellington's mastery of tactics formed the basis of his art of war:

> One must understand the mechanism and power of the individual soldier; then that of a company, a battalion, or brigade, and so on, before one can venture to group divisions and move an army. I believe I owe most of my success to the attention I always paid to the inferior part of tactics as a regimental officer. There were few men in the army who knew these details better than I did; it is the foundation of all military knowledge. When you are sure that you know the power of your tools and the way to handle them, you are able to give your mind altogether to the greater considerations which the presence of the enemy forces upon you.[11]

Wellington was an infantryman. He did not have a sizeable cavalry force until 1811 and lacked confidence in its experience and discipline, although in fact it generally served him well and played a key role at both Salamanca and Waterloo. Similarly, he had few guns in his early campaigns and used them to support his infantry, rather than massing them as Napoleon did as a powerful offensive weapon.

Wellington's infantry was highly trained and never suffered sufficiently heavy casualties for its quality to be undermined. It used a variety of tactical formations, including assault columns and hollow squares to resist cavalry. But such was the discipline of Wellington's battalions that he regularly deployed them in lines just two ranks deep to maximise their firepower. He also relied heavily on the recently developed light infantry arm to counter the swarms of skirmishers that preceded French attacks. Wellington's most famous tactic was to hide his battalions behind the crest of a ridge and surprise the attacking French infantry columns at the last moment to give them no time to deploy into line for a firefight. The British lines would fire a volley or two at close range and then rout the French with a bayonet charge.

In his overall conduct of a battle, Wellington was able to rely on the tactical superiority of his infantry. He was fortunate that he never had to face Napoleon's Grand Army in its heyday, 1805–7, and in the Peninsula he encountered French troops that were generally either of inferior quality or demoralised by repeated defeats. Furthermore, the difficult terrain of many Peninsular battlefields contributed to the disjointed nature of French assaults and made it difficult to mount combined-arms attacks. It was only at Waterloo that Wellington had to contend with powerful French cavalry and artillery and, ironically, the French on that occasion attacked for most of the day with unsupported cavalry or with infantry alone.

When on the defensive, Wellington used his eye for the ground to select a naturally strong position. He carefully secured his flanks and garrisoned any farms or villages that could serve as strongpoints against frontal attack. Then he simply kept his balance and smashed each successive enemy attack. He held that 'the great secret of battle is to have a reserve'[12] and he skilfully drew units from quiet sectors to achieve local superiority at attacked points. Thus, his defensive battles were highly flexible and active and at the end he sometimes even switched to the offensive and drove his exhausted attackers from the field, for instance at Quatre Bras.

Wellington, despite being seen primarily as a defensive general, attacked at most of his battles, particularly in India where boldness and a reputation for invincibility were enough to triumph over numerically superior but indisciplined or poorly led enemies. In the early years of the Peninsular War, he was actually accused of rashness by political opponents and from 1812 onwards, he repeatedly drubbed the French in bold, offensive strokes. In fact, he was even more ambitious than the results of some of his battles suggest: at both Vitoria and Orthez, he had hoped to trap and destroy the French army rather than merely defeat it.

His key aim was to win battles as cheaply and decisively as possible, without the heavy casualties inherent in attritional encounters like Talavera or Waterloo. He therefore preferred when possible to outflank his enemy, or at least to combine outflanking moves with frontal attacks (as at Roliça and Orthez), even if he thereby had to take the risk of dividing his army into two or more sections. Likewise, he never became dogmatic and could be counted on to do just one thing, namely the unexpected. When attacking across the Bidassoa river in October 1813, for example, he did so near the tidal estuary, which the French had believed to be impassable.

Thus Wellington in both strategy and tactics demonstrated a high degree of flexibility, surprise and manoeuvre. The other hallmark of his warfare was opportunism, for although he planned carefully, he was highly pragmatic and swift to exploit unexpected developments. He explained that the French marshals:

> planned their campaigns just as you might make a splendid piece of harness. It looks very well; and answers very well; until it gets broken; and then you are done for. Now I made my campaigns of ropes. If anything went wrong, I tied a knot; and went on.[13]

Wellington's headquarters were small but effective. The staff work was divided between his Military Secretary, his Quartermaster-General and his Adjutant-General, but he went personally into detail and was in effect his own Chief-of-Staff. His military success was underpinned by his remarkable system of logistics, which used a combination of river transport, ox-carts and mules to move supplies from ports and depots to the front. He had a relatively small army and was able to keep it supplied owing to Britain's economic strength and maritime supremacy. The French, in contrast, had to rely heavily on marauding and as a result were less disciplined and less able to keep an army concentrated; moreover they antagonised the local people.

In addition Wellington took a close interest in military intelligence and usually knew far more about his enemies than they knew about him. He explained that:

> All the business of war, and indeed all the business of life, is to endeavour to find out what you don't know by what you do; that's what I called 'guessing what was on the other side of the hill.'[14]

He read widely, rode long distances in reconnaissance and sent 'observing officers' to act as his eyes and ears behind enemy lines. To supplement this, he corresponded with informants and paid well to ensure that he promptly received despatches that had been intercepted by Spanish guerrillas.

But Wellington also had to operate under constraints and one of his most pressing problems was Britain's limited manpower. So many troops were required for home defence and overseas garrisons that it would have been impossible to replace Wellington's army had it been destroyed. He was fully aware of the restrictions this placed on him. 'I could lick those fellows any day,' he commented in 1810, 'but it would cost me 10,000 men, and as this is the last army England has, we must take care of it.'[15]

A further handicap was his appalling shortage of engineers, which made sieges the weakest aspect of his art of war. His sieges were often rushed and bloody as he had to take fortresses quickly, before the French could concentrate to relieve them.

Wellington had close personal links with the British Tory Government and enjoyed its active support, despite his outspoken and often unreasonable complaints. Yet his political connections did not solve all his difficulties, for he had limited authority in non-operational matters. For example, he lacked the authority to appoint subordinates and only in 1813 was he permitted to send incompetent generals home.

If there was a secret to Wellington's success, it was that he always paid close, personal attention to detail, though without losing sight of the larger picture. His complaint of 1811 about unreliable subordinates encapsulates his thinking in this respect:

> I am obliged to be everywhere, and if absent from any operation, something goes wrong. It is to be hoped that the general and other officers of the army will at last acquire that experience which will teach them that success can only be attained by attention to the most minute details; and by tracing every point of every operation from its origin to its conclusion, and ascertaining that the whole is understood by those who are to execute it.[16]

To do this, he needed to be physically fit, decisive and highly self-confident. An officer noted:

> Lord Wellington's simplicity of manner in the delivery of orders, and in command, is quite that of an able man. He has nothing of the truncheon about him; nothing foul-mouthed, important, or fussy: his orders, on the field, are all short, quick, clear, and to the purpose.[17]

Unflappability was another key part of his image as a commander. Ensign Rees Gronow of the 1st Guards wrote of him and his staff on the morning of Waterloo that 'they all seemed as gay and unconcerned as if they were riding to meet the hounds in some quiet English county.'[18] But Wellington did not always manage to hide his inner tension. At Salamanca, Private William Wheeler of the 51st Light Infantry recalled how Wellington 'waited some time anxiously looking towards the hill, as the enemy's fire was very brisk . . . his Lordship looked as serious as a Judge going to pass sentence of death.'[19] He was also deeply depressed by the butchery of Assaye, Badajoz and Waterloo and to a lesser degree by that of Talavera and Vitoria.

Subordinates admired or loathed him, but were never indifferent. Most trusted him implicitly and as Johnny Kincaid of the 95th Rifles explained:

> We would rather see his long nose in the fight than a reinforcement of ten thousand men any day. Indeed, there was a charm not only about himself but all connected with him, for which no odds could compensate.[20]

Wellington for his part wrote privately that 'the best troops we have, probably the best in the world, are the British infantry.'[21] But people tend to remember instead the sarcastic words that slipped from him in moments of anger, notorious phrases like 'the scum of the earth', which he used to denounce the disorder during the retreat from Burgos. By unfairly condemning all his men for the failings of a few, he caused lasting resentment, notably when he criticised the conduct of his gunners at Waterloo.

He has likewise been accused of not giving sufficient praise, but this flaw was in fact limited to his written despatches, for he made a point of encouraging his men verbally in battle. At Salamanca, he exclaimed to his cavalry commander: 'By God, Cotton, I never saw anything so beautiful in my life; the day is *yours.'*[22] Similarly, Sergeant Duncan Robertson of the 92nd Highlanders recorded that during the advance on Paris after Waterloo:

> The Duke of Wellington in person came up and thanked us for the manner in which we had conducted ourselves during the engagement, and lavished the highest eulogiums upon us.[23]

In fact, Wellington could be a surprisingly supportive commander, as he showed after Brigadier-General Robert Craufurd's notorious mishandling of the action on the Coa in July 1810. 'If I am to be hanged for it,' he remarked, 'I cannot accuse a man who I believe has meant well, and whose error was one of judgement, not of intention.' Although in fits of anger he could reduce men to tears, he was usually reasonable. 'I like to convince people rather than stand on mere authority,' he explained.[24] He was rigid in matters of discipline and integrity and did not hesitate to flog or hang looters; yet at the same time, William Grattan of the 88th Foot thought that:

> [He] was a most indulgent commander; he never harassed us with reviews, or petty annoyances, which so far from promoting discipline, or doing good in any way, have a contrary effect.[25]

Wellington is remembered today primarily for four achievements. First, he and his brothers helped establish British imperial power in India. Second, he helped restore the British Army's prestige and self-confidence after the American War of Independence (1775–83) and the often disappointing operations against Revolutionary France. Third, he helped bring down Napoleon, first indirectly during the Peninsular War and then, in 1815, directly on a battlefield. He himself said that 'Waterloo did more than any other battle I know of, towards the true object of all battles – the peace of the world.'[26] Fourth, by the end of his life he had become a national symbol, the supreme British ideal of a selfless, devoted and incorruptible public servant.

The Battle of Toulouse: 10 April 1814

'The real reason why I succeeded in my own campaigns,' Wellington noted, 'is because I was always on the spot – I saw everything, and did everything for myself.'[27]

But in the final year of the Peninsular War, he commanded a larger army than normal and often had to operate on a wide front. At Vitoria in June 1813, for example, he had to divide his army into four, widely separated prongs to try and trap the French and, since he could not be everywhere in person, this led to serious problems in co-ordinating his attacks. He had experienced even greater difficulties during the subsequent fighting in the Pyrenees and later complained that:

> It is a great disadvantage when the Officer Commanding in Chief must be absent, and probably at a distance. For this reason there is nothing I dislike so much as these extended operations, which I cannot direct myself.[28]

This basic problem turned Toulouse on 10 April 1814 into Wellington's shoddiest battle. It revealed the limitations of his highly personal style of command to such an extent that Lieutenant-Colonel Sir John Colborne, commander of the 52nd Light Infantry, claimed that 'it was the worst arranged battle that could be, nothing but mistakes.'[29]

Wellington at this stage of the war was extremely self-confident and had brought his army to a peak of fighting efficiency while the French under Marshal Soult were increasingly demoralised. Such was Wellington's mood that he did not hesitate to attack Soult in a strong position at Orthez in February 1814. He then followed Soult eastwards and on 26 March arrived in front of Toulouse, the main city and arsenal in south-western France.

Toulouse had 65,000 inhabitants and was protected by formidable natural and man-made defences. The inner fortifications consisted of the

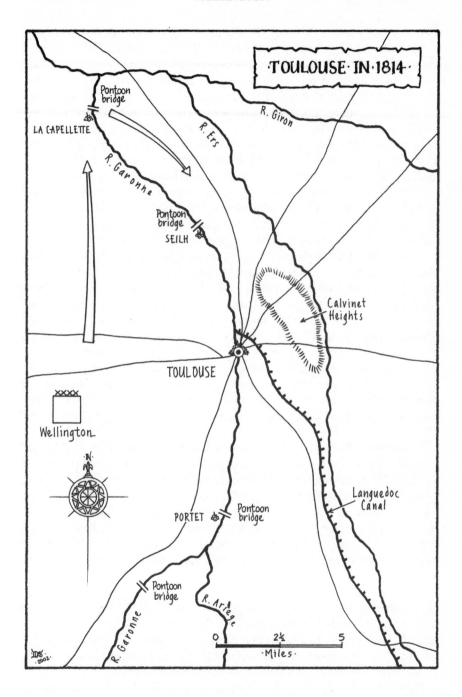

mediaeval city walls, although these were not proof against siege artillery. It was primarily the outer defences of watercourses that made Toulouse so strong. The city was covered to the west by the Garonne river, except for the strongly fortified suburb of St Cyprien on the far bank. About half-a-mile outside the city to the north and east was the Languedoc canal, which was 100 yards wide, unfordable and well fortified at its locks and bridges. A mile east of the city, outside the canal, lay a range of hills called the Calvinet heights which were three miles long and thirty-five yards higher than the ground on either side. Finally, to the east of these hills, the unfordable and steeply banked Ers river flowed from south to north.

In short, Toulouse was protected by watercourses to the east, north and west, like a castle surrounded by moats. But it had two weak points: first, it had no water defences to the south and second, it was dominated by the Calvinet heights to the east. If Wellington could seize these hills, he would be able to bring up guns and force Toulouse to surrender. His problem was that to get there, he would have to cross the Garonne to the east bank, yet at the same time he could not take his whole army across without exposing his lines of communication westward to the Atlantic coast. Hence he would have to operate on both banks of the Garonne simultaneously and would be obliged to move units around Toulouse if he wanted to reinforce part of his army. Soult, in contrast, had the advantage of operating on interior lines: by using a bridge over the Garonne within the city, he could quickly concentrate troops for a powerful counter-attack on either bank. Fortunately, as Wellington knew, Soult was not a bold general in battle and usually failed to press home his attacks.

Wellington initially decided to attack Toulouse from the south, but had to abort his attempt to cross the Garonne five miles south of the city on the night of 27–28 March when he discovered that he did not have enough pontoons. He had in fact ignored the advice of his senior engineer officer, who had warned that he could not bridge a wide river. Major George Napier of the 52nd Light Infantry remarked that he had never seen Wellington in such a rage, but further frustration was to follow.[30] An attempt to cross the Garonne farther upstream failed on the night of 30–31 March: 13,000 troops under Lieutenant-General Sir Rowland Hill successfully passed over it eight miles south of the city, but were checked by another river, the lower Ariège, and found that the water-logged terrain had no roads fit to bear guns. Wellington personally went to see for himself. According to his Judge Advocate-General, he 'has spent his mornings in riding all over the country to reconnoitre; and he dispatches all his other multitude of business at odd hours and times.'[31]

Wellington ordered Hill to return to the west bank of the Garonne on the night of 1–2 April. He now had no choice but to cross north of Toulouse and then sweep round to the east. Soult immediately realised this and hastened the fortification of the Calvinet heights. Meanwhile, Wellington's staff officers found a suitable spot for his pontoon bridge eleven miles north of Toulouse, at the hamlet of La Capellette. He himself inspected the ground on 3 April[32] and that night his army shifted northwards, while leaving some units west of Toulouse. At dawn on the 4th the pontoon bridge was established and 19,000 troops under Marshal William Carr Beresford crossed over. John Malcolm of the 42nd Highlanders noticed Wellington watching the operation, 'surrounded by a crowd of French peasantry, men, women and children, to whom he behaved with great affability and good humour.'[33] Wellington himself crossed to the east bank that morning and reconnoitred to within six miles of Toulouse.

But the bridge broke that evening, for the Garonne was swollen from heavy rain and melted snow from the Pyrenees. Beresford was cut off on the east bank and it would be three days before the bridge could be re-established. Wellington kept his cool. He related how:

> In this awkward situation, when the army was divided, I used to cross over [in a boat] every morning to the other side (where Beresford lay) and return at night. I thought the troops might be out of spirits at seeing themselves in a position so exposed; but not a bit – they didn't mind it at all.[34]

In fact, they were disappointed that Soult did not attack. Wellington had drawn up twenty-two guns on the west bank to command the flat fields on the opposite side.

It was on one of his crossings to the bridgehead that Wellington was nearly shot by one of his own sentries after forgetting the countersign. The sentry recognised him in the nick of time and delightedly blessed his hooked nose, which he said he would rather see than 10,000 men. According to Wellington, this was the finest compliment ever paid him.

On the morning of the 8th the pontoon bridge was finally back in operation. Another 9,000 troops crossed to the east bank and Wellington pushed southwards in two columns along either side of the Ers river. Two brigades of French light cavalry withdrew before his advance, destroying each bridge over the Ers as they did so until a bold charge by Colonel Vivian's 18th Hussars managed to seize one at Croix d'Orade, three miles north-east of Toulouse. 'Well done, the Eighteenth,' Wellington exclaimed in delight, 'by God, well done.'[35]

To shorten his communications with Hill's troops west of Toulouse, Wellington ordered the pontoon bridge over the Garonne to be relocated five miles farther south, at Seilh. This would allow the Light Division to reinforce him on the east bank ready for an attack on Soult on the 9th. But the transfer of the bridge took longer than expected and was accomplished only at 3.00 pm on the 9th, forcing Wellington to postpone the battle. The Light Division crossed only at dawn on the 10th. 'Lord Wellington was more vexed, and in a greater state of anger, than he usually is when things go wrong even without any good cause,' noted his Judge Advocate-General. 'He said his whole plans for the day were frustrated and nothing could be done.'[36]

Resigned to attacking on the 10th, Wellington issued his orders. His army was to operate in three sections to the west, north and east of Toulouse. On the west bank of the Garonne, Hill was to feint against the fortified suburb of St Cyprien, but without risking heavy casualties.

The central section of Wellington's army would contain the 3rd and Light Divisions, plus two cavalry brigades and General Don Manuel Freire's two divisions of Spanish infantry. Both the 3rd and Light Divisions were to stand north of Toulouse and, like Hill, were merely to skirmish, since the French defences along the Languedoc canal on this side were all but impregnable. In contrast, Freire's Spaniards north-east of the city were to make a full-blooded assault against the northern end of the Calvinet heights, once they saw the main attack go in east of the city.

This main attack would be delivered by the third section of the army, namely the 4th and 6th Divisions and two hussar brigades under Beresford. The assault would hit the most vulnerable sector of the Calvinet heights, the southern end, where they were not so strongly fortified. The only question was how to get there. Beresford had been advancing during the last couple of days along the east bank of the Ers up to Croix d'Orade. It seems that Wellington initially hoped to secure additional bridges over the Ers farther south. This would allow the 4th Division to march southwards along the east bank of the river and out of range of the French guns on the heights before turning west, crossing at the bridge of Les Bordes and sweeping straight on up the heights. But on the evening of the 9th Wellington was informed that the tracks east of the Ers were impracticable and that the bridge of Les Bordes had been blown up. He had to change his plan: the 4th and 6th Divisions would both have to cross the Ers at Croix d'Orade and march southwards along the west bank to reach their assault positions opposite the far end of the heights. This meant that Beresford would have to march for about three miles under artillery fire across the front of the French-held heights. One of his hussar brigades would lead the advance, while the other would cover his flank by going down the east bank of the Ers to try and seize any bridges that remained intact. Wellington sensibly allowed Beresford discretion in judging exactly how far to march before he launched his attack.

Wellington could field nearly 49,000 troops, of whom 10,000 were Spaniards and 13,000 Portuguese. Soult had 42,000 men, but these included over 7,000 conscripts. Two of his seven infantry divisions were on the Calvinet heights with a third in close support. The other four held

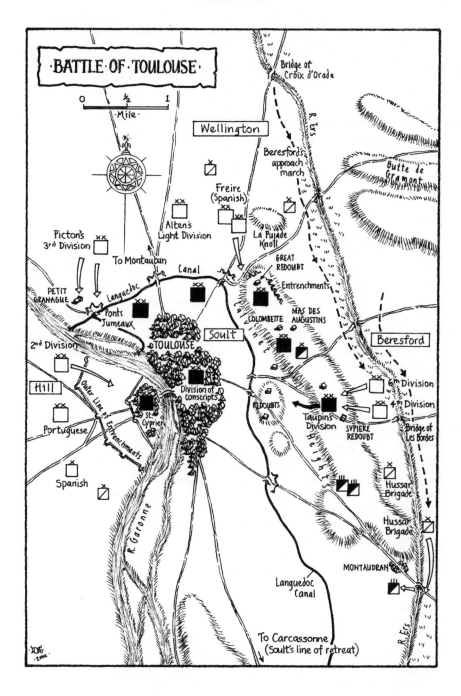

·BATTLE·OF·TOULOUSE·

0   ½   1
·Mile·

·N·

Wellington

Bridge of
Croix d'Orade

R. Ers

Beresford's
approach
march

Butte de
Gramont

Freire
(Spanish)

Alten's
Light Division

La Pujade
Knoll

GREAT
REDOUBT

Picton's
3rd Division

To Montauban

Canal

Entrenchments

COLOMBETTE

MAS DES
AUGUSTINS

PETIT
GRANAGUE

Languedoc

Ponts
Jumeaux

Soult

Beresford

TOULOUSE

2nd Division

Hill

St Cyprien

Division of
conscripts

REDOUBTS

Taupin's
Division

SVPIERE
REDOUBT

6th Division

4th Division

Bridge of
Les Bordes

Portuguese

Outer Line of Entrenchments

Heights

Hussar
Brigade

Spanish

R. Garonne

Hussar
Brigade

MONTAUDRAN

R. Ers

Languedoc
Canal

To Carcassonne
(Soult's line of retreat)

125

the canal line, the St Cyprien suburb and the city itself. Since Toulouse was a major arsenal, Soult had been able to supplement the field artillery that accompanied his army with a varied collection of heavier pieces of greater range and calibre, which he placed on the city walls and in his fortifications. However, he was short of skilled gunners and this reduced the effect of his superior numbers of guns.

Wellington's army was on the move early on the 10th. It was Easter Sunday. John Malcolm of the 42nd Highlanders, part of the 6th Division, saw Wellington and his staff 'riding back from the front at a hard trot.' Malcolm easily recognised him, even at a distance, 'by the peculiarly erect carriage of his head, and the white cravat which he always wore. Some of the men called out, *there goes Wellington, my lads, we shall have some hot work presently.*'[37]

At 6.00 am three shots from Wellington's cannon at Croix d'Orade signalled the start of the battle.[38] Over to the west of Toulouse, Sir Rowland Hill opened his diversionary operations against the St Cyprien suburb and quickly penetrated the outer line of entrenchments. Sensibly, he did not attempt to storm the strong inner line. But far from reinforcing the suburb as Wellington had hoped, Soult later withdrew a brigade to act as a reserve for the troops on the Calvinet heights.

By now, the battle had flared up north of Toulouse. The Light Division in accordance with Wellington's orders restricted itself to skirmishing in front of the Languedoc canal. But the 3rd Division under its impatient commander, Lieutenant-General Sir Thomas Picton, was bloodily repulsed in a series of unauthorised assaults on the fortified canal bridgehead of the Ponts Jumeaux.

Farther east, Freire's Spanish infantry occupied a knoll called La Pujade, from where Portuguese guns fired on the northern end of the Calvinet heights. Wellington initially watched the battle from the Butte de Gramont, a mound on the east bank of the Ers one-and-a-half miles south of Croix d'Orade, but later moved forward to La Pujade.

Beresford's advance, meanwhile, proved frustratingly slow. His troops had to struggle across muddy, ploughed fields and began to come under artillery fire from the Calvinet heights to the west. Luckily, it was not as heavy as it might have been, partly because Soult's redoubts had been placed well back from the eastern edge of the heights, with the result that Beresford's men were outside the effective range of the French guns. Although Beresford had two artillery batteries, he left them behind as they had trouble in keeping up with him; they instead unlimbered and bombarded the northern end of the heights.

The battle so far had gone reasonably to plan. But its synchronisation suddenly broke down when Freire attacked prematurely with 5,500 of his Spanish infantry. Why he did so remains a mystery. He had asked Wellington to give his Spaniards an important role to play and this desire for distinction probably made him impatient. Perhaps he mistook the fire of Beresford's artillery to be the signal for the start of the main assault. Whatever the answer, the Spaniards advanced heroically, but unexpectedly encountered a sunken road as they approached the Great Redoubt at the top of the heights. With the momentum of their advance thus broken, they disintegrated under a hail of fire and fled back down the slopes, provoking Wellington to exclaim: 'Well, d__n me, if I ever saw ten thousand men run a race before.' In fact, not all the Spaniards fled, for one regiment, the Tiradores de Cantabria, gallantly stood and held its ground until Wellington had it recalled. He then galloped over to help rally the fugitives, but it was two hours before they could recover.

Wellington on seeing the premature Spanish attack had ordered Beresford to abandon his march, wheel to the west and assault the Calvinet heights. Beresford received this order only after the Spaniards had been routed and sensibly ignored it. Wellington's other reaction to the crisis was to plug the gap left by the Spaniards. He turned to his Adjutant-General, Sir Edward Pakenham. 'There I am,' he said, 'with nothing between me and the enemy.'

'Well,' answered Pakenham, 'I suppose you will order up the Light Division now.'

But Wellington refused to commit this crack division, his reserve, to an attack: 'I'll be hanged if I do.'[39] Nonetheless, he pulled it eastwards and added a brigade of heavy dragoons, in case Soult tried to exploit his success and cut Beresford off from the rest of the army. In the event, the French remained in their defensive positions.

Beresford's units at last reached the end of their approach march and turned to face the Calvinet heights before advancing up the slopes. The 6th Division formed the right, or northern, wing and the 4th Division the left. Each division had three brigades arrayed one behind the other and since each brigade was formed up in a two-deep line, Beresford's entire formation of 11,000 infantry had a depth of six ranks and covered a front of one-and-a-half miles. It had been impossible for Beresford to screen his march or hide his intention, so Soult had time to summon reinforcements. General Eloi-Charlemagne Taupin's division of 5,500 men had arrived behind the crest of the heights at the threatened point; another brigade was on the way. To replace these troops in reserve, Soult withdrew a brigade from the St Cyprien suburb.

As Beresford's two divisions came up the slopes, Soult exclaimed: 'here they are, General Taupin; I make you a present of them.'[40] Taupin immediately advanced in two massed columns down the forward face of the ridge to meet the attack, masking as he did so the line of fire of the nearest French fortification, the Sypière Redoubt. But his impressive advance soon foundered. Beresford had with him a small detachment of the Mounted Rocket Corps, which fired some highly erratic Congreve rockets that helped unnerve the French. Taupin hesitated and made the mistake of trying to deploy under the deadly fire of the British lines. He had bravely if foolhardily decided to lead from the front and fell mortally wounded, while his surviving men streamed back up the hill, infecting with their panic the garrison of the Sypière Redoubt, which abandoned its post and fled.

Beresford hence established a foothold on the heights, but was not yet ready to follow this up and drive the French from the northern end, for he had left his batteries behind during his approach march. He also informed Wellington that he wanted the Spaniards to make a second diversionary assault on the northern end of the heights. In the meantime, he deployed the 6th Division ready to attack north-westwards along the crest. The 4th Division faced Toulouse to guard Beresford's western flank and his two brigades of hussars acted as a covering force farther south.

A two-hour lull ensued. Those who could not see what was happening on the heights found the silence unsettling. Picton assumed that Beresford had been repulsed and that he alone could now snatch victory from the jaws of defeat. Already that morning he had been bloodily repulsed in attacking the Ponts Jumeaux north-west of Toulouse and he now attacked them again, equally fruitlessly. He lost over 300 men, including a brigadier wounded and a colonel killed.

Freire's Spaniards meanwhile rallied and the battle at last flared up again on the heights with attacks by both Freire from the north and the 6th Division from the south. The Spaniards lost half their senior officers and were again repulsed, but tied down a French division in the north while Beresford attacked half-a-mile to the south. Spearheading the 6th Division's advance were the 42nd and 79th Highlanders, who stormed the Mas des Augustins and Colombette Redoubts, only to be hurled back by a powerful counter-attack. The French regained the redoubts, lost them and once again recaptured them. Beresford had to commit the last brigade of the 6th Division finally to break their resistance. The cost was appalling. The 42nd Highlanders lost fifty-five per cent of their strength and the 79th forty-four per cent. But the battle was won, for the crucial heights were in Beresford's hands, except in the extreme north, where the French still held the Great Redoubt and the adjacent entrenchments. But even here, they were under fire from Beresford's skirmishers and from a battery of the Royal Horse Artillery that Wellington had sent. Beresford's two batteries were also present, but were running out of ammunition.

Late in the afternoon, Soult conceded defeat and ordered his troops to evacuate the Great Redoubt and retire within the canal line. They did so without undue trouble and even managed to bring their guns back into the city. Wellington, who had arrived on the heights, watched Beresford's men occupying the abandoned positions. Night fell and towards 9.00 pm the last skirmishes petered out.

1. *Napoleon at the battle of Montereau in 1814.*

2. *Napoleon slightly wounded at Ratisbon in 1809. Casualty rates among generals during the Napoleonic wars were high. (ASKB)*

3. *Eugène de Beauharnais. (ASKB)*

4. *Lasalle receiving the keys of Stettin, 1806. (ASKB)*

5. *Moore. (ASKB)*

6. *Wellington at Waterloo. (ASKB)*

7. *Hill. (ASKB)*

8. *Archduke Charles. (ASKB)*

9. *Aftermath of the battle of Leipzig in 1813. Kneeling in the centre are Tsar Alexander I of Russia, Emperor Francis I of Austria and King Frederick William III of Prussia. Blücher is standing to the left of Alexander, while the allied supreme commander, Schwarzenberg, is on horseback to the right of Frederick William. Schwarzenberg's position was undermined by the presence of the allied monarchs, as this picture suggests. (ASKB)*

10. *Blücher. (ASKB)*

11. *Gneisenau. (ASKB)*

12. *The city of Laon today.*

13. *Barclay de Tolly, painted by George Dawe. In the background is the hill of Montmartre in Paris, where Barclay fought on 30 March 1814. It was this picture that inspired Pushkin to write his poem 'The Commander'. (ASKB)*

14. *Bagration. (ASKB)*

15. *The battle of Smolensk, 1812. Napoleon's troops assault the city in the background. (ASKB)*

16. *Kutusov. (ASKB)*

17. *Napoleon's army crosses the Beresina during the retreat from Moscow in 1812. (ASKB)*

Wellington had to spend the whole of the next day replenishing ammunition, burying the dead and re-organising his army. Soult had already decided to evacuate Toulouse, so as not to be trapped inside the city and forced to surrender. Wellington's cavalry had not yet been able to seal off the southern side of Toulouse and on the night of 11–12 April, Soult duly marched out along the Carcassonne road, leaving behind only those of his men too badly wounded to be moved, including three generals.

Wellington entered Toulouse to popular acclaim on the morning of the 12th and that evening received news from Paris that Napoleon had abdicated on the 6th, meaning that the battle need not have been fought at all. But the predominant emotion was relief that the long struggle was finally over. Wellington took a moment to absorb the full implications of the news and then suddenly exclaimed 'you don't say so, upon my honour!' and twisted round, clicking his fingers and cheering 'hurrah!' Hostilities with Soult formally ended six days later, yet Toulouse had been a disappointing end to Wellington's long series of Peninsular victories. John Colborne of the 52nd Light Infantry pointed out that isolated attacks were made; he thought it a most extraordinary battle and went so far as to claim: 'I think the Duke almost deserved to have been beaten.'[41] In contrast to the French casualties of 3,200, Wellington lost over 4,500 men, of whom as many as 1,900 were Spanish. 'In the whole of my experience,' he claimed, 'I never saw an army so strongly posted as the French at the battle of Toulouse.'[42]

The main lesson to be drawn from the battle is just how difficult it was to exercise effective command and control with primitive means of communication over armies covering a large extent of ground. Napoleon used a semaphore telegraph at Austerlitz in 1805, as did Archduke Charles at Aspern–Essling four years later. Generals sometimes fired a pre-arranged number of cannon-shots, or used beacons or Congreve rockets as signals, but for the most part messages travelled only at the speed of a galloping horse. Toulouse illustrates many of the problems that could ensue.

NOTES

1   P. Guedalla, *The Duke* (1931), pp.3, 5
2   E. Longford, *Wellington: pillar of state* (1972), p.148
3   G. Gleig, *The life of the Duke of Wellington* (1939), p.5
4   E. Longford, *Wellington: the years of the sword* (1969), p.19
5   Earl of Ellesmere, *Personal reminiscences of the Duke of Wellington* (1903), p.161
6   C. Oman, *A history of the Peninsular war* (1902–30), v.5, p.473
7   Longford, *Wellington: the years of the sword*, p.389
8   But note that the extent to which Wellington's British troops at Waterloo consisted of young and untried troops has been seriously questioned by

C. Atkinson, 'An "Infamous Army"', in *Journal of the Society for Army Historical Research* (1954). Likewise, Wellington's staff by the time of the battle was far from inexperienced: see J. Edmonds, 'Wellington's staff at Waterloo', in *Journal of the Society for Army Historical Research* (1933).

9   A. Brett-James, *The hundred days* (1964), p.183

10   Longford, *Wellington: the years of the sword*, p.300

11   J. Croker, *The Croker papers* (1885), v.1, p.337

12   H. Maxwell, *Life of Wellington* (1900), v.2, p.139

13   W. Fraser, *Words on Wellington* (nd), p.28

14   *The Croker papers* (1884), v.3, p.275

15   M. Glover, *Wellington as military commander* (1968), p.148

16   J. Gurwood, ed., *The dispatches of Field Marshal the Duke of Wellington* (1834–8), v.7, p.567

17   M. Sherer, *Recollections of the Peninsula* (1825), p.151

18   R. Gronow, *The reminiscences and recollections of Captain Gronow* (1984), p.186

19   B. Liddell Hart, ed., *The letters of Private Wheeler 1809–1828* (1951), pp.87–8; see also W. Tomkinson, *The diary of a cavalry officer* (1894), pp.188–9

20   J. Kincaid, *Adventures in the Rifle Brigade and random shots from a rifleman* (1981), pp.36–7

21   Maxwell, *op. cit.*, v.2, p.109

22   Lady Combermere and W. Knollys, ed., *Memoirs and correspondence of Field-Marshal Viscount Combermere* (1866), v.1, p.274

23   D. Robertson, *The journal of Sergeant D. Robertson* (1842), p.162

24   J. Fortescue, *History of the British army* (1899–1930), v.7, p.484; *The Croker papers* (1885), v.1, p.346

25   W. Grattan, *Adventures with the Connaught Rangers, 1809–1814* (1989), p.50

26   *The Croker papers* (1885), v.2, p.235

27   Earl of Stanhope, *Notes on conversations with the Duke of Wellington* (1938), p.182

28   Guedalla, *op. cit.*, p.240

29   G. Moore Smith, *The life of Colborne* (1903), pp.205–6

30   G. Napier, *The early military life of General Sir George T. Napier* (1886), p.211

31   G. Larpent, ed., *The private journal of F.S. Larpent* (1853), v.3, p.95

32   C. Vivian, *Richard Hussey Vivian* (1897), p.235

33   J. Malcolm, 'Reminiscences of a campaign in the Pyrenees and south of France,' in *Memorials of the late war* (1828), v.1, p.290

34   Maxwell, *op. cit.*, v.1, p.370

35   Fortescue, *op. cit.*, v.10, p.76; Vivian fell wounded in this action.

36   Larpent, *op. cit.*, v.3, p.126

37   Malcolm, *op. cit.*, v.1, p.292

38   J.-P. Escalettes, *10 avril 1814: la bataille de Toulouse* (1999), p.69

39   Fortescue, *op. cit.*, v.10, p.84

40   *Ibid*, v.10, p.85

41   Moore Smith, *op. cit.*, p.206

42   Maxwell, *op. cit.*, v.1, pp.371–2

CHAPTER VI
Hill

'That young man will rise to be one of the first soldiers of the age.' So spoke Lieutenant-General Charles O'Hara, commander of the allied troops besieged at Toulon by the French Revolutionaries in 1793. 'That young man' was his ADC, Captain Rowland Hill, who was 21 years old.[1] But although Hill eventually commanded the British Army, his star never shone as brightly as it deserved in the glittering galaxy of Peninsular War generals, because everyone's eyes followed the blazing meteor that was Wellington.

Rowland, one of the sixteen children of Sir John Hill, was born on 11 August 1772 at Prees Hall in Shropshire, just three miles from the Welsh border. Even as a child, he displayed the characteristics that would make him one of the best-loved of British generals. 'He was extremely good-natured and amiable,' recalled a fellow schoolboy, 'ever ready to assist a lad out of a scrape, and never tumbled into one himself.'[2] He loved the country life, but suffered from delicate health and was remarkably squeamish. He passed out when a fellow pupil cut his finger and would faint again soon after becoming a soldier, when he saw a prize-fight. The puzzle is how he later coped with the carnage of the battlefield. 'I have still the same feelings,' he explained after he had won fame, 'but in the excitement of battle all individual sensation is lost sight of.'[3]

His parents suggested a career in law, but he had other plans. 'I have a dislike to the law,' he wrote to his mother in March 1790, 'and am sure I should neither be happy, nor make any figure, as a lawyer. The profession which I should like best, and I hope you and Papa will not object to, is the army.'[4] Hill's father duly bought him a commission as an ensign in the 38th Foot, with leave of absence to study at the military school in Strasbourg. In January 1791 he was back in England and two months later was appointed a lieutenant in the 53rd (Shropshire) Foot. He had leave to return to Strasbourg but stayed there only a few weeks because of the troubles in Revolutionary France. He joined the 53rd at Edinburgh in January 1792 and a year later, after recruiting a company of men, was made a captain.

War broke out between France and Britain at the beginning of 1793 and

131

that August a fleet under Admiral Lord Hood landed a British, Spanish, Neapolitan and Sardinian expeditionary force at the southern French port of Toulon, which had declared for the royalist cause and was under siege from French Revolutionary forces. A week later, Lord Mulgrave arrived to take command and appointed Captain Rowland Hill to his staff. At Toulon, Hill served as ADC to three successive commanders, Lord Mulgrave, Lieutenant-General O'Hara and Major-General David Dundas, and favourably impressed them all. During a sortie, he had to conduct a retreat back within the city's fortifications after O'Hara was captured. In December 1793 he was sent home with despatches that informed the Government that Toulon could no longer be held; indeed, it was evacuated shortly afterwards.

Among those who noticed Hill at Toulon was his fellow ADC, Thomas Graham, who became a close friend and was later one of Wellington's generals. Early in 1794 Graham raised an infantry regiment, which became the 90th Foot, and he offered Hill a command in it as a major for raising a certain quota of men. Three months later, Hill was a lieutenant-colonel and commander of the regiment at the age of 23.

The summer of 1795 saw him take part with the 90th in an expedition to the Ile d'Yeu off the western coast of France. The aim was to take the island as a base from which to support French royalists against the Revolutionary regime. Badly planned British expeditions were not uncommon during the Revolutionary wars, but this was one of the most foolhardy. Although the British captured the island, they had few supplies and would have starved to death had it not been for the Royal Navy's exertions. The troops had no regrets when they were finally evacuated in December.

In 1800 the 90th went to Gibraltar and a year later Hill, by now a full colonel, commanded the regiment in the campaign to expel the French army that Napoleon had left in Egypt. The British under Lieutenant-General Sir Ralph Abercromby landed at Aboukir Bay in March 1801, pushed inland and clashed with the French at Mandara on the 13th. The 90th formed the advanced guard of the leading brigade, but stood firm and coolly repelled a cavalry attack. Hill himself was wounded in the right temple by a blow that knocked him unconscious and would have killed him had it not been for the brass binding on the front of his helmet. He recovered in a month, rejoined his regiment and commanded it at the surrender of Cairo and during the siege of Alexandria. After the successful conclusion of the campaign, he returned to England in April 1802.

The following spring found him with the 90th in Ireland, where his calm efficiency was invaluable. Insurrection and a French invasion were distinct possibilities in the aftermath of the crushed rebellion of 1798. In August 1803 he took up an appointment as a brigadier-general on the staff and as part of his duties inspected locations where the French might land.

Hill was promoted to major-general in October 1805 and at the end of the year commanded a brigade in Lord Cathcart's expedition to Hanover. But he saw no action, for the expedition was recalled in February 1806 after Napoleon smashed the Austro-Russian army at Austerlitz. The most significant aspect of the expedition for Hill was his first meeting with Major-General Sir Arthur Wellesley, who commanded a brigade in the same venture.

On his return, Hill served briefly on Lieutenant-General Sir John Moore's staff in southern England and in early 1807 returned to Ireland. The following year he joined the British expeditionary force that landed in Portugal under Sir Arthur Wellesley to expel the French occupation forces. Hill was heavily engaged at Roliça on 17 August 1808, although his brigade stood in reserve at Vimeiro four days later. The victorious Wellesley was then superseded and later returned home. Under the controversial Convention of Cintra, the defeated French troops in Portugal, cut off by uprisings in Spain, were repatriated on British ships.

Command of the British army in Portugal passed into the hands of Sir John Moore, who boldly advanced into Spain to support the Spanish armies. But Moore was forced to withdraw after Napoleon intervened with massive reinforcements and scattered the Spanish armies. Hill endured this horrific winter retreat to Coruña on the north-western coast of Spain. Moore checked the French pursuit in a battle outside the port on 16 January 1809, but lost his life. Hill's brigade was not heavily engaged in the battle and helped cover the subsequent embarkation of the army. On his return to England, he showed exemplary care for his exhausted troops.

He was soon back with Wellesley in Portugal, for Moore had left 10,000 troops there and the French, busy overrunning Spain, had not yet had a chance to march on Lisbon. The arrival of reinforcements and the incorporation of Portuguese troops into Wellesley's army increased its size and as a result Hill was given command of a division. Wellesley first expelled a French corps that had entered northern Portugal by launching a bold daylight crossing of the Douro river at Oporto on 12 May. Hill was among the first to cross and took over command on the far bank when Lieutenant-General Edward Paget was wounded. By successfully holding the bridgehead, he covered the arrival of sufficient troops to defeat the French.

In June 1809 Hill took command of the 2nd Division. Wellesley, having driven the French from northern Portugal, now thrust deep into central Spain, where he fought a desperate, two-day battle at Talavera after the French unexpectedly concentrated against him and his Spanish ally, General Don Gregorio Garcia de la Cuesta. The action began on the afternoon of 27 July and flared up again after dusk when the French made a surprise attack. The top of the Medellin hill in the centre of the British position suddenly blazed with musketry. Hill later recalled:

Not having an idea that the enemy were so near, I said to myself that I was sure it was the old Buffs [the 3rd Foot], as usual, making some blunder.[5]

He immediately rode up the Medellin to put things right, only to run straight into the French. Someone seized his arm, but Hill shook him off and galloped away under a hail of fire. It was not the least of his many narrow escapes, for a companion had been shot dead at his side. He quickly collected a brigade and with it drove the French off the Medellin before they could consolidate their position.

The French renewed the battle next morning. Hill now firmly occupied the Medellin but saw heavy French columns advancing against him. Losing some of his cool in the excitement of the moment, he even swore when British skirmishers masked his field of fire as they retired. 'Damn their filing, let them come in anyhow!' he exclaimed in one of only two recorded instances of him cursing.[6] In the ensuing clash, the French were beaten off and although Hill was struck by a musketball near the left ear, he recovered after a couple of days.

The Talavera campaign ended with Wellesley having to retreat back to the Portuguese frontier in August. During the winter of 1809–10 Napoleon sent over 100,000 extra troops into Spain in a bid to subdue the Peninsula once and for all. Wellesley (now Viscount Wellington) was reduced to defending Portugal. Only two roads suitable for a large army crossed the country's rugged eastern frontier. Wellington himself guarded the northern corridor, around the fortress of Ciudad Rodrigo, but he gave Hill a detached force of 12,000 men to guard the southern corridor near Badajoz. Hill's detachment amounted to a corps command, although it was never formalised as such, and had as its nucleus his own 2nd Division and a Portuguese division.

Marshal André Massena, ordered by Napoleon to drive Wellington into the sea, decided to invade Portugal through the northern corridor and by the end of August had taken the fortresses of Ciudad Rodrigo and Almeida. Then, in September, he called in his outlying units and began his advance on Lisbon. Hill had been guarding the Portuguese frontier farther south against the threat posed by the French II Corps, but once this corps marched north to join Massena, Hill made a parallel move and joined Wellington on the ridge of Busaco early on 26 September. His arrival enabled Wellington to accept battle the next day. The French attacked the ridge head-on in the centre and north, but Hill, who was stationed at the southern end, was unengaged.

Wellington repelled all Massena's assaults at Busaco, but had to retreat to Lisbon when he was subsequently outflanked in the north. He withdrew into the safety of the fortifications of Torres Vedras which sealed off the city and waited until starvation forced Massena to retreat

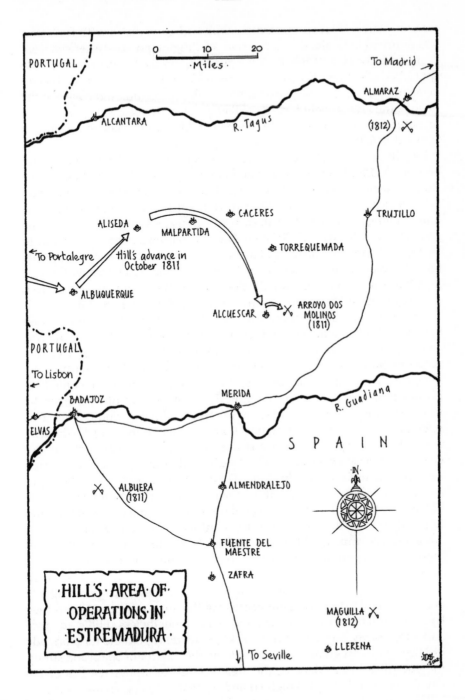

PORTUGAL

To Madrid

ALMARAZ

(1812)

ALCANTARA

R. Tagus

TRUJILLO

CACERES

ALISEDA

MALPARTIDA

TORREQUEMADA

To Portalegre

Hill's advance in
October 1811

ALBUQUERQUE

ALCUESCAR

ARROYO DOS
MOLINOS
(1811)

PORTUGAL

To Lisbon

BADAJOZ

MERIDA

R. Guadiana

ELVAS

S P A I N

·N·

ALBUERA
(1811)

ALMENDRALEJO

FUENTE DEL
MAESTRE

ZAFRA

·HILL'S ·AREA ·OF·
OPERATIONS ·IN·
ESTREMADURA·

MAGUILLA
(1812)

LLERENA

To Seville

0   10   20
·Miles·

135

early in March 1811. Unfortunately, Hill had gone down with fever and had returned to England on sick leave. Wellington pursued Massena from Portugal in April and resumed his positions on the Spanish frontier. He appointed Marshal William Carr Beresford to command Hill's old detachment, which was guarding the southern corridor and covering the siege of the French-held fortress of Badajoz. But Beresford suffered heavy casualties when attacked by the French at Albuera in May and narrowly avoided defeat.

Luckily, Hill was able to resume his former command at the beginning of June. Wellington personally joined him in the south, intending to take Badajoz while Hill covered the siege, but had to abandon the operation and fall back when two of the French armies in Spain concentrated against him. Wellington returned north early in August, leaving Hill to guard the southern corridor with 12,000 men. Hill was reinforced later in the year to 16,000 and some Spanish regular forces were also in the area. Opposite him, in Estremadura, stood a French corps of about 13,000 under General Jean-Baptiste Drouet, Count d'Erlon, which had been detached from Marshal Jean-de-Dieu Soult's army operating in southern Spain.

The surprising thing about Hill was his boldness as a commander. Steady and reliable men do not usually make daring leaders, but he was an exception. In October 1811, for instance, he thrashed one of d'Erlon's divisions under General Jean-Baptiste Girard after a dawn assault on the village of Arroyo dos Molinos. After this success, Hill remained quietly in his positions for a couple of months. Then, at the end of December, he received orders from Wellington to divert Marshal Soult, who was operating in southern Spain against both the coastal city of Tarifa (held by a small Anglo-Spanish garrison) and a Spanish regular army under General Francisco Ballesteros. On the 27th Hill duly advanced eastwards into Spain with the bulk of his force. For a moment it seemed as if he might surprise an exposed division at the town of Merida, thirty-four miles east of Badajoz, but the French discovered his approach in the nick of time and hurriedly retreated. Hill then pushed southwards for fourteen miles up to Almendralejo, causing d'Erlon to fall back before him. He sent out a small mobile detachment to press farther south and then withdrew to Portugal in the middle of January 1812 after learning that the French had abandoned their operations against Tarifa. In fact, they had given up not because of Hill's diversion, but because of the impossible conditions they had encountered in prosecuting the siege. Nonetheless, Hill's advance had temporarily pushed d'Erlon back and made it possible for a brigade of 3,000 Spanish regular troops to raid into the interior of Spain and stir up the guerrillas in La Mancha, the area around the upper reaches of the Guadiana river. Hill was knighted and promoted to lieutenant-general.

The war now swung against the French. In January 1812 Wellington recaptured Ciudad Rodrigo, which had been in French hands since July

1810. This success opened the northern corridor into Spain and Wellington then brought the bulk of his army south to join Hill and seize the city of Badajoz, so as to open the southern corridor as well. To guard against outside interference in the siege, Wellington pushed out two covering forces: 19,000 men under Lieutenant-General Sir Thomas Graham to the south-east and 14,000 under Hill to the east. Graham and Hill pushed d'Erlon's 12,000 men right back; Soult in early April brought 13,000 reinforcements from southern Spain, but lacked the strength to break through to Badajoz because Hill on Wellington's orders united with Graham at Albuera, thirteen miles south-east of the city. In any case, Badajoz fell on the 6th: Soult was too late and could do nothing but return south, leaving d'Erlon as an observing force.

Wellington for his part returned northwards, leaving Hill with 14,000 men in the southern corridor. Wellington planned to take the offensive into Spain and ordered Hill to carry out a preliminary raid against the strategically important French pontoon bridge over the Tagus at Almaraz, 100 miles north-east of Badajoz. Hill left most of his troops in Estremadura and took the remaining 6,000 to Almaraz, where he brilliantly destroyed the pontoon bridge and neighbouring forts before returning safely. The success of the raid severely hindered communications between Marshal Soult's army in southern Spain and Marshal Auguste Marmont's army in the centre. Wellington could now advance against Marmont, confident that Soult could not readily intervene.

On 22 July Wellington decisively smashed Marmont's army at Salamanca, while Hill and a Spanish regular army under General Ballesteros between them kept Soult distracted in southern Spain. In the course of these operations, Hill advanced against d'Erlon in Estremadura to relieve the pressure on Ballesteros, who had suffered a defeat on 1 June. This led to the action of Maguilla on 11 June, when a British cavalry brigade under the inept Major-General Sir John Slade was routed after being sent on reconnaissance. Despite this minor fiasco, Hill had successfully drawn more of Soult's troops on to himself and retired on Albuera. After a quiet fortnight, he advanced once more against d'Erlon on 2 July, heading south-eastwards and trying to cut him off by turning his western flank. But despite blocking the road to Seville, he failed to trap d'Erlon, who continued his retreat in a more easterly direction. Hill thereupon halted at Zafra, forty miles south-east of Badajoz, where he could continue to contain d'Erlon during Wellington's more important operations in the north.

After Wellington's triumphant entry into Madrid, Soult reluctantly evacuated southern Spain and towards the end of August fell back north-eastwards to unite with the other French armies. This freed Hill to move north. Wellington meanwhile detached four of his divisions at Madrid and took the rest north to besiege the city of Burgos. When Hill arrived south of Madrid at the end of September, he added to his command the four divisions he found there, thus bringing his detachment to a total of 36,000 men. His role was to remain near Madrid to guard Wellington's southern flank during the operations against Burgos. Wellington hoped that with Burgos in his hands he would be able to hold on to his positions deep inside Spain. But the siege failed and he had to fall back on 21 October as the French armies in Spain concentrated against him.

The situation was potentially disastrous. Hill was confronted near Madrid by over 60,000 French troops under Marshal Soult and Napoleon's brother, King Joseph of Spain. Unfortunately, the autumn rains were late, so the Tagus river south of the city was still fordable and useless as a defence line. On 28 October, as Wellington withdrew from Burgos, Hill similarly began a retreat that took him past Madrid and across the Guadarrama mountains. Thus Wellington and Hill each guarded the other's line of retreat as they fell back to unite around Salamanca on 8 November. Soult tried in vain to catch Hill and on finally meeting him twenty-six years later, exclaimed:

> What! have I found you at last? You, whom I followed so long without ever being able to overtake you.[7]

After linking up, Wellington and Hill fell back to the safety of Portugal. The year had ended in disappointment after the high hopes of Salamanca, but their efforts had not been in vain. One result of the campaign was that the French had evacuated southern Spain for good, thus removing the need for Hill to be detached to guard the southern corridor.

In December 1812 Wellington went to Cadiz for talks with the *Cortes*, or Spanish Parliament, and left Hill to command the army until his return in January 1813. All remained quiet during this time and, indeed, life in the Peninsula was not all fighting. According to Lieutenant Robert Blakeney of the 28th Foot, Hill was

> as keen at unkennelling a Spanish fox as at starting a French general out of his sleep, and in either amusement was the foremost to cry, 'Tally ho!' or, 'There they go!'[8]

Hill did all he could to add to his troops' amusements. A subaltern of the 34th Foot recorded:

> He patronized an amateur theatre, which was very well got up. We had amongst so many regiments capital actors, scene-painters, and really a first-rate company . . . After the play we all went in our stage dresses to the General's supper-table, where we *did* enjoy ourselves to the full, a singular-looking group of painted actors and actresses. I

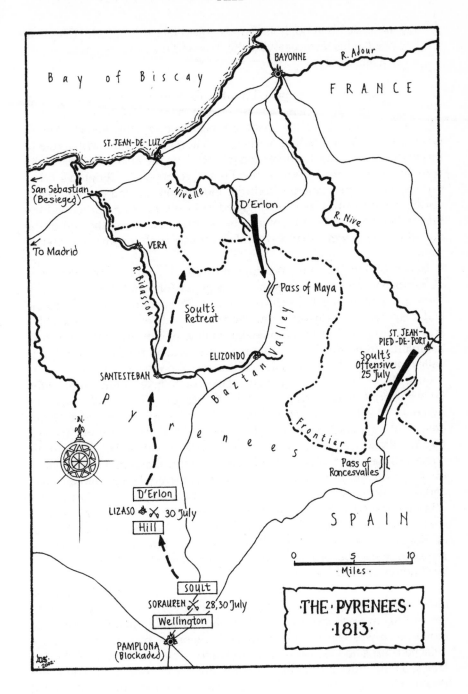

Bay of Biscay

R. Adour

BAYONNE

FRANCE

ST. JEAN-DE-LUZ

San Sebastian
(Besieged)

R. Niveille

D'Erlon

R. Nive

To Madrid

VERA

R. Bidassoa

Pass of Maya

Soult's
Retreat

Baztan Valley

ST. JEAN-
PIED-DE-PORT

Soult's
Offensive
25 July

ELIZONDO

SANTESTEBAN

P
y
r
e
n
e
e
s

Frontier

Pass of
Roncesvalles

·N·

D'Erlon

LIZASO   30 July

Hill

SPAIN

0   5   10
· Miles ·

Soult

SORAUREN   28,30 July

Wellington

THE · PYRENEES ·
· 1813 ·

PAMPLONA
(Blockaded)

can now see his good, honest, benevolent face shining with delight at the head of his table, enjoying the *scene* and the songs that went round until a late hour.[9]

The campaigning season opened in May 1813 with a dazzling display of Wellington on the offensive. He swept across northern Spain by repeatedly outflanking the positions occupied by the French, before turning inwards and falling on them at Vitoria on 21 June. Hill's role in this battle was to launch a diversionary attack on the Puebla heights in the west to draw in and weaken the French reserves. Wellington's other prongs would then emerge from the mountains and fall on the French northern flank. Hill was soon engaged in heavy fighting but gained the Puebla heights and held them against counter-attacks; by the end of the day, the French were shattered and streaming back towards the French frontier.

To consolidate his gains, Wellington resolved to take the Spanish cities of San Sebastian on the coast and Pamplona forty miles inland, which were still held by isolated French garrisons. To cover these operations, he had to spread his army out along the Spanish side of the Pyrenees. Hill's area of responsibility was the Baztan valley, twenty-five miles north of Pamplona, from which he drove the French early in July. Through this valley ran one of the three main roads across the western Pyrenees.

On 25 July Marshal Soult, sent by Napoleon to take command of all the French forces in the area, launched a surprise offensive through the Pyrenees in a bid to break the blockade of Pamplona. As part of this onslaught, a detached corps of 20,000 men under d'Erlon attacked through the Maya pass at the head of the Baztan valley. Hill reached the scene at the end of the day to find that his subordinates had mismanaged the situation and lost the pass. Being outnumbered, he ordered a retreat and concentrated his corps six miles farther back at Elizondo. Fortunately d'Erlon pursued feebly, but matters were more serious fifteen miles to the south-east, where the bulk of Soult's troops had broken through the pass at Roncesvalles. Sir Thomas Picton and Sir Lowry Cole thereupon retreated with the 3rd and 4th Divisions almost to Pamplona itself. Wellington arrived in the nick of time to check Soult at the Battle of Sorauren on the 28th. Hill, who had been ordered by Wellington to fall back southwards and join him, was delayed by a storm and on the 30th was still six miles to the north-west. It was on the 30th that Soult began to move north-westwards from Sorauren, intent on picking up d'Erlon's detached corps and retreating back to France. To cover the move, d'Erlon attacked Hill with superior numbers and drove him back about a mile. But Wellington meanwhile smashed the rest of Soult's army as it moved across his front at Sorauren and Hill subsequently helped to pursue the defeated French units back across the frontier.

Hill returned to his former task of covering the blockade of Pamplona, until released by the surrender of that city on 31 October. Meanwhile, the British Government suggested that he should be sent to take command of the British, Sicilian and Spanish troops in Catalonia on the Mediterranean coast of Spain, where Lieutenant-General Sir John Murray had been mishandling a diversionary operation against a French army under Marshal Louis Suchet. This independent command would have given Hill more scope for his talents, but Wellington could not spare him.

By this stage, Wellington had fought his way on to French soil and on 10 November broke out of the Pyrenees when he smashed through the French fortified lines above the Nivelle river. Hill commanded Wellington's eastern wing in this battle.

Wellington was now south of the city of Bayonne near the Atlantic coast, but was hemmed in between the sea to the west and the Nive river to the east. On 9 December he therefore pushed Hill's command over the Nive to occupy the east bank. Soult first counter-attacked Wellington on the west bank on 10–12 December and then on the 13th switched his attention to Hill on the other side. Heavy rains swelled the Nive and swept away a pontoon bridge, leaving Hill partly cut off. He had just 14,000 men, while Soult advanced against him with over 30,000. This, the Battle of St Pierre, was Hill's finest hour. Gone was his usual calm manner. He even swore, 'damn it, this won't do,' as he rode over to rally the 71st Light Infantry, which had been abandoned by its cowardly commander, Colonel Sir Nathaniel Peacocke. Wellington later remarked that if Hill had begun to swear, they must all mind what they were about. Another battalion commander also lost his nerve and retreated, but Hill was equal to it all: he personally rallied his units and led forward his reserves, just as Wellington would have done. Reinforcements began to reach Hill just as his counter-attack made the French retire. Wellington rode up but declined to take over command. 'My dear Hill,' he exclaimed, 'the day's your own.'[10] But the cost had been heavy: nearly 1,700 of Hill's men had been killed or wounded and few of his staff had escaped unhurt.

Hill served faithfully until the end of the Peninsular War but never again escaped from his master's shadow. Wellington resumed the offensive in the middle of February 1814 and pursued Soult's field army eastwards, away from the coast. He attacked Soult at the Battle of Orthez on 27 February, but Hill saw action only in the closing stages, when he outflanked Soult's position in the east and helped precipitate a rout. On 2 March he encountered 8,000 French troops on a ridge near the Aire river and drove them off. Later that month, he attacked again at Tarbes, but these were minor actions compared with the Battle of Toulouse on 10 April, which Wellington won after hard fighting. Hill made only a diversionary assault, but significantly, did exactly what was required of him, whereas Picton with the 3rd Division launched an all-out attack instead of a feint. Following the battle, Wellington received news from Paris of Napoleon's abdication, which shortly brought the Peninsular War to an end.

Honours and a warm welcome greeted Hill on his return home. On 1 June he accepted his seat in the House of Lords as Baron Hill of Almaraz and of Hawkstone (later of Hardwick Grange). To commemorate his achievements, a column 133 feet high was built just outside Shrewsbury and would be finished on 18 June 1816.[11]

Hill resolved to spend his remaining years on his Shropshire estate. He was not keen to accept command of an expedition against the Americans: Major-General Robert Ross went instead and was killed on his way to attack Baltimore. Hill was therefore in England when Napoleon escaped from exile on the island of Elba in the spring of 1815. Since Wellington was in Vienna, command of the Anglo-Dutch-German forces protecting the United Netherlands rested for the time being with the young and rash Prince of Orange, the heir to the Dutch throne. The British Cabinet, terrified lest the prince prematurely start an action on the French frontier, turned to Hill, who happened to be in London. He took it all in his stride, without any fuss. At dinner that day, he calmly told his sister, 'I cannot go to the opera with you this evening; I am off for the continent to-morrow morning.'[12] He reached Brussels on the evening of 1 April and kept matters under control until Wellington arrived on the 5th.

Hill was given command of the II Corps and posted in Flanders to guard Wellington's western flank and communications with Ostend on the Channel coast. But rather than attempt an encircling move, Napoleon on 15 June invaded at a point thirty miles south-east of Hill's headquarters in a bid to divide Wellington from his Prussian allies. Hill did not arrive in time for the battle Wellington fought against a wing of the French army at Quatre Bras on 16 June. But he visited the Duke at Quatre Bras on the following morning and Sergeant Duncan Robertson of the 92nd Highlanders recalled how:

> We all stood up and gave him three hearty cheers, as we had long been under his command in the Peninsula, and loved him dearly, on account of his kind and fatherly conduct towards us. When he came among us he spoke in a very kindly manner, and inquired concerning our welfare.[13]

The cheering so astonished Wellington that he hurriedly emerged from a little hut, thinking that it announced the approach of the French. He laughed when he realised the true cause.[14]

Wellington retreated later that day to take up a new position near the village of Waterloo and Hill's troops joined him there. For both Wellington and the British Army, the victory of Waterloo on the 18th was the climax of the Napoleonic wars. But not for Hill. Wellington exercised close, personal command over his whole army throughout the day. He divided his front into three sectors and placed Hill in charge of the western one. Wellington thought that Napoleon might try to outflank him to the west, but had the reliable Hill in a position to block such a move. Since Napoleon attacked only frontally, Hill did not cut so prominent a figure as Wellington's other senior subordinates. Scattered references in eyewitness accounts offer glimpses of him during the battle. Sergeant William Wheeler of the 51st Light Infantry remembered how Hill visited his regiment. He seemed tired, Wheeler thought, and he drank some water from one of the men's canteens.[15] He watched the fight from an exposed vantage point under heavy fire.

During the massed French cavalry charges in the afternoon, Wellington ordered Hill to bring forward some of his infantry from reserve in the west to reinforce the embattled centre. Hill sent Colonel du Plat's King's German Legion brigade to the front and personally brought up Major-General Frederick Adam's brigade of British light infantry.[16] Later on, he cheered a charge by the 13th Light Dragoons, who had served under his command in the Peninsula: 'at them, my old friends, the 13th.'[17]

He was with Adam's brigade when Napoleon's Guard attacked in the evening and suffered concussion and bad bruising when his horse was shot beneath him. His staff feared he was dead and were delighted when he rejoined them after half-an-hour. For much of the day, he had been in the thick of the action, but he barely features in accounts of the battle. No doubt he was content with Wellington's simple yet sincere praise in the Waterloo Despatch: 'I am also particularly indebted to General Lord Hill for his assistance and conduct upon this, as upon all former occasions.'[18]

No fewer than four of Hill's brothers served at Waterloo, one of them, Lieutenant-Colonel Clement Hill, as his ADC. All these brothers survived the battle, but two were wounded. Thoughtful as ever, Hill sent one of his siblings to the battlefield to find his horse, either to bury it if dead or put it out of its misery if wounded. It was dead: in fact, it had been shot in five places. Hill once again had escaped by a miracle.[19] Six days after the battle, he wrote to his sister: 'I verily believe there never was so tremendous a battle fought as that of Waterloo; and it is astonishing how any one could escape.'[20]

Afterwards, Hill marched with Wellington's triumphant army to Paris and following a spell of leave in England returned to France to serve as Second-in-Command of the allied Army of Occupation until the last troops withdrew in 1818. During these years, he had another narrow escape, this time while boar-hunting. When charged by a furious boar, he coolly waited until the right moment and then killed it with a spear thrust through the heart. Once his service in France was over, he retired to live as a country squire in his beloved Shropshire and although he remained Colonel of the 53rd Foot, he turned down offers of employment. Then, in 1825, he became a full general and apparently grew bored with his now inactive life. After all, he was still only in his mid-50s and in 1828 he welcomed his appointment as Commander-in-Chief of the British Army. Even now, he still worked under Wellington's shadow and influence. The Duke had been Commander-in-Chief before him and would re-assume the position in 1842. Hill strove to improve conditions for the soldiers and conscientiously handled routine matters such as the distribution of patronage. A political opponent observed in the House of Commons that:

> He felt bound as a soldier to bear his testimony to the honest and impartial manner in which Lord Hill had distributed the patronage of the army. He believed that never for one moment since that noble Lord had taken office had he given way to private feeling or political bias in his distribution of the army patronage at his disposal.[21]

Hill was as popular as ever and the Reverend Edwin Sidney, his biographer, commented that 'it was impossible to have any intercourse with him, and not to come away with a glow of kindly feeling.'[22] But Hill was forced by failing health and the pressures of the job to resign command of the Army in 1842 and after bring created viscount he died peacefully at Hardwick Grange on 10 December, aged 70. He had never married.

They buried the 'soldier's friend' at the little village church of Hadnall, four miles north-east of Shrewsbury. It was a private ceremony, but many people came in tribute and among them was a recruiting party of the 53rd Foot. This was one of Hill's old regiments and the men had come of their own accord to pay their respect as he passed by on his final journey.

'Daddy Hill'

Of Wellington's generals, none were so treasured in the hearts of the rank and file as 'Daddy Hill'. The historian Sir Charles Oman described him as 'a man brimming over with the milk of human kindness.'[23] His generosity to all who met him made him a legend throughout the army, but nowhere more so than in the 2nd Division, which he personally commanded from June 1809 to March 1813 and which afterwards remained as part of his corps. Every soldier of the division knew Hill as 'our father', which, commented Lieutenant Robert Blakeney, was 'a title more honourable than all the well-earned brilliant stars which decorated his breast.'[24] According to a subaltern of the 92nd Highlanders, Hill's sole delight:

> consisted in providing for his troops, – seeing them comfortable,

contented, and happy, – easing them at all times of as much fatigue as his duty would permit, – and, when an opportunity offered, in directing with proper effect their warlike energies against the enemy.[25]

Another officer wrote:

He was the very picture of an English country gentleman: to the soldiers who came from the rural districts of old England he represented *home*; his fresh complexion, placid face, kind eyes, kind voice, the absence of all parade or noise in his manner delighted them . . . His attention to all their wants and comforts, his visits to the sick in hospital, his vigilant protection of the poor peasantry, his just severity to marauders, his generous treatment of such French prisoners and wounded as fell into his hands, made for him a warm place in the hearts of his soldiery; and where'er the survivors of that army are now scattered, assuredly Hill's name and image are clearly cherished still.[26]

They loved Hill, too, for his sense of humour. James Hope of the 92nd Highlanders fondly remembered one Sunday during the Peninsular War. A young clergyman had just arrived from England and took divine service with the 2nd Division. A drum served as an altar, but the young man assumed it was there to enable the troops to see him and jumped on top of it:

When the first ebullition of surprise had subsided, a titter ran along the inside of the square like a running fire. Sir Rowland Hill preserved his gravity with difficulty, and General Chowne was forced to turn his back.[27]

Hill's approach worked wonders among the rank and file. As a British officer noted, 'the displeasure of Sir Rowland was worse to them than the loudest anger of other generals.'[28] Hill cared deeply for the lives of his soldiers, who used to say that 'with Hill, both life and victory may be ours.'[29] The same could not be said for some of Wellington's other generals, such as Picton or Craufurd.

Hill was a man of contrasts: the lover of animals, yet the keen hunter; the mild-mannered gentleman, yet the ruthless soldier. He sometimes acquired a different character in battle, for example when he suddenly drew his sword and led the charge at Arroyo dos Molinos. At other times, he was his usual, calm self. Rifleman Benjamin Harris recalled how at Roliça Hill rallied the brave but baffled soldiers of the 29th Foot, made them fire at the French and then had them charge:

It seemed to me that few men could have conducted the business with more coolness and quietude of manner, under such a storm of balls as he was exposed to. Indeed, I have never forgotten him from that day.[30]

No one knows how Hill would have fared in supreme command, in Wellington's shoes. But he demonstrated at Arroyo dos Molinos, at Almaraz and again at St Pierre than he was fully equal to the challenge of independent command. Nor did he resent his subordinate position. Wellington wrote:

More than thirty-five years have elapsed since I had the satisfaction of being first connected with and assisted by him in the public service; and I must say that, from that moment up to the latest period of his valuable and honourable life, nothing ever occurred to interrupt for one moment the friendly and intimate relations which subsisted between us.[31]

Hill was anxious to serve his country, but was not personally ambitious. Wellington even wondered: 'I am not quite sure that he does not shrink from responsibility.'[32] But he trusted him as he trusted few of his other generals. 'The best of Hill,' he observed, 'is that I always know where to find him.'[33]

The Battle of Arroyo dos Molinos: 28 October 1811

The situation in the Peninsula in the second half of 1811 was one of stalemate. Wellington had successfully cleared the French from Portugal but was not yet able to break out into Spain. Only in 1812 would the balance of forces swing more in his favour and permit a bold thrust deep into the interior. For the moment, he sought to capture the frontier fortresses of first Badajoz in the south and then Ciudad Rodrigo in the north and thus open the two principal invasion routes into Spain. Both attempts failed, as each time the French concentrated two of their armies against him and forced him to fall back.

But the threat to Ciudad Rodrigo in August did set off an important chain reaction. Marshal Auguste Marmont was keen to contain Wellington in Portugal, so he placed great importance on the fortress and assembled 58,000 men to relieve it. Marmont's concentration drew in one of his divisions from farther south and this left a gap in the French dispositions along the Portuguese border immediately south of the Tagus river. To compound this problem, about 3,600 Spanish troops under General Francisco Castaños were raiding in the area and threatening to cut communications between Marmont's Army of Portugal and Soult's

Army of the South in Andalusia. This forced an outlying part of Soult's army, the V Corps under General Jean-Baptiste Drouet, Count d'Erlon, to send General Jean-Baptiste Girard's division northwards to occupy the area between the Guadiana and the Tagus. This left Girard dangerously isolated, for the remainder of d'Erlon's over-extended corps lay on the other side of the Guadiana, with its headquarters thirty miles to the south of it at Zafra.

Hill, who at this time was guarding the southern corridor with a detached force, saw his chance. On 15 October he sought, and soon obtained, permission from Wellington to strike at Girard, who by now had swept back Castaños' Spaniards and reached the enticingly unplundered region around Caçeres, fifty miles north of the Guadiana. Girard had 5,000 infantry and almost 1,000 cavalry, plus one battery. Hill had to leave some of his 16,000 troops in Portugal to watch the rest of d'Erlon's corps. That left him with a strike force of 7,000 British and Portuguese infantry, besides 900 cavalry and two batteries.

Hill concentrated these troops on 22 October at Portalegre, just inside Portugal and forty miles north-west of Badajoz. Next day he marched eastwards for over twenty-five miles to Albuquerque. His Spanish allies informed him that Girard was still at Caçeres, forty miles to the north-east. On the 24th he therefore pushed over twenty miles north-eastwards to Aliseda, where he united with a contingent of Spanish allies: 2,000 infantry under Brigadier-General Pablo Morillo and 600 horsemen under General Penne Villemur. This brought his command to over 10,000 troops.

The Spanish cavalry drove in Girard's outposts on the 25th. Hill then advanced that night along atrocious roads up to Malpartida, eight miles from Caçeres, but learnt on the morning of the 26th that Girard had retreated southwards. It turned out that d'Erlon, having learnt from traitorous Spanish officers of Hill's intention, had ordered Girard to return from Caçeres to the town of Merida on the Guadiana. The over-confident Girard had initially dismissed d'Erlon's fears and only moved after the order had been repeated.[34]

Despite this setback, Hill resolved to pursue. He marched early on the 27th and learnt that Girard was heading for Arroyo Molinos de Montanchez. (This is the full, correct name of the village, although the battle honour is known officially as Arroyo dos Molinos.)[35] He was determined to make a forced march to cut Girard off and his men responded magnificently, marching twenty-eight miles through mountainous terrain in bad weather, while Girard covered only twelve. By nightfall Hill's leading units had reached Alcuescar, only five miles west of Girard at Arroyo. Hill had caught up with his quarry and now had to spring the surprise. Despite his numerous cavalry, Girard did not realise that his enemy was so near.

Hill's men fell out of their ranks to find what cover they could for the night on the exposed ground and had orders to parade at 2.00 am. 'A terrible stormy night, with strong wind, and abundance of rain, made our position truly miserable,' noted Captain Charles Cadell of the 28th Foot. 'Our tents were all blown down, and we were obliged to lie under those wet covers without having any thing warm to comfort us.'[36] No fires could be lit with the French so near and troops surrounded the nearby villages to prevent any pro-French inhabitants alerting Girard. In fact, these precautions failed to stop two Spanish collaborators from reaching Arroyo during the night. Luckily, Girard dismissed their warning.[37]

At 2.00 am on the 28th the order to march came in whispers. 'The whole night was one continual pour of rain,' remembered a soldier of the 71st Light Infantry. 'Weary and wet to the skin, we trudged on, without exchanging a word; nothing breaking the silence of the night save the howling of the wolves.'[38]

Hill's plan was to trap Girard against the steep, rugged slopes of the Sierra de Montanchez, a two-mile-long mountain range that overlooked the village of Arroyo from the east. Five roads left the village. One, heading northwards, was the route along which Girard had arrived the previous day. Another led westwards to Alcuescar: Hill would march along this road to reach Arroyo. That left three roads along which Girard could continue his retreat. The first led south-westwards to Merida and the second south-eastwards to Medellin. The third initially ran south-eastwards, but then swept round the end of the Sierra and headed for Trujillo in the north-east. Hill had to block all three of these roads to trap Girard. He decided to attack in two prongs. A frontal attack on Arroyo itself would be made from the west by a brigade of British infantry under Colonel Stewart[39], supported by Morillo's Spanish infantry and by three guns. Meanwhile, Hill's other British infantry brigade, led by Major-General Kenneth Howard and supported by three Portuguese battalions, would sweep round the village to the south and cut the roads. The British and Spanish cavalry, under Lieutenant-General Sir William Erskine, would operate between the two prongs in support.

By dawn Hill's force was less than half-a-mile from Arroyo. The rain blew from the direction of Hill's advance and made French sentries huddle under trees and turn their backs to the wind. Unknown to Hill, part of Girard's division had already left the village: a brigade of infantry and a cavalry regiment had marched off an hour earlier. But 4,000 men were still slowly filing out of it and preparing to move off and Girard himself, blissfully ignorant of the impending catastrophe, was at breakfast.

Suddenly, the leading British troops ran into a picket. Some of the Frenchmen managed to escape and raise the alarm. Hill ordered the 71st Light Infantry to clean the wet powder from the priming pans of their muskets and to form up in column. 'God be with you,' he called to them,

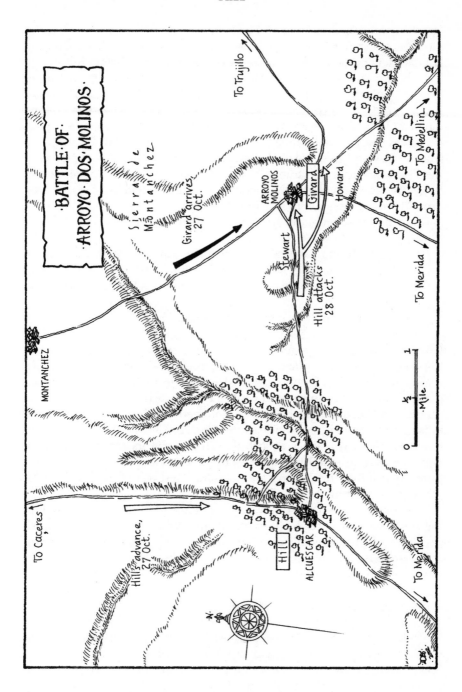

BATTLE·OF·
ARROYO·DOS·MOLINOS

'quick march.' It was 7.00 am. He drew his sword and with a shout of 'hurrah' spurred his horse forward. The 71st and the 92nd (Gordon) Highlanders burst into the village with orders to charge straight through it to the far side without stopping. Above the din came the wailing of bagpipes playing, appropriately enough, 'Hey, Johnnie Cope, are ye wakin' yet?' which commemorated Bonnie Prince Charlie's devastating dawn attack on Lieutenant-General Sir John Cope at Prestonpans in 1745.

Prince Prosper d'Aremberg, commander of the 27th Chasseurs à Cheval, was captured and Girard nearly shared the same fate. A soldier of the 71st saw him rush, frantic with rage, out of a house: 'never shall I forget the grotesque figure he made as he threw his cocked hat upon the ground and stamped on it, gnashing his teeth.'[40]

Duncan Robertson of the 92nd Highlanders noted that:

> Owing to the narrowness of the street, and the compact way in which we were at the time, their shot told with deadly effect. Our front section dashed forward at a rapid pace, and quickly dislodged them. The greatest uproar and confusion now prevailed in the town, and the work of death was going on at a fearful rate.[41]

Girard frantically tried to form his infantry in two hollow squares outside the eastern end of the village, hoping to march away covered by his two regiments of cavalry. But the 71st fired at them from the cover of some old garden walls, although in many cases the muskets refused to go off as the powder had been dampened by the rain. Then the 92nd emerged from the village and formed into line ready to charge Girard's flank. The High-landers boiled with rage as French shots felled officers and comrades, but were not permitted to reply until their line was complete. Three of Hill's guns opened up with canister and then the 92nd were finally unleashed, while the 71st vaulted the garden walls.

The French hurried off southwards along the Merida road, only to find their advance blocked by General Penne Villemur's gallant Spanish cavalry. Girard ordered his own outnumbered horsemen to charge to win time, while he and his infantry veered off to the east to gain the Trujillo road beneath the Sierra de Montanchez. The French cavalry, checked by Villemur's Spaniards, were overthrown following the belated arrival of some British hussars and light dragoons.

Meanwhile, Hill's other prong had been advancing round the south of the village and now sent forward three British light infantry companies to dash ahead, cut the Trujillo road and trap Girard against the mountains. Some French guns dashed past, but Hill ordered the light companies to press on and leave them to be captured by the 13th Light Dragoons. Hill, galloping on ahead with an ADC, was joined by the light companies on the Trujillo road just as the French infantry column came up. He forbade the men to fire and ordered a bayonet charge in order to win time for reinforcements to arrive. Lieutenant Robert Blakeney of the 28th Foot gallantly led the charge.

Girard could have swept these three light companies aside by sheer weight of numbers, but lost his nerve and ordered his troops to escape over the mountains on their left. His men scrambled up the steep slopes. The rain had now ceased and the spirits of Hill's men soared. 'The weather was very fine, and it was a most gratifying sight for us to see the enemy scampering up the mountain in every direction,' wrote Charles Cadell.

Many of Girard's men found themselves below sheer cliffs, trapped on both sides by Hill's troops and forced to surrender. But Girard himself and 500 men successfully reached the top of the heights and made off, pursued by Morillo's bloodthirsty Spaniards. 'The enemy's troops were by this time in the utmost panic,' reported Hill. 'His cavalry was flying in every direction, the infantry threw away their arms, and the only effort of either was to escape.'[42]

Ensign George Bell of the 34th Foot remembered the scene vividly. 'A thick mist rolled down the craggy steep mountain behind the town,' he noted. 'There was a terrifying cheer, such as is not known except among British troops on the battleground; it drowned the clatter of musketry.'[43] Another subaltern recalled that 'our share of the business, among the rocks, was a scene of laughter and diversion, rather than of bloodshed and peril.' He and his comrades chased the French closely and 'quite mixed with them, and made prisoners at every step; until the number of pursuers being diminished by exhaustion and fatigue, and being encumbered with arms, ammunition, and knapsacks, all which such of the enemy as escaped threw from them, we desisted from the pursuit.'[44]

Hill had triumphed once more. He had inflicted losses of about 500 killed and an unknown number of wounded. He had taken 1,300 prisoners and half a battery and temporarily cut communications between the Army of Portugal and the Army of the South. All this had cost him merely seven dead, sixty-four wounded and one missing; his Spanish allies had lost another thirty men. As a result of the action, the 2nd Division won the nickname 'The Surprisers', while the 34th Foot captured all the drums belonging to the French 34th Regiment. Hill had truly earned the knighthood that he won for the action, but modestly wrote that:

> It certainly proved more fortunate than I had reason to calculate upon. I was always confident that there could be no difficulty in dislodging Girard from Caceres, but I feared that as I advanced he would walk off.[45]

Girard himself had been wounded in the action, but he and 400 or 500 of his men eventually made their way back through the mountains to rejoin d'Erlon's corps. The three regiments which had marched from Arroyo an hour before Hill attacked also escaped. Hill vainly pursued them up to Merida, before falling back and entering Portalegre in early November, to the cheers of the inhabitants.

Major Moyle Sherer concluded:

> One thing in our success at Arroyo de Molinos gratified our division highly; it was a triumph for our General, a triumph *all his own*. He gained great credit for this well-conducted enterprise, and he gained what, to one of his mild, kind, and humane character, was still more valuable, a solid and [relatively] bloodless victory.[46]

NOTES

1   E. Sidney, *The life of Lord Hill, G.C.B.* (1845), p.16
2   *Ibid*, p.6
3   *Ibid*, pp.7–8
4   *Ibid*, p.8
5   C. Oman, *A history of the Peninsular war* (1902–30), v.2, p.517
6   E. Longford, *Wellington: the years of the sword* (1969), p.194
7   G. Gleig, *The life of the Duke of Wellington* (1939), p.334
8   R. Blakeney, *A boy in the Peninsular war* (1899), p.214
9   G. Bell, *Rough notes by an old soldier during fifty years' service* (1867), v.1, pp.78–9
10 Longford, *op. cit.*, p.338
11 A sketch of the column appears in *The Gentleman's Magazine* (July–December 1817), p.393
12 J. Cole, *Memoirs of British generals distinguished during the Peninsular war* (1856), v.2, p.219
13 D. Robertson, *The journal of Sergeant D. Robertson* (1982), pp.149–50
14 J. Hope, *The military memoirs of an infantry officer* (1833), pp.416–17
15 B. Liddell Hart, ed., *The letters of Private Wheeler 1809–1828* (1951), p.174
16 W. Siborne, *History of the Waterloo campaign* (1990), pp.299, 301
17 H. Siborne, ed., *The Waterloo letters* (1983), p.137
18 A Near Observer, *The battle of Waterloo* (1816), p.164
19 Sidney, *op. cit.*, pp.307, 311–12
20 Cole, *op. cit.*, v.2, p.220
21 *The Gentleman's Magazine* (January–June 1843), p.531
22 Sidney, *op. cit.*, p.394
23 C. Oman, *Wellington's army 1809–1814* (1993), p.115
24 Blakeney, *op. cit.*, p.368
25 Hope, *op. cit.*, p.338
26 Sidney, *op. cit.*, p.228–9
27 Hope, *op. cit.*, pp.192–3
28 Sidney, *op. cit.*, pp.228–9
29 *The Gentleman's Magazine* (January–June 1843), p.532
30 C. Hibbert, ed., *The recollections of Rifleman Harris* (1985), p.16
31 Sidney, *op. cit.*, p.389
32 Second Duke of Wellington, ed., *Supplementary despatches, correspondence, and*

memoranda of Field Marshal Arthur Duke of Wellington, K.G. (1858–64), v.8, p.547

33   G. Moore Smith, *The life of John Colborne* (1903), p.140
34   See J. Drouet d'Erlon, *Vie militaire* (1844), p.69
35   See J. Fortescue, *History of the British army* (1899–1930), v.8, p.272
36   C. Cadell, *Narrative of the campaigns of the Twenty-Eighth Regiment* (1835), p.115
37   Blakeney, *op. cit.*, p.236; George Wrottesley, *Life and correspondence of Field Marshal Sir John Burgoyne* (1873), v.1, p.148
38   C. Hibbert, ed., *A soldier of the Seventy-First* (London, 1975), p.68
39   Confusingly, the commander of this brigade was Major-General Howard, but in this action he instead led the other British infantry brigade.
40   Hibbert, *A soldier of the Seventy-First*, p.69
41   Robertson, *op. cit.*, p.79
42   C. Kelly, *The battle of Waterloo* (1831), p.455
43   Bell, *op. cit.*, v.1, p.16
44   M. Sherer, *Recollections of the Peninsula* (1827), pp.236–7
45   A. Delavoye, *Life of Thomas Graham* (1880), p.613
46   Sherer, *op. cit.*, p.241

CHAPTER VII
Archduke Charles

That Archduke Charles was the foremost Austrian general of the Napoleonic era has never been disputed. Yet despite his physical bravery in battle, he tended to be cautious, indecisive and unable to hide his bouts of despondency. It is difficult to avoid the conclusion that he has been seriously over-estimated as a commander.

Charles was born on 5 September 1771 in the Italian city of Florence. He was the third son of Grand Duke Leopold of Tuscany and Maria Ludovica, the daughter of King Charles III of Spain. Although his paternal grandmother was the Austrian Empress Maria Theresa, he and his family led an unostentatious lifestyle in Tuscany. He spent a happy, loving and unrestrained childhood, and was often rolling around in the grass and shouting himself hoarse as he played with some of his fifteen brothers and sisters. His aunt wrote to Maria Theresa that 'Charles, the third son, is the most delightful child of the whole family. He is small, but strong and very lovely.'[1]

Even as a boy, Charles wanted to be a soldier and took a lively interest when the conversation turned to battles or sieges or when he heard the beating of a drum or saw soldiers passing by. But his father shared none of his love for the military: he disbanded nearly the whole of his small Tuscan Army and refused Charles's requests to be allowed to drill. Nonetheless, Charles was encouraged by the enthusiasm of his older brothers' military tutor, Major Federigo Manfredini, and his assistant, Lieutenant Lelio Spanocchi.

Charles enjoyed perfect health until in March 1779 he had a feverish cold, during which he suffered the first of the epileptic attacks that would plague him for the rest of his life. His illness hardened him mentally by contributing to a certain isolation and loneliness and he later complained bitterly of the unsympathetic attitude of most of his tutors. He trained himself to suppress his emotions and formed a set of principles to guide him through life. He also tried to gain physical toughness through exercise on both foot and horse.

Empress Maria Theresa died in 1780 and was succeeded by Charles's uncle, Emperor Joseph II. After Joseph's death in February 1790, Charles's father became Emperor Leopold II. Charles accordingly went to live in Vienna. The change of climate from sunny Tuscany caused him initially to suffer from rheumatic fever and whooping cough, but he devoted these months of enforced inactivity to studying the military profession. His father subsequently allowed him to attend meetings of the Bohemian and Hungarian Court Chancelleries, which gave him at a young age valuable experience of political and military administration.

When Leopold died in March 1792, Charles's older brother, Francis, succeeded to the throne. That same year, Charles also lost his mother and was therefore adopted by his aunt and uncle, Field Marshal Duke Albert of Saschen-Teschen, the joint governors of the Austrian Netherlands, an area roughly corresponding to modern Belgium and Luxembourg. He now received professional military guidance from Colonel Carl von Lindenau, a former adjutant to Frederick the Great of Prussia who had won something of a reputation with his books on tactics but whose conservative influence contributed to Charles's overly methodical approach to war.

Charles soon saw action, for Revolutionary France after declaring war in April 1792 sought to seize the Austrian Netherlands. Following a failed offensive in the spring, General Charles Dumouriez invaded with the Army of the North in the autumn. The Austrians were commanded by Duke Albert of Saschen-Teschen and Charles had his baptism of fire in November at the Battle of Jemappes near Mons. He acquitted himself well in command of a brigade, despite being only 21. But the French won Jemappes through sheer weight of numbers and induced the Austrians to fall right back towards Cologne in the north-east, abandoning Brussels.

After a harsh winter which seriously degraded his army, Dumouriez was ordered to invade Holland early in 1793. But he was forced to retreat when 40,000 Austrians under Field Marshal Prince Josias von Coburg-Saalfeld advanced from the area of Cologne against his right rear. Charles at his own request commanded Coburg's advanced guard and won distinction when he defeated 9,000 French troops at Aldenhoven on 1 March. It was here that he proved his fitness to command and won the confidence of the Austrian rank and file with his courage under fire. He surprised the French by attacking over the crest of a ridge and quickly drove them from their entrenchments. 'These French think they are invincible,' he exclaimed to the Latour Regiment of dragoons. 'It's up to you, brave Walloons, to make them flee!'[2] The French lost 2,000 men and retreated westwards, abandoning the siege of Maastricht.[3]

Dumouriez counter-attacked Coburg with 45,000 troops at Neerwinden on 18 March, a fiercely contested battle in which Charles was heavily engaged. Dumouriez was routed, but only after Charles had helped dissuade the lacklustre Coburg from conceding defeat. As a result of Neerwinden, Dumouriez negotiated a convention to allow his units to retreat safely back to France in return for abandoning the Austrian Netherlands; fearing for his life as a result of his defeat, he then deserted to the allies. But Coburg cautiously renounced a thrust on Paris and instead began methodically reducing and masking the frontier fortresses. Charles was appointed Governor-General of the Austrian Netherlands and his new responsibilities sometimes prevented him from accompanying the army.

The French now rallied, defeated Coburg at the Battle of Wattignies in October 1793 and relieved the fortress of Maubeuge. The following year, they exploited allied disunity and poor co-operation to regain the Austrian Netherlands with a series of victories. One of the key battles was Tourcoing near Lille. The allies made the error of attacking on 17 May in six widely separated columns and became increasingly vulnerable to counter-attack. Orders arrived that night for Charles to march his column northwards to help support two of the others, but he had been incapacitated by an epileptic attack. His staff not only refused to wake him, but failed to take action themselves. By the time he had recovered next day, the battle had been lost.

A month later, Charles commanded the left wing of Coburg's army at the viciously contested Battle of Fleurus, twenty-six miles south of Brussels. Coburg was outnumbered, failed to concentrate his assaults and eventually ordered a retreat. By the end of August 1794, the Austrians along with their Dutch and British allies had been driven from Belgium for good.

By the time an armistice was agreed in autumn 1795, Charles was on leave to recover from nervous strain. He pondered the lessons of the recent fighting and suggested in his treatise, *On war against the new Franks*, that the Austrians had lost principally because of the caution, defensive-mindedness and egotism of their commanders.

Such problems were exemplified by the intrigues against Field Marshal Charles von Clerfayt, who had replaced Coburg in the autumn of 1794 and who now commanded the Austrian Army on the Lower Rhine. Charles took an active part in these intrigues and on Clerfayt's removal in February 1796, was appointed to replace him at the age of 24. In May, after taking up his command, he produced a set of directions, *Observationspunkte*, to instruct his senior officers on tactics against the French and encourage them to train their troops in using initiative. Unfortunately, he lacked sufficient time to enforce the application of his ideas and was saddled with mediocre and sometimes unco-operative subordinates.

Initially, two Austrian armies defended the Rhine river: one under Charles in the north and another under General Dagobert Wurmser in the south. But in the middle of June Wurmser left with 25,000 of his men to help defend northern Italy against Napoleon Bonaparte. Charles, who also took over the troops that Wurmser left behind, now had 130,000 men and was the sole Austrian commander in this theatre. However, his authority was limited by the suspicious Emperor Francis. In particular, he was obliged to heed his senior subordinates in the councils-of-war that according to Austrian regulations had to be held on important issues.

The French, in contrast to the Austrians, fielded two armies on the Rhine, under Generals Jean Moreau (78,000 men) and Jean-Baptiste Jourdan (72,000). Their aim was to encircle Charles with a two-pronged offensive, but they were not subject to an overall commander and co-operated poorly.

Jourdan made the first move, when he crossed the Rhine at Düsseldorf in the north and advanced until checked by Charles at Wetzlar on 15 June. He then fell back, but had enabled Moreau to cross the Rhine 200 miles farther south at Strasbourg. Charles detached 36,000 men under General Alexander Wartensleben to watch Jourdan and marched south to meet Moreau. Jourdan naturally resumed the offensive in the north, defeated Wartensleben and pressed eastwards.

Charles steadily retreated across southern Germany, leaving behind 30,000 troops tied up in the garrisons of Mainz and Mannheim in the vain hope that the French would detach a large force against these fortresses. He also lost 10,000 troops which had been contributed by some of the German states of the Holy Roman Empire, but whose rulers defected in the face of the French advance. Despite these problems, and despite Wartensleben's refusal to join him in the south, Charles turned at bay and on 11 August clashed indecisively with Moreau at Neresheim, 100 miles east of the Rhine. He then retired south-eastwards across the Danube, followed by Moreau who thus drew away from Jourdan in the north. This allowed Charles to launch a masterly counter-stroke. First, he detached General Maximilien Baillet de Latour with 35,000 men to observe Moreau. Then, with his remaining 28,000, he recrossed the Danube and marched north to join Wartensleben and tackle Jourdan. He beat a French division on 22 August and two days later thrashed Jourdan himself at Amberg. Jourdan retreated ninety miles westwards to Würzburg, where he suffered a further defeat on 3 September. He then withdrew to the Rhine, pursued by Charles and harassed by local inhabitants antagonised by French looting. Charles continually outflanked Jourdan by marching along a better road to the south and could thereby prevent him from trying to join Moreau.

Charles switched back to the southern sector, where Latour had suffered a reverse. Moreau withdrew on hearing of Jourdan's defeats and was twice beaten by Charles towards the end of October before pulling back across the Rhine. When the French requested an armistice in this theatre, Charles wanted to accept, but was overruled by Vienna, which insisted that he take the last two French-held fortresses on the Rhine. This was done in the first weeks of 1797. For Charles, it was a triumphant end

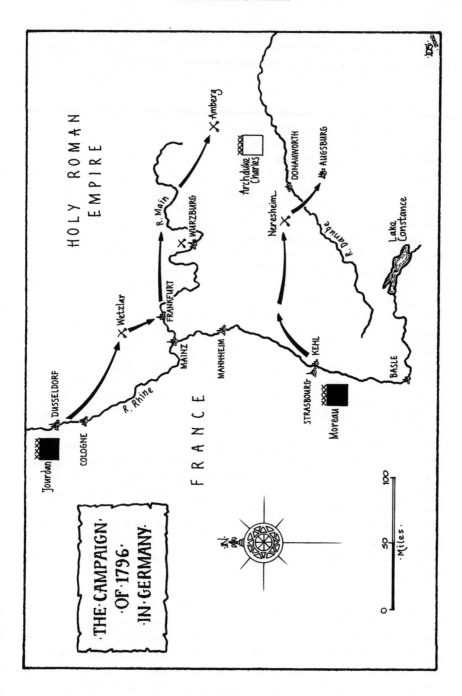

to a campaign in which he had used his central position to outmanoeuvre his two opponents and beat them piecemeal. The campaign would be much analysed by admirers and he himself wrote *The principles of strategy illustrated by the description of the campaign of 1796 in Germany*, a three-volume work published in 1814.

But while Charles had been winning a reputation on the Rhine, the young Napoleon Bonaparte had inflicted a series of defeats on the Austrian army in northern Italy. Charles as a result was transferred to this front in February 1797 to replace General Josef Alvintzy and try to prevent an invasion of Austria herself. It was unfortunate that he had to leave Germany, where he had so distinguished himself, and measure himself against a more dangerous opponent. Furthermore, he was attacked in March before he and his demoralised troops were ready. He retreated, convinced that he could do no more than save his army from destruction. He abandoned the line of the Tagliamento river and lost heavily in a series of piecemeal actions, without significantly delaying the French. Napoleon's leading units actually reached the Semmering pass, just seventy-five miles south of Vienna.

In fact, the Austrian situation was better than Charles realised, for Napoleon's rapid advance had over-extended his lines of communication. Napoleon, having outrun his supplies, wrote to Charles at the end of March and cynically suggested an armistice to end the bloodshed. Charles readily passed the message to Vienna, where initial resolve had weakened as the French approached. Following the preliminary Peace of Leoben that April, Austria lost both prestige and territory under the Treaty of Campo Formio in October.

In December Charles was appointed Governor and Captain-General of the province of Bohemia, based in Prague. Fifteen months later, in March 1799, Austria again went to war with Revolutionary France, this time as part of a coalition including Britain and Russia. Napoleon at this time was leading an expedition in Egypt and Syria, but in his absence three French armies took the offensive against the Austrians in southern Germany, Switzerland and northern Italy.

Jourdan, who commanded the northernmost of these armies, crossed the Rhine with 40,000 troops and thrust eastwards through the Black Forest. His opponent, once again, was Archduke Charles, who was now at the head of the 72,000-strong Austrian army in southern Germany. Charles slowly advanced westwards between the Alps in the south and the Danube in the north. On 21 March he clashed with the French and drove them from the position of Ostrach, but did not pursue. Four days later, he decided to occupy the strategic crossroads at Stockach, at the northern end of Lake Constance. The battle that ensued initially swung against Charles, until the arrival of reinforcements gave him superior numbers. He instantly counter-attacked at the head of his troops, assuming personal command because of the ineptitude of several of his generals and exposing himself to such danger that he was urged by his men to retire. Although he finally won the battle, he suffered heavier casualties and again failed to pursue.

When Charles finally advanced towards the Rhine, he was halted by an order from Vienna. The *Hofkriegsrat*, or Palace War Council, wanted him to wait until the French Army of Helvetia under General André Massena had evacuated Switzerland farther south. Charles in any case was aghast at the thought of another battle like Stockach and went on leave to recover from nervous strain before rejoining his army.

In May 1799 Charles disobeyed his orders and, after detaching 20,000 men to cover southern Germany, linked up with 25,000 Austrian troops already operating in Switzerland under General Friedrich von Hotze. Massena, who had united Jourdan's survivors with his own army, withdrew to a fortified position in the mountains immediately north of Zürich. Charles attacked him here on 4 June, but was repelled with heavy casualties and merely induced Massena to abandon Zürich and withdraw his centre to an even more dominating position. Charles occupied the city on the 6th, but wisely declined to resume his attacks.

A two-month lull ensued. Vienna again intervened following strategic discussions with Britain and Russia, her coalition partners. The allied armies were to be re-arranged in accordance with a plan originating with the British Foreign Secretary, Lord William Grenville. Charles was to move north, being replaced in Switzerland by Russian forces, including those currently operating under Field Marshal Prince Alexander Suvorov in northern Italy, where the Austrians were keen to re-establish their former dominance. The Russians were meant to drive Massena from Switzerland and then attack into France itself. Charles, meanwhile, was to relieve the fortress of Philippsburg, capture Mannheim and cross the Rhine into France, partly to distract the enemy from the landing of an Anglo-Russian expedition under the Duke of York in Holland.

Meanwhile, Massena had become active again in the middle of August. Charles saw an opportunity to threaten his northern flank and communications with France by crossing the Aare river at Döttingen, nineteen miles north-west of Zürich. On the morning of 17 August, he had nearly 45,000 men in position, but found that his staff had miscalculated the number of pontoons necessary to bridge the river. Then the mist lifted and the pontoniers were shot down by light infantrymen posted on the far bank. An hour later, the French had assembled 10,000 troops, obliging Charles to abandon the attack and all hope of forcing Massena to evacuate Switzerland.[4]

Twelve days later, Charles began marching northwards. He left behind Hotze with 18,000 troops to help 28,000 Russians under General Alexander Rimski-Korsakov hold Switzerland until Suvorov's 20,000 men could arrive from northern Italy. But in Charles's absence, the French drubbed the outnumbered Korsakov and Hotze and then forced Suvorov to make a desperate fighting retreat over the mountains to safety. As Charles had foreseen, his premature removal from Switzerland resulted in the loss of that key strategic region to the French. He himself in his operations farther north briefly took Mannheim before falling back, while the Duke of York was forced to withdraw from Holland by the end of November.

Fighting died down, but strained nerves caused Charles to retire to Bohemia in February 1800. In his absence, an armistice was concluded in June. But, against his advice, the Austrians renewed hostilities in November and were quickly worsted, suffering a particularly serious defeat at Hohenlinden, twenty miles east of Munich. Charles in these circumstances could not be left inactive and on 17 December replaced one of his brothers, the 18-year-old Archduke John, as commander of the Austrian army in southern Germany. But as Moreau's Army of the Rhine thrust eastwards on Vienna, Charles saw that the situation was hopeless and within a week secured an armistice that led to the Peace of Lunéville in February 1801.

Despite the disappointing end to the war, Charles's popularity was at its height. Since his 1796 campaign, he had been hailed as the Saviour of Germany and the *Diet*, or noble assembly, of the Holy Roman Empire wanted to erect a statue in his honour.[5] In January 1801 he was appointed Field Marshal and president of the *Hofkriegsrat* by his brother, the Emperor Francis, and given a mandate to produce a plan for military reform.

Charles believed that the worst problems lay not with the Army itself, but with the bureaucratic and over-centralised Government and administrative machinery. A *Staats und Konferenz Ministerium* was duly set up to try and provide more co-ordination of internal and external affairs and within this organisation Charles was entrusted with the War Ministry, with responsibility for the Army and Navy. Although such changes made for greater administrative efficiency, they proved short-lived for Charles and his reforms antagonised entrenched reactionary interests. Charles through his powerful position and reluctance to confine himself to strictly military matters also aroused the suspicious nature of the Emperor Francis, who was wary of too much authority being concentrated in one person. It did not help that Charles outshone Francis in intellect and often also in popularity; relations between the two had been tense since 1797.

Only some of Charles's reforms were aimed directly at improving the Army, but were generally sensible if cautious measures. For example, he managed against opposition to reduce the term of enlistment from life to between ten and fourteen years, partly to rejuvenate the ranks and partly to increase the popularity of military service. Another significant step was the establishment in 1801 of the Quartermaster-General Staff on a permanent footing, it hitherto having been active only in wartime. Nonetheless, it remained too small and unsystematic and only became truly effective by 1813.

Although his reforms were limited and needed time to take effect, Charles from 1803 onwards was confronted by an increasingly powerful war party in Vienna. He knew that Austria was not ready to resume hostilities with France (where Napoleon had seized power), but was outmanoeuvred by his opponents, led by General Karl Mack von Leiberich. Charles remained as War Minister, but lost effective power and the *Hofkriegsrat*, which he had subordinated to the War Ministry, was restored to its former status early in 1805. In April that year, Mack was appointed Quartermaster-General, or Chief-of-Staff, and hurriedly reformed the Army's tactics and organisation in the last few months of peace. Unfortunately, as Charles had anticipated, this merely confused the situation, since the new methods were applied inconsistently through the Army because of the lack of time.

A Third Coalition of allied powers took shape in 1805, intent on renewing hostilities on the continent and crushing Napoleon's Empire. The Austrians were keen to regain lost territory in northern Italy and assigned Charles with their main army of over 90,000 men to Venetia, their remaining Italian province. A further 22,000 Austrian troops under Archduke John were in the mountainous Tyrol region, covering Charles's northern flank, while another secondary army, under Mack, was on the Danube north of the Alps. Charles believed that Italy would see the key fighting, not least as it offered the shortest route to Vienna. But Napoleon instead took the offensive in the Danube valley north of the Alps, quickly forcing Mack's army to surrender at Ulm in October, taking Vienna and decisively crushing the Russians at Austerlitz on 2 December.

Charles, meanwhile, had been pessimistic from the start. His opponent in northern Italy was his old enemy, Marshal Massena. Charles had fortified a position on a ridge at Caldiero, six miles east of the city of Verona. Flooded ricefields guarded the plain to the south up to the Adige river, while the Alpine foothills made the position difficult to outflank to the north. Massena attacked, but was numerically inferior and, despite bitter fighting on 29 and 30 October, achieved nothing. On the 31st he tried to outflank Charles by an assault across the Adige, but was again checked.

Charles then received news of Mack's disaster at Ulm and on 1 November began to retreat north-eastwards, pursued by Massena. He united with Archduke John's units from the Tyrol, but was too distant to prevent the allied defeat at Austerlitz. Emperor Francis secured an armistice on 4 December and on the 23rd sent Charles to try and obtain milder peace terms for Austria. In fact, all such entreaties were in vain and the Peace of Pressburg was signed early on the 27th. Charles had an interview with Napoleon that day at which they discussed military matters at length. Napoleon even offered to make Charles the Austrian emperor, but Charles declined to usurp his brother.

In contrast to the disgraced Mack, Charles had emerged with his reputation intact. His prospects immediately rose again. In February 1806 he was appointed Generalissimo, the supreme commander of the Austrian armed forces, with authority over the *Hofkriegsrat*, and initiated another period of reform. This time, he concentrated directly on improving the Army rather than repeating his attempt to overhaul the Empire's administrative machinery, but there were limits to what he could achieve. The financial drain of over seven years of war since 1792 and the loss of large tracts of territory in successive peace treaties had seriously weakened the Austrian economy. Charles was spied on by the Emperor Francis, intrigued against by opponents and hindered by resistance within the Army to the implementation of his changes.

He himself was conservative by instinct and unwilling to push through radical measures that might have threatened the stability of the Habsburg monarchy. He had to strike a balance and guard against the external threat from Napoleon without undermining the Austrian Empire's internal supports, the foremost of which was a professional, long-service Army set apart from the rest of society and led predominantly by aristocratic senior officers. Thus he did not attempt to make the officer corps less socially exclusive. Nor did he favour the idea of raising militias, partly because he sensibly doubted their combat value and partly because he feared that they would give the people access to weapons and training that might subsequently be used in revolts. He finally accepted the creation of the *Landwehr*, or national militia, in June 1808 only because its potential threat to the Habsburg monarchy was outweighed by both the danger from Napoleon and the greater cost of expanding the regular Army. Even then, the *Landwehr* was not raised in regions where the loyalty of the Empire's subject peoples was suspect.

More positively, Charles tried to improve the often brutal life of the rank and file in order to boost morale and make army service more attractive. In 1807, for example, he abolished capital punishment, although he would find himself obliged to reinstate it in the middle of the 1809 campaign. He also reversed some of the less successful changes that Mack had made to regimental organisation and he added two reserve battalions to each of the Army's German infantry regiments to alleviate the problems of finding trained replacements in time of war. Charles addressed the shortage of light infantry by creating nine new *Jäger* battalions and he designated the third rank of line battalions to deploy as skirmishers when necessary. But Austrian skirmishers still lacked the spontaneity and aggressiveness of their French counterparts, being over-drilled and over-controlled.

Drawing on his experience of fighting the French, Charles directed the publication of a series of tactical manuals to instruct his officers. He also produced new regulations. Those for the infantry were introduced in 1807, but were not radically new, did little to simplify the notoriously complicated drill and in many cases simply recognised changes that had already been made informally. Charles notably retained the three-deep line as a standard formation for both attack and defence. But he did add a degree of flexibility in tactics by prescribing some use of assault columns. He also formally introduced the mass, a column of infantry, usually a battalion strong, that could be closed up to form a tightly packed body of troops. This formation was vulnerable to artillery fire but capable of beating off cavalry and of manoeuvring more readily than the hollow square and would prove effective in 1809.

Although Charles produced new regulations for the cavalry, he did not substantially alter its tactics, nor solve its shortage of men and horses. In contrast, he introduced significant changes for the artillery. Hitherto, most of the Austrian guns had been distributed among the infantry regiments. In one of his most effective reforms, Charles increased the number of field guns to 760 and created eight-gun batteries which were assigned to infantry and cavalry brigades and also to corps level as a reserve. This allowed the Austrian artillery to be concentrated more readily into powerful massed batteries, although unimaginative officers often failed to appreciate the potential for this.

Charles also turned his attention to the high command. In 1805 and during previous campaigns, the Army had lacked any permanent formations higher than the regiment. Charles belatedly introduced corps on the French model when the Army mobilised in February 1809, just two months before the outbreak of war. Each corps had between 10,000 and 30,000 men, with its own staff and a combination of infantry, cavalry and artillery organised into permanent divisions. This new organisation made the Army more flexible and resilient, but to work to its full potential required bold and energetic corps commanders capable of using initiative. Charles never had enough generals with the necessary experience or confidence, while the Austrian staff lacked the efficiency and systematic training to compensate for this. Nor did he attempt to instruct his generals through large-scale manoeuvres, partly because of the financial cost of such exercises. In 1808 he helped found *Österreichisch-militärische Zeit-schrifte*, a journal intended to educate the officer corps using examples from military history, but whether it had any significant impact is doubtful. He himself failed whole-heartedly to embrace Napoleon's more aggressive methods of war, as he showed in *Principles of the higher art of war for generals of the Austrian Army*, a work published under his name in

1806 and which for the most part advocated the conventional principles of eighteenth-century strategy.

In short, Charles's reforms were limited and had little time to take effect. The Austrian Army therefore remained slow-moving and poorly led, but nonetheless would prove a more robust opponent in 1809 than it had been four years earlier. To a minister who subsequently ridiculed Austrian military prowess, Napoleon would remark: 'it is evident you were not at [the Battle of] Wagram.'[6]

Charles had rightly argued against joining Prussia and Russia in the campaigns of 1806–7, which ended victoriously for Napoleon. But the war party, led by Emperor Francis's wife Ludovica, was still determined to avenge Austria's defeat of 1805. At the end of 1808 Napoleon was trying to subdue Spain over 1,000 miles away and this seemed so good an opportunity that on 23 December Austria secretly resolved to go to war, a decision that received final confirmation in February 1809.

The Austrians, learning from 1805, intended to make the Danube their main theatre of war. They would send only two corps under Archduke John into northern Italy, while Charles himself remained with six regular and two reserve corps on the Danube. Another corps, supported by *Landwehr*, would operate in the north under Archduke Ferdinand d'Este against one of Napoleon's satellite states, the Duchy of Warsaw, while also keeping an eye on Russia, which had an alliance with Napoleon but in practice was neutral.

Charles initially planned to advance north of the Danube from Bohemia into central Germany, seconded by just two of his eight corps on the south bank of the river. But, assailed by doubts, he reverted to his usual caution, particularly when it became clear that Prussian support would not be forthcoming. Despite opposition from his Chief-of-Staff, who was promptly replaced, he decided that the bulk of his forces would operate south of the Danube in the corridor between that river and the Alps, mainly so as to keep Vienna fully covered. He accordingly reversed his plan, with six corps on the south bank and only two in support to the north. It was a safer strategy, but one less likely to deliver the quick and decisive blow that Charles needed. It took a month to transfer the troops across the Danube, time that Napoleon used to begin to build up his forces in southern Germany.

Hostilities broke out on 10 April, when Charles invaded Bavaria, Napoleon's ally. He had over 200,000 men, whereas only 170,000 of Napoleon's troops were in southern Germany and most of them were either French conscripts or German auxiliaries. Unfortunately, the Austrian Army upheld its reputation for slow-marching and the weather was bad. But Napoleon was not yet personally present and his absence led to his Chief-of-Staff, Marshal Alexandre Berthier, mismanaging the concentration of the army, so that his troops were grouped into two wings

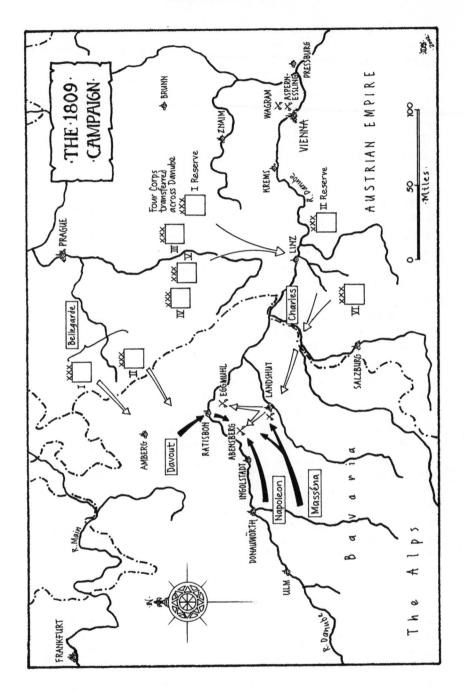

around Ratisbon in the north-east and Augsburg in the south-west. In between was a gap of seventy miles, covered only by 30,000 Bavarian troops. Charles advanced up the Danube valley, pushed back the Bavarians and was in a perfect position to penetrate the gap, separate the two wings of Napoleon's army and defeat them piecemeal. The situation when Napoleon arrived on 17 April was critical, but the Austrians did not move fast enough to exploit it.

There followed five days of fighting. On the 19th Charles saw a chance to crush Marshal Louis Davout's isolated III Corps at the city of Ratisbon on the Danube. He hoped to crush Davout against one of the two Austrian corps operating north of the river and therefore moved northwards on Ratisbon with three of his corps. But his move was executed too slowly. On Napoleon's orders, Davout left a small garrison in Ratisbon and successfully fought his way eight miles south-westwards to link up with the Bavarians in the centre.

The initiative now slipped from Charles's grasp. His attempt to trap Davout exposed him to a dangerous counter-stroke, since it over-extended his army at the same time as Napoleon was gradually concentrating his own forces. On the next day, 20 April, Napoleon smashed through Charles's weak centre in the Battle of Abensberg and split his army in two. Charles himself seems to have been inactive for most of the day and may have had an epileptic attack.

On the 21st Davout and the Bavarians in the north advanced eastwards against the bulk of Charles's army, while the severed Austrian southern wing under General Johann von Hiller escaped over the Isar river at Landshut, despite Napoleon's bid to cut its line of retreat. (Hiller would make his own way eastwards along the south bank of the Danube, later crossing the river and reuniting with Charles.)

Fortunately for Charles, the French garrison of Ratisbon had surrendered on the evening of the 20th after expending its ammunition and this allowed him to bring one of his two corps north of the Danube over the city's bridge to the south bank. He planned to use this fresh corps, plus two others, in a powerful offensive against Davout's weak northern flank, while another corps engaged Davout frontally. The stage was set for the Battle of Eggmühl on 22 April, the dramatic final act of this phase of the war.

Charles again found that his army moved too slowly. Only at 1.00 pm did his offensive begin to put pressure on Davout and by then Napoleon had brought reinforcements from the south and smashed into Charles's southern flank. Charles sensibly aborted his offensive and pulled back to a new position where he hoped to check Napoleon's advance. A massive cavalry clash ensued in which the outnumbered Austrians were overthrown and Charles himself nearly captured. But at 10.00 pm Napoleon's troops halted, too exhausted to push farther north. Charles was left hemmed in against the Danube, but managed during the night to evacuate his army to the safety of the north bank at Ratisbon. Then, on the 23rd, he left a rearguard in the city and retreated north-eastwards.

Napoleon had lost his chance to deal Charles a decisive blow. Rather than pursue him directly into Bohemia, Napoleon instead advanced on Vienna along the south bank of the Danube. Still stunned by the shock of his defeats, Charles wrote to the French Emperor:

> Sire, Your Majesty has announced to me his arrival by a thunder of artillery, without giving me the time to compliment him. Hardly was I informed of your presence than I was able to sense it by the losses that you caused me ... I feel flattered, Sire, to fight the greatest captain of the century. I would be more fortunate if destiny had chosen me to obtain for my country the benefit of a durable peace.[7]

This message was similar to one that Tsar Alexander of Russia had sent Napoleon after the Battle of Austerlitz in 1805. By giving an impression of weakness, it earned Napoleon's contempt and probably contributed to his over-confidence in the next few weeks.

Charles had at least avoided the destruction of his army, but the fighting had shown that despite his reforms, it was incapable of manoeuvring or striking with the speed and vigour of Napoleon's forces. The Austrian corps commanders were simply not up to their responsibilities and co-operated poorly. Charles's only hope in future was to fight a straight-forward battle of attrition in which his army was united under his personal control. He re-organised his forces accordingly, creating an Advanced Guard for the whole army and a Reserve of cavalry and grenadiers that would remain under his immediate control.

Napoleon's occupation of Vienna on 13 May failed to destroy the determination of the Austrian Government to fight on. He therefore had to cross to the north bank of the Danube and bring Charles to battle. His first bid to cross the river, using the island of Lobau four miles east of Vienna as a stepping stone, was over-hasty and ended in near-disaster when Charles unexpectedly advanced his army across the Marchfeld, the large plain on the north bank, and prevented him from breaking out of his bridgehead at Aspern–Essling on 20–1 May. After desperate fighting, Napoleon recognised failure and evacuated his troops back over the river.

This setback made it even more imperative for Napoleon to crush Charles and end the war quickly and decisively, for Europe was restless and renewed revolt raged in the Tyrol. For the next six weeks, Charles vainly hoped that Aspern–Essling would lead to Prussian intervention, spark an uprising against the French in southern Germany or bring Napoleon to the negotiating table. In the meantime, he passively awaited events and was joined by reinforcements, including 7,000 men of dubious value from the *Landwehr*. At Wagram, he would field 137,000 troops and 414 guns. But Napoleon, too, was collecting additional forces and would be able to confront Charles with a massive army of 190,000 men and 617 guns.

Only at the beginning of July did Charles realise that another onslaught was imminent. He found it difficult to decide whether to occupy a forward position near the Danube or remain farther north. On 1 July he took up advanced positions behind fortifications that he had built between the villages of Aspern, Essling and Gross-Enzersdorf, but two days later pulled most of his army back six miles to the northern edge of the Marchfeld, where he drew it up along the Russbach stream on either side of the village of Deutsch-Wagram. Only the VI Corps and the army's Advanced Guard were left near the Danube. This meant that Charles would no longer be in a position to launch an immediate counter-attack while Napoleon was trying to transfer his army over the river, but equally he would run less risk of being imperilled by an assault at an unexpected point.

On the evening of 4 July Charles sent an order to his brother, Archduke John, who with a detached force was guarding a stretch of the Danube around Pressburg, thirty miles to the east. John was instructed immediately to bring the bulk of his troops westwards. But Napoleon crossed the Danube that night, in a carefully planned operation that led to the two-day Battle of Wagram. He again used the island of Lobau as a base, but crossed the final arm of the Danube from the island's eastern side, thus outflanking Charles's fortifications before sweeping northwards across the Marchfeld. In the evening of the 5th he attacked the Austrian army on the low hills north of the Russbach, but was beaten back towards 10.00 pm after Charles personally rallied the Austrian I Corps to prevent a breakthrough.

Charles was slightly wounded in the shoulder, but adopted a bold and ambitious plan for the following day, hoping that surprise would compensate for his numerical inferiority. He intended to cut Napoleon off from the Danube with a powerful thrust from the west, seconded by an attack in the east, where Archduke John should arrive with 13,000 troops from Pressburg. But it was unrealistic to expect the offensive to begin at 4.00 am given that Charles issued his orders only at midnight. Even worse, his two-pronged assault would force his army to fight on the outside of a long arc, while Napoleon occupied the shorter inner side. This would dangerously weaken Charles's centre and leave him with only the V Corps in reserve. This was stationed six miles to the west to guard the rear and would be too distant to intervene. Furthermore, Archduke John would not arrive in time, partly because he received his orders late and partly because he failed to hasten.

Austrian co-ordination quickly broke down on 6 July. Charles's main attack in the west was made by two corps under Generals Johann Klenau and Carl Kolowrat-Krakowski. But they received their orders late and had to march five miles before reaching Napoleon's open western flank. Their onslaught was therefore delayed by three hours, obliging Charles to suspend his secondary attack in the east. Napoleon reacted decisively to secure his endangered western wing. He pulled Marshal André Massena's corps out of his front line and shifted it southwards to check the Austrian push.

At the same time, Marshal Davout's corps in the north-east began to overwhelm the Austrian left wing. Charles brought up reinforcements and fiercely counter-attacked Davout, but won only a temporary respite. Then, in the centre, Napoleon committed 8,000 men under General Jacques Macdonald in a massive, hollow oblong formation in an attempt to smash his way through. The Austrians fought Macdonald to a standstill, but were now being remorselessly forced back on the wings. Charles knew that he could not risk the destruction of his army and ordered a retreat. He skilfully covered the withdrawal of his two wings by putting up a stout resistance in the centre and then pulled back altogether. The French were too exhausted to launch a pursuit until the afternoon of the following day.

Wagram was a murderous battle. Austrian casualties numbered over 23,000 in killed and wounded, plus several thousand more captured or missing, yet Napoleon had not won the decisive victory for which he had hoped. The Austrian army survived intact and withdrew from the battlefield with 7,000 prisoners, three eagle standards and twenty-one enemy guns. Despite having the advantage of numbers, Napoleon had come close to defeat. Yet Charles in his Order of the Day of 7 July spoke pessimistically of the 'disastrous result' and instead of accepting responsibility unfairly blamed his troops. Accusing them of disorder, he threatened to use the death penalty to punish cries of alarm and if necessary to decimate and disband guilty regiments.

Wagram had broken Charles's will to fight on. He retreated north-westwards into Moravia and after some bitter rearguard actions decided on his own initiative to seek an armistice, which he signed on 12 July. This independent action infuriated Emperor Francis. Charles was dismissed as supreme commander of the Austrian forces and on the 23rd resigned command of his army. Never again did he see active service. For the first half of the Napoleonic wars, he had been Austria's rising star, but thereafter he was replaced by Field Marshal Prince Karl von Schwarzenberg, a steadier, if less inspired, general. In 1810 Charles reluctantly represented the absent Napoleon at his marriage to Marie-Louise, the daughter of Emperor Francis, in Vienna. His only other position of note was the Governorship of Mainz on the Rhine in 1815.

That same year he married Princess Henrietta of Nassau-Weilburg and had six children, including a daughter who became Queen of Naples and four sons who all entered the Army. The eldest was Field Marshal the Archduke Albert, who won fame as a commander in 1866, when he beat the Italians at Custoza, less than twenty miles from his father's old battlefield of Caldiero. Charles succeeded to the Duchy of Saschen-Teschen in 1822 and in 1830 was briefly considered as a possible king for Belgium or Poland. He passed away in Vienna on 30 April 1847, at the age of 75.

Archduke Charles

Charles was physically unimpressive, being thin, weak-chinned and barely five foot tall. Yet his reputation is formidable. The Duke of Wellington was rarely lavish with praise, but responded vigorously when asked if Charles was a great officer. 'Why, he knows more about it than all of us put together,' he exclaimed and added that 'us' included even Napoleon:

> We are none of us worthy to fasten the latchets of his shoes, if I am to judge from his book and his plans of campaign. But his mind or his health has, they tell me, a very peculiar defect. He is admirable for five or six hours, and whatever can be done in this time will be done perfectly; but after that he falls into a kind of epileptic stupor, does not know what he is about, has no opinion of his own, and does whatever the man at his elbow tells him.[8]

This glowing reference was certainly an exaggeration and Charles's standing has also been inflated by official Habsburg biographers. In reality, he tended to be cautious, methodical and reluctant to risk anything that might endanger his army and therefore the Habsburg Empire. His writings on the art of war reflected his conventional, eighteenth-century outlook: he was more concerned with manoeuvring, occupying strategic points and protecting his communications than with destroying the enemy. He lacked the killer instinct and was one of those of whom Napoleon said:

> There are in Europe many good generals, but they see too many things at once. I see only one thing, namely the enemy's main body. I try to crush it, confident that secondary matters will then settle themselves.[9]

Charles in many ways was a likeable man, despite his tendency to be pedantic and to blame others when things went wrong. He insisted that 'a man of war must be a man of honour' and during the 1796 campaign chivalrously ordered his own surgeon to care for the heroic French General François Marceau-Desgraviers, who had been wounded and captured. When Marceau died, Charles had his body returned to the French and commanded the Austrian guns to fire a funeral salute. But this sensitivity also tended to make him pessimistic, especially after a setback. Defeats brought from Charles both shaken nerves and advice to make peace, rather than an iron resolve to fight on.

He was at his best on a battlefield and in a crisis. He was able instantly to spot the critical moment of a battle and throughout his career threw himself into the thick of a fight to try and save the situation. He did this most memorably at Aspern–Essling, but also notably at Stockach and Wagram. It was primarily through his inspirational leadership in battle that he won the devotion of his men: lack of physical courage was never one of his flaws.

After his death, Charles rapidly recovered popularity in Austria. Today, you can see his statue in the *Heldenplatz*, or 'Heroes' Square', in Vienna. It depicts Charles on horseback, at the moment when he supposedly seized a flag at the crisis of Aspern–Essling to rally his troops. Charles had many faults as a commander, but the moment depicted by that statue symbolises his claim to be a great general.

The Battle of Aspern–Essling: 21–22 May 1809

By the end of May 1809, the war against Napoleon had gone seriously wrong. A series of Austrian defeats in Bavaria towards the end of April had uncovered Vienna on the south bank of the Danube, which now lay in Napoleon's hands.

On the other side of the river there lay an open plain called the Marchfeld, which extended northwards for up to eight miles. Charles knew it well, for it was a favourite location for Austrian peacetime manoeuvres. He arrived with the bulk of his army on the low hills north of this plain on 16 and 17 May, too late to save Vienna. The Danube, which separated the two armies, was wider and stronger than usual, for the onset of spring was causing snow to melt in the Alps. The Tabor bridge linking Vienna with the north bank had been destroyed by the Austrians on 12 May and was the only one in the vicinity. Nor could it be repaired as the Austrians had occupied the village of Florisdorf at the northern end.

But Charles knew that Napoleon had bridging equipment and therefore stationed patrols and outposts along the edge of the Danube to watch for any offensive moves. He received additional information from local people who slipped across from the south bank and also from an observation post on top of the Bissam hill, some eight miles north of Vienna, which transmitted reports to him by semaphore telegraph. Napoleon, in contrast, was operating in the dark and wrongly assumed that Charles was retreating northwards with the bulk of his army into Moravia.

Rather than spread his 110,000 troops out along the river bank, Charles sensibly kept the bulk of them more concentrated and out of sight several miles to the north. He intended to advance into the Marchfeld only after ascertaining the whereabouts of Napoleon's main landing. Instead of trying to prevent Napoleon from crossing, he would therefore counter-attack him immediately after he had crossed, while he had little room for manoeuvre and was in the potentially disastrous position of having the river at his back.

Napoleon, after detaching units to guard his communications along the Danube, had a strike force of 80,000 men. One point where he might cross was a mile north-west of the Tabor bridge at the village of Nussdorf, where a minor French attack had already failed on 13 May. The other obvious place lay six miles south-east of Vienna, near the village of Kaiser-Ebersdorf. Here, a sandbank and two islands, the Lobgrund and Lobau, offered three stepping stones across the river. The distance from bank to bank was two miles, but of that distance the island of Lobau alone accounted for one mile. To cross the river here would require the construction of four sections of a bridge of a combined length of 868 yards, using pontoons, trestles and rafts.

Charles suspected that if Napoleon attacked at Kaiser-Ebersdorf at all, it would be merely a secondary attack, with the main thrust coming at Nussdorf. So when he learnt on the morning of the 19th that French troops had landed on the Lobgrund, he merely alerted his army to be ready to march. In the evening, following further reports of activity in the area, he moved his three rearmost corps forward a couple of miles and pushed an advanced guard into the Marchfeld at the villages of Deutsch-Wagram and Aderklaa.

On the morning of the 20th Charles joined his advanced guard at Aderklaa, six miles north of the Danube, and waited for Napoleon to reveal his hand. That afternoon he learnt from his observers on the Bissam hill that Napoleon was completing a bridge over the Danube at Kaiser-Ebersdorf and beginning to push troops across. Charles refused to make an immediate counter-attack, but towards 3.00 pm ordered some preliminary moves. To guard his western flank, he would leave the V Corps strung out along a forty-mile stretch of the Danube including the Nussdorf sector. (Even farther west, opposite Linz 100 miles away, he had already detached the III Corps during his retreat from Ratisbon in April.) The remaining corps were ordered forward a mile or two to stand along the northern edge of the Marchfeld from the village of Stammersdorf in the west to Deutsch-Wagram seven miles to the east. These positions were just six miles from Napoleon's bridgehead, but were screened by a strong Austrian cavalry force. Furthermore, as a result of defective staff work, three of the corps would have to march during the night to reach their new positions and this, ironically, would work in Charles's favour, since the marching troops would not light campfires and thereby reveal their strength and proximity.

Also on the 20th Charles issued a proclamation which was read to all his units:

> Tomorrow or the day after, a battle will be fought. Its outcome is likely to decide the destiny of the monarchy and the fate of each individual. The only choice is between eternal disgrace and immortal fame. I count on the valour of the army, on the example and spirit of enterprise of the officers. Great rewards or great penalties must follow the result of this battle.
>
> The corps commanders must assemble their generals, and they in turn their staff officers, and urge on them emphatically that it is a question in the present moment only of victory or death. But the soldiers, too, must realise this fact and must fully display their sense of honour, their patriotism and their devotion to their sovereign.
>
> This crucial battle will be fought under the eyes of our Emperor and of the oppressed inhabitants of our capital city, who count on the valour of the army to deliver them.[10]

The address may have lacked the vigour and style of Napoleon's electrifying proclamations, but it drew cheers from all along the Austrian lines.[11]

Sunday 21 May dawned bright and sunny. After concluding at 9.00 am that Napoleon was crossing at Kaiser-Ebersdorf in strength, Charles decided to order a general advance. His army totalled about 98,000 men and 292 guns (not including the V Corps, which would take no part in the battle). The Chief-of-Staff, General Maximilian von Wimpffen, drew up a plan of attack[12] and Charles himself briefed his assembled corps commanders. He aimed to drive Napoleon from the north bank of the Danube back to the island of Lobau, to destroy the bridge over that arm of the river and to occupy the bank with a strong force, especially of artillery. At noon, therefore, five Austrian columns would press southwards on a six-mile front. The first three, a total of 55,700 troops, would be formed by the VI, I and II Corps, while the Fourth and Fifth Columns would be provided by the IV Corps of 24,500 men. The Cavalry Reserve, 6,700 men strong, would occupy the centre of the army to connect the two wings, while the Reserve of 11,400 grenadiers would remain at Gerasdorf, five miles north of Napoleon's bridgehead. It is surprising that the western wing was so disproportionately strong, but Charles apparently expected Napoleon to thrust north-westwards from the bridgehead up the Danube to cover the crossing of more troops at Nussdorf. Charles announced that

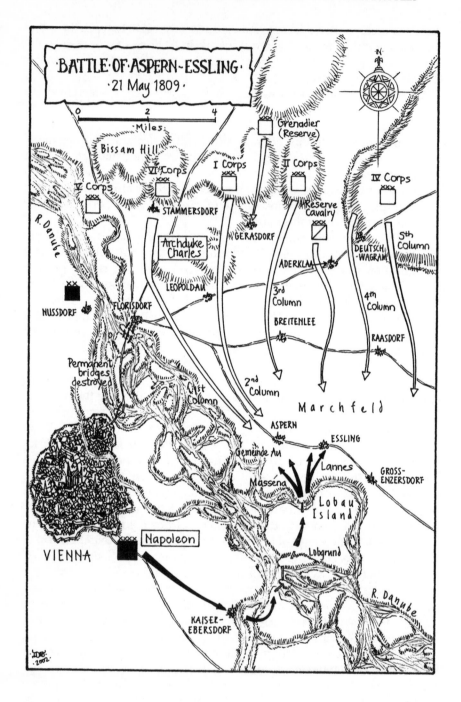

he would accompany the Second Column and exhorted his subordinates to advance in a cool and orderly manner and to co-ordinate their infantry, cavalry and artillery.

Clouds of dust and a slight ridge in the Marchfeld screened the Austrian columns and it was not until 1.00 pm that Napoleon learnt of their approach. Charles for his part did not appreciate just how small a bridgehead the French had so far established on the north bank. Unknown to him, a section of Napoleon's bridge had been broken the previous evening when a detachment of Austrian engineers posted five miles upstream had floated a boat down the Danube. Napoleon, not expecting to encounter opposition, had neglected to protect the bridge with palisades and it had been out of action for nine hours. Although repaired, it had been severed again at 10.00 am. As a result, Napoleon had been unable to push as far northwards as Charles had anticipated and this meant that the Austrians had farther to march before they met opposition. Charles would also encounter serious problems of co-ordination as his five columns would be operating around the outside of a semi-circular bridgehead and the easternmost columns would have farther to march to get into position. As a result, the columns would come into action one after the other, from west to east, instead of arriving simultaneously.

Napoleon's bridgehead rested on two villages, Aspern in the west and the smaller Essling one-and-a-half miles to the east. These were linked by a road, together with a ditch and embankment constructed as flood defences. To the south of Aspern was a heavily wooded area called the Gemeinde Au. The eastern flank was weaker, as the ground between Essling and the Danube was more open to attack. Napoleon, moreover, was totally dependent on his bridge, the highly vulnerable umbilical cord that enabled him to pour additional units and ammunition into the bridgehead and to evacuate his wounded. At the moment, he had only 24,000 men and forty guns on the north bank.

The battle started towards 2.30 pm with some poorly co-ordinated Austrian assaults on Aspern. These failed totally, as did their attempts to seize the Gemeinde Au south of the village, for despite Charles's reforms, the French had a definite edge over the Austrians in open-order fighting in such wooded terrain. The third Austrian column now joined the first two and soon set Aspern on fire with its guns.

By 5.00 pm Aspern had been under attack for two hours. But Essling had been undisturbed because the Austrian Fourth and Fifth Columns had farther to march. Charles in his frustration ordered Aspern to be captured at all costs and another assault was made. But the commander of the leading brigade was wounded, obliging Charles personally to urge the units on despite the hail of fire around him. His troops seized the village but then lost the eastern part and fighting continued for the rest of the evening. Napoleon had entrusted the defence of Aspern to Marshal André Massena, who was memorably described by a French staff officer:

Thoughout this awful struggle Massena stood beneath the great elms on the green opposite the church, calmly indifferent to the fall of the branches brought down upon his head by the showers of grape shot and bullets, keenly alive to all that was going on, his look and voice, stern ... inspiring all who surrounded him with irresistible strength.[13]

Napoleon had deployed his cavalry between Aspern and Essling. These horsemen charged repeatedly, but were checked with heavy loss by Charles's battalion masses and by his Cavalry Reserve under General Johann, Prince zu Liechtenstein. Only at 6.00 pm did the Austrians finally attack Essling. General Franz, Prince zu Rosenberg-Orsini, the commander of the IV Corps, failed to co-ordinate his two columns, whose piecemeal attacks from the north and east made no impression. The biggest obstacle was a massive granary building on the northern outskirts of the village which served the French as a formidable bastion.

The Austrians retired slightly after dusk, except at Aspern, where they still held the western side of the village. At his headquarters in the village of Breitenlee, three miles to the north, Charles prepared for a renewal of the battle the next day. He ordered his troops to be under arms by dawn and his cavalry not to unsaddle. All the generals and staff officers were to bivouac near their troops and the corps commanders were instructed to send out patrols to try and ascertain if the French were evacuating the bridgehead. Ammunition was to be replenished, supplies requisitioned and the wounded evacuated. Disappointed by the poor co-ordination of his attacks, Charles again stressed the importance of keeping up communications between the various columns. He commanded his Reserve of grenadiers to move forward and join him at Breitenlee and ordered fireships and floating mills to be sent down the river to try and destroy Napoleon's bridge. He wanted reports to be forwarded to his headquarters and announced that he would be with the Second Column by dawn, from where he would give further directions.[14]

Fighting resumed as early as 3.00 am, in the mist that shrouded the banks of the Danube. Napoleon, despite being reinforced in the night, had available only 71,000 men and 152 guns, but soon regained the whole of Aspern by 7.00 am. At Essling, the Austrians renewed their attacks from two directions, but with minimal success. Then, towards 7.00 am, Napoleon unleashed a massive onslaught between these two villages. His aim was to smash Charles's army in two and create enough room in the bridgehead to allow the III Corps under Marshal Louis Davout to arrive from the south bank of the Danube, deploy and clinch the victory. The offensive was entrusted to Marshal Lannes, who advanced with three infantry divisions on a diagonal front, supported by an array of cavalry.

This mass of troops gradually ground forward about a mile and threatened to overwhelm Charles's centre. Charles personally intervened as some of his units broke in the face of cavalry charges and close-range artillery fire. He reputedly even seized the flag of the Infantry Regiment No.15 (Zach)[15] in order to rally the men. He later modestly protested that the flag was heavy and that a little chap like himself could hardly have carried it, but his intervention marked the turn of the tide. He had called up more batteries and his corps of grenadiers from reserve and now used them to shore up his front line. Napoleon's hopes of a breakthrough slowly faded in a hail of fire.

At 9.00 am Napoleon's bridge over the Danube was again broken, between the island of Lobau and the south bank. This disastrous rupture meant that troops and ammunition could not be brought across. Lannes, who in fact had already been fought to a standstill by the Austrians, was ordered to halt and an hour later to fall back to his original position.

At 10.00 am Charles learnt of the break in the bridge. He made another unsuccessful attack on Essling, but finally managed to take Aspern for good. Meanwhile, he massed nearly 200 of his guns into a formidable battery (made possible by his earlier reforms of the army) and towards 2.00 pm began pounding Napoleon's centre.

Towards 3.00 pm Charles launched a co-ordinated assault on Essling and personally led a brigade of grenadiers in support. This time he seized nearly all the village and threatened to punch a hole right through the French eastern wing. Napoleon sent part of his Imperial Guard under Generals Georges Mouton and Jean Rapp to extricate the garrison of Essling and fall back. But Rapp disobeyed and counter-attacked, expelling the Austrians and restoring the situation. Napoleon later told him: 'if ever you did well in not executing my orders, it is today, for the salvation of the army depended on the capture of Essling.'[16]

It was unfortunate for Charles that he could not count on his subordinates showing such initiative. Appalled by his heavy losses, he suspended his assaults and left it to his artillery to pulverise Napoleon's over-crowded troops. One of the victims of this cannonade was Marshal Lannes, who had both his legs mangled by a cannonball and died nine days later.

The fighting ended in the evening and the Austrians settled down to spend a second uneasy night on the battlefield. Charles did not try to exploit his success, as he did not wish to lose more troops simply to accelerate Napoleon's now inevitable evacuation of the bridgehead. When General Johann von Hiller, the commander of VI Corps, prepared to thrust eastwards from Aspern, he was sharply ordered to desist by the Chief-of-Staff, General Wimpffen.

The French evacuated their positions that night and crossed to the island of Lobau. It took four more days before the bridge connecting Lobau with the south bank was re-established, but Charles remained passive and did not even bombard the island, perhaps because he assumed that enough blood had already been shed to bring Napoleon to the negotiating table.

Casualties at Aspern–Essling numbered about 20,000 for Charles and 23,000 for Napoleon. Charles owed the victory partly to Napoleon's over-confidence and partly also to being able to fight a battle in which Napoleon did not have room to manoeuvre. But Charles's own contribution had been crucial, particularly his personal intervention during the crisis on the second day.

The Austrian trophies – three guns, a couple of flags, seven ammunition waggons and 3,000 prisoners – do not indicate an overwhelming triumph and Napoleon reversed his check just six weeks later at Wagram. But at Aspern–Essling Charles showed that Napoleon could be defeated on the battlefield. Indeed, the outcome deeply shocked the French Emperor. For the whole day after the battle he remained shattered by exhaustion and by the low, sullen ache of personal defeat.

NOTES

1. O. Criste et al., *Erzherzog Karl: Der Feldherr und seine Armee* (1913), p.1
2. The regiment was recruited from Walloons, the French-speaking inhabitants of the southern half of the Austrian Netherlands.
3. O. Criste, *Erzherzog Carl von Österreich* (1912), v.1, pp.80–2
4. *Ibid*, v.2, pp.107–8
5. The Holy Roman Empire comprised over 300 often minute territorial units in central Europe. Its nominal ruler was the Austrian Emperor Francis and it was dissolved following Napoleon's defeat of Austria in the 1805 campaign.
6. D. Chandler, *The campaigns of Napoleon* (1966), p.667
7. J. Pelet, *Mémoires sur la guerre de 1809* (1824), v.2, pp.178–9
8. J. Croker, *The Croker papers* (1885), v.1, p.338
9. Chandler, *op. cit.*, p.141
10. M. von Angeli, *Erzherzog Carl von Österreich als Feldherr und Heeresorganisator* (1896–8), v.4, pp.307–8. The Emperor Francis would be at the village of Stammersdorf during the battle.
11. Captain de Maleissye-Melun, trans., *Sous les aigles autrichiennes: souvenirs du Chevalier de Grueber* (1909), pp.96–7
12. This plan is quoted in W. Müller, *Relation of the operations and battles of the Austrian and French armies in the year 1809* (1810).
13. A. Bell, ed., *Memoirs of Baron Lejeune* (1897), v.1, p.271
14. Angeli, *op. cit.*, v.4, pp.333–4
15. Austrian infantry regiments bore both a numerical designation and the name of their *Inhaber*, or Proprietor.
16. D. Lacroix, ed., *Mémoires du général Rapp* (nd), p.144

CHAPTER VIII
Blücher and Gneisenau

Field Marshal Gebhard Leberecht von Blücher was sometimes so un-balanced that he believed he was pregnant with an elephant. Yet he was also one of the greatest leaders of this era and his obsession with beating Napoleon made him the heart and soul of the allied campaigns of 1813–15. He redeemed all his flaws with an outstanding moral and physical courage and repeatedly decided the outcome of operations through sheer fighting spirit.

Blücher was born on 16 December 1742 at Gross-Renzow near Rostock on the Baltic coast. This area now lies in eastern Germany, but at the time formed part of the Duchy of Mecklenburg-Schwerin, which adjoined Prussia. Blücher sprang from a minor noble family and had eight brothers and a sister. He did not study hard at school and remained weak at spelling and grammar all his life and even as an army commander was unable to read a map. His father, a former infantry captain, wanted him to become a farmer and sent him at the age of 14 to relatives on the Baltic island of Rügen, fifty miles north-east of Rostock, to learn how to run an estate. But Swedish troops descended on the island following the start of the Seven Years' War in 1756. In 1757 Blücher enlisted in the Swedish Mörner Hussar Regiment and saw action against Frederick the Great's Prussia.

In 1760 he was captured by, and subsequently served with, a regiment of Prussian hussars. Its commander, Colonel Wilhelm von Belling, took Blücher under his wing and was a wonderfully eccentric man. 'Thou seest, dear Heavenly Father, the sad plight of thy servant Belling,' he would pray. 'Grant him soon a nice little war that he may better his condition and continue to praise Thy name, Amen.'[1] But Blücher, who was by now a lieutenant, saw little action after the Seven Years' War and instead endured the tedium of garrison life in various small towns. Gambling, drinking and womanising were among his favourite hobbies, as were duels and practical jokes.

Promoted to captain in 1771, he went to Poland, which was at the centre of a dispute between Prussia and Russia. When Polish partisans murdered Prussian troops, Blücher was determined to take revenge and in 1772 even had a priest shot on suspicion of involvement. This unsavoury incident nearly wrecked his career. His patron, Belling, had left the regiment and had been replaced by a man who disliked Blücher and passed him over for promotion. Blücher twice protested to Frederick the Great, but the execution of the priest told against him, for Frederick wanted to win over the Poles. In 1773 Blücher was informed that he had leave to resign and that he could go to the devil as soon as he pleased; not for the last time did he have cause to regret an impulsive action.

Blücher was now in his early 30s. He married the daughter of a landowner in East Prussia, became a farmer and after four years bought his own estate in Pomerania. He also took a post in local government and struggled to learn some French. But his repeated requests for reinstatement in the Army won him nothing but silence until after Frederick the Great died in 1786. An interview with the new king led to Blücher rejoining his old regiment of hussars with the rank of major: at the age of 44, after a fourteen-year gap, Blücher was back in the saddle. He was even given the rank and seniority that he would have held had he remained in the Army and in 1790 was promoted to colonel. But his alcoholism worsened when his wife died the following year.

War with Revolutionary France broke out in 1792 and at last Blücher had the prospect of seeing some more active service. His first clash with the French came in 1793 and for the next two years he was continually engaged in small-scale actions in the Austrian Netherlands and on the Maas, Saar and Rhine rivers. He won a reputation not merely for bravery but for boldness and tactical skill. He repeatedly snatched triumphs from seemingly impossible odds through a combination of bluff, surprise and a ferocious charge. The details of these campaigns are unimportant; it is sufficient to note that Blücher's mentality and methods during these actions as a cavalry officer were those that would distinguish him as an army commander twenty years later.

This highly satisfying time came to an end in April 1795, when Prussia made peace; she would remain neutral until 1806. Blücher took the opportunity to remarry and served in mundane administrative roles in some of Prussia's outlying territories near the Dutch border. In 1801 he was promoted to lieutenant-general and the following August occupied the province of Münster, a small ecclesiastical territory near the Rhine that Prussia had annexed in agreement with France as compensation for the ceding of Prussian lands on the west bank of the river. Blücher's conduct in Münster was firm but fair and so successful that the local authorities asked for him to be made their governor.

During these years Blücher watched Napoleon's increasingly threatening moves with alarm and vainly urged the Prussian King, Frederick William III, to take decisive action. But Prussia failed to join the Austrians and Russians in the field in 1805 and following their crushing defeat at Austerlitz was confronted by a dangerously altered balance of power.

At the beginning of October 1806, Frederick William belatedly demanded that Napoleon withdraw all French troops to the west bank of the Rhine. Unfortunately, Prussia had an outdated army and was practically isolated, for Austria remained neutral following her recent defeat and the Russians were too distant to lend immediate support. Prussia's southern neighbour Saxony was bullied into an alliance, but reluctantly supplied only 20,000 troops.

After rapidly concentrating his army, Napoleon seized the initiative and thrust north-eastwards into Saxony in the direction of Berlin. He then swept round to the west and on the 14th fell on the Prussian forces on the battlefields of Jena and Auerstädt. Blücher led a small cavalry force at Auerstädt, where 27,000 French soldiers under Marshal Louis Davout defeated 63,500 Prussians. Blücher gallantly charged several times, but lacked adequate support, had his horse shot beneath him and was bloodily repulsed. Meanwhile, Napoleon himself with 96,000 men beat the remaining 53,000 Prussian troops twelve miles farther south at Jena.

In the aftermath of Jena–Auerstädt, General Prince Friedrich von Hohenlohe-Ingelfingen assumed command of the surviving Prussian forces and retreated north-eastwards as Napoleon launched a relentless pursuit. Blücher with a detached force marched sometimes with Hohenlohe's main body, sometimes by a separate route and fought several rearguard actions. When Hohenlohe surrendered at Prenzlau on 28 October, Blücher was on his own with 22,000 troops. He wanted to launch a counter-offensive, but was forced by the reality of the situation to retreat north-westwards in the hope of being evacuated by sea. He managed on 5 November to reach Lübeck, a neutral free city near the Danish border. He ruthlessly entered and demanded supplies, but was attacked the next day. When the French broke into the city, he managed to slip away northwards with some horsemen, but had to surrender on the 7th after running out of food and ammunition. Nonetheless, he had won valuable time for the Russians to prepare for a tough campaign against Napoleon in Eastern Prussia that winter.

In April 1807, after a polite interview with Napoleon, Blücher was exchanged for General (later Marshal) Claude Victor, but saw no more fighting since Napoleon and Tsar Alexander I of Russia agreed to peace at Tilsit in July. Prussia was humiliated and partly dismantled, but some of her citizens sought to avenge the disaster and as a preliminary step undertook a reform of the Army. Blücher, now Governor-General of Pomerania, did not have the intellect to play a close role in this, but kept in touch with men like Gerhard von Scharnhorst and August von Gneisenau who served on the Military Reorganisation Commission.

When Austria again went to war with Napoleon in April 1809, Blücher

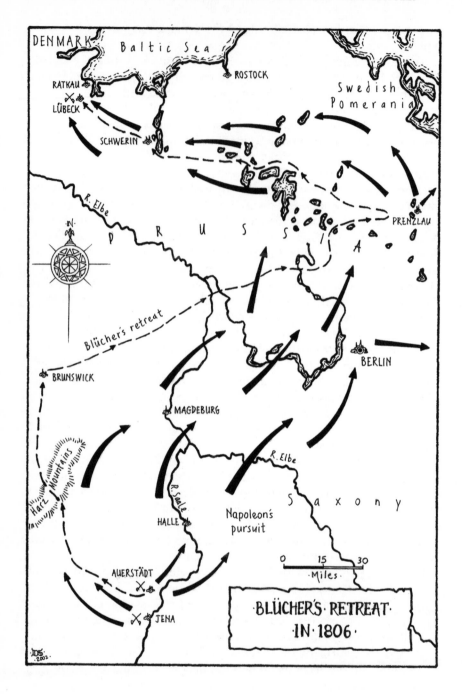

sought to persuade his King to join her, or at the very least to give him 30,000 men with which to liberate Prussia. But his appeals were to no avail and when Austria sought peace in July, he dropped into the blackest despair. He suffered from depression, delusions, emaciation and trembling hands, all of them classic symptoms of excessive alcohol intake. He grew paranoid and once grappled with what he imagined was the ghost of an officer whom he had had dismissed. Sometimes, he believed that his head was made of stone and wanted it to be hit with a hammer, while the dreaded elephant came in 1811. To be pregnant with an elephant is Berlin slang for 'I'm losing my temper', but Blücher seems to have meant it literally; perhaps in his case it began as a figure of speech and became a delusion.[2]

Blücher's resilience brought recovery. He helped secretly to train Prussian troops, but was caught in the act by a French consul. Under French pressure, the Prussian King dismissed him from the Army in November 1811, but sent him money and a promise to employ him again as soon as possible. Blücher retired to his estates near Breslau, while Napoleon in June 1812 launched a disastrous invasion of Russia that practically destroyed his Grand Army.

In the aftermath of this catastrophe, the year 1813 opened in Prussia with the promise of liberation. Napoleon returned to Paris to raise a fresh army and the battered forces he left behind fell back to the Elbe river, abandoning most of Prussia. At the end of February the Prussian King signed an alliance with Russia and the following month declared war on France. Popular clamour ensured that Blücher received command of the Russo-Prussian Army of Silesia, despite some criticisms of his age and temperament. He wrote excitedly that he was 'itching in every finger to grasp the sword'[3] and at the age of 70 was at last about to make his name as a commander. Had he died at this stage, he would have been but an heroic footnote to the disasters of 1806. Only the years 1813–15 established him as a great general.

The allies fielded a main army flanked by two supporting armies, including the Army of Silesia on the southern wing. But as they pushed westwards, Napoleon returned from Paris with his fresh troops and a fierce battle ensued at Lützen on 2 May. Napoleon had the advantage of numbers, but had too few cavalry and too many raw conscripts. Blücher calmly puffed away at his pipe as he watched the fighting. Every now and again, he would call 'Schmidt!' and hold his pipe behind him for an orderly to replace with one full of tobacco. To shouted warnings of a shell that fell nearby, he retorted, 'well, let the hellish thing alone!' It burst harmlessly.[4] That afternoon he attacked but was wounded and had his horse shot beneath him. He hurriedly had the injury dressed and returned to the fray. The battle swung in favour of the French, but Blücher led a final cavalry charge that nearly reached Napoleon himself and discouraged the French from being too bold. Next morning the allies retreated unhindered. They turned at bay at Bautzen, where they fought a defensive battle on 20–1 May. They lost and again retreated, but five days later, Blücher ambushed Napoleon's advanced guard at Haynau and seized eighteen guns.

An armistice followed early in June, for both sides needed time to draw breath before the next round. During this pause, a new man came to occupy a crucial place at Blücher's right hand. For Blücher, however inspirational as a leader, needed a highly intelligent Chief-of-Staff to direct the army for him, particularly as he had no previous experience of army command and had not seen action for seven years. General Gerhard von Scharnhorst had filled this role until his untimely death from an infected wound received at the Battle of Lützen. His replacement was August Wilhelm Anton Neithardt von Gneisenau.

Born in Saxony on 27 October 1760, Gneisenau came from humble origins. His father was a lieutenant in the Austrian artillery during the Seven Years' War; his mother died shortly after his birth while fleeing from the advancing Prussian army of Frederick the Great. Gneisenau is said to have slipped from her arms and to have been found in the road by a soldier. While his father travelled to seek employment, Gneisenau was left in the care of a poor family and endured poverty and neglect until at the age of 9 he was cared for by his maternal grandparents.

Aged 17, he went to study at Erfurt University and two years later joined an Austrian hussar regiment stationed in the city. In 1782 he transferred to the service of the Margrave of Ansbach-Bayreuth as an officer, at the same time seeking to help his career by adopting the noble name of von Gneisenau, from a castle in Austria where his family had its origins. He served with an Ansbach contingent under the British flag in America in 1782 during the War of Independence there and followed the conflict with interest, although he did not see action.

Gneisenau obtained a commission in the Prussian Army in 1786, but spent most of the next twenty years as a junior officer doing routine garrison duties. During that time, he married and studied the military profession. Although he took part in the actions that accompanied the partition of Poland in 1793–5, it was only in 1806 that he finally had a chance to distinguish himself. He fought at the Battles of Saalfeld (where he was wounded in the leg) and Jena and then joined King Frederick William III in East Prussia. After being promoted major, he was sent in the spring of 1807 to command the beleaguered Prussian fortress of Colberg on the Baltic coast, which he did with great spirit, mobilising the townsfolk to support the defence and holding out until after the Peace of Tilsit. This was at a time when other fortresses across Prussia fell like nine-pins in the aftermath of Jena–Auerstädt. Gneisenau won the prestigious *Pour le Mérite* decoration, as well as great renown and promotion to lieutenant-colonel.

·CAMPAIGN·OF·1813·
Showing Army locations at end of
Armistice ~ mid·August·

In July 1807 he joined the Military Reorganisation Commission, the body set up to suggest improvements to the Prussian Army. Gneisenau was responsible, in particular, for much of the new tactical doctrine for light infantry, in which he had spent much of his career. But like several of his colleagues, he realised that military reform on its own was not enough and sought far-reaching political and social changes to replace the widespread apathy of 1806 with patriotic fervour. He wanted a national army based on universal service to supplant the traditional, more insular army of professional soldiers. He also dreamed of a mass insurrection of the Prussian people liberating the country and leading to constitutional government. He was destined for disappointment, for after limited progress political and social reform ground to a halt in the face of the King's conservatism and powerful entrenched interests. Gneisenau resigned his commission after the King refused to join Austria against Napoleon in 1809, but subsequently went on diplomatic missions to Russia, Sweden and Britain until the outbreak of war in March 1813.

Following his appointment as Chief-of-Staff, Gneisenau quickly forged an effective relationship with Blücher. He also fostered teamwork among the headquarters staff as a whole by debating issues openly. Blücher similarly harangued those around him, hoping that this would create a robust, fighting spirit that would transmit itself through the army when his staff officers left to carry messages to subordinates. But Carl von Müffling, one of the senior staff members, believed that this openness could cause problems: for instance, if Blücher and Gneisenau publicly ruled out a retreat, they would have difficulty in reversing that decision without loss of face.[5]

By August 1813, when the spring armistice expired, Napoleon's situation had worsened. Austria had joined the coalition and Swedish troops under the former French Marshal Bernadotte, now Crown Prince of Sweden, also took the field. The allies therefore managed to place three armies in a semi-circle around Napoleon in central Europe. These were Prince Karl von Schwarzenberg's Army of Bohemia to the south; Blücher's Army of Silesia to the east; and Bernadotte's Army of the North. The terms of the armistice ruled that hostilities could not begin again until 17 August, but Blücher impatiently violated it and opened his offensive westwards three days early. His Army of Silesia numbered 95,000 men, but included poorly equipped and trained Prussian militia as well as Russian and Prussian regulars.

The allied strategy was to exploit their numerical superiority and avoid a battle with Napoleon in person except on favourable terms. Any army targeted by him was to retire while the others attacked his detached forces and menaced his lines of communication. The result was to deny Napoleon a decisive victory and force him to march back and forth to meet each successive threat. Thus, when he advanced against the Army of

Silesia on 21 August, he merely chased it back eastwards in disorder. Blücher hated retreats, but was not wholly blind to their potential advantages. 'I am well in health,' he wrote, 'and very happy to have played a trick on the great man. He ought to be furious at not having been able to make me accept battle.'[6]

Only when Napoleon left the area did Blücher return to the offensive. By then, Blücher faced a mere covering force under Marshal Macdonald, which he smashed at the Battle of Katzbach on 26 August, taking 18,000 prisoners and 100 guns and boosting the morale and cohesion of his own forces. Early in September Napoleon switched his attention back to Blücher, counter-attacked his advance guard and caused him to retreat for a second time. But a fourth allied army, General Levin von Bennigsen's newly arrived Army of Poland, reinforced Schwarzenberg's Army of Bohemia in the south and released Blücher to join the lacklustre Bernadotte in the north. Operations now revolved around Napoleon's new base, the city of Leipzig. To the north of the city, Blücher fought his way over the Elbe river at Wartenburg on 3 October, reluctantly followed by Bernadotte, his nominal superior. Napoleon headed north to counter-attack, but instead of tamely retiring back across the Elbe, Blücher and Bernadotte unexpectedly evaded Napoleon's blow by going westwards.

Napoleon, having failed to catch Blücher, returned southwards to Leipzig. All four allied armies gradually drew up in a vast circle around the city and between 16 and 19 October attacked Napoleon on three sides with superior numbers. Blücher in the north was exasperated by Bernadotte's reluctance to become seriously engaged; it did not help matters that Bernadotte, formerly a French marshal, had been one of Blücher's opponents in 1806. On the third day of the battle, Napoleon began to retreat and the next day, the allies attacked his rearguards holding Leipzig itself. Blücher badly wanted to be the first into the city and yelled his usual battle cry *vorwärts! vorwärts!* His Russian soldiers eventually realised what he was shouting and promptly nicknamed him Marshal Forwards. At last the fighting was over and Napoleon had suffered a disastrous defeat. Blücher greeted the Emperor of Austria, the Tsar of Russia and the King of Prussia inside the city and as a reward for his role was made Field Marshal.

The victorious allies pressed westwards up to the Rhine, the eastern frontier of France. The main allied invasion force consisted of Blücher's Army of Silesia and Schwarzenberg's Army of Bohemia, while additional forces were operating in support in Belgium, northern Italy and south-western France. Schwarzenberg entered eastern France through Switzerland in December 1813 and Blücher crossed the Rhine farther north on New Year's Day, 1814.

Blücher and Schwarzenberg outnumbered Napoleon by more than two to one, but would take three months to reach Paris. Some allied statesmen, fearful of heavy casualties, hoped to use limited military operations to put pressure on Napoleon for a negotiated settlement. The Austrians, for example, did not necessarily want to see Napoleon toppled, for a weak France could become a Russian satellite. Blücher took on a significance out of proportion to the numbers under his command as he was exceptional in having a clear military aim and an unshakeable resolve to achieve it. 'We must go to Paris,' he demanded. 'Napoleon has paid his visits to all the capitals of Europe; should we be less polite?'[7]

After raising more conscripts, Napoleon reached the front and counter-attacked towards the end of January. His initial target was Blücher's Army of Silesia, which he attacked on 29 January at the town of Brienne, ninety miles east of Paris. Unforgettable scenes ensued as French cannonballs struck the Château of Brienne, where Blücher had established his headquarters and was in the middle of dinner. Among his guests was a French prisoner, who so enjoyed the company that he insisted on staying when Blücher suggested that he withdraw to safety. In contrast, a local man was terrified. Blücher bluntly asked him if he owned the château, received a reply in the negative and then told him: 'you may be quite easy; the castle is solidly built, the cost of the repairs will not be considerable, and at any rate you will not have to pay for them.'[8] Blücher and his guests finished eating and then went to watch the fighting from the terrace. But the battle soon came to them when a French infantry brigade attacked the château. Blücher and Gneisenau rode off just in time as the leading French skirmishers opened fire on the courtyard.

Driven from Brienne, Blücher fell back five miles on to Schwarzenberg's army, before turning at bay and defeating Napoleon at La Rothière on 1 February. Blücher and Schwarzenberg then separated again, partly because of the problems of supplying large numbers of concentrated troops in winter. Both their armies headed for Paris, but along routes thirty miles apart. Flushed with victory, Blücher became dangerously over-confident and allowed his forces to become over-extended. 'The route to Paris is free,' he wrote on 10 February. 'I do not believe that Napoleon will engage in another battle.'[9]

In fact, Napoleon launched a surprise attack northwards into the southern flank of Blücher's advance. He caught the Army of Silesia strung out along the road to Paris and between 10 and 14 February inflicted four defeats one after the other: Champaubert, Montmirail, Château Thierry and Vauchamps. Blücher was personally present at Vauchamps and narrowly survived a fighting retreat in which he was knocked over and nearly captured or trampled underfoot. The Army of Silesia reeled from this swift succession of blows, having lost at least 16,000 men, or a third of its strength.

Both Blücher and Schwarzenberg retreated eastwards to regroup. On 25 February the allied high command transferred two corps from

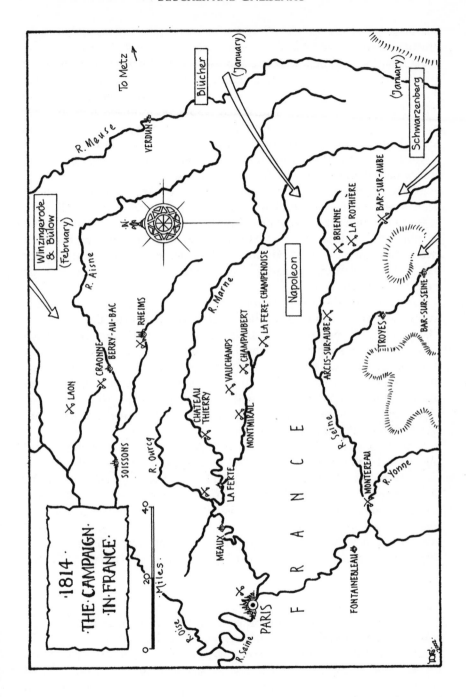

·1814·
·THE· CAMPAIGN·
·IN·FRANCE·

Miles
0   20   40

To Metz

Blücher (January)

Schwarzenberg (January)

R. Meuse

VERDUN

Winzingerode & Bülow (February)

R. Aisne

R. RHEIMS

BERRY-AU-BAC

CRAONNE

LAON

SOISSONS

R. Ourcq

R. Marne

CHATEAU THIERRY

VAUCHAMPS

CHAMPAUBERT

MONTMIRAIL

LA FERTÉ

LA FERTÉ-CHAMPENOISE

Napoleon

BRIENNE

LA ROTHIÈRE

BAR-SUR-AUBE

ARCIS-SUR-AUBE

TROYES

BAR-SUR-SEINE

R. Seine

R. Yonne

MONTEREAU

MEAUX

FONTAINEBLEAU

PARIS

R. Oise

R. Seine

F R A N C E

Bernadotte's Army of the North currently operating in Belgium to Blücher's Army of Silesia. These corps, General Ferdinand von Winzingerode's 30,000 Russians and General Friedrich von Bülow's 17,000 Prussians, more than compensated for his recent losses. He therefore resolved to march again on Paris, on the way picking up these reinforcements from the north. When Napoleon followed him, Blücher hurriedly abandoned his advance, retreated northwards, united with his reinforcements and repelled Napoleon at Laon on 9–10 March.

But the strain had been too much. Blücher collapsed from exhaustion and remained in a poor state for the rest of the campaign. Yet Napoleon, who had swung south again, lost the battle of Arcis-sur-Aube against Schwarzenberg. He then took the risk of leaving open the road to Paris in order to threaten Schwarzenberg's lines of communication to the east. But the allies called his bluff, ignored the threat to their rear and marched their two armies directly on Paris. Blücher had begun to recover, but could barely ride a horse and instead lay in a carriage with a lady's green silk hat shading his inflamed eyes.

In Napoleon's absence, only about 40,000 French troops were available to defend Paris. A short but bitter battle ensued outside the city on 30 March, with Blücher attacking from the north and Schwarzenberg from the east. Blücher spent most of the day in his carriage, until he could bear it no longer and then he mounted a horse and directed an assault against the hill of Montmartre. The French marshals left in charge of the defence bowed to the inevitable and surrendered the city in the early hours of the 31st. Napoleon rushed back with his army to try and save his capital, but was too late and abdicated on 6 April.

After two years of high command, Blücher was left mentally and physically bankrupt and was terrified that he might be dying. He gave up command of the Army of Silesia, which he had led from the banks of the Oder river to the walls of Paris, but gradually recovered his spirits and was granted the title Prince of Wahlstadt. Gneisenau, who had likewise resigned as Chief-of-Staff, became a count. Blücher at this time met Wellington, who had won fame in the Peninsular War, and on a visit to England in June caused the people to go wild with joy, cheering 'Blücher for ever!' and demanding locks of his hair. He then retired to his estates, little suspecting that he had yet to add a final chapter to the story of his career.

In the spring of 1815 Napoleon escaped from exile, marched on Paris and swiftly regained power. Blücher was delighted at the prospect of renewed war, as he felt that France had not been properly punished, nor Prussia adequately rewarded, for their roles in the late wars. He was given command of the Prussian Army of the Lower Rhine, which together with Wellington's Anglo-Dutch-German army would defend the United Netherlands. Gneisenau once more served as Blücher's Chief-of-Staff, for although he had wanted an independent command in order to win personal renown, he was condemned by lack of seniority to his former position.

Napoleon suddenly invaded the United Netherlands on 15 June and thrust northwards on Brussels. Wellington and Blücher needed to concentrate their dispersed troops from cantonments and in order to win time, Blücher gave battle at Ligny on the 16th with three-quarters of his army. The result was a serious, but inconclusive, Prussian defeat. Blücher himself led a cavalry charge in the twilight to check Napoleon's advance, but crashed to the ground and was nearly captured when his horse was shot beneath him. Although eventually rescued by his ADC, Lieutenant-Colonel August von Nostitz, he was left badly bruised.

In the temporary absence of his chief, Gneisenau ordered a retreat twelve miles northwards on Wavre, where the Prussian army rallied during the 17th. Wellington meanwhile occupied a parallel position nine miles to the west, near the village of Waterloo. Napoleon took most of his army to tackle Wellington, but sent a detachment under Marshal Emmanuel de Grouchy to pursue the Prussians.

Blücher, now back in the saddle, promised to join Wellington at Waterloo and overcame Gneisenau's anxieties about the dangers of this move. Thus on the 18th, despite the difficulties of their cross-country march, a succession of Prussian units eventually arrived at Waterloo and attacked Napoleon's flank. Blücher concentrated his efforts against the village of Plancenoit in the south-eastern corner of the battlefield in a bid to cut Napoleon's line of retreat. 'If only we had the cursed village,' he swore.[10] His attacks forced Napoleon to divert 13,000 troops from his reserves and thereby saved Wellington. As dusk fell, the battle finally ended in a decisive allied victory. As in 1813–14, Blücher had been essential to the outcome. Even though he was the least brilliant of the three commanders-in-chief, he was the only one not to fight the campaign under serious illusions and his fierce loyalty and determination tipped the scales.

Wellington and Blücher now marched on Paris. Napoleon abdicated, leaving a Provisional Government that surrendered on 3 July after the Prussians fought their way round to the unfortified southern side of the capital. Blücher embarked on a short-lived spree of vengeance by extorting reparations and vainly attempting to blow up the Bridge of Jena, before returning to Prussia in the winter of 1815–16. Exhausted and sick of war, he died aged 77 at Krieblowitz in Silesia on 12 September 1819.

Gneisenau survived his master by twelve years, but never had the chance to distinguish himself as a great commander. He died a disappointed man, for by 1819 his hopes of constitutional reform in Prussia were finally crushed by entrenched conservative interests. He retired in 1816 from ill-health and frustration, although he was appointed

Governor of Berlin in 1818 and Field Marshal on the tenth anniversary of Waterloo in 1825. He died from cholera at Posen on 21 August 1831, while commanding a Prussian Army of Observation during a Polish revolt against Russian rule.

Papa Blücher

Blücher was an unlikely hero. A British hussar captain who saw him in Paris after Waterloo wrote that 'he is an uncouth-looking old man and was spitting over a bridge when I saw him.'[11] Yet as a fighting general, he equalled Marshal Ney in his ability to inspire troops. His pipe was always in his mouth, the word 'Forwards' always on his lips and the smell of powder always in his nostrils.

The lesson from his life is the value of persistence. According to Müffling:

> It was no secret to Europe that old Prince Blücher ... understood nothing whatever of the conduct of a war; so little, indeed, that when a plan was submitted to him for approval, even relating to some unimportant operation, he could not form any clear idea of it, or judge whether it were good or bad.[12]

But he repeatedly turned the tide by sheer force of personality and readiness to take risks. Even when he lost, he always bounced back. In fact, few great generals have been beaten so often. As Müffling noted, Blücher had often used his physical strength in hand-to-hand fighting early in his career:

> In this way he had gradually convinced himself that there was no military predicament from which one could not ultimately extricate oneself by fighting, man to man.[13]

Blücher was one of the few generals who did not fear Napoleon. He admitted in private to a grudging admiration for his opponent: 'if you had brought Napoleon to me I could not have received him but with the greatest respect, in spite of the fact that he has often called me a drunken hussar. He is still a tremendously brave man.'[14] But in public, Blücher referred scathingly to 'Mr Napoleon', or 'the swaggerer Napoleon'. He personally commanded against the French Emperor at Brienne, La Rothière, Vauchamps, Craonne, Laon and Ligny. Of these, he lost four and won two and, as part of an allied force, he also helped beat Napoleon at Leipzig and Waterloo. No other general had such a record against Napoleon.[15] Similarly, few have had so many narrow escapes from death or capture. He was wounded at Lützen, nearly captured at Brienne and Ligny and almost trampled underfoot at Vauchamps.

There should be no illusions about Blücher. He was ruthless and hard-headed and had few scruples at transferring from Swedish to Prussian service at the start of his career. In his late 20s, he indulged in dubious transactions involving stolen horses[16] and in 1806 did not hesitate to take over and extort supplies from the neutral free city of Lübeck. Nor did he have any qualms in violating the armistice in August 1813, for to him the end justified the means. He saw the world in black and white and this is what made him intensely loyal. That was one of his greatest strengths, as Müffling made clear when he advised Wellington in 1815:

> You may depend upon this: when the Prince has agreed to any operation in common, he will keep his word, should even the whole Prussian army be annihilated in the act.[17]

Blücher could also be depended upon to seek quick and decisive outcomes, but this was not always a virtue. As Wellington recalled, Blücher was 'a very fine fellow, and whenever there was any question of fighting, always ready and eager – if anything too eager.'[18] For Blücher had the temperament of an hussar and repeatedly strayed into the realms of mental instability. His obsessive nature led to fixations: war with France; the march on Paris; the execution of Napoleon. He craved excitement, was happiest in a battle and, when there was no fighting, found release instead in reckless gambling. His physical bravery stemmed from a deep religious faith. He prayed before and after every battle and believed in predestination, the idea that God had fixed the course and extent of everyone's life. His surgeon, Dr Carl Bieske, recorded that Blücher never, even in the greatest danger,

> had an idea of being shot dead, and thought that, if he had not felt certain of it, he would have lost his head as many others, for every man in a greater or less degree, previous to a battle and when going into it, has an instinctive dread in his bosom; and he who knows how [best to] overcome it is the bravest after all.[19]

Blücher valued most the cheers of his soldiers and the nickname 'Marshal Forwards'. He led by example. If he came across stragglers on the march, he might dismount and walk behind them. When his army was short of food, he shared its hardships and allowed only boiled potatoes to be served at his table. 'He always knew,' recorded his surgeon, 'at the proper moment how to work upon the soldiers' feelings, and only a few comforting words were necessary, and at once toil, hunger and thirst, and all the hardships of war were forgotten.'[20] His leadership transcended distinctions of nationality, for he knew how to address the human heart. His Russian troops sometimes called him 'the little Suvorov', after their most famous general of the Revolutionary wars. The Cossacks even convinced themselves that Blücher was one of them, that he had really been born near the Don river. Indeed, that was the key to Blücher's success as a leader: he made his soldiers feel that he was one of them.

Commanders who are too familiar with their troops risk losing the authority imparted by reserve, but Blücher avoided this partly by force of character and partly by his age. He did talk to his men like a mere subaltern of hussars, yet at the same time, he was older than his 'children' and this helped give him a natural authority.

Blücher has become a legend. His eccentricities, his jokes, his image as a fire-breathing and none-too-bright Prussian have become fixed in stone. Yet the real Blücher was more complex than the legend. His man-management skills were just as important as his determination. Although not well educated, he was thoroughly experienced in human nature and capably handled such difficult colleagues as Bernadotte and General Hans von Yorck. While he could be ruthless, he usually wore a velvet glove on his iron fist. He quickly won the hearts and minds of the people of Münster when he occupied that province in 1802, although his long hatred of France prevented him from helping Wellington establish a lasting peace after Waterloo. But perhaps the least recognised of Blücher's qualities was his humility. By recognising his limitations and accepting advice from Gneisenau and other members of his staff, he was able to neutralise many of his weaknesses.

Gneisenau

Individually, both Blücher and Gneisenau had serious flaws, but together, they made a formidable command team. Blücher once joked that he was the only man who could kiss his own head and proved it by kissing Gneisenau.

Gneisenau is a difficult man to assess. He was both liked and respected by many of his colleagues. 'I have had the happy lot to be in the society of many remarkable men,' observed Professor Henry Steffens, 'but I never regretted having a conversation interrupted [as much] as I have done when with Gneisenau.'[21]

Yet Gneisenau was not as easy a colleague as his chief. He tended to be tempestuous, perhaps as a result of his unstable childhood, and fought several duels as a young officer. He was a visionary and allowed idealism to unbalance his judgement, as he showed with his unrealistic hopes of a popular uprising to free Prussia from French domination. As the Prussian King remarked, Gneisenau was too clever for his own good. Similarly, he often pressed his troops too hard and although he justified this on the grounds that high targets were necessary to produce good results, he seems to have ignored the effect of relentless marching on discipline and cohesion.

According to Müffling, Gneisenau had tended to be bold in 1813, but became markedly more timid in 1814 under the influence of advisers who argued that Prussia after the end of the war with France would need an intact army to counter potential threats from her traditional rivals Austria and Russia.[22] His excessive caution and distrust of allies was equally prominent during the Waterloo campaign.

Yet despite his flaws, Gneisenau deserves greater recognition. One of his foremost achievements was to help develop the Prussian system of command, whereby subordinates were allowed to use their initiative in pursuit of clearly defined general objectives. This allowed them to react to developments without wasting time seeking fresh orders, although problems could occur if too much freedom was given to excessively headstrong subordinates.

Even more importantly, Gneisenau helped foster the development of the Prussian General Staff. The campaigns of 1813–15 saw staff officers, trained in a common doctrine, assigned for the first time to all Prussian generals at army, corps and brigade level. In other armies, a Chief-of-Staff usually merely put into effect a general's commands; in the Prussian Army, in contrast, he was a partner rather than a subordinate. The idea was that since the Prussians lacked a general with Napoleon's genius, they would rely on the collective genius of the General Staff. The common training of the staff officers would help give coherence to the operations of the various units to which they were attached. The concept of the General Staff was not fully developed until the middle of the nineteenth century under General Helmuth von Moltke, but Gneisenau played a crucial role during its infancy. In spring 1813, for example, he noticed that some Prussian generals were reluctant to heed their Chiefs-of-Staff. He therefore insisted, with Blücher's support, that the Chiefs-of-Staff share responsibility for decisions with their generals and ensured that they could complain directly to himself, the Chief of the General Staff, if they were ignored.

The partnership between Blücher and Gneisenau served as a model for subsequent Prussian and German armies, although the balance of authority shifted even more from Commander-in-Chief to Chief-of-Staff with the growing influence of the General Staff. Such combinations of a charismatic leader and an intellectually gifted Chief-of-Staff included Wilhelm I and Moltke in 1870–1 and Hindenburg and Ludendorff in 1914–18.

The Battle of Laon: 9–10 March 1814

Quelle affaire! exclaimed a triumphant Blücher on the evening of Waterloo. Even he had never fought so tremendous a contest. But while Waterloo is the most famous of his battles, it is not the most instructive. It superbly illustrates his iron determination and his obsession with the offensive, but little else.

More can be learnt from the little-known Battle of Laon during the 1814 campaign. The extent of Blücher's contribution to the decisions of his command team is usually difficult to determine. But because he fell ill during Laon and was totally incapacitated on the second day of the battle, it is possible to identify the extent of his role. On that second day, Gneisenau alone had to take the decisions, even though Blücher remained officially in command. The episode revealed that Blücher was indispensable and that Gneisenau, however talented as Chief-of-Staff, was unfit for independent command.

The lead-up to the battle began in the last week of February, when Blücher seized the initiative and advanced on Paris. Two of Napoleon's marshals, Edouard Mortier and Auguste Marmont, were covering the city with two detached corps but had only 10,000 men and would be unable to check Blücher for long. Napoleon therefore hurried westwards with 30,000 of his troops, hoping to trap Blücher against the Marne river, sandwiched between himself in the east and his two marshals in the west.

On 27 February Blücher began to cross to the north bank of the Marne at La Ferté, thirty-four miles east of Paris, and unsuccessfully assaulted Mortier and Marmont along the Ourcq river on both 28 February and 1 March. He intended to renew his attacks, but received reports of French troops in his rear and promptly transferred the rest of his army across the Marne. Later on 1 March, after being informed that Napoleon himself was on the way, he ordered a retreat northwards.

Napoleon, who had no bridging equipment, temporarily found himself brought up short by the Marne. Having failed to destroy the Army of Silesia, he instead resolved to drive it far to the north beyond the fortress of Laon, which would serve as a bulwark on the road to Paris should Blücher attempt a renewed advance. After containing Blücher, Napoleon intended to thrust eastwards and pick up the isolated garrisons of Metz and Verdun before turning south to fall on the communications of Schwarzenberg's Army of Bohemia.

Blücher continued to fall back northwards in the hope of collecting reinforcements, although he was unaware of their exact location. Two corps, under Generals Friedrich von Bülow and Ferdinand von Winzingerode, had been detached from Bernadotte's Army of the North currently operating against French forces in Belgium and had moved into north-eastern France. Blücher had ordered Winzingerode to join him farther south, but discovered on the morning of 3 March that both Winzingerode and Bülow were on their own initiative trying to capture the city of Soissons to ease his retreat.

The morale of Blücher's troops plummeted as they trudged on. Supplies

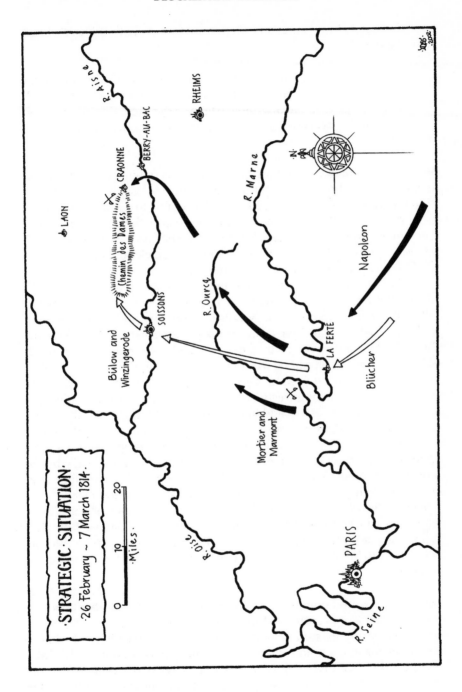

STRATEGIC · SITUATION ·
· 26 February ~ 7 March 1814 ·

· Miles ·
0   10   20

R. Aisne

R. Marne

R. Oise

R. Seine

R. Ourcq

Chemin des Dames

RHEIMS

BERRY-AU-BAC

CRAONNE

LAON

SOISSONS

LA FERTÉ

PARIS

Napoleon

Blücher

Bülow and Winzingerode

Mortier and Marmont

were short and Professor Henry Steffens, who was with Blücher's head-quarters, noted:

> In March, when Napoleon was in our rear and all communication was nearly cut off, our want became greater, and was felt severely amongst the men; the discipline began at the same time to fail; there was plunder everywhere; houses were sacked, and the inhabitants fled.[23]

Blücher now had to cross the swollen Aisne river, which flowed from east to west across his line of retreat. But after Soissons capitulated to Winzingerode and Bülow on 3 March, he was able to transfer his army to the north bank by the end of the next day using both the city's stone bridge and three pontoon bridges.[24] Now that he had united with his reinforcements, he had 100,000 men, mostly in the vicinity of Soissons but with cavalry posts farther east along the Aisne.

On the 5th Napoleon outflanked him twenty-five miles to the east by seizing the bridge over the Aisne at Berry-au-Bac; he then intended to follow the main road north-westwards to Laon. But Blücher countered by marching eastwards for sixteen miles along the plateau of the Chemin des Dames, which ran parallel to the Aisne and four miles to the north. Blücher as a result would be in a position to fall on the western flank of any French advance on Laon. Faced with this threat, Napoleon on the evening of the 6th swung westwards to drive what he took to be Blücher's rearguard from the eastern end of the Chemin des Dames near the village of Craonne. The fighting ended indecisively, but both sides prepared to resume the battle next morning. Blücher planned to keep part of his army on the Chemin des Dames to resist a frontal attack from the east, while he sent Winzingerode with one corps and a force of 11,000 cavalry on a wide circular movement to fall on Napoleon's northern flank and rear.

The Battle of Craonne raged bitterly for the whole of the 7th as Napoleon attacked westwards along the Chemin des Dames. But when Winzingerode's outflanking move failed to materialise in time, Blücher was forced to break contact and retreat on Laon. Napoleon had won the battle, but at a cost he could not afford: his casualties numbered over 5,500, while he inflicted under 4,800. He was also deluded into believing that Blücher would now retire far to the north and that another attack on his rearguard would suffice to hurry him on his way.

Blücher's army massed at Laon on the morning of the 8th. It had been retreating for a week and was in poor spirits. His Russian troops also resented the fact that they had suffered heavily at Craonne without their Prussian comrades being engaged. Furthermore, Bülow and Winzingerode's newly joined corps did not yet see themselves as an integral part of the army. Bülow's Prussians were horror-struck at the sight of their ragged and starving countrymen in the Army of Silesia and resented the fact that they had to share their supplies now that Blücher in falling back northwards had abandoned his original lines of communication. In short, the Army of Silesia had serious morale problems that could be cured only by a victory.

There is no mystery as to why Blücher chose to fight at Laon. It was both an important road junction and a superb defensive position, for the town stood on a flat-topped hill that rose abruptly 330 feet above the surrounding terrain, with slopes sometimes as steep as thirty degrees. The countryside to the north was flat and open, but to the south it was rough, marshy and wooded and would impede Napoleon's moves. Furthermore the villages of Ardon and Semilly at the foot of the hill served as advanced bastions.

Blücher now had about 90,000 troops and 176 guns. He entrusted the defence of Laon itself in the centre of his position to Bülow's Prussian corps. Bülow infested the southern and western slopes of the hill with skirmishers and stationed two battalions in each of the villages of Ardon and Semilly, while fifty guns on the top of the hill dominated the approaches. Blücher's western wing was provided by a Russian corps under Winzingerode, while the eastern wing consisted of two Prussian corps under Generals Hans von Yorck and Friedrich Kleist, which blocked the road from Berry-au-Bac. That left a reserve of two Russian corps under Generals Louis de Langeron and Fabian von der Osten-Sacken, which were hidden behind the hill of Laon. Small detachments were stationed well forward on the Soissons and Berry-au-Bac roads to give timely warning of any enemy approach from the south-west or south-east.

After Craonne, Napoleon had taken 27,000 of his men westwards along the Chemin des Dames to reach the Soissons road, which he then followed north-eastwards on Laon. But he detached 9,500 troops under Marshal Marmont to advance separately on Laon by the Berry-au-Bac road. Although he and Marmont were initially fifteen miles apart, their roads converged on Laon.

A preliminary action occurred on the evening of 8 March, when Napoleon's advanced guard chased a small Russian detachment from the village of Urcel on the Soissons road. It pressed on, but was unable to penetrate Etouvelles, three miles south-west of Laon, as the road led across a marsh which did not allow movement on either side. The Army of Silesia settled down for the night in its positions around Laon. General Winzingerode had managed to find lodgings in a mental hospital.[25]

The Battle of Laon began in the early hours of 9 March, when the French renewed their advance along the Soissons road. Marshal Ney surprised the Russian detachment at Etouvelles at 1.30 am, but was unable to capture the village of Chivy, half-a-mile to the north, until 4.00 am. A small detachment under General Gaspard Gourgaud, one of Napoleon's

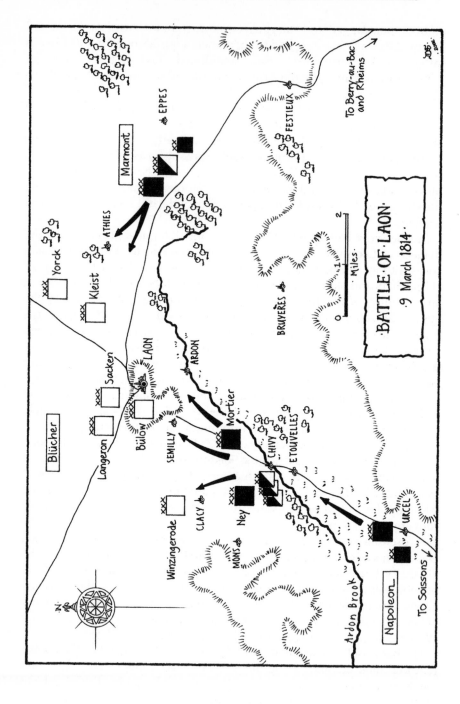

BATTLE·OF·LAON·
·9 March 1814·

orderly officers, had been sent to outflank the allied positions to the west and thus to ease Ney's advance, but had been delayed by poor roads and heavy snow and had lost its way.

Towards 5.30 am French dragoons arrived before Laon, but had lost all chance of making a surprise attack and withdrew under heavy fire. Visibility was minimal. 'When day broke,' wrote Carl von Müffling, one of Blücher's senior staff officers, 'the fog was so thick that we were unable to see a hundred paces before us.'[26] Snow had fallen heavily during the night and although it now ceased, it remained bitterly cold. From 7.00 am onwards, more French units arrived before Laon and attacked the villages of Ardon and Semilly. A company of Young Guardsmen even penetrated to the top of the hill before being driven back.

Blücher and Gneisenau directed the battle from the ruined ramparts on the south-western side of Laon. But Blücher was suffering from fever and inflamed eyes and although he spent some time on horseback, he was in no condition to ride for the whole day. For once, therefore, he was unable to lead from the front and had to direct the battle from the rear while seated on a wicker chair.[27] He could hardly have had a better observation post, for once the fog lifted towards 11.00 am, he could see the battlefield laid out below him. Professor Henry Steffens explained:

> It was not one continued battle, but different corps of the enemy as they came in sight were attacked, and engagements were taking place at several points distinct from each other at the same time. We saw all with perfect ease.

At one stage, Steffens saw a Russian square come under fierce attack:

> A mass of cavalry tried to hew a road into the middle of them; but they were not to be broken; they waved every way, and curved and bent, but always drew closer again into a dense mass as if they had been one single living body. It was a grand, a wonderful sight! . . . The generals themselves viewed the spectacle with amazement; Gneisenau was loud in his delight.[28]

Even at the top of the hill, Blücher had his share of danger and narrowly escaped death or injury when a cannonball smashed through a nearby windmill and wounded three officers with flying splinters of wood.[29]

Blücher and his command team planned initially to stay on the defensive and to attack only when Napoleon's intentions had become clear. Even Blücher became cautious, partly because he was ill and partly because a French prisoner had exaggerated Napoleon's strength. Whereas Napoleon in fact had only 36,500 men (including Marmont), Blücher and Gneisenau believed him to have 90,000. Blücher therefore assumed that the handful of French troops assaulting Laon from the south-west was merely a feint and that the bulk of Napoleon's troops had yet to arrive. He was strengthened in this belief towards noon when a message arrived from his son, who commanded a cavalry outpost at Festieux, seven miles to the south-east. Colonel Blücher reported that a strong French column (in fact Marmont's detachment) was advancing north-westwards on Laon.

If at this stage Blücher and his colleagues had committed their reserves on their western wing, they could have smashed Napoleon's forces here. But since the overall situation was unclear, they ordered only Winzingerode's corps to assail Napoleon's western flank near the village of Clacy. Blücher's aim, apparently, was to gauge whether the French forces on the Soissons road represented a feint or a serious attack: if they retired, this would indicate that Napoleon planned to make his real attack with the eastern column. But if they resisted, then the eastern column would probably come to them.

The lacklustre Winzingerode feebly probed the French positions and pulled back when he was counter-attacked by Marshal Ney. An allied officer, Woldemar von Löwenstern, revealed that Winzingerode spent most of the day on a mound from where he had a good view:

> Some cannon-balls came to visit us, but we hardly paid them any attention. I was astonished to see him so calm and quiet and so immobile. I do not remember having seen him on horseback for a single moment, except when he arrived and when he retired. His conduct during this whole day was totally peaceful and in-different.[30]

As a result of the stout French resistance to Winzingerode, Blücher decided that he needed to isolate Napoleon from his eastern column. He therefore ordered the recapture of the village of Ardon, which lay at the foot of the hill of Laon on the southern side. One of Bülow's infantry brigades duly seized the village, but on advancing farther was ordered to halt. This uncharacteristic command reflected Blücher's fears that the brigade could become dangerously exposed if the French eastern column turned off the Berry-au-Bac road and headed westwards across country through the village of Bruyères. Blücher resolved to wait until the battle developed further before he committed himself to an all-out attack and in the meantime, he sent Müffling to find out the strength and location of the French eastern column.

It was now 1.00 pm. Napoleon belatedly came forward to see the situation for himself, having been over-confident that his troops would not meet serious resistance. He decided to press home the attack, but when he mounted a heavy assault towards 4.30 pm, he found that the woods and marshy ground prevented his cavalry and artillery from adequately supporting his infantry. The French seized the village of Clacy by 6.30 pm, but were unable to advance across the easier terrain farther north in the face of concentrated artillery fire. Dusk descended on the snow-covered battlefield towards 7.00 pm. Napoleon had little to show for the day's fighting, for the stubborn hill-top town of Laon remained firmly in Blücher's hands.

The French eastern column that had caused Blücher such anxiety in fact consisted only of Marshal Marmont's 9,500 men and had been delayed by fog and Marmont's caution. It finally arrived east of Laon towards 5.00 pm and took the village of Athies from a Prussian advanced post. Marmont's men bivouacked around campfires, while he went to sleep in a château at Eppes, three miles away. Before doing so, he sent 1,000 men under Colonel Fabvier westwards towards the village of Bruyères, three-and-a-half miles south-east of Laon, to establish contact with Napoleon.

Blücher and Gneisenau heard Marmont's gunfire during the action at Athies and realised that Marmont was not heading westwards to link up with Napoleon. They therefore ordered a powerful counter-attack by their eastern wing, namely the Prussian corps of Yorck and Kleist. The army's reserves under Sacken and Langeron were to shift eastwards in support.

Despite his illness, Blücher had remained at his command post on the hill of Laon. Müffling recorded:

> When I returned from the left wing, just as it began to grow dark, to the point where the Field-Marshal had remained since the morning, I found him still on the same spot; and it was not until he had given all the orders for the day that we led him to his dwelling.[31]

Yorck attacked shortly after 7.00 pm and caught Marmont's men by surprise. Marmont arrived to find his troops fleeing south-eastwards and later wrote:

> Never shall I forget the music that accompanied our march. Light infantry cornets sounded, the enemy stopped and directed fire on us for some minutes. Silence followed, until a new music, announcing a new fire, sounded. Luckily, as the enemy was very close at the moment he fired, almost all his shots went too high.[32]

Kleist's corps sought to cut Marmont's escape route along the road to Berry-au-Bac. But Colonel Fabvier, whom Marmont had earlier detached to establish contact with Napoleon, heard the fighting and marched back eastwards. His 1,000 men and two guns sufficed to clear the road. Another undeserved stroke of good luck completed Marmont's salvation. Farther to the south-east, the road, having hitherto traversed open countryside, passed through a range of hills at Festieux. But when allied cavalry tried to block this defile, they were seen off by a mere 125 veterans of the Old Guard who happened to be passing through with a supply convoy.

Marmont finally rallied his troops at Corbeny, six miles north-west of Berry-au-Bac, having lost 3,500 men and forty-five of his fifty-five guns. He had only himself to blame for the setback: he no longer believed that Napoleon could win the war and was merely obeying orders, without zeal or initiative.

A succession of three ADCs reached Laon between 9.00 and 11.00 pm with increasingly good news of the outcome of the attack on Marmont. Blücher delightedly exclaimed: 'Upon my honour, you old Yorckists are worthy and reliable fellows. If I could not rely on you, the sky would fall.'[33] Then, with Gneisenau and Müffling, he planned what to do the next day. At about midnight, orders were sent for a bold outflanking move involving the corps of Sacken, Langeron, Yorck and Kleist sweeping round from the east on a wide axis to threaten Napoleon's line of retreat.[34]

News of Marmont's disaster reached Napoleon towards 5.00 am on the 10th. He was initially furious, but resolved to stand his ground, partly to cover Marmont's withdrawal, partly as he apparently still hoped that Blücher would resume his retreat and evacuate Laon.

Napoleon should have paid a heavy price for remaining in his exposed positions. That he did not do so was due to the illness that had struck down Blücher, thus paralysing the Army of Silesia and foiling its bold outflanking move. For on the morning of the 10th, Blücher found his eyes were so inflamed that he had to cover them with a bandage and was unable to leave his room. He could barely sign his name and suddenly seemed strangely indifferent to the battle.

At dawn, Müffling found Blücher's ante-room crowded with officers:

> Amongst them I observed many Russian generals, who were come to congratulate him on the result of the previous day, and also some inquisitive people and critics, and those croakers who are to be found at all head-quarters, when great events frighten them.[35]

Indeed, Blücher's collapse unnerved his subordinates, who missed his rumbustious energy and self-confidence. The Russian General Louis de Langeron was next in seniority and dreaded the prospect of having to take over. 'For God's sake,' he exclaimed at one stage, 'let us take this corpse along with us!'[36] Gneisenau was effectively in command, but he was junior to several of the corps commanders and so Blücher, although incapacitated, remained nominally in charge.

Suddenly saddled with supreme responsibility, Gneisenau cancelled the bold outflanking move that had been ordered the previous night and settled instead for the safe and unambitious policy of holding Laon. It was simply too good a defensive position: it offered a security that Gneisenau was loath to leave for the hazards of the country farther south.

So that day, the Army of Silesia made only limited frontal attacks west of Laon. When Winzingerode's Russians took heavy losses in vain attempts to seize the village of Clacy, Gneisenau drew some of Bülow's Prussians from Laon to act in support. Ironically, this worsened the situation, for Napoleon spotted the Prussian battalions moving out and mistakenly assumed that they were evacuating their position. He hence attacked and, although ultimately repelled, added to Gneisenau's caution. Then, towards the end of the day, Napoleon finally recognised failure and slipped away under the cover of darkness. Only on the 11th did Cossacks and other allied troops mount a pursuit and they failed to show much vigour after falling into an ambush.

The two days of fighting had cost the French 6,500 casualties. 'My losses are not very great,' Blücher wrote to his wife. 'The enemy has lost many men, for he wanted to take my position by brute force.'[37] Even so, Napoleon had extracted himself from a potential disaster and three days later he recaptured the city of Rheims, thus dramatically repairing the damage to his reputation. He then struck once more at Schwarzenberg's army farther south.

The Army of Silesia remained inactive for a week after Laon. Gneisenau's caution was one problem, but so too was shortage of supplies. Furthermore, the battle had failed to heal the tensions between the Russian and Prussian contingents. The Prussians had been heavily engaged at Laon, but Gneisenau's caution on the second day had exasperated the Russian corps commanders who suspected that he had called off the pursuit of Marmont by the Prussian corps of Yorck and Kleist to avoid further casualties.

Ironically, Yorck himself thought that Gneisenau's motive had been to rob him of the glory. On top of this, Yorck was subsequently ordered to take up quarters in an area already stripped of resources. This was too much. Yorck, who viewed obedience as an optional extra, rather than the essence of military service, abruptly left in his coach and was brought back only by an appeal from Blücher. 'Old comrade,' Blücher scribbled, with his ADC guiding his hand, 'history should not have to relate such things of us! Be sensible and come back!'[38]

Such were the problems that followed the battle and they showed conclusively that Blücher, whatever his intellectual limitations, was indispensable at the head of his army, not merely to act as a figurehead, but to boost morale and cohesion and provide the sheer driving force that enabled his army to play such a prominent role in the campaigns of 1813–15.

NOTES

1   E. Henderson, *Blücher and the uprising of Prussia against Napoleon 1806–1815* (1911), p.3
2   Earl of Stanhope, *Notes of conversations with the Duke of Wellington* (1938), p.120; A. Horne, *How far from Austerlitz?* (1996), p.198
3   Henderson, *op. cit.*, p.79
4   *Ibid*, pp.100–1
5   C. von Müffling, *The memoirs of Baron von Müffling* (1997), pp.39–40
6   P. Vermeil de Conchard, *Marshal Blücher as portrayed in his correspondence* (1896), p.18
7   Müffling, *op. cit.*, p.419
8   *Ibid*, pp.105–6
9   Vermeil de Conchard, *op. cit.*, p.34
10 W. von Unger, *Blücher* (1907–8), v.2, p.302
11 P. Carew, 'A hussar of the hundred days,' in *Blackwood's Magazine* (November 1945)
12 Müffling, *op. cit.*, p.225
13 A. Brett-James, *Europe against Napoleon* (1970), p.45
14 R. Parkinson, *Hussar general: the life of Blücher, man of Waterloo* (1975), p.244
15 Blücher also shared in the allied defeats of Lützen and Bautzen in 1813 at Napoleon's hands. In 1806 he fought at Auerstädt while Napoleon won Jena less than fifteen miles away. In 1814 Napoleon beat elements of the Army of Silesia at the Battles of Champaubert, Montmirail and Château Thierry, but Blücher was not personally present.
16 Parkinson, *op. cit.*, p.12
17 Müffling, *op. cit.*, p.217
18 Stanhope, *op. cit.*, p.120
19 Vermeil de Conchard, *op. cit.*, p.78
20 *Ibid*, p.79
21 H. Steffens, *Adventures on the road to Paris, during the campaigns of 1813–14* (1848), p.74
22 Müffling, *op. cit.*, pp.148–53, 472
23 Steffens, *op. cit.*, pp.145–6
24 The cowardice of the commandant of Soissons in capitulating has caused considerable controversy. But Blücher would probably have escaped without serious loss even if Soissons had held out, although the city's bridge certainly eased the transfer of his army. See F. Loraine Petre, *Napoleon at bay* (1994), pp.111–15.
25 M. Weil, ed., *Mémoires du général-major russe Baron de Löwenstern* (1903), v.2, p.342
26 Müffling, *op. cit.*, p.484
27 Unger, *Blücher*, v.2, p.212
28 Steffens, *op cit.*, p.152
29 Unger, *Blücher*, v.2, p.213; Vermeil de Conchard, *op. cit.*, p.36
30 Weil, *op. cit.*, v.2, p.347
31 Müffling, *op. cit.*, p.164
32 A. Marmont, *Mémoires du maréchal Marmont, duc de Raguse* (1857), v.6, pp.213–14
33 Unger, *Blücher*, v.2, p.214
34 Müffling claimed that this plan originated wholly with him, but, as the great French historian Henry Houssaye wrote acidly, 'so says Müffling, who

always attributes good advice to himself.' See H. Houssaye, *Napoleon and the campaign of 1814* (1914), trans. R. McClintock, pp.168–9.

35   Müffling, *op. cit.*, p.167
36   *Ibid*, p.174
37   W. von Unger, *Blüchers Briefe* (1913), pp.231–2
38   Henderson, *op. cit.*, p.244

CHAPTER IX

Bagration and Barclay de Tolly

Napoleon's retreat from Moscow in the winter of 1812 is the most famous disaster of military history. But it constituted only the final part of his mighty invasion of Russia and has overshadowed the almost fatal problems that the Russians had encountered in the summer during their own demoralising retreat in the face of Napoleon's advance. Despite his own difficulties, Napoleon could in fact have won a decisive victory in the first weeks of the campaign.

Two Russian generals figured prominently in these crucial early stages: Prince Peter Ivanovich Bagration and Prince Mikhail Bogdanovich Barclay de Tolly. They differed sharply in both background and character and unfortunately this produced a monstrous personality clash. Of the two, Bagration has always been the popular hero. An eyewitness, Sir Robert Wilson, has described him brilliantly:

> Bagrathion was by birth a Georgian, of short stature, with strong dark features, and eyes flashing with Asiatic fire. Gentle, gracious, generous, chivalrously brave, he was beloved by every one, and admired by all who witnessed his exploits. No officer ever excelled him in the direction of an advance or rear guard; nor had any officer's capacity in these commands ever been more severely tested.[1]

Bagration was born in 1765 in the city of Kizliar in the Caucasus and came from an ancient Georgian royal dynasty. When Russia annexed the Kingdom of Georgia in 1801, the Bagrations simply entered the Russian nobility. The family was renowned not merely for martial prowess: one of Bagration's nephews would discover the cyanide process for extracting gold from ore.

Bagration himself followed his father into the Russian Army in 1782. These were the years of Catherine the Great's reign, when an expansionist Russia repeatedly clashed with her three great enemies: the Swedes in the north, the Poles in the west and the Ottoman Turks in the south. Bagration soon saw action, first against the Turks in the Caucasus (1787–92) and then as a colonel during the Polish rebellion of 1794. During this time, he came under the wing of one of Russia's foremost commanders, the inspirational Alexander Suvorov, whose insistence on vigorous bayonet charges rather than more methodical tactics left a lasting impression.

Bagration's next taste of action came in 1799 during Suvorov's famous campaign to wrest northern Italy from the French. Napoleon Bonaparte had seized this area from Austria two years previously, but was now campaigning in Egypt and Syria. Suvorov arrived in April 1799 with about 20,000 Russian troops and then, incorporating into his command the Austrian forces in this theatre, pushed westwards along the southern edge of the Alps. On 21 April Bagration, as part of the allied advanced guard, helped to take the town of Brescia. This was a minor success, but won Bagration promotion to major-general because it was the first victory in which the Russians had taken part. Eager to add to his glory, he attacked a French rearguard the next day at Palazzolo on the Oglio river but was bloodily repulsed.

On the 26th Bagration with 3,000 troops was again checked, this time at the walled town of Lecco at the northern end of the Adda river, which formed the new defence line of the French Army of Italy as it covered Milan. Despite Bagration's failure, Suvorov managed by the end of the 27th to establish bridgeheads across the Adda farther south. Among the prisoners he took was General Philibert Sérurier, a future marshal under Napoleon. Sérurier rightly criticised Bagration's fervour, only to be told by Suvorov: 'What do you expect? We Russians understand nothing. We are without rules and without tactics.'[2]

Demoralised by its defeats, the Army of Italy fell right back to near Genoa. But Suvorov then had to march eastwards to reinforce an Austrian detachment against a French army advancing from southern Italy under General Jacques Macdonald. Three days of battle followed on the Tidone and Trebbia rivers, forty miles south-east of Milan. The fighting began on 17 June with the leading Russians arriving exhausted on the battlefield. Suvorov ordered his men to attack immediately and brushed aside Bagration's remonstrations that the relentless marching had left no more than forty men in each company. 'And Macdonald does not have even twenty in his! Attack with what the good Lord has sent you! Hurrah!'

Bagration was in the thick of the fight both that day and the next. But the climax came on the 19th, when Macdonald took the offensive and began to make headway. Bagration told Suvorov that things were going badly. 'Not so good, Prince Peter,' Suvorov replied. Then he called for his horse and personally led Bagration's electrified men against the French. Fighting continued into the evening, but Macdonald decided to retreat, having suffered heavy casualties.

After this victory, Suvorov marched back westwards to tackle the Army of Italy, now reinforced by Macdonald's remnants and commanded by General Barthélemy Joubert. The two sides clashed twenty-five miles north of Genoa on 15 August and Bagration was bloodily repulsed as he repeatedly attacked the walled town of Novi in the centre. But Joubert was killed and his army finally vanquished in the afternoon after its flanks were driven in.

By now, the French retained in northern Italy only the city of Genoa. Suvorov was ordered to take his Russians northwards into Switzerland to join the Austro-Russian forces already operating there under Generals Alexander Rimski-Korsakov and Friedrich von Hotze and defeat the French Army of Helvetia under General André Massena.

Suvorov found his advance through the Alps blocked at the St Gotthard pass, but despite the mountainous terrain broke through with the help of Bagration, who fought his way along the heights overlooking the pass to menace the French eastern flank. The French merely fell back to an even better position at the Devil's Bridge, which crossed a chasm and could be attacked only after passing through a gorge. Suvorov desperately fought his way through and continued his advance northwards, with Bagration leading the way. But towards the end of September, he learned that Massena had already beaten Korsakov and Hotze. Left dangerously isolated, he immediately began to retreat.

With the advanced guard, Bagration successfully fought his way eastwards along a gorge, driving back a French brigade that was blocking the army's escape route. Then, on 5 October, he took over the rearguard for the next stage of the retreat, south to the upper Rhine and then down the river to lower and less exposed ground. He did not distinguish himself during this phase, retreating too soon after the rest of the troops and at one point apparently leaving his command under French attack to cope as best it could on its own.[3]

Suvorov, despite the bitter winter conditions and the shortage of food and ammunition, brought the bulk of his men to safety. Tsar Paul I ordered his troops to return home, but arbitrarily refused Suvorov the honour of a parade into St Petersburg. Stricken with sorrow, Suvorov died in May 1800 within three weeks of his return. Bagration, sent by Paul to report on Suvorov's condition, was able to bid farewell to his mentor. He later recalled how Suvorov:

> coming to himself, . . . looked at me, and in his big eyes the look of life was no more. He gazed long at me, as if getting to know who I was; then he said, 'Ah! . . . it's you, Peter! How are you?' and he was silent and forgot himself.[4]

Bagration married in 1800, but not very happily. His wife, Katharina, had an illegitimate daughter two years later by the Austrian statesman, Prince Clemens von Metternich, and was later mistress to both Tsar Alexander I and the slippery French politician, Charles-Maurice de Talleyrand.

Bagration for his part would have an affair in 1807 with the 19-year-old Grand Duchess Catherine Pavlovna, Tsar Alexander's favourite sister.

It was Paul's murder in 1801 that brought the young Alexander to the throne. When war broke out with Napoleon four years later, Bagration marched with the leading Russian army commanded by General Mikhail Kutusov to join an Austrian army under General Karl Mack von Leiberich in the Danube valley. But Napoleon forced Mack to surrender at Ulm before the Russians could arrive, obliging Kutusov to beat a retreat back down the Danube.

Bagration proved his valour and skill as Kutusov's rearguard commander and on 4–5 November fought a bitter delaying action near Amstetten. Kutusov managed to get his army over to the north bank of the Danube and headed north-eastwards to join a Russian army under General Friedrich Buxhöwden. But the French seized a bridge over the Danube at Vienna and thrust due north in a bid to block the retreat. Kutusov detached Bagration to occupy a defile near the village of Schöngraben, twenty-five miles north-west of Vienna, and win time while the rest of his army passed behind. Knowing that it was virtually a suicide mission, Kutusov made the sign of the cross on Bagration's forehead.

Bagration was heavily outnumbered, but fortified his position. During the battle that ensued on 16 November, he beat off the French, defied a surrender summons, repeatedly counter-attacked and finally slipped away under the cover of darkness with the surviving half of his command. He rejoined Kutusov, who hugged him and exclaimed: 'I don't ask you what you have lost. You are alive: that's enough for me.'[5]

Kutusov successfully united with Buxhöwden's army on the 19th and was joined by additional Russian and Austrian troops. But Napoleon skilfully exploited the belligerent mood of Tsar Alexander and his suite to lure the allies into attacking him at Austerlitz on 2 December. Bagration commanded the right wing in the northern sector of the battlefield, while the mass of the allied army made an outflanking attack in the south. Napoleon's sudden counter stroke smashed the weak allied centre, but in the north Bagration retreated in good order, despite being slightly wounded in the thigh. His resistance could not save the army but did limit the extent of the disaster and enabled many fugitives to escape. He alone of the Russian generals emerged from the campaign with increased stature, since Kutusov was unfairly made a scapegoat by the Tsar.

By his decisive victory, Napoleon forced Austria to make peace and the Russians to withdraw from central Europe. But ten months later, in October 1806, Prussia belatedly abandoned her neutrality. Napoleon quickly smashed the Prussian Army and then advanced into East Prussia and Poland, where the Russians were again taking the field. During the bitter fighting that followed, Bagration regularly acted as the Russian rearguard commander and fought several delaying actions. He was heavily engaged at Eylau in February 1807 and it was in his honour that the town of Preussisch-Eylau was renamed Bagrationovsk following its incorporation into the Soviet Union after World War Two. In June 1807 he saw action at Guttstadt and Heilsberg and also at Friedland, where he formed the allied left wing, which, bearing the brunt of Napoleon's devastating attack, was trapped against the Alle river and crushed.

Napoleon triumphantly concluded the war by securing an alliance with Russia in the Peace of Tilsit. This allowed Russia to turn her attention to other foes. In February 1808 Bagration took part in the invasion of Finland, which wrested that province from the Swedes. Then, in the spring of 1809, the Russians mounted a remarkable attack by three columns across the frozen Gulf of Bothnia to carry the war into Sweden itself. The role of Bagration's column, the strongest of the three, was to capture the strategically important Åland Islands, which lay midway between Finland and the Swedish capital, Stockholm. Bagration, whose column was accompanied by the Minister of War, Alexei Arakcheev, set off from Abo on 10 March across the desolate icescape. He took the Åland Islands and pursued the Swedish garrison. He captured forty guns, thousands of muskets and even some ships trapped in the frozen harbours and also sent a cavalry detachment to raid the Swedish coast just sixty miles from Stockholm. Although the Åland Islands were a sticking point in subsequent peace negotiations, they remained in Russian hands and Bagration, like Barclay de Tolly, was appointed a full general in recognition of his conduct.

Bagration was then transferred to fight the Turks, who had been at war with Russia since 1806. He took command of the Army of the Danube for nearly a year from August 1809. He operated on what is now the border between Bulgaria and Romania, but had mixed fortunes, partly as he had to cope with a typhus epidemic and severe shortages of supplies. Although he won some actions, he was beaten by the Turks at the Battle of Tataritza in October 1809 and had to abandon the siege of Silistria. He was consequently replaced. Then, in 1812, following the deterioration of Russia's relations with France, he found himself at the head of the 2nd Army of the West, 48,000 men strong and positioned on the western frontier. North of him stood the 127,000 troops of the 1st Army of the West, under Barclay de Tolly.

Unlike Bagration, Barclay attained high rank by merit not birth. He was the great-grandson of a Scotsman who had settled in Livonia, which became part of the Russian empire in 1721. He was born at Luhdegrosshof, fifty miles south of Riga, on 27 December 1761. His father had been a subaltern in the Russian Army, while his mother's family had served with the Swedes. Barclay's two surviving brothers both had military careers and one of them became a general.

Barclay lived from the age of 3 with foster-parents in St Petersburg since his father was in debt. His foster-father had served under Frederick the Great and had Lutheran ideals of discipline and hard work. Barclay proved good at mathematics and finance, learnt French and German and was encouraged by his foster-parents to read avidly.

He officially entered the Russian Army as a lance-corporal when he was 6 years old, but only actually served from the age of 15. His military career initially progressed slowly, for after being promoted to cornet in 1778, he reached the rank of lieutenant only after eight years. But war broke out with the Ottoman Turks in 1787 and brought Barclay to the notice of several commanders who furthered his advancement. Foremost among these was General Prince Victor-Amadeus Anhalt-Bernburg, whom Barclay served as adjutant. When the prince was mortally wounded in 1790, he gave his sword to Barclay, who took it with him throughout the rest of his career. The highpoint of Barclay's service against the Turks was the storming of the fortress of Ochakov in December 1788, in which he displayed his characteristic coolness in the face of danger.

In April 1790 Barclay arrived in Finland where the Swedes had started an indecisive conflict that ended in August and the following year he married a cousin, Auguste von Smitten. They were deeply in love and although only one of their children survived to adulthood, they fostered others. By now, Barclay had fought both the Turks and the Swedes and in 1792 and 1794 he saw action against the Poles as a battalion commander. He had acquired a valuable range of experience, in the infantry and cavalry and on the staff, and attained the rank of major-general in 1799.

Barclay was not present at Austerlitz in 1805, but had his share of the fighting in East Prussia and Poland a year later and particularly distinguished himself at Pultusk on 26 December 1806. Even he was shaken after this battle when, while looking for one of his batteries, he mistook a French unit for a friendly force and narrowly escaped with his life.

Fighting flared up again in the middle of January 1807 when the Russians under General Levin Bennigsen tried to surprise Napoleon in his winter quarters and had to retreat before his powerful riposte. Barclay, commanding one of the three Russian rearguards that were under Bagration's overall command, fought some desperate actions, particularly at Hof on 6 February. The next day was the eve of the bloody Battle of Eylau and it saw Barclay heavily involved in a preliminary action, the defence of the town of Preussisch-Eylau against heavy French attacks. He personally led a cavalry charge in the evening to drive the enemy back, but had to leave the field after being badly wounded in the arm.

Tsar Alexander visited Barclay while he was in hospital in Memel and later that year promoted him to lieutenant-general. As a result of his wound, Barclay did not share in the defeat of Friedland that June and had time to consider how to counter Napoleon should he continue into Russia.

As it happened, Napoleon concluded peace at Tilsit in July 1807, but Barclay decided that the correct strategy would have been to withdraw into the interior.

In February 1808, during the Russian invasion of Finland, Barclay commanded a division in reserve. The Russians initially made good progress against the Swedes, but were then heavily counter-attacked. Barclay took part in the fighting that ensued and learnt much from the conflict, not least from the effect that enemy irregulars had on his supply lines. He was given leave after falling ill in July, but joined Alexander's councils-of-war back in St Petersburg.

By the end of 1808, Russia had reversed a series of setbacks and conquered all of Finland. The next phase was the attack over the frozen Gulf of Bothnia on Sweden proper, with Barclay leading the central column and capturing the town of Umeå. The campaign ended when the Swedes obtained an armistice after overthrowing their mad king, Gustavus IV, in March 1809, but Barclay's health had been permanently impaired by the harsh winter conditions. In April 1809 he became both Commander-in-Chief and Governor-General in Finland. Alexander knew that he was appointing Barclay over the heads of senior men, but ignored the outcry. Barclay justified the trust placed in him and won the Finns over to Russian rule. Since Alexander had ordered the armistice to be broken off, Barclay continued to prosecute the war against Sweden, but without any dramatic success before the conclusion of peace in September 1809.

As a result of his loyalty and administrative skills, Barclay was made Minister of War in January 1810. He did much to modernise the Russian Army in the next two years leading up to Napoleon's invasion, even though inertia and shortage of time limited the effectiveness of many of his reforms.

He re-organised the Ministry of War, actively gathered intelligence and began to establish fortifications and depots in western Russia (few of which would in fact be ready in time). He redeployed more troops to this front and positioned them to reflect Napoleon's reported moves; he also urged Alexander to free further units by ending the war with the Ottoman Turks.

Barclay more than doubled the Russian Army's strength to around 490,000 by three huge levies of serfs and tried to soften the notoriously cruel treatment of the rank and file. But the Russians were still heavily outnumbered when hostilities broke out and despite greater emphasis on musketry training, still carried a wide variety of often poor quality firearms.

Barclay introduced new regulations at the beginning of 1812 to replace those of Peter the Great. These *Regulations for the functioning of a large army in the field* (better known as the *Yellow Book*) set out in detail the functions of the various branches and levels of command and would remain basically unchanged for half-a-century. Unfortunately, Barclay found it harder to improve the notoriously inefficient Russian staff or increase the quality and numbers of junior officers.

In April 1812 Barclay organised the three armies on Russia's western frontier into corps, for the Russians had hitherto lacked any permanent formations higher than the division. That same month, he took up an appointment as commander of the 1st Army of the West: although officially still Minister of War, he left its business in the hands of a subordinate.

The Russians deployed their three Armies of the West too near the frontier and on a ridiculously long front. The 3rd Army, south of the Pripet marshes, would confront only forces guarding the southern flank of Napoleon's invasion, but in the crucial northern sector, Barclay's 1st Army and Bagration's 2nd covered over 300 miles, from the Baltic Sea in the north to the Pripet marshes in the south. The Russians ran the risk of being beaten piecemeal before they could concentrate and would have done better to deploy farther back, ready to move once Napoleon had revealed the direction of his main thrust. Their faulty dispositions stemmed partly from a serious underestimation of Napoleon's numbers and partly from the indecision of Tsar Alexander over which strategy to adopt. Among the options considered were defensive operations along the frontier, a retreat into the interior and even a pre-emptive strike into the Duchy of Warsaw. Alexander paid too much attention to one of his advisers, General Ernst von Phull, who wanted Barclay to retreat north-eastwards on to a fortified camp at Drissa. The idea was that after Napoleon arrived in front of this camp, Bagration would strike against his vulnerable flank and rear from the south.

When Napoleon invaded on 24 June, Barclay duly fell back to Drissa, only to find that the fortified camp was incomplete and that Napoleon could simply march straight past its southern flank and cut him off from Bagration. Alexander belatedly realised the foolishness of Phull's plan and Barclay resumed his retreat on 14 July, this time heading south-eastwards to draw closer to Bagration.

Alexander now accepted that his place was in the interior and took his leave of Barclay on the evening of the 16th. 'Goodbye General,' he told him. 'I recommend my Army to you. Do not forget that it is the only one I have. Always bear this in mind.'[6] Unfortunately, Alexander lacked the strength of character to make clear that Barclay was now Commander-in-Chief, with authority over Bagration. Lieutenant Carl von Clausewitz, a Prussian observer, admitted that:

> How the matter really stood as to the command, no one exactly knew, and I think that even now a writer would have difficulty in explicitly defining, without admitting that the Emperor had adopted a half measure.[7]

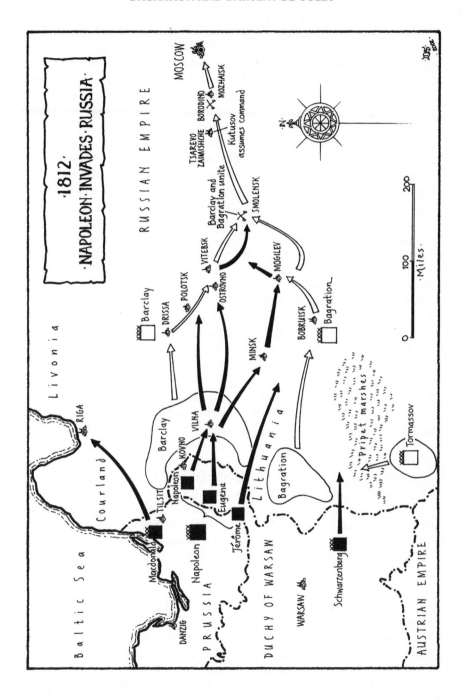

Barclay was unaware of Bagration's exact location, but knew that he had to join him as soon as possible. On the 25th Barclay's rearguard saw action near the village of Ostrovno and for a while he seemed willing to offer battle ten miles farther east, at Vitebsk. Napoleon did not attack immediately and instead waited for his rearmost units to come up. But Barclay slipped away before dawn on the 28th. By now he had heard from Bagration and was intent on uniting with him at the city of Smolensk, eighty miles to the south-east. Napoleon, meanwhile, had to halt for over a week at Vitebsk to rest and collect his troops.

During this time, Bagration had been retreating under alternate conditions of pouring rain and scorching sun. Napoleon had wanted three corps under his younger brother, Prince Jérôme Bonaparte, to pin him down while another corps under Marshal Louis Davout descended from the north to cut his line of retreat. But Jérôme by some oversight had been placed too far back from the frontier and although he marched as fast as possible, he could merely harass Bagration's rearguard.

Bagration was prevented by Davout's presence from heading directly to join Barclay. He therefore retired eastwards to the fortress of Bobruisk, crossed the Beresina river and then advanced north-eastwards towards Vitebsk, only to find himself blocked by Davout south of Mogilev on 23 July. Davout, who did not have all his corps with him, was in fact heavily outnumbered, but chose a tough defensive position behind a ravine. Bagration was so over-confident that he sent an ADC to suggest that Davout should retire and avoid an unnecessary battle. Davout refused and then checked Bagration's repeated attacks across the ravine. Bagration disengaged, fell back, crossed to the east bank of the Dnieper river and successfully marched north-eastwards on Smolensk, unpursued by Davout's exhausted corps.

Barclay by now was being heavily criticised. Many senior figures indignantly railed against the policy of retreating without a battle and pointedly referred to Barclay as 'The Minister', rather than as general or commander. He found himself almost isolated even in his own headquarters: his Chief-of-Staff, General Alexei Ermolov, for example, was a friend of Bagration and thus a vocal critic. The presence in his suite of a German staff officer, Colonel Ludwig von Wolzogen, only worsened matters, for the xenophobic Russians saw him as a fat, poisonous spider who exerted a sinister influence. Barclay himself was sometimes seen as a foreigner because of his ancestry and German accent.

Bagration was among the most vituperative of Barclay's accusers and informed one of Tsar Alexander's favourites that 'a man must really be a traitor to the Tsar and the country to lead us to destruction in this way.'[8] Bagration never understood, or refused to accept, that the Russian armies simply had to retreat to avoid destruction. Part of the problem stemmed from the period when Alexander had been personally present with

Barclay's army and had repeatedly sent Bagration orders to join Barclay in the north. Bagration had resented these impossible demands and wrongly assumed that Barclay was behind them. Thus distance served to increase misunderstandings, rather than soften the friction between the two men.

Bagration's complaints bordered on the hysterical. 'I am not to blame,' he wrote. 'I cannot defend the whole of Russia on my own.' He even wanted Barclay to attack in the north in order to divert enemy attention from himself. Although Barclay remained calm, his position was increasingly undermined. Alexander did not rate Bagration highly as a general, but could not afford to ignore the clamour against Barclay, for he remembered how his own father, Paul I, had been murdered after antagonising the Russian nobility.

Barclay and Bagration successfully united at Smolensk on 3 August. Their first move was a half-hearted counter-offensive to the north-west, but this was quickly aborted as Napoleon advanced. After a bloody defensive battle at Smolensk on the 17th, Barclay ordered a resumption of the retreat and fought his way out of danger.

Smolensk marked the start of a new phase, for the Russians after falling back from their exposed and over-extended forward positions no longer ran the risk of being outmanoeuvred and destroyed piecemeal. Barclay thus saved the Russian armies and contributed to Napoleon's eventual destruction, but in doing so retreated between 400 and 500 miles in seven weeks. For this, Russian pride demanded that Barclay no longer be in charge of their armies. On 17 August Tsar Alexander had assembled a committee to decide on a Commander-in-Chief to co-ordinate Russia's armies. The verdict was unanimous in favour of General Mikhail Kutusov.

Meanwhile, Barclay knew that he had to fight a major battle west of Moscow, but was unable to find a strong defensive position amid the open and gently rolling countryside. Barclay sent his Quartermaster-General, Colonel Toll, to select the best available battleground, but found that Toll's choice, a spot fifty miles east of Smolensk near Dorogobuzh, was unsuitable and so continued the retreat to Tsarevo-Zaimishche, 100 miles from Moscow.

Barclay learnt of Kutusov's appointment on 27 August from a blunt and official notification. He took the news with dignity, and apparently some relief,[9] and two days later showed the newly arrived Kutusov the position at Tsarevo-Zaimishche. Kutusov at first approved, but abandoned it on the morning of the 30th.

Borodino, just eighty miles west of Moscow, was the ground on which Kutusov finally halted and fought a pitched battle on 7 September. Barclay's 1st Army held the northern sector, with Bagration's 2nd Army in the south. Kutusov exercised a loose control from the rear and left direction of the fighting almost totally to his two army commanders and their subordinates. Barclay began the battle in a depressed state of mind, for he had been treated badly and wished to find release in a hero's death. Unusually for him, he had donned full-dress uniform with decorations. Major von Löwenstern described how Barclay:

> galloped along the whole extent of the line and continuously exposed himself to the greatest dangers, but did not for a moment lose his calm attitude. He was in his general's embroidered uniform, with all his decorations and his plumed hat. He was a sharp contrast with several of the other generals who for the most part had none of the distinctive marks of their ranks and who carefully hid their decorations so as not to be noticed by the enemy sharpshooters.[10]

But he did not die. By a quirk of fate, it was Bagration who fell, when he was shot in the leg towards 10.00 am while counter-attacking the enemy in his sector. He bravely tried to hide the injury, but found the effort too much and collapsed. His men caught him just in time, laid him on the ground and then, despite his reluctance to leave the field, carried him to the rear. So often had he escaped death and tight corners that they had come to believe him to be invincible. Rumours immediately spread that he had been killed and morale slumped.

Major Woldemar von Löwenstern, ADC to Barclay de Tolly, was also wounded and found Bagration at a medical post. He was lying on the grass, surrounded by doctors and staff officers, and was bearing the pain heroically as the ball was extracted from his leg. 'What is General Barclay doing?' he asked. 'Tell him that the fate of the army is in his hands. All goes well up to now.' Then he noticed that Löwenstern, too, was injured and added: 'Ah, go and have your wound dressed.'[11] Another eyewitness described how blood had soaked Bagration's clothes and splashed his head, how his uniform was unbuttoned and how a boot had been removed. 'His face, covered with dark patches of gun powder, was pale but calm' and he stared intently at the horizon as he listened to the thunder of the guns.[12]

They took the wounded Bagration to Moscow and, when that city was evacuated, farther into the interior of Russia. But in spirit, he never left his command. To the last, noted the British observer Sir Robert Wilson, Bagration 'was as anxious for all the details of what was passing as if he had been still at the head of his army.' Wilson told him that Alexander had refused to agree to any peace treaty while an armed Frenchman remained in Russia. Bagration squeezed Wilson's hand and said: 'dear General, you have made me die happy, for then Russia will assuredly not be disgraced.'[13] He died on 24 September, aged 46; twenty-seven years later, his remains were reburied in the Great Redoubt at Borodino.

Fortified by rum and a bit of bread, Barclay fought on at Borodino. He seemed to have forgotten his death wish in the heat of battle, now that so much depended on him. His conduct went far to wiping out the slanders that he was a traitor and when he passed the Russian Guard, he even heard cheering.[14]

The Russians were so mauled by the end of the battle that Kutusov had to resume the retreat. This brought him on 13 September to the western outskirts of Moscow, where General Levin Bennigsen had managed to pick a lousy position. Barclay bluntly said, 'the only thing I desire is to be killed if we are mad enough to fight here where we are'[15] and at a council-of-war held that day at Fili his views were echoed by others. He correctly advised the abandonment of Moscow; this eased Kutusov's decision to do just that, but led to Barclay being used as a scapegoat.

Barclay and Miloradovitch ably handled the retreat through Moscow; Kutusov then moved his forces by a circular route to a camp at Tarutino forty-six miles south-west of the city. Here, Barclay fell ill and suffered further humiliation at the end of September when Kutusov ordered the 1st and 2nd Armies to be merged into one. Barclay as a result lacked any meaningful role and so obtained six months' sick leave and set out for his home at Beckhof near the Baltic. His ADC, Lieutenant-Colonel von Löwenstern, claimed that the army suddenly thought of itself as orphaned when it saw Barclay depart.[16] But the mood in Russia as a whole was grim. Kutusov had sought in a letter to the Tsar to put the blame for the abandonment of Moscow on Barclay's loss of Smolensk. To safeguard his own position, the Tsar weakly acquiesced and allowed the letter's publication; Barclay as a result was nearly attacked by a mob on his way to Beckhof.

Relaxation with his family restored Barclay's health and made him keen to rejoin the fight. In February 1813 he assumed command of the 3rd Army of the West, in place of the incompetent Admiral Paul Chichagov. His popularity had already begun to recover as the military situation improved with Napoleon's disastrous retreat from Russia at the end of 1812. Indeed, a corps commander in 3rd Army noted:

> The admiral . . . left immediately, pursued by the curses and hatred of his whole army, which saw Barclay arrive like one for whose arrival it had prayed for a long time. It was a real day of celebration for us.[17]

Barclay's army was in fact little more than a corps in terms of numbers and was further weakened by detachments. But he took the fortress of Thorn on the Vistula river in April and then marched westwards as part of the advance of the Russians and their newly liberated Prussian allies.

Napoleon, who had meanwhile raised a replacement army in France, now returned to central Europe, counter-attacked the allies and beat them at Lützen on 2 May. Barclay did not arrive in time for this battle, but saw action later that month at Bautzen, where he helped defend the allied northern wing against a potentially dangerous outflanking move.

Following Bautzen, the allies retreated and General Ludwig Wittgenstein resigned as Commander-in-Chief because he found it impossible to cope with continually being overruled by Tsar Alexander, who accompanied him in the field. On 31 May Alexander appointed Barclay to fill the vacancy, thus atoning for his supersession after Smolensk. Shortly afterwards, on 4 June, Napoleon agreed to the armistice of Pleischwitz, which would last, with an extension, until 10 August. Barclay took advantage of this breathing space to overhaul the Russian forces. He had wanted the Russians to fall right back to reorganise in the safety of Poland, even though this would have exposed his Prussian allies and reduced the likelihood of neutral Austria joining the allied coalition. Fortunately, Prussian protests persuaded the Russians to retire only as far as Reichenbach in Silesia.

By the time the armistice expired in August, Austria had joined Russia, Prussia and Sweden in the field in central Europe. Barclay commanded a combined Russo-Prussian army that formed part of the Army of Bohemia under the Austrian Field Marshal Prince Karl von Schwarzenberg. Although Schwarzenberg was also the allied Supreme Commander, Barclay had little respect for his generalship and relations between the two were tense.

Towards the end of August, Barclay took part in the Battle of Dresden, when the Army of Bohemia attacked 20,000 troops under Marshal Gouvion St Cyr but had to retreat when Napoleon arrived with reinforcements and launched a powerful counter-attack. It was a serious defeat, but was reversed three days later when Barclay's units smashed an exposed French corps under General Dominique Vandamme at Kulm, a victory that restored allied morale, even though it resulted more from luck than skill.

The climax of the campaign was the mighty Battle of Leipzig in October, when four allied armies converged against Napoleon from the north, east and south and after four days of fighting inflicted a massive defeat. Barclay fought with distinction in the southern sector and was created a count on the field of battle by Tsar Alexander.

When Napoleon retreated across the Rhine that November, Barclay favoured concluding peace so as not to spill even more Russian blood far from home. But Napoleon's rejection of an allied peace offer set the stage for an invasion of France. For the 1814 campaign, Barclay was given 32,000 crack Russian and Prussian troops. This force, part of Schwarzenberg's Army of Bohemia (now called the Main Army), was to act as a reserve and Barclay had orders from the Tsar to keep it intact for an eagerly awaited victory parade into Paris. However, Barclay saw action on 20 March when Schwarzenberg repulsed Napoleon's small army at the Battle of Arcis-sur-

Aube. Then, as Napoleon threatened Schwarzenberg's lines of communication by manoeuvring to the east, Barclay characteristically advised caution: he wanted to follow Napoleon rather than boldly call his bluff and march on Paris. It was Tsar Alexander who ensured that the allies advanced on the exposed French capital. When the allies reached the city at the end of March, Barclay took part in the fighting outside against the troops that Napoleon had left to guard it. As a result of this action, Barclay won the rank of Field Marshal and after entering Paris in triumph took command of the allied Army of Silesia, in place of the Prussian Field Marshal Blücher who had fallen ill.

Following a visit to England that June, Barclay returned to Warsaw and again sought to reform the Russian Army. When Napoleon returned from exile in March 1815, Barclay led an army back to France, but Napoleon's defeat at Waterloo removed any need for the Russians to fight. Barclay was made a prince, but did not long survive the end of the wars, for his health had begun to fail. In 1818 he took two years' leave, intending to travel in Europe with his family, but it was not to be. On 25 May he died aged 56 at Insterburg in East Prussia and today rests with his wife in a massive mausoleum at Beckhof in Estonia.

Bagration

Bagration was one of Russia's most famous warriors, a born soldier whose panache was equalled only by the most famous of Napoleon's marshals. His chivalrous image was immortalised at Borodino when he saw the French 57th Infantry advance to the attack and shouted his admiration: 'Bravo, gentlemen, it's superb!' His long, hooked nose gave him the appearance of an eagle and his nickname *Bog-Rati-On*, 'god of the Army', said it all. Yet he was a man you either loved or hated. He was brave and disloyal in equal measure, veered erratically between charm and rudeness and was as feared for his temper as he was adored for his kindness to the rank-and-file.

It was as a rearguard commander that he truly excelled. Denis Davidov, who served with him as an adjutant before winning fame as a partisan leader in 1812, explained that Bagration's technique was to manoeuvre constantly as he retired, so as to intimidate the foe without becoming seriously engaged. 'This,' Davidov remarked, 'is an operation that calls for a shrewd grasp of the situation, coolness, a sharp eye and quick reactions – qualities with which Bagration was so well endowed.'[18]

But otherwise, Bagration has been over-estimated: he was no strategist, as even Tsar Alexander realised[19], and acted on impulse, not calculation. He lacked the cool, rational judgement so vital in war and could be reckless. Suvorov's influence was to blame here. 'Reconnaissances,' the old warrior had once exclaimed:

I do not desire them. They are of no use except to timid natures, and to let the enemy know that one is coming. The enemy is always to be found when wanted. Columns – the bayonet, the naked weapon – the attack and piercing of the enemy's line – these are my recon-naissances![20]

Disloyalty was Bagration's worst fault. He had no qualms about intriguing against Barclay, or shamelessly flattering those who could advance his interests. His xenophobia amounted to paranoia, yet he himself as a native Georgian was not a true Russian. His reputation must now be seriously questioned.

Barclay de Tolly

Barclay was a big man in every sense of the word and impressed observers with his imposing height and large, bald head, as well as with his courage under fire. Indeed, his physical bravery has never been questioned and his powers of endurance were likewise greater than those of most men. According to Löwenstern, he 'never felt the need for rest and still less for restoring himself with a good meal, which meant that we, his ADCs, often had empty stomachs.'

Barclay soon established his competence as a tactician, but as a strategist was sound rather than brilliant and indeed, his own ADC, Lieutenant-Colonel von Löwenstern, thought that he was 'a man of great commonsense, without having a remarkable mind.'[21] He tended to be cautious: following the spring 1813 armistice he advocated withdrawing to the safety of Poland and in March 1814 opposed the idea of calling Napoleon's bluff and marching on Paris. But his apparent indecision during the 1812 campaign was caused mostly by circumstances beyond his control, especially the Tsar's interference and the outcry against retreat. Indeed, few generals have suffered more from unfair criticism. Barclay's efforts to save Russia in 1812 earned him the scornful nickname *boltai da i tolko*, 'all bark and no bite'.

It was as an administrator and reformer of the Russian Army before Napoleon's invasion that Barclay deserves particular credit. As a leader of troops, in contrast, he lacked the charisma of the dynamic Bagration. He was too stiff and formal and was seen as a foreigner, while his conscientiousness bordered on pedantry. Although he led by example and took good care of his soldiers, he found it difficult to hide his despair from them in 1812. 'In his melancholy and troubled countenance,' noted Lieutenant Carl von Clausewitz, 'every soldier had read the desperate condition of the state and the army.'[22]

Yet Barclay showed true greatness of spirit when he continued to serve after being superseded by Kutusov in August 1812. He was totally loyal to the Tsar and, apart from the darkest days of 1812, enjoyed Alexander's favour, partly because he was not a protégé of Suvorov. Alexander did not favour the unorthodox methods of the eccentric Suvorov and preferred steadier, conventional soldiers like Barclay and Bennigsen to Suvorovites like Kutusov and Bagration.

Barclay's motto, 'loyalty and patience', sums up his life and career. He was one of the great men of the age, but has been overshadowed by both Kutusov and Bagration. One of the few Russians to recognise his greatness was Alexander Pushkin (1799–1837), who wrote one of his finest poems, 'The Commander', after seeing his impressive portrait by George Dawe.

The Battle of Smolensk: 17 August 1812

Smolensk was the first great battle of the 1812 campaign, but dashed Napoleon's hopes of a decisive victory. On the Russian side, much of the battle's interest lies in the almost fatal lack of co-operation between Barclay and Bagration.

Smolensk is 230 miles west of Moscow and 280 east of the Niemen river. Barclay could not abandon it without at least a pretence of defending it, for it was the country's third most important city and stood inside old Russia rather than the recently acquired western provinces. At the time of the battle, it had nearly 20,000 inhabitants. The old part of the city lay on the south bank of the Dnieper and was surrounded by a wall thirty feet high and up to six feet thick. A shoddy earthen fort, the Royal Citadel, had been built at the south-western corner. But most of the houses of Smolensk were built of wood and would shortly fuel one of history's greatest bonfires. Outside the wall lay the city's suburbs. One of them, that of St Petersburg, stood on the north bank of the Dnieper and was linked by only one bridge, but the water was just four feet deep and the Russians would add two pontoon bridges for the battle.

Barclay's army reached Smolensk on 1 August, followed by Bagration's two days later. Seeking to improve relations, Barclay courteously went out in full-dress uniform to meet Bagration and this helped thaw the frosty atmosphere. Bagration voluntarily placed himself under Barclay, giving the Russians a united force of 116,000 men. At a council-of-war on the 6th, Barclay faced some demands for a counter-offensive against Napoleon and although he was reluctant to risk the army, he was equally wary of creating further antagonism. He therefore agreed to an offensive, but insisted that they stay within three days' march of Smolensk. His ignorance of the exact locations of Napoleon's forces added to his caution and not surprisingly, in these circumstances Bagration's co-operation proved short-lived.

The Russian counter-offensive began on the 7th. Barclay left a division under General Dmitri Neverovski south of the Dnieper to guard Smolensk while the rest of the units were operating on the north bank. He himself advanced north-westwards, while Bagration pushed due west. Next day, Russian forces thrashed some of Napoleon's cavalry at Inkovo, twenty-five miles from Smolensk, but discovered from captured documents that news of their offensive had leaked to the enemy. A letter from one of the Tsar's ADCs had been intercepted, but the Russians did not know this at the time and instead blamed treachery. Their suspicion of Barclay's Prussian adviser, Colonel Ludwig von Wolzogen, did much to undermine Barclay's authority.

To make matters worse, Barclay halted after receiving faulty intelligence of enemy dispositions. Even his devoted ADC, Major von Löwenstern, wrote of subsequent events:

> Barclay hesitated . . . it was the first time that I was not wholly happy with the way he was. He was restless, he exhausted the army with continual marches in miry and impassable tracks and by changes of position without purpose.[23]

After hearing that Napoleon himself was on the way, Barclay apparently resolved to stand and fight, but early on the 15th received news that Napoleon had crossed the Dnieper seventy-five miles west of Smolensk and was now advancing on the city along the south bank. He realised that Napoleon intended to sweep anti-clockwise around his southern flank in a bid to seize Smolensk in his rear and cut him off from Moscow. If Napoleon's manoeuvre worked, the Russians would be forced to fight a decisive, and probably fatal, battle.

Luckily, Barclay had left General Neverovski's 27th Division south of the Dnieper. These 9,000 men delayed Napoleon's leading forces at the defile of Krasnoe, thirty miles south-west of Smolensk, before withdrawing in good order despite heavy losses. Napoleon's cavalry were therefore prevented from seizing the city on the evening of the 14th. Furthermore, Barclay's caution meant that the main Russian forces had not strayed far from Smolensk. He and Bagration now raced back eastwards, with Bagration sending General Nikolai Raevsky's VII Corps on ahead to hold the city until reinforced.

It was only on the morning of the 16th that Napoleon's troops began to arrive before Smolensk. His semi-circle of units south of the city was completed when V and I Corps under Prince Poniatowski and Marshal Davout arrived to join Ney's III Corps and Murat's cavalry.

By now, the two Russian armies had begun to mass on the heights north of the Dnieper. That night, in the Royal Citadel, Barclay and Bagration discussed the situation and apparently agreed that at dawn Bagration would march eastwards for Dorogobuzh, fifty miles down the road to Moscow, to assure the Russian line of retreat against a wide encircling

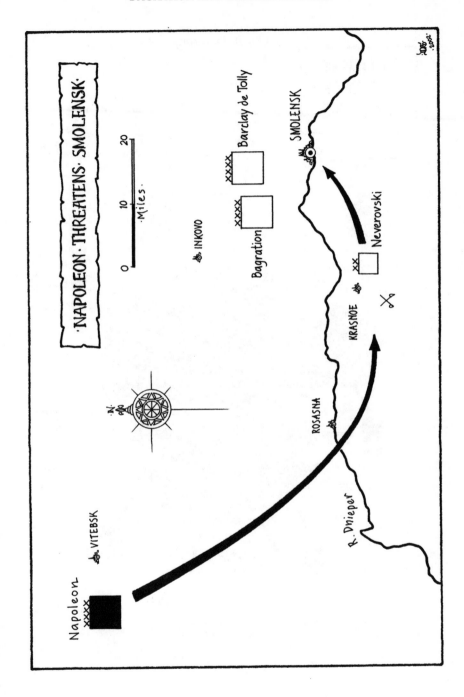

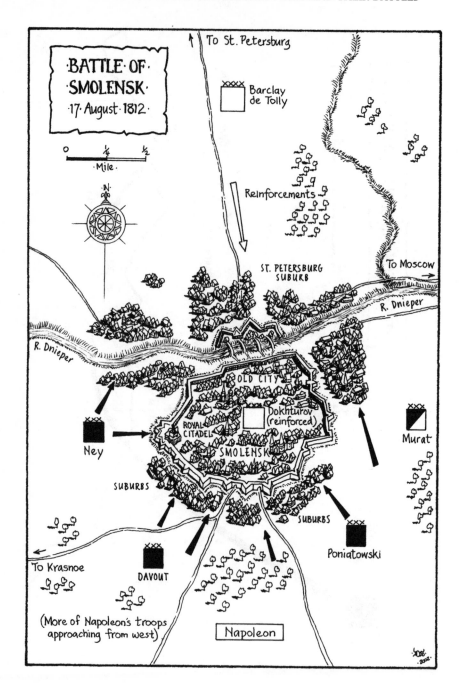

To St. Petersburg

BATTLE OF
SMOLENSK
17 August 1812

Barclay
de Tolly

0   ¼   ½
·Mile·

·N·

Reinforcements

ST. PETERSBURG
SUBURB

To Moscow

R. Dnieper

R. Dnieper

OLD CITY

Dokhturov
(reinforced)

ROYAL
CITADEL

SMOLENSK

Ney

Murat

SUBURBS

SUBURBS

Poniatowski

To Krasnoe

DAVOUT

(More of Napoleon's troops
approaching from west)

Napoleon

move. As it happened, Napoleon would be content at first simply to attack Smolensk frontally.

Dawn broke on Monday 17 August. Bagration left early on as agreed. The bulk of General Raevsky's VII Corps, which formed part of his army, was relieved in Smolensk and rejoined him, leaving the city's defence to General Dmitri Dokhturov's VI Corps (from Barclay's 1st Army), plus some attached units, a total of 20,000 men. The city wall bristled with light artillery, while the rest of Barclay's troops stood on the heights north of the Dnieper in reserve.

Towards 8.00 am Dokhturov attacked out of the city and cleared the suburbs of some enemy troops who had entered them during the night. Barclay watched this preliminary fighting from the city wall and to support Dokhturov set up batteries on the north bank of the Dnieper to direct fire on Napoleon's troops on the western and eastern sides of the city.

Major von Löwenstern recalled how during the cannonade at the start of the battle, Barclay:

> went everywhere and stopped on our extreme left, on a height, next to a church which masked a 12-pounder battery . . . He ordered it to fire at once; the enemy replied from the other side of the river and the action was hot. General Barclay seemed not to care about the imminent danger which surrounded him and gave his orders with the utmost coolness.

But the French noticed that the Russians had no troops to protect this 12-pounder battery and sent some cavalry to ford the river and try and take it. Löwenstern had to charge them with Barclay's escort before a regiment of Russian lancers reached the scene.[24]

Napoleon hoped at first that the Russians would leave the city and fight in the open country and so he attacked only at 2.00 pm. It took four hours of fighting before his troops conquered the suburbs and then began to assault the walled old city. Dokhturov, sick as he was with dysentery, stoutly held on and appealed for reinforcements. Barclay sent the 4th Division under Prince Eugen von Württemberg together with a *Jäger* regiment, followed later by two more regiments of *Jägers*. The additional troops boosted Dokhturov's strength to almost 30,000 and enabled him to check the enemy assaults.

Napoleon had to resort to bombarding Smolensk. He had no siege artillery and his field guns could not breach the stout walls, but his howitzers lobbed shells into the city and set fire to its wooden houses. These fires united into a vast conflagration. The fire, noted the British observer Sir Robert Wilson, enveloped 'the northern suburb in a volume of flames that extended above half a mile; a spectacle that no person present can forget, and a calamity (for it was a holy city) which every Russian resolved to avenge.'[25]

To control growing disorder in the city, Barclay ordered seven men to be shot. The Russians had lost about 6,000 troops and while Napoleon had suffered worse casualties, he could afford them more readily given his numerical superiority. As night fell, the gunfire gradually died away and towards 11.00 pm Barclay gave orders to abandon Smolensk, knowing that it was untenable. His situation was not eased by the arrival of a letter from Bagration, idiotically urging him to hang on to the city. The contents of the letter were soon widely known and approved of by many of Barclay's subordinates.

Sir Robert Wilson went into Smolensk to see the situation at first hand. He reported to Barclay that the generals there believed that they could hold out for another ten days if adequately supplied. What Wilson did not realise was that Napoleon by that time would have outflanked Smolensk to the east and cut the Russians off from Moscow. Barclay's problems grew. Grand Duke Constantine, brother to the Tsar, came with General Levin Bennigsen at the head of a group of generals who insisted, through the Grand Duke, that Barclay switch to the offensive. Barclay bluntly refused to discuss the matter and sent them packing.

The evacuation proceeded during the night. Barclay ordered the two supposedly miraculous icons of the Holy Virgin to be saved from the blazing city: they would be shown to the troops on the eve of the Battle of Borodino to boost their morale. Major von Löwenstern recalled how Barclay 'spent the whole night under the stars. He had eaten nothing all day and the only nourishment he took was a little milk that I offered him.'[26]

Groups of Napoleon's troops infiltrated the gutted city in the early hours of the 18th in search of loot and found it abandoned. Its desolation symbolised Napoleon's empty success, but did not seem to dampen his spirits. 'Within a month we shall be in Moscow,' he boasted. 'In six weeks we shall have peace.'[27] But in reality he was far from confident and consulted his senior subordinates as to whether to stay at Smolensk or continue the pursuit.

Barclay's army still stood on the high ground two miles north of Smolensk, with a rearguard in the St Petersburg suburb. At 8.00 am some of Napoleon's troops crossed the Dnieper but were vigorously counter-attacked. Barclay learnt from prisoners that Smolensk was full of artillery and ammunition waggons and promptly ordered shells to be lobbed into it. He remained in position throughout the 18th, so as to keep Napoleon guessing whether he was going to head east for Moscow or north for St Petersburg. Towards 6.00 pm Napoleon's troops finally established pontoon bridges across the Dnieper and forced back Barclay's rearguard, but then halted.

That night, Barclay marched his army off in two columns along parallel by-roads, intending to rejoin the main Moscow road at a safe distance east of Smolensk. But the routes were not properly reconnoitred and in the darkness some units actually went round in a circle. Barclay and his southernmost column found themselves at dawn on the 19th still dangerously close to the French outposts near Smolensk.

Barclay calmly detached a rearguard and then, taking advantage of daylight, marched the rest of the column off to the north-east. But he was still in danger of being cut off should Napoleon thrust eastwards along the Moscow road while he himself was still struggling along the tracks farther north. Napoleon, moreover, might try to cross the Dnieper to the east of Smolensk rather than pass his whole army across the bridges north of the city. Bagration, despite Barclay's orders to detach strong rearguards as he retired along the Moscow road two days before, had negligently left only four regiments of Cossacks a couple of miles east of Smolensk. Fortunately, Barclay had subsequently sent General Paul Tuchkov III with a mixed force of 2,400 men to reinforce these Cossacks.

Napoleon and his subordinates failed to act with vigour. Marshal Ney's corps drove back Barclay's rearguard at about 8.00 am and advanced eastwards down the Moscow road, supported by Marshal Davout's corps and some of the reserve cavalry.

Tuchkov's detachment, meanwhile, had occupied a strong position blocking the road four miles east of Smolensk and near the village of Valutino Gora. Tuchkov had to make a stand here to cover the retreat of Barclay's forces on the tracks farther north until after they had rejoined the Moscow road at the crossroads of Lubino a couple of miles to the east.

When Tuchkov was attacked by the foremost French units towards 1.30 pm, Napoleon went forward to see for himself. He concluded that it was only a minor clash and returned to Smolensk after ordering Davout to support Ney with General Charles Gudin's division. Tuchkov had been reinforced by Barclay to a total of 8,000 men, but had pulled back half-a-mile under heavy pressure. He now held another strong position on high ground east of the Stragan river, where he beat off renewed onslaughts with the help of additional troops that Barclay had assembled. The French had a clear advantage in numbers but the difficult terrain favoured the defensive.

The action might now have swung decisively in Napoleon's favour. That morning, he had ordered General Andoche Junot's VIII Corps to cross the Dnieper by a recently discovered ford at Prudichevo, three miles south-east of Smolensk. Junot did so and towards 5.00 pm was ready to fall on Tuchkov's vulnerable southern flank. But he then halted and did nothing, despite being urged by colleagues to advance.

Even so, Tuchkov was hard-pressed and at one point came to tell Barclay that he could no longer hold on. 'Return to your post,' Barclay retorted, 'and get yourself killed, for if you come back from there, I will

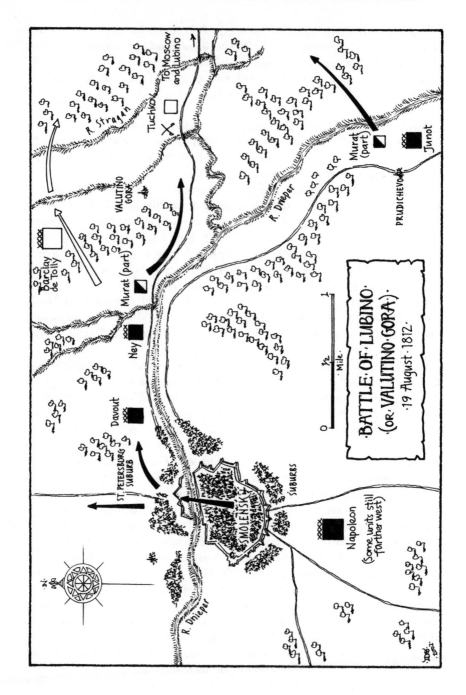

Battle of Lubino (or Valutino Gora) 19 August 1812.

have you shot.'[28] Tuchkov obeyed and was later wounded and captured.

Sir Robert Wilson, one of Barclay's harshest critics, had nothing but praise for his fearlessness.[29] Towards 7.00 pm, Ney put in a final, full-blooded attack which, as Wilson recalled, brought the action to a thunderous climax:

> The Russians in the valley, unable to resist such great superiority, had given way. The centre was shaking and its rear flying, when Barclay arrived and, placing himself at the head of the rallying fugitives, charged forward, electrifying all by his personal example, and giving an impulse that snatched victory from the enemy and attached it firmly and finally for the remainder of the combat, to the Russian standards.[30]

Barclay's battle cry was 'Victory or death! We must preserve this post or perish!' He almost fell into the hands of enemy lancers when he found himself unable to make his horse move. Löwenstern dismounted and noted how Barclay, 'with the greatest calm and without saying a word descended from his horse, nimbly mounted the one that I presented to him and continued on his way.' Löwenstern himself took Barclay's horse and somehow forced it to move off.[31]

By the end of the day, Ney had at last driven the Russians from their positions, but was unable to inflict decisive damage as darkness had long since fallen. Barclay's army by now had safely regained the Moscow road and was marching off eastwards to catch up with Bagration, as yet unpursued by the exhausted French forces.

Napoleon lost nearly 9,000 men at Lubino, 3,000 more than the Russians. Among his casualties was Charles Gudin, a promising general who died from wounds received in the final attack. The ordeal of the wounded had only just begun: such was the shortage of proper dressings that hay and the city archives had to be used instead.

Between 7 and 19 August the Russians had tried each of the three options open to them: they had first launched a counter-offensive, then returned to defend Smolensk and finally resumed their retreat. The apparent indecision did nothing to improve Russian morale, yet the significance of the Battle of Smolensk lies in what did not happen. Barclay's army was neither cut off nor badly damaged and this was due to his commonsense as much as to the errors of the enemy. Smolensk, in fact, marked the end of the beginning, for thereafter the whole character of the campaign dramatically altered. As Barclay informed the Tsar: 'thanks to my junction with Bagration, Napoleon's manoeuvres were thwarted as never before.'[32] No longer could Napoleon hope to defeat Russia's two principal armies separately, by manoeuvre and at relatively little cost. He would instead fight the brutal bloodbath of Borodino.

NOTES

1   R. Wilson, *Narrative of events during the invasion of Russia* (1860), p.156
2   C. Andolenko, *Histoire de l'armée Russe* (1967), p.142
3   C. Duffy, *Eagles over the Alps: Suvorov in Italy and Switzerland, 1799* (1999), p.248
4   W. Blease, *Suvorof* (1920), p.351
5   A. Mikhailovsky-Danilevsky, *Relation de la campagne de 1805 (Austerlitz)* (1846), p.174
6   A. Brett-James, *1812: eyewitness accounts of Napoleon's defeat in Russia* (1967), p.78
7   C. von Clausewitz, *The campaign of 1812 in Russia* (1992), p.112
8   Brett-James, *op. cit.*, p.71
9   M. Weil, ed., *Mémoires du général-major russe Baron de Löwenstern* (1903), v.1, p.250
10 *Ibid*, v.1, pp.268–9
11 *Ibid*, v.1, p.260
12 E. Tarlé, *Napoleon's invasion of Russia 1812* (1942), pp.138–9
13 Wilson, *op. cit.*, pp.156–7
14 Weil, *op. cit.*, v.1, p.256
15 Brett-James, *op. cit.*, p.155
16 Weil, *op. cit.*, v.1, p.290; Löwenstern was promoted after Borodino.
17 La Société d'histoire contemporaine, *Mémoires de Langeron* (1902), p.138
18 G. Troubetzkoy, ed., *In the service of the Tsar against Napoleon: the memoirs of Denis Davidov, 1806–1814* (1999), p.28
19 Brett-James, *op. cit.*, p.110
20 L. Shadwell, *Mountain warfare, illustrated by the campaign of 1799 in Switzerland* (1875), p.183
21 Weil, *op. cit.*, v.1, p.291
22 Clausewitz, *op. cit.*, pp.142–3
23 Weil, *op. cit.*, v.1, p.219
24 *Ibid*, v.1, pp.220–1
25 Wilson, *op. cit.*, p.104
26 Weil, *op. cit.*, v.1, p.222
27 Brett-James, *op. cit.*, p.94
28 Weil, *op. cit.*, v.1, pp.228–9
29 The Russians called it the Battle of Lubino, but the French know it as Valutino Gora.
30 Wilson, *op. cit.*, pp.94–5
31 Weil, *op. cit.*, v.1, p.229
32 Brett-James, *op. cit.*, p.79

CHAPTER X

Kutusov

Field Marshal Prince Mikhail Larionovich Golenishchev-Kutusov opposed Napoleon at two of the greatest battles of the Napoleonic wars: Austerlitz and Borodino. He enjoys a prominent role in Leo Tolstoy's epic novel *War and Peace* and is still venerated in Russia today, but at the time faced widespread criticism. In fact, his perceived greatness as a general evolved only gradually and stemmed largely from his prominence during Napoleon's mighty invasion of the motherland in 1812. The significance of that epic struggle in Russian history has rightly or wrongly placed the mantle of greatness on the general who commanded in that supreme hour.

As the son of a general, Kutusov almost inevitably became a soldier. His father, an engineer who had served in Peter the Great's Army, belonged to one of Russia's ancient noble families and had connections at the highest levels. Kutusov was born at St Petersburg, Russia's political capital, on 16 September 1745 and was the eldest of three children. His mother died when he was young, but he soon had a wisdom beyond his years, for he was an intelligent and inquisitive child who liked to spend much of his time in the company of adults. He also mingled at an early age with the Russian court as a result of his father's position and this experience later proved invaluable.

When he was 12, Kutusov went to the military engineering school, where he received both general and specifically military education. He proved particularly adept at mathematics, mastered French and German and also understood English, Swedish, Turkish, Polish and Latin. He was a popular, high-spirited and fun-loving young man and left the school in 1761 to serve as an ensign.

Kutusov was slightly too late to see action in the Seven Years' War, from which Russia withdrew in 1762. But he had the good fortune to serve for a while under Colonel Alexander Suvorov, an inspirational leader who unlike most Russian officers cared for the rank-and-file and quickly won their devotion. He encouraged them to use their initiative, seize opportunities and assault vigorously with the bayonet.

Throughout his career, Kutusov was a diplomat as well as a soldier. Late in 1762 he became ADC to the Governor of Revel in Estonia, where he exercised his renowned charm and tact. Yet he longed to see active service and fortunately these were the years of Catherine the Great's reign (1762–96), during which expansionist Russia fought a series of wars. In 1764 Kutusov entered Poland, as part of Catherine's unscrupulous military intervention in Polish internal affairs, and the following year he had his baptism of fire under the walls of Warsaw, as a 23-year-old infantry captain. Small-scale actions followed. 'When we were in Poland, we led a happy life,' he remembered. 'We were often engaged with the Poles, but I still understood nothing of war.'[1]

Then war broke out with the Ottoman Turks in 1768 and fighting raged in the area immediately north-west of the Black Sea. Kutusov arrived here two years later, helped to storm Turkish strongholds along the Pruth and Danube rivers and gradually built a reputation for courage under fire. During this time, he served for a while on the staff of Peter Rumiantsev, the highly capable and well read commander of the Russian 1st Army. Rumiantsev, like Suvorov, inspired Kutusov deeply, particularly with his recognition that military operations should not be seen in isolation but as part of the wider political and diplomatic situation. Rumiantsev favoured manoeuvre and avoided battles unless they offered a decisive victory.

Few young men have so glittered with the promise of a distinguished military career as Kutusov did at that stage of his life, but in 1772 he almost wrecked it all. Carried away by his love of fun, he mimicked Rumiantsev, was reported by a sneak and consequently dismissed from his army. It was a crucial formative experience, for it made Kutusov suspicious, self-reliant and adept at hiding his thoughts and emotions.

Luckily, the setback proved only temporary and later that same year he joined the Russian 2nd Army operating in the Crimea against the Tartars. He personally seized a flag during the assault on Alushta and was nearly killed when a musketball went though the edge of his head, narrowly missing his brain and right eye. Miraculously, he survived, but suffered so severely from dizziness and other after-effects that he had to leave the Army in 1773 with his career once again apparently over.

He toured Europe to seek treatment for his injuries and in the process widened his horizons, particularly in discussions with Frederick the Great of Prussia and with the foremost Austrian generals. He went home in 1776, older, wiser and restored to health and late that year returned to the Crimea to serve under Suvorov. The war with the Turks had ended in 1774 to Russia's advantage, although it looked likely to flare up again. Suvorov's patronage meanwhile helped Kutusov to rise to the rank of colonel in 1777, brigadier-general in 1782 and major-general in 1784. He married in 1778: he was a womaniser, but his wife tolerated his infidelities and bore him six children.

In 1787 Catherine the Great provoked the Ottoman Turks into declaring war on Russia and Austria. But her hopes of a quick victory were soon shattered, particularly by the obstinate resistance of the port of Ochakov on the north-western shores of the Black Sea. During this siege, Kutusov was again seriously injured when a musketball eerily struck his head in much the same spot as his previous wound fifteen years before. The doctors did not believe he would survive. One later wrote: 'if we had heard of this and not seen it with our own eyes, we would have regarded it as a fairy tale.' He added that 'destiny is clearly keeping Kutusov's head for some great conception, since it has preserved it after two so extraordinary wounds.'[2] Kutusov was left with headaches and a crooked eye, but again defied all odds and seemed to make a full recovery.

In December 1790 Kutusov served under Suvorov during the siege of Izmail, which lay on one of the arms of the Danube delta as it flowed into the Black Sea. He personally rallied his men during the assault and was in the thick of the fighting. The fortress fell, at an horrendous cost in both Turkish and Russian lives.

Success won Kutusov the governorship of Izmail and during this period he successfully attacked a nearby concentration of Turkish forces in June 1791. But by now the war had exhausted both sides. Austria had withdrawn from the conflict and Russia concluded peace in January 1792.

That same year, a Russian army again intervened in Poland and occupied Warsaw. Kutusov was with that army, but left before Poland was finally partitioned in 1795 between Austria, Prussia and Russia. For in the summer of 1793 he took up an appointment at Constantinople as Russian ambassador to the Turks and proved an instant success, winning over his former foes with his charm and delighting in the dinners and social events. He later remembered it as the happiest year of his life.

His next appointment was governor of the south-eastern part of Finland, an area that the Swedes had lost in the peace treaties of 1721 and 1743. He reached his new base, the city of Viborg seventy-five miles north-west of St Petersburg, early in 1795. He set to work preparing defences along the border, for the Swedes had attempted unsuccessfully to recover their lost territory in 1788 and seemed likely to try again.

Catherine the Great's patronage had helped Kutusov in the early stages of his career, but ended with her death in 1796. Never again did he enjoy the favour of a Russian ruler. Tsar Paul I set about restoring strict discipline in the Army. In some respects, this was badly needed, for many aristocratic officers shamefully neglected their duties, yet Paul went so far that perfection on the parade ground took precedence over fighting fitness. Suvorov, who voiced his opposition to Paul's methods, was temporarily dismissed in 1797 and Kutusov was lucky to escape by taking up an appointment as ambassador to Berlin that same year. This enabled him to meet the leading Prussian military figures and to discuss with them the methods used by the French Revolutionary armies. He then served as Governor-General at Vilna in Lithuania, a province acquired by Russia in

1795 during the partition of Poland. Unfortunately, this prevented him from seeing action under Suvorov, who in 1799 won fame against the French in northern Italy and Switzerland.

In 1800 Kutusov returned to St Petersburg to act as Governor-General of the city. Intrigue was in the air, for Paul had alienated the influential Russian nobility and was becoming increasingly unstable. Kutusov avoided involvement, but thereby incurred the distrust of the plotters, who included Paul's son Alexander. The storm finally broke in March 1801, when Paul was murdered and the 24-year-old Alexander became Tsar. Insecure, indecisive and consumed with guilt, Alexander distrusted all but his favourites. Kutusov was soon dismissed from the capital to the village of Goroshki, where he spent his time managing his estates. He was 57 years old and had little prospect of seeing any more active service, particularly as Russia's foreign affairs were unusually peaceful. He suffered from poor health, rheumatism and now also from blindness in his injured right eye. In 1804 he complained to his wife, who had remained at St Petersburg, that:

> It is a dull business trying to put the estate on its feet when everything is in such ruin. Upon my word, sometimes I feel like throwing up everything in despair and resigning myself to the will of God . . . I am haunted by the fear of spending my old age in penury and want, and of having laboured, encountered danger and suffered wounds in vain. And this sad thought distracts me from everything and makes me incapable.[3]

Nonetheless, he kept abreast of developments in the wider world and discussed religion and philosophy with his visitors. He might at this point have died with his initially promising career left unfulfilled. He was saved by Napoleon, now Emperor of the French, who by his high-handed actions provoked Britain, Russia and Austria to form the Third Coalition. Joined by Sweden and Naples, the allies planned an array of thrusts against the French Empire from the north, east and south of Europe.

Suvorov's death in 1800 had left Kutusov as Russia's foremost general and it was unthinkable to go to war without him. He was given command of the leading Russian army and sent to link up with the Austrians on the Danube, but was late setting off, made slow progress and endured such hardships as a result of inadequate supplies that he lost 11,000 of his troops. To make matters worse, the Austrians did not realise that the Julian calendar used by the Russians was twelve days behind the Gregorian one used by western Europe. Furthermore, Kutusov was ordered to detach one of his six columns to the Turkish border and it rejoined him only in time for the Battle of Austerlitz.

Kutusov marched south-westwards into the Habsburg Empire and then along the southern bank of the Danube to reinforce the Austrian army of General Karl Mack von Leiberich, which had already advanced into Bavaria in southern Germany. But Napoleon had seized the initiative and struck a pre-emptive blow, surrounding Mack and forcing him to surrender at Ulm on 20 October. Kutusov accordingly began to retreat on the 29th. By now, he had barely 27,000 Russians and although he also commanded 20,000 Austrians who had avoided the trap at Ulm, these were soon defeated and dispersed. He initially retired eastwards along the southern bank of the Danube, fighting rearguard actions on the tributaries that joined the river from the Alps in the south. Although the Austrians wanted him to defend Vienna, Kutusov knew that it was more important to keep his army intact and therefore crossed to the north bank of the Danube at Krems on 9 November.

At this stage, only three widely separated French divisions were on the north bank. Kutusov therefore switched to the offensive and on 11 November fell on one of these divisions, just 6,000 men strong, at Dürenstein with 25,000 troops. But his plan was over-ambitious and clumsily executed: it would have worked against the Turks, but not against highly trained and disciplined French troops under the inspirational leadership of Marshal Edouard Mortier. The unco-ordinated advance of Kutusov's six columns meant that barely 10,000 of his troops saw action and as a result of the superior French tactics, they suffered well over twice as many casualties. The battle ended when another French division arrived to rescue the one under attack.

Chastened by this dismal failure, Kutusov pulled back north-eastwards towards Znaim. The French by now had seized a bridge over the Danube at Vienna and were pouring on to the north bank to threaten his line of retreat. Kutusov detached General Peter Bagration at the defile of Schöngraben with a rearguard of 6,800 men to allow the rest of the army to escape. Kutusov gained a day by sending ADCs to deceive Marshal Joachim Murat, who was leading the pursuit, into halting and concluding an armistice that Kutusov had no intention of ratifying. Murat attacked only on 16 November after receiving orders to do so from a furious Napoleon in Vienna. Bagration was forced to retreat, but only after fierce fighting and was able to rejoin Kutusov despite heavy casualties.

Thus Kutusov saved his command by a combination of bluff and battle and after picking up some surviving Austrian units he finally united with the main Russian army under General Friedrich Buxhöwden near Wischau on 19 November. These forces, together with Kutusov's sixth column which finally rejoined him, fell back to Olmütz, where the arrival of the Russian Imperial Guard brought Austro-Russian numbers to 73,000.

Napoleon had shot his bolt and was now deep in hostile country with his units dispersed over a wide area. He could not advance farther without his men starving. Kutusov wanted to continue retreating north-eastwards, into Galicia, so as to avoid a premature battle and gain time for the approach of Archduke Charles's Austrian army from northern Italy and for Prussia to mobilise and join the allies in the field.

But the young Tsar Alexander was present at allied headquarters and wanted a battle. Officially, Kutusov was Commander-in-Chief, but in reality had little say and was scorned by the arrogant young nobles in the Tsar's entourage as 'General Dawdler'. Prince Adam Czartoryski, the influential Russian deputy foreign minister, complained that:

> Alexander no longer listened to our advice. He did not believe what we endlessly repeated to him, namely that his presence would take from General Kutusov the means of directing prudently the army's moves. This was all the more to be feared, given the general's timorous character and his habits of playing the courtier.[4]

The Austrian General Franz Weyrother drew up the plan of attack for the battle that ensued at Austerlitz. He held a final briefing on the evening of 1 December, but Alexander did not attend and Kutusov, who was present, actually dozed off. The plan was for a powerful outflanking thrust to crush Napoleon's southern wing and roll up his battle line. Unfortunately, this ambitious move would over-extend the allies and fatally weaken their centre on the Pratzen heights.

The morning of 2 December found Kutusov still on the Pratzen with the allied Fourth Column, which had been delayed by congestion and was yet to join the leading three columns assaulting Napoleon's southern wing. Then hooves thundered as Tsar Alexander galloped up and opened one of the most celebrated battlefield exchanges.

'Mikhail Larionovich!' he stormed. 'Why are you not proceeding farther?'

Kutusov explained that he was waiting for all the columns to get in position, a reply which enraged the Tsar: 'We are not in Tsaritsyn Meadow, where we do not start a parade until all the regiments have arrived!'

'Your Majesty!' retorted Kutusov, 'it is precisely because we are not in Tsaritsyn Meadow that I am not commencing. But, if you order . . .'[5]

Thus the crucial Pratzen heights slowly emptied of troops. Then, shortly after 9.00 am, a staff officer shouted in alarm as he spotted French forces advancing towards him to seize the heights. Kutusov tried to limit the impending disaster by recalling troops to the Pratzen, but was too late.

Kutusov never forgot the trauma of Austerlitz. He was under a hail of fire and felt a musketball tear open a painful wound in his cheek. When Tsar Alexander sent his surgeon, Kutusov told him: 'thank His Majesty, assure him that my wound is not dangerous.' Then he pointed at the foe.

'There is the injury that is mortal.'[6] He saw his horse killed under him and his son-in-law slain at his side; all he could do was to try and salvage as much as possible and retire eastwards.

Alexander unfairly blamed Kutusov:

> At the battle of Austerlitz, I was young and inexperienced. Kutusov told us that we ought to do the opposite to what we wanted, but he should have persevered in his opinion.[7]

Kutusov returned to St Petersburg and another temporary, and this time partial, eclipse. Although appointed Military-Governor of Kiev in October 1806, he was passed over for command of the Russian forces that resumed the struggle with Napoleon in East Prussia and Poland that winter. Early in 1807, after another outbreak of war with the Ottoman Turks, he transferred to the headquarters of the Army of the Danube, but found it impossible to work with its increasingly unbalanced commander, Field Marshal Prince Prozorovski. He was recalled in 1809 to take up the post of Military-Governor of Lithuania, but in March 1811 was back with the Army of the Danube, this time as its commander.

Tsar Alexander had concluded peace with Napoleon in 1807, but relations were breaking down and the Minister of War, Mikhail Barclay de Tolly, feared a war on two fronts: against both Turks and French. Kutusov was told to bring the war with the Turks to a prompt but honourable end. He had only 46,000 men but concentrated his forces. He repulsed a Turkish attack at Rustchuk on the Danube in July 1811, but declined to exploit his victory. This made the Turks over-confident and when they attacked again in September, he caught them as they crossed the Danube and surrounded them in their entrenched camp, before settling down to wait until they came to terms. Annoyed at the time that this was taking, Alexander vainly pressed Kutusov to attack and then appointed Admiral Paul Chichagov as his replacement. In the event, Chichagov arrived a day after Kutusov secured an armistice with the Turks and this led to the signing, on 28 May 1812, of the Treaty of Bucharest, the moderate terms of which gave Russia Bessarabia.

This timely peace with the Turks later enabled Chichagov to move troops northwards in time to intervene during Napoleon's retreat from Moscow. But a cynical subordinate, General Louis de Langeron, wrote:

> Kutusov has left. He touched us deeply on his departure. He was very amiable and moving. Let the Lord give him a Field Marshal's baton, tranquillity, thirty women – but not an army.[8]

Hostilities finally broke out in the north on 24 June 1812 when Napoleon crossed the Niemen river into Russia at the head of a massive army.

Outnumbered, the main two Russian armies on this front retreated before him and at the beginning of August united at Smolensk under the command of Barclay de Tolly. They fought a tough but limited battle here and then continued their retreat.

Alexander's hostility to Kutusov decreased as the situation worsened. Kutusov was soon back in St Petersburg and in August attended the Supreme State Council. Barclay's withdrawal was the only sensible strategy to follow, but provoked outrage from the patriotic and influential Russian nobility. Barclay was duly superseded by Kutusov's appointment as Commander-in-Chief on 20 August. Alexander was unenthusiastic, but, as he later explained to Admiral Chichagov, 'I did not have much choice. General Kutusov was the only one I had available and public opinion wanted his appointment.'[9] Alexander ensured that one of his favourites, General Levin von Bennigsen, was made Kutusov's Chief-of-Staff.

Kutusov, who had always been devout, prayed at Kazan Cathedral before he left St Petersburg. His daughter asked him whether he really hoped to defeat Napoleon. 'Defeat him?' the old man replied. 'No. But I hope to deceive him.'[10] He left the city on 23 August. Let us consider him at this supreme moment of his career. Sir Robert Wilson, a British observer, described him as:

> A bon vivant – polished, courteous, shrewd as a Greek, naturally intelligent as an Asiatic and well instructed as a European – he was more disposed to trust to diplomacy for his success than to martial prowess, for which by his age and the state of his constitution he was no longer qualified.

Despite the injury to his eye, added Wilson, 'the expression of his countenance was still engagingly intellectual.'[11]

Kutusov reached his command on 29 August and initially approved of a defensive position that Barclay had selected at Tsarevo-Zaimishche. But he changed his mind overnight and ordered a resumption of the retreat. Nonetheless, he realised that he would have to fight a major battle to save Moscow, the religious capital of Russia.[12] He therefore fought at Borodino on 7 September, but suffered such massive losses that he was obliged to resume the retreat. Alexander promoted him to the rank of Field Marshal after receiving his report on the battle, which misleadingly presented it as a victory.

Bennigsen, Kutusov's Chief-of-Staff, now selected a position immediately south-west of Moscow and Kutusov halted here as if about to give battle. But Barclay reported on 13 September that the Russians would suffer a disaster if they gave battle in such a bad position against such numerical odds. Kutusov then summoned a council-of-war of his senior subordinates in a peasant's hut at Fili on the western outskirts of Moscow, in the hope that this would advocate the abandonment of Moscow and hence relieve him of having to take such an unpopular decision alone. In fact, the majority of those present wanted to stand and fight; only Barclay and three others advocated retreat. Kutusov listened to the arguments and then took the decision to retreat. The loss of Moscow was not the loss of Russia. To preserve the army intact was to deny victory to the foe. He stood up. 'I order the retreat.'[13]

The loneliness of high command weighed heavily on Kutusov that night. 'I will force these cursed French to eat horsemeat, as the Turks did last year,' he raged.[14] In fact, Kutusov's decision to abandon Moscow denied Napoleon his last chance to force Alexander to the peace table by a decisive military victory. Perhaps no other Russian general could have made this decision and remained in command. Alexander would never forgive Kutusov, but realised that the aged field marshal's popularity with his troops and the absence of any obvious replacement made it impossible to sack him.

After retreating through Moscow, Kutusov first headed south-eastwards and then craftily circled round south of the city. By the end of September, he had reached Tarutino, forty-six miles south-west of Moscow. He was now in a position to block the roads that led southwards and south-westwards from Moscow to the fertile provinces in southern Russia and to the arms-production centre of Tula. He realised that he had left open the road that ran north-westwards from Moscow to St Petersburg but was confident that exhaustion and shortage of supplies would prevent Napoleon from marching the 400 miles to that city. Even if Napoleon did try to do so, Kutusov in the south could attack his rear.

While he waited at Tarutino for Napoleon to make the first move, Kutusov prepared his troops for the next phase of the campaign and formally merged the two armies under his command[15] into one. Russian reinforcements flooded in, while Napoleon's numbers continued to drop.

Napoleon wasted five weeks in Moscow in the vain hope of a peace settlement. Cossacks and partisans meanwhile harassed his communications, attacking isolated parties of troops and destroying supplies. Kutusov knew the value of the Cossacks, with whom he had served in the Crimea in the early 1770s, but was wary of encouraging the partisans, lest these armed peasants subsequently turn against Russia's rulers.

Kutusov's subordinates were keen to fight a significant action using regular troops, but Kutusov was reluctant to risk serious Russian losses. Nor did he want to hurry Napoleon's evacuation of Moscow, for the longer the French Emperor remained, the greater would be his difficulties, particularly as winter began to close in. Yet Kutusov felt impelled to do something to placate both his critics and the irate Tsar. Thus elements of his army attacked French outposts near Vinkovo (north of Tarutino) on 18

October. The assault surprised the foe, but Kutusov withheld reinforcements in order to prevent the action from escalating into a major clash. He thereby lessened some of the pressure on him and unnerved Napoleon, yet at little cost to his army. The action also revealed serious shortcomings in Russian staffwork and co-ordination that probably reinforced Kutusov's belief that the Russians were still no match for the Grand Army in a pitched battle.

Napoleon had already decided to abandon Moscow, but the clash at Vinkovo caused him to do so a day early, on 19 October. By now, he had irretrievably lost the initiative and no longer enjoyed numerical superiority, for he had only 95,000 men immediately under his hand to pit against Kutusov's 110,000.

Even before Napoleon's arrival at Moscow, Alexander and his advisers had planned a counter-offensive involving Russian forces from subordinate theatres operating against the flanks of Napoleon's long and vulnerable lines of communication. They intended to mount a pincer move, with 40,000 men under General Ludwig Wittgenstein thrusting southwards and 64,000 under Admiral Chichagov advancing north from the area south of the Pripet marshes. These two prongs were to unite 375 miles west of Moscow, near Borisov, where the Beresina river gave them the chance to trap Napoleon's army as it retreated. Kutusov with the main Russian army would meanwhile follow and harass Napoleon's withdrawal. This was the plan that the Russians now sought to put into effect.

Rather than retreat along the devastated route of his advance, Napoleon hoped to head south-westwards to reach his depots at Smolensk via the more fertile southerly provinces. Kutusov belatedly learnt of this move and sent General Dmitri Dokhturov with a corps of infantry and another of cavalry to check it at Malojaroslavets. The ensuing battle began early on 24 October and ended with Dokhturov being driven back. Kutusov failed to support him with more than a single corps, instead drawing up the rest of his army a mile farther south. He resolved, should Napoleon press home his advance, to retire rather than fight.

Although Napoleon won the Battle of Malojaroslavets, he decided to retreat along his line of advance after being unnerved by a brush with Cossacks while reconnoitring on the 25th. He may also have been intimidated by the strong position that Kutusov had occupied with the bulk of his army. For Napoleon knew that he could not risk another bloody battle, any more than Kutusov could. It was an interesting predicament, but Napoleon's nerve gave way first: his Grand Army abandoned any attempt to break through to the south and headed north-westwards to rejoin the route it had used during its march on Moscow. This moment marked the beginning of the end.

Kutusov realised by 28 October that Napoleon had been deflected. He himself had begun to retreat towards Kaluga, but now halted and ordered

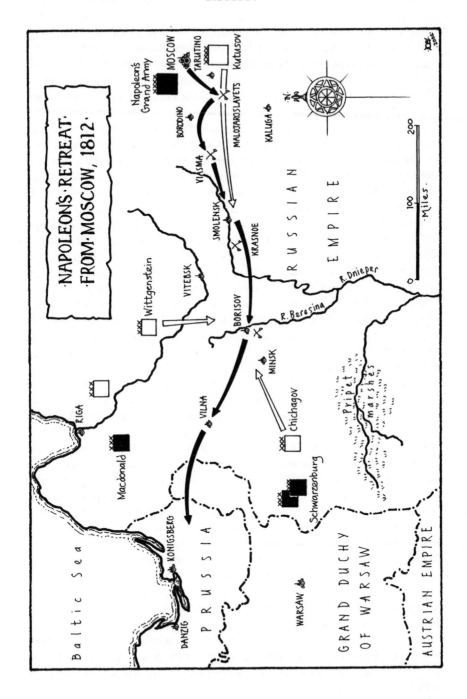

NAPOLEON'S RETREAT FROM MOSCOW, 1812

a pursuit. He realised that if he merely pressed along the road that Napoleon's army was following, he would repeatedly run into rearguard actions, so he kept the bulk of his troops to the south of it. They thus shadowed Napoleon's retreat and were constantly in a position to check any attempt that he might make to turn off the main road and head for the fertile southerly provinces.

Kutusov did not want to waste Russian lives by pursuing faster than necessary. He was also afraid to meet Napoleon in a full-scale battle with the insufficiently trained and hardened reinforcements that he had received at Tarutino. A lost battle, he explained, would have endangered all the advantages he presently enjoyed. Why should he risk all, just to accelerate what cold, hunger and exhaustion would inevitably produce?[16]

Hence Russian attempts to block Napoleon's retreat were limited and half-hearted. On 3 November they failed to cut off his rearguard at Viazma, 100 miles east of Smolensk. Next day, the first snow began to fall. Then, on the 9th, a whole French brigade surrendered, indicating the extent to which the morale of Napoleon's troops had slumped.

Napoleon's army successfully reached Smolensk and began to leave it on 12 November on the next stage of its retreat. But it became strung out and several days of fighting ensued as Kutusov's advanced guard tried to intercept some of the rearmost corps near Krasnoe. Napoleon promptly turned round with his Guard, marched back eastwards, hurled back the Russians and rescued Marshal Davout's corps. Despite this rebuff, Alexander created Kutusov the Prince of Smolensk, more to celebrate the recapture of the city than to recognise any military virtues that he might have.

Napoleon hurried westwards to try and escape before the Russian forces closed in from the northern and southern flanks. A Russian corps under General Wittgenstein was held at bay by detached forces as it pushed down from the north, but Admiral Chichagov arrived with 34,000 men from the south to oppose any attempt to bridge the Beresina river, which had been melted by an untimely thaw and had become a formidable obstacle across Napoleon's line of retreat. Yet much of the Grand Army managed to escape over two bridges thrown over the river after Napoleon deceived Chichagov into moving to the wrong place.

Kutusov's intervention on the Beresina in support of Chichagov might have destroyed the Grand Army, captured Napoleon and put an end to the long wars. But he was wary after the drubbing he had received at Krasnoe and suffered badly during these weeks from exhaustion, headaches, frostbite and rheumatism. One of the few improvements was the replacement in December of Bennigsen, his disloyal Chief-of-Staff, with General Peter Konovnitsyn.

The last of Napoleon's survivors stumbled out of Russia in mid-December, leaving behind over 400,000 of their comrades and more than

1,000 guns. But the Russians for their part had lost over 250,000 men[17] and Kutusov was reluctant to advance farther west, partly as his army needed rest and reorganisation and partly as he feared, with some justice, that the benefits of Napoleon's downfall would go primarily to Britain.[18]

But Tsar Alexander had joined the army on 23 December and was determined to lead a crusade to liberate Europe. Early in 1813 Prussia switched sides and joined Russia in the field. Kutusov was appointed as allied Commander-in-Chief in February but, exhausted by his exertions, died on 28 April at Bunzlau in Silesia, at the age of 67. The authorities knew that his passing would undermine the morale of the Russian soldiers and therefore kept it quiet for some days. They took his body back to St Petersburg and laid it to rest in Kazan Cathedral, reputedly on the spot where he had prayed prior to joining the army before Borodino. But his heart they buried separately, in a simple churchyard near Bunzlau (now the town of Boleslawiec in Poland).

Just days after Kutusov's death, Napoleon counter-attacked the allies with a newly raised army at Lützen on 2 May and again at Bautzen on 20–1 May, forcing them to fall back and vindicating Kutusov's caution. The allies then secured an armistice and used the respite to prepare for the resumption of hostilities in August. Austria now joined them and that October, they dealt Napoleon a crushing blow at Leipzig, after which his downfall was but a matter of time.

The saviour of Russia?

The young Kutusov's talents had promised a brilliant career, but there was nothing inevitable about his rise. Twice he suffered a head wound that would have killed most men and twice he was recalled to command against Napoleon when his career had seemed to be over.

Kutusov lived most of his life in the 1700s and in mind and method was an eighteenth-century commander. The strategy of evasion that he employed so effectively in 1812 was a standard eighteenth-century procedure. But Kutusov's old-fashioned approach could prove a handicap. One of his most serious flaws in 1812 was his antiquated command style. Although Barclay de Tolly had set out in his new regulations how a general should command and use his staff, Kutusov did not follow these new rules, partly because he had not kept up-to-date with such developments during his years out of favour and partly because he could not trust all his staff officers, some of whom were incapable and others disloyal. Kutusov's primitive command methods were sufficient against the Turks, but proved deficient at Borodino against Napoleon's more sophisticated system.

Kutusov's leadership skills, on the other hand, were one of his greatest strengths. 'When he spoke to a soldier,' asserted one historian, 'he tried to be like him, an unsubtle, simple Russian, a hearty and well-disposed grandfather.'[19] He knew that high morale was a battle-winner. 'The good humour of the soldier vouches for his bravery,'[20] he declared and he played shamelessly on his troops' simple yet unshakeable patriotism and religious faith. He never missed a chance to praise them. 'Honour and glory to you!' he told them. 'Fine fellows!'[21] When in 1812 he saw soldiers polishing equipment, he told them:

> I don't want any of this. I want to see whether you are in good health, my children. A soldier has no time for smartness during a campaign. He must rest after his tiring efforts and prepare for victory.[22]

Deceit was an integral part of Kutusov's character. Sometimes it was a vice, sometimes a virtue. He was a slippery man, an experienced diplomat who liked to keep his options open and to avoid committing himself in writing if he could help it. Suvorov had recognised Kutusov's craftiness early on: 'he is shrewd, very shrewd; nobody can fool him.'[23] Napoleon himself called him the sly old fox of the north, while another French opponent, General Philippe de Ségur, noted that he 'calculated every-thing. His genius was slow, vindictive, and above all, crafty – the true Tartar character!' He knew 'the art of preparing an implacable war with a fawning, supple and patient policy.'[24] Such was Kutusov's deceit that even today we can not be sure how far he had a master plan and how far he was guided by circumstances.

Old age, the cumulative effects of wounds and the colossal strain of responsibility took their toll. Kutusov declined from the recklessly brave young officer to the stout, tired and battle-scarred old general who commanded at Borodino from a stool instead of a saddle. General Langeron recalled how:

> Kutusov almost never mounted a horse, but travelled in his carriage. He used to sleep fifteen hours a day, he was heavy and indecisive and was not personally present at any action. His generals received no orders, or received them late.[25]

Lieutenant-Colonel Woldemar von Löwenstern, who served both Barclay de Tolly and Kutusov as an ADC, commented that with Barclay, 'you risked your life every day. With [Kutusov], in contrast, you risked living for ever.'[26]

Kutusov was devious, unfaithful to his wife and, in later years, downright lazy. He could also be vindictive, not least in his treatment of Barclay de Tolly. As one who knew him claimed, 'he imperceptibly undermines anyone whom he [suspects] of sharing in his glory, just as a worm gnaws at a lovely and hated sapling.'[27] Yet it is hard totally to dislike him. He could be a man of immense charm and wit, as the success of his diplomatic postings proved. His orderly wrote:

> Kutusov, it might be said, did not so much speak as play with his tongue. He was a Mozart or a Rossini, who enchanted the ear with his conversational bow. No one was more adept at playing upon the emotions, and no one was subtler in the art of cajoling or seducing, if that was what he had to do.[28]

Execrated by many while he lived, Kutusov was revered after he died. Leo Tolstoy, author of the epic *War and Peace*, presented a sympathetic picture that emphasised Kutusov's wisdom, played down his faults and portrayed him as the personification of the Russian people. Soviet Russia in turn seized on his legend for its own ends and inspired its soldiers with the coveted Order of Kutusov during the Great Patriotic War of 1941–5. But the truth was more down to earth: Kutusov had the usual human failings, women and wine being just two of the more prominent.

Kutusov never actually beat Napoleon in battle and, indeed, feared to cross swords with him. This is where he was inferior to Wellington, Blücher and Archduke Charles. His success in 1812 owed nothing to any skill on the battlefield. It was made possible by Barclay de Tolly's actions in the early stages of Napoleon's invasion and by Alexander's resolve never to negotiate while French troops remained in Russia. In fact, few of the foremost generals of this era have been so overrated.

The Battle of Borodino: 7 September 1812

Except for Waterloo, no Napoleonic battle exerts such fascination as Borodino. It was neither the largest nor the bloodiest battle of the age, for that distinction belongs to Leipzig in 1813, where the casualties numbered at least 100,000, in contrast to the 70,000 odd of Borodino. But Borodino has an intensity of horror uniquely its own.

The battleground that inspires such strong emotions lies eighty miles west of Moscow. It remains much the same as it was in 1812: a constricted, undulating killing ground. Across the northern sector flowed the Kalatsha river, which although fordable had steep banks. Two parallel roads, two miles apart, also swept across the battlefield, from Smolensk in the west to Moscow in the east. The southernmost, or old, road ran through woods and the village of Utitsa. The new road in the north crossed the Kalatsha river at the village of Borodino.

The selection of the Borodino position has been variously attributed to three of Kutusov's officers: Lieutenant-Colonel Harting; Colonel Toll; and General Levin von Bennigsen, his Chief-of-Staff.[29] The Russians in fact

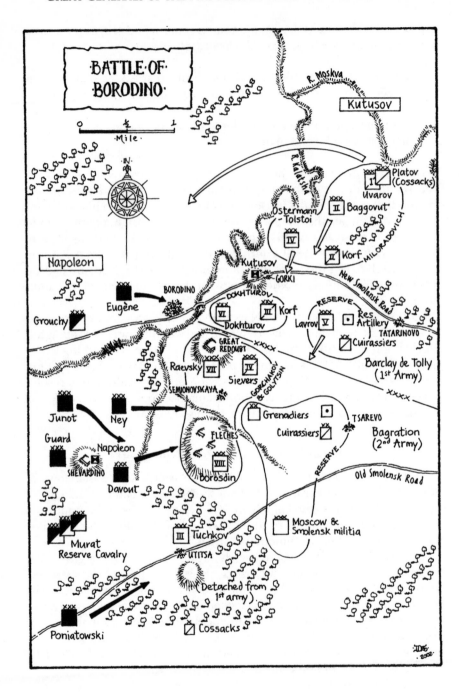

had little choice: the battleground was not ideal as a defensive site, but was the best available one west of Moscow.

Kutusov inspected the field four days before the battle, on 3 September, accompanied as legend would have it by an eagle circling overhead. The first Russian units arrived that day and began to fortify a hill in the centre, which would become known as the Great Redoubt, or the Raevsky Redoubt after the commander of the Russian VII Corps defending it.

Kutusov expected Napoleon to make his main attack along the new road to Moscow and placed Barclay de Tolly's strong 1st Army in the northern sector, behind the Kalatsha river, to cover this approach. Bagration's weaker 2nd Army held the southern sector, which Kutusov examined on 4 September. Barclay de Tolly saw that there were insufficient troops here and wanted to shift his entire 1st Army southwards to shorten 2nd Army's front. But Kutusov ignored the suggestion and Bagration had to make do with the artificial support of two or three flèches, fortifications constructed in the form of arrowheads, pointed at the foe and left open at the rear to facilitate Russian counter-attacks.

Kutusov had placed an infantry division, supported by cavalry and guns, in the Schevardino Redoubt a mile in front of his main position, partly to gain time and partly to help him judge where Napoleon intended to attack his main battle-line. But the decision to hold the redoubt turned out to be a major mistake, for when it was attacked on the evening of the 5th its doomed defence cost the Russians 6,000 men and three guns, a sacrifice out of all proportion to any advantages gained.

After this preliminary action, the next day was strangely quiet. Kutusov, worried by Napoleon's dispositions, had reinforced his extreme southern wing with General Nikolai Tuchkov I's III Corps. He took this unit from the reserves of the 1st Army, but did not bother to inform Barclay and, when Barclay found out, merely assured him that it would not happen again. He also sent, with Tuchkov, 1,500 Cossacks and 7,000 Moscow militiamen, but none of these second-rate troops would be of much use in a pitched battle, except to add to Bagration's apparent strength.

The transfer of Tuchkov's corps meant that Kutusov had depleted his reserves before the battle had even begun, thus disobeying his own orders that they were to be used economically. He had clearly blundered in not following Barclay's advice to shift the whole of 1st Army southwards: as it was, he could now reinforce the weak southern sector only by depleting his reserves or wrecking the chain of command by detaching individual 1st Army units to the 2nd Army sector.

Kutusov's Chief-of-Staff, General Bennigsen, now interfered. Kutusov had wanted Tuchkov to remain hidden in the woods of Utitsa at the end of the southern wing, ready to sally forth at an advantageous moment and fall on the flank of enemy troops as they attacked Bagration farther north.

But, unknown to Kutusov, Bennigsen moved the corps out of the woods and into the open. This breakdown in communication between Kutusov and his Chief-of-Staff reflects well on neither man, but was mostly Bennigsen's fault. 'That man will spoil everything,' said Barclay de Tolly:

> He is jealous and envious. His conceit makes him think that he alone is capable of giving battles and of bringing them to a successful close. He certainly has talent, but he wants to use it only for his own profit. The common, sacred cause is nothing to him. I regard him as a real pest for the army.[30]

That afternoon, Russian soldiers saw a stout man on a large white horse riding round their positions. It was Kutusov exhorting his units. He knew better than anyone how to inspire his simple peasant soldiers. He told them that their children needed protection; he reminded them of their beloved Tsar; he inflamed them with the memory of the city of Smolensk in flames. Above all, he hammered home the message that they were defending the soil of mother Russia and they must hold on to the last drop of their blood. He ensured that they could rest and also played his trump card: the Holy Icon of the Black Virgin. The Russians had saved this image, which they believed to have miraculous powers, from the flames of Smolensk and Kutusov and his soldiers now knelt before it in awe and devotion.[31] Major Woldemar von Löwenstern, ADC to Barclay de Tolly, recorded that 'the army's morale was admirable. Soldiers, officers and generals all burned with the desire to fight or die.'[32]

That night, at his headquarters at the Tatarinovo farmhouse, nearly two miles behind the Russian front line, Kutusov still anxiously pondered where Napoleon would attack. But he made no more changes to his dispositions and so in the end presumably still anticipated the main thrust to come in the north. In fact, the old fox had completely misjudged the situation, for the brunt of Napoleon's onslaughts was going to fall on Bagration's over-extended 2nd Army. Some commentators have argued that Kutusov deliberately kept his southern wing weak, in order to encourage Napoleon to attack this sector frontally rather than try and outflank the northern end of the Russian line. But if this were so, Kutusov would have ensured that reserves could be quickly transferred southwards. He did not. The simple truth is that he allowed his overriding fear for the northern flank to blind him to other weaknesses. Indeed, he seems to have overlooked the fact that the open terrain to the south of his position was more vulnerable to an outflanking move than the steep-sided Kalatsha river in the north.

Against Napoleon's 130,000 men and 587 guns, Kutusov had 120,000 troops and 640 cannon, but of these, his 7,000 Cossacks were fit only for harassment and his 10,000 militiamen from Smolensk and Moscow were too poorly equipped to be of any fighting value. However, General Alexei Ermolov, the chief-of-staff of 1st Army, placed a cordon of these militia, supported by gendarmes, along the Russian rear to stop fugitives leaving the battlefield and to take care of the wounded, thus leaving the regulars with no excuse to leave the ranks.[33]

Borodino was a crowded battlefield, with the Russian formations drawn up close behind each other and in full view of their opponents. This limited the chances of a breakthrough, but was suicidal in the presence of massed enemy cannon. For its part, the Russian artillery had orders not to follow its usual practice of withdrawing the guns to safety whenever threatened. Instead, they were to stand and fight it out side-by-side with the infantry to the bitter end.

The Russian command structure was top-heavy. Kutusov's two immediate subordinates were the army commanders, Barclay de Tolly and Bagration. Within each army, sector commanders had authority over two or more corps. For example, Prince Alexei Gorchakov commanded Bagration's northern wing, which contained VII and VIII Corps and the IV Cavalry Corps. As the battle progressed, this situation became more complicated, since units were transferred from 1st Army to reinforce 2nd Army. Roving senior officers such as Bennigsen and Ermolov further confused the situation by intervening wherever they saw fit. Kutusov himself seemed resolved to let the coming battle unfold with minimal supervision. In his orders, he spoke of merely reacting to the enemy moves and of leaving it to his subordinates to act as they saw best. Once the battle was won, he said, he would issue instructions for the pursuit.[34]

Dawn on Monday 7 September found Kutusov already at his command post in the northern sector of the battlefield, on a knoll immediately west of the village of Gorki and a mile east of Borodino. He wore a dark green coat and white peaked cap and was discussing the impending battle with some of his staff towards 6.00 am when guns boomed from Napoleon's positions. Kutusov dismounted and sat on a stool, as if about to watch a show rather than command an army.

Russian guns now riposted to Napoleon's artillery and enjoyed the advantage of having the rising sun behind them. In the north, a French infantry division seized Borodino village on the west bank of the Kalatsha from a crack Russian Lifeguard *Jäger* regiment, which had been placed in this exposed position against Barclay de Tolly's advice. The French were checked by a fierce Russian counter-attack, but Barclay sensibly did not attempt to regain the village and instead ordered the bridge over the Kalatsha here to be burnt.

After an intense preliminary bombardment in the southern sector, French infantry assaulted Bagration's flèches. Their assaults, although initially successful, were repeatedly hurled back by Russian counter-attacks. So far, the Russians were holding their own, but had already begun seriously to weaken their reserves and to complicate their dispositions. Reinforcements marched to support the hard-pressed Bagration: the bulk of II Corps from 1st Army, plus some guns and Guard infantry from reserve.

The folly of Kutusov's unbalanced dispositions now became clear. II Corps had to run a terrible gauntlet of fire as it marched the three miles across the battlefield to the far southern wing, and as it passed the centre of the line it had to detach two regiments and some guns to restore the situation at the Great Redoubt. Meanwhile, Tuchkov's III Corps at the southern end of the line had detached a division to reinforce Bagration in the flèches and now had to fall back after setting fire to Utitsa village.

Kutusov was remarkably removed from the battle, cocooned as he was in a clique of noble officers and champagne bottles. Every general needs moral support from his staff, but can insulate himself from reality if his retinue numbers 200 or 300 people.[35] Löwenstern visited Kutusov several times during the battle and found him 'surrounded by an enormous staff [and] so placed as to see only very little and to be seen even less. The cannon-balls were something unknown for all these gentlemen.'[36] Indeed, Löwenstern welcomed these visits for they provided a complete break from the dangers and exhaustion of the front; unfortunately, they never lasted more than quarter-of-an-hour.

Kutusov relied on Colonel Toll, the Quartermaster-General of 1st Army, to roam about the battlefield and act as his eyes and ears, even telling him at one point: 'Karl, whatever you say, I'll do.'[37] Kutusov would have done better to have followed the systematic staff procedures that Barclay de Tolly had set out in his regulations, *The Yellow Book*. This would have given him a greater grip on the battle and brought some badly needed regularity into his command arrangements. As it was, Löwenstern noted, 'of the headquarters, I saw only General Bennigsen and Colonel Toll appear on the battlefield.'[38] Napoleon, handicapped by a bad cold and a bladder affliction, would, like Kutusov, exercise command by remote control from a single command post. But at least Napoleon could rely on a tried-and-tested system of staff support and a logical command structure.

Kutusov occasionally mounted his white horse and rode short distances, but mainly stayed at Gorki, too far from the critical southern sector, which was out of sight. Nonetheless, he deserves blame not so much for failure to intervene, but for the haphazard nature of his interventions. He interfered at inconvenient moments, enough to be a nuisance, but not enough to exert a strong influence on events. For example, Barclay de Tolly had formally ordered General Lavroff, commander of the V Corps in reserve, not to detach any units, as he planned to use the corps in the evening to defeat Napoleon's army once it had exhausted itself in repeated assaults. But now Barclay's ADC, Major von Löwenstern, found that Lavroff had broken under the strain of being under fire:

> I found him in a piteous state, almost paralysed, unable either to walk or to mount a horse. He was incapacity personified ... How astonished I was when he told me that, a moment ago, Count Toll had arrived from Kutusov and had just taken from him two regiments of the Guard and two cavalry regiments, to lead them to support the left wing.

Löwenstern told Barclay, who exploded with fury:

> I can truly say that it was the first time that I saw him lose his temper. He, who was so calm, so perfectly in control of himself . . .

Although Kutusov had emphasised that the reserves must not be used too quickly, he had himself done precisely that. Barclay had to gallop over and entreat Kutusov to leave intact what remained of the V Corps and above all not to use the cavalry.

Bad news arrived shortly after 10.00 am: Bagration had been seriously wounded. Kutusov was visibly shaken, for Bagration was one of his favourites, and he ordered Prince Eugen von Württemburg to take command of the 2nd Army. But the prince was only 24, understandably lost his nerve and appealed for support. Kutusov cannily begged him to return, on the grounds that he had realised that he needed him at Gorki and to replace him sent General Dmitri Dokhturov, a steady and capable old veteran who until then had been commanding VI Corps. This botched transfer of command cost vital time and did nothing to limit the confusion. The fall of other Russian generals in the southern sector compounded the crisis and although a Russian counter-attack temporarily recaptured the flèches, the pressure continued to mount.

A powerful French onslaught on the Great Redoubt provoked another crisis, until several senior Russian officers, each reacting separately, organised counter-attacks which happened to converge on the redoubt at about the same time. So bitter was the struggle that a French prisoner, General Charles Bonnamy, suffered thirteen bayonet wounds. Kutusov took one look at the mangled man and shouted 'doctor!' He then exchanged a few words before Bonnamy was taken to the rear.

The Russians also lost heavily in the struggle for the redoubt. Major-General Alexander Kutaisov, commander of the Reserve Artillery of 1st Army, disappeared after leading an infantry attack, leaving the empty, blood-stained saddle of his horse to testify to his fate. He was a brave young man, but with his responsibilities had no business to be playing the role of an infantry captain. His death prevented many of his guns from being brought into action, so that although the Russians had more artillery than Napoleon, they failed to exploit this superiority.

In the south, the battered 2nd Army finally lost the flèches for good after one of its units, the 7th Combined Grenadier Division, had been practically wiped out. The French pressed home their advance and seized the destroyed village of Semionovskaya 500 yards north of the flèches, thus creating a dent in the Russian battle-line. To the south of the Great Redoubt, the Russian front had now been bent back in a vulnerable hinge as the 2nd Army was driven in. The French promptly massed their artillery opposite this point and viciously raked the Russian line to both north and east. Worst hit was General Borosdin's VIII Corps, which might have disintegrated altogether had Napoleon committed his crack Imperial Guard. But the onslaught never came, partly because dense, white smoke hid the chaos in Russian lines, partly because Napoleon was reluctant to risk the possible destruction of his final reserve. Furthermore, a descent of Russian horsemen on his northern flank distracted him from the centre. Kutusov deserves little credit for this crucial move: the idea originated, ironically enough, with Matvei Platov, the dynamic but rather stupid Cossack leader. Colonel Toll conveyed the suggestion to Kutusov, who merely grunted, 'it's good, take it!'

The actual onslaught rapidly degenerated into an anti-climax. At around noon Platov's 2,000 Cossacks and General Sergei Uvarov's I Cavalry Corps of 2,500 regulars crossed the Kalatsha river at the northern end of the Russian line. Uvarov cautiously probed south-westwards and drove back a cavalry division before being checked by French infantry formed in squares. Platov could do little, for his Cossacks were mere mounted raiders. Lacking infantry support and accompanied by only one battery, the Russian horsemen had to fall back. 'May God forgive you!' Kutusov exclaimed to Uvarov. The bitter remark indicated what great expectations the Russians had placed on the move. Little did Kutusov know that the diversion, limited though it was, had caused such alarm that Napoleon had reinforced his northern wing with a division from his Imperial Guard, while a third attack on the Great Redoubt had been postponed.

But all this time, Napoleon's massed guns were relentlessly smashing the Russian line. At about 1.00 pm Major von Löwenstern reached General Ivan Ostermann-Tolstoi, the commander of IV Corps. 'I found him exposed to the most murderous fire that I have seen,' wrote Löwenstern:

> His corps had almost disintegrated. As I talked to him, the cannonballs rained down in such numbers around and next to us and even in our group that at one moment I saw only horses knocked over, men killed and all of us splattered with earth.

Löwenstern had some harsh criticism of the corps commander:

Although as brave as his sword, Count Ostermann did not have the necessary qualities to be a good general. He is very indecisive and when he is in the thick of the action and has, above all, exposed all his men, he believes that he has done everything and leaves the rest to chance . . . They are fighting, they are killing, for him that is the main thing . . . At the moment, he was more engaged than anyone. Those were his tactics, but no orders, no dispositions came from him and he did not have any reserve.[39]

Most Russian generals, like Ostermann, required closer supervision than Kutusov was able to provide from Gorki.

After 2.00 pm, following a two-hour lull, the delayed assault on the Great Redoubt finally went in. The strongpoint fell to a massive cavalry charge, backed up by a renewed infantry push and preceded by an awesome bombardment by 400 guns. The gallant defenders were wiped out, but Russian cavalry charges checked a subsequent French push eastwards. Napoleon still did not dare to commit his Imperial Guard and the battle ended in clashes of massed cavalry. Napoleon had driven the Russians back a mile, but at such heavy cost that he could do no more.

That evening Barclay sent one of his staff, Colonel Ludwig von Wolzogen, to inform Kutusov of the situation and to ask him for orders. Barclay told Wolzogen that he wanted the reply in writing as 'you have to be careful with Kutusov.' To his disgust, Wolzogen found Kutusov's large entourage far behind the front line. He began to tell Kutusov of the shattered state of the army and of the lost positions, only to be shouted down:

With which vulgar camp-follower have you been getting drunk, that you make me so absurd a report? I know best how the battle has gone! The French attacks have been successfully beaten back everywhere, so that tomorrow I shall place myself at the head of the army to drive the enemy without more ado from the sacred soil of Russia!

Kutusov's sycophantic suite duly burst into applause.[40] Wolzogen eventually returned to Barclay with orders to draw up the army into a new defence line, but to make no moves unless Napoleon resumed the battle. The Russians duly fell back 1,000 yards to straighten out their front.

Wolzogen believed that Kutusov's outburst was merely a bluff designed to save the prestige of his position as Commander-in-Chief and hide the fact that he had already decided to retreat.[41] But in fact, Kutusov seems to have miscalculated badly. Had he accepted the reality of the situation, he would have prepared the Tsar for the now inevitable loss of Moscow. Instead, his initial report, sent on the evening of the battle, gave Alexander the false hope of a major victory at Borodino, so much so that he awarded Kutusov a field marshal's baton and 100,000 silver roubles. Thus the subsequent shock of disillusionment would hit Alexander all the harder.

The truth is that Kutusov was too out of touch to know the state of his army and had to send Colonel Toll and another adjutant on a tour of inspection. On their return, they reported devastating losses and low levels of ammunition, finally forcing Kutusov in the early hours of 8 September to announce a retreat.

During the night the French fell back from the positions that they had so bloodily conquered, including the Great Redoubt, and made no attempt to hinder the Russian evacuation of the battlefield, which was complete by 10.00 am on the 8th. The success of the retreat was due to Barclay de Tolly's careful preparations and had nothing to do with Kutusov. Only in the afternoon of the 8th did Marshal Murat's cavalry attempt a pursuit and they were checked west of Mozhaisk, just seven-and-a-half miles east of Borodino.

Carnage littered the battlefield. Guns were the real battlefield killers of the Napoleonic wars. At Borodino, there were 1,227 of them, or 4.8 guns for every 1,000 soldiers, a ratio unequalled at any other battle of the era. Twenty-nine per cent of those who fought at Borodino became casualties, so it was small wonder that Napoleon rated it as the most terrible of his battles. The generals on both sides had suffered horribly, with Napoleon losing forty-seven of them killed and wounded and the Russians twenty-three.

Napoleon had won the battle, but indecisively and at an horrendous cost. Nothing short of the destruction of Kutusov's army would have been a meaningful victory, yet Kutusov could claim little of the credit for the outcome, for his initial dispositions had been faulty and his command methods had caused chaos. The real heroes of Borodino were Bagration and Barclay de Tolly, without whom the Russians would have suffered a disaster. In fact, Kutusov's only positive contribution of any significance was made before the battle began, for he more than anyone boosted the morale of his troops after their long retreat.

NOTES

1   A. Mikhailovsky-Danilevsky, *Vie du feld-maréchal Koutouzoff* (1850), trans. A. Fizelier, p.5
2   *Ibid*, p.12
3   M. Bragin, *Field Marshal Kutuzov* (1944), trans. J. Fineberg, p.17
4   A. Czartoryski, *Mémoires du Prince Adam Czartoryski* (1887), v.1, p.403
5   Bragin, *op. cit.*, p.36
6   A. Mikhailovsky-Danilevsky, *Relation de la campagne de 1805 (Austerlitz)* (1846), pp.247–8
7   Mikhailovsky-Danilevsky, *Vie du feld-maréchal Koutouzoff*, p.50

8   E. Tarlé, *Napoleon's invasion of Russia 1812* (1942), p.124
9   P. Chichagov, *Mémoires inédits de l'amiral Tchitchagoff* (1858), p.43
10 R. Parkinson, *The fox of the north* (1976), p.1
11 R. Wilson, *Narrative of events during the invasion of Russia* (1860), pp.130–1
12 St Petersburg was the political capital.
13 Mikhailovsky-Danilevsky, *Vie du feld-maréchal Koutouzoff*, pp.92–3
14 *Ibid*, p.93
15 These were the 1st and 2nd Armies of the West, which at the start of the campaign operated separately under Barclay de Tolly and Bagration, but which united at Smolensk in August.
16 La Société d'histoire contemporaine, *Mémoires de Langeron* (1902), p.40
17 A. Brett-James, *1812: eyewitness accounts of Napoleon's defeat in Russia* (1967), p.264
18 C. von Müffling, *The memoirs of Baron von Müffling* (1997), p.31; Wilson, *op. cit.*, p.131
19 Tarlé, *op. cit.*, p.124
20 Parkinson, *op. cit.*, p.125
21 Bragin, *op. cit.*, p.25
22 *Ibid*, p.60
23 *Ibid*, p.27
24 P. de Ségur, *History of the expedition to Russia* (1825), v.1, pp.307–8
25 La Société d'histoire contemporaine, *op. cit.*, p.39
26 M. Weil, ed., *Mémoires du général-major russe Baron de Löwenstern* (1903) v.1, p.292
27 Tarlé, *op. cit.*, p.123
28 *Idem*
29 See E. Cazalas, *Mémoires du général Bennigsen* (nd), p.80.
30 M.-H. Weil, ed., *op. cit.*, v.1, p.269
31 Löwenstern stated that Kutusov 'showed himself little'. This does not seem to have been true for 6 September. Naturally, however, he would not have been able to see all his soldiers.
32 Weil, *op. cit.*, v.1, p.253
33 *Ibid*, v.1, p.273
34 D. Smith, *Borodino* (1998), p.57
35 Weil, *op. cit.*, v.1, p.269
36 *Ibid*, v.1, p.261
37 M. & D. Josselson, *The commander: a life of Barclay de Tolly* (1980), p.142
38 Weil, *op. cit.*, v.1, p.269
39 Weil, *op. cit.*, v.1, p.263
40 J. von Wolzogen, *Memoiren des königl. preuss. Generals Ludwig Freiherrn von Wolzogen* (1851), pp.145–7
41 This was also the interpretation of one of Kutusov's adjutants, Golitsyn. See C. Duffy, *Borodino and the war of 1812* (1972), p.134

Further Reading

Introduction

For the background to the Napoleonic era, try Michael Glover, *The Napoleonic wars: an illustrated history 1792–1815* (London, 1979) and Charles Esdaile, *The wars of Napoleon* (London, 1995). Atlases include Vincent Esposito and John Elting, *A military history and atlas of the Napoleonic wars* (New York, 1965; reissued London, 1999) and Jean-Claude Quennevat, *Atlas de la Grande Armée: Napoléon et ses campagnes* (Paris, 1966).

Some reference books are particularly useful: Digby Smith, *The Greenhill Napoleonic wars data book* (London, 1998); David Chandler, *A dictionary of the Napoleonic wars* (London, 1979); Philip Haythornthwaite, *The Napoleonic source book* (London, 1990) and *Who was who in the Napoleonic wars* (London, 1998); Georges Six, *Dictionnaire biographique des généraux et amiraux français de la Révolution et de l'Empire* (Paris, 1934), 2v and his analytical accompanying work *Les généraux de la Révolution et de l'Empire* (Paris, 1947). See also David Chandler, ed., *Napoleon's marshals* (London, 1987; reissued 1998) and Tony Linck, *Napoleon's generals: the Waterloo campaign* (Chicago, nd). For a guide to specialised research, refer to Donald Horward, *Napoleonic military history: a bibliography* (London, 1986).

Chapter I: Napoleon

Napoleon is so controversial a figure that some biographies hardly seem to describe the same man. Compare the warm portrait in Vincent Cronin, *Napoleon* (London, 1971) with the scathing indictment in Correlli Barnett's *Bonaparte* (New York, 1973). Pieter Geyl gives a useful survey of the arguments in *Napoleon: for and against* (London, 1948; reissued 1987).

The indispensable work on Napoleon's military mind and methods is David Chandler's *The campaigns of Napoleon* (London, 1966). See also Owen Connelly, *Blundering to glory: Napoleon's military campaigns* (Wilmington, 1987); John Elting, *Swords around a throne: Napoleon's Grande Armée* (London, 1988) and Sir James Marshall-Cornwall, *Napoleon as military commander* (London, 1967).

For Austerlitz, see Christopher Duffy, *Austerlitz 1805* (London, 1977); and Scott Bowden, *Napoleon and Austerlitz* (Chicago, 1997).

Chapter II: Eugène de Beauharnais

Carola Oman, daughter of the historian Sir Charles Oman, produced *Napoleon's viceroy: Eugène de Beauharnais* (London, 1966), an important study but one that concentrates on the man rather than the soldier, besides being occasionally inaccurate and confusing for those with little prior knowledge of the subject. Other biographies of Eugène do exist, but mostly in French or German. See, for example, Violette Montagu, *Eugène de Beauharnais: the adopted son of Napoleon* (London, 1913); Frédéric Vaudoncourt, *Histoire politique et militaire du Prince Eugène* (Paris, 1828), 2v; Françoise de Bernardy, *Eugène de Beauharnais* (Paris, 1973) and Prince Alphonso Adalbert, *Eugen Beauharnais, der Stiefsohn Napoleons* (Munich, 1950). Some of these are subjective: General Frédéric Vaudoncourt, for example, was a friend of Eugène. Valuable primary evidence exists in André du Casse, ed., *Mémoires et correspondance politique et militaire du Prince Eugène* (Paris, 1858–60), 10v. Also of interest are Owen Connelly, *Napoleon's satellite kingdoms* (New York, 1965) and Musée national des châteaux de Malmaison et Bois-Préau, *Eugène de Beauharnais: honneur et fidélité* (Paris, 1999).

For Eugène's record as a soldier, read Robert Epstein, *Prince Eugène at war, 1809: a study of the role of Prince Eugène de Beauharnais in the Franco-Austrian war of 1809* (Arlington, 1984) and Frederick Schneid, *Soldiers of Napoleon's Kingdom of Italy* (Oxford, 1995). Eugène's defence of the Kingdom of Italy in 1813–14 is covered in: Reuben Rath, *The fall of the Napoleonic Kingdom of Italy* (New York, 1941); Maurice Weil, *Le Prince Eugène et Murat 1813–1814* (Paris, 1902), 5v; Camillo Vacani, *Bataille du Mincio du 8 Février 1814 entre l'armée du prince Eugène et celle du maréchal comte de Bellegarde* (Milan, 1857) and Georg vom Holtz, *Die Innerösterreichische Armee, 1813 und 1814* (Vienna, 1912). For a biography of Eugène's opponent at the Mincio, see Karl von Smola, *Das Leben des Feldmarschalls Heinrich Grafen von Bellegarde* (Vienna, 1847).

Chapter III: Lasalle

The outstanding biography of Lasalle is François Hourtoulle, *Le général comte Charles Lasalle 1775–1809* (Paris, 1979). Note also: Robinet de Cléry, *D'Essling à Wagram: Lasalle* (Paris, 1891); Marcel Dupont, *Le général Lasalle* (Paris, 1929) and Tancrède Martel, *Un galant chevalier: le général Lasalle (1775–1809)* (Paris, 1929). No biography of Lasalle yet exists in English, but David Johnson, *The French cavalry, 1792–1815* (London, 1989) vividly conveys the spirit of Napoleon's mounted arm.

For the Battle of Medellin, see especially Sir Charles Oman, *A history of the Peninsular war* (Oxford, 1902–30; reissued London, 1995–7), v.2; and Albert de Rocca, *In the Peninsula with a French hussar* (London, 1990).

Chapter IV: Moore

The standard biographies are: Roger Parkinson, *Moore of Corunna* (London, 1975) and Carola Oman, *Sir John Moore* (London, 1953). See also Sir John Maurice, ed., *The diary of Sir John Moore* (London, 1904), 2v.

David Gates, *The British light infantry arm c.1790–1815* (London, 1987) reassesses Moore's role at Shorncliffe, while D.W. Davies presents a provocative re-interpretation of the Coruña campaign in: *Sir John Moore's Peninsular campaign, 1808–1809* (The Hague, 1974).

For the Battle of Coruña, see Christopher Hibbert, *Corunna* (London, 1961); Sir Charles Oman, *A history of the Peninsular war* (Oxford, 1902–30; reissued London, 1995–7), v.1 and Sir John Fortescue, *History of the British army* (London, 1899–1930), v.6.

Chapter V: Wellington

Among the best studies of Wellington's military career are: Elizabeth Longford, *Wellington: the years of the sword* (London, 1969); Sir Herbert Maxwell, *The life of Wellington* (London, 1900), 2v and Jac Weller's famous trilogy: *Wellington in India* (London, 1972; reissued 1993), *Wellington in the Peninsula* (London, 1962; reissued 1999) and *Wellington at Waterloo* (London, 1967; reissued 1998). A supplementary collection of Weller's essays is entitled: *On Wellington: the Duke and his art of war* (London, 1998). See also Ian Robertson, *Wellington at war in the Peninsula 1808–1814: an overview and guide* (Barnsley, 2000) and Andrew Uffindell, *The National Army Museum book of Wellington's armies,* due to be published in October 2003.

Paddy Griffith, ed., *Wellington commander* (Chichester, 1985) provides a readable survey, which can be supplemented with Antony Brett-James's edited selection of the Duke's correspondence: *Wellington at war, 1794–1815* (London, 1961). Relevant essays will be found in the new, ninth volume to Sir Charles Oman's *A history of the Peninsular war* (London, 1999), edited by Paddy Griffith, and also in Norman Gash, ed., *Wellington: studies in the military and political career of the First Duke of Wellington* (Manchester, 1990).

For some fascinating specialised studies, see Robin Thomas, 'Wellington in the Low Countries, 1794–1795,' in *The International History Review* (1989) and Stephen G.P. Ward, *Wellington's headquarters: a study of the administrative problems in the Peninsula, 1809–1814* (Oxford, 1957). Rory Muir puts Wellington in perspective by examining the role of the British government in *Britain and the defeat of Napoleon 1807–1815* (London, 1996), while Charles Esdaile provides a fresh view of Wellington in the Peninsula in *The Duke of Wellington and the command of the Spanish Army, 1812–14* (London, 1990). For detail on Waterloo, see Andrew Uffindell and Michael Corum, *On the fields of glory: the battlefields of the 1815 campaign* (London, 1996). Andrew Roberts traces the fascinating evolution of the way in which Wellington and Napoleon viewed each other in: *Napoleon and Wellington* (London, 2001).

Wellington's reminiscences can be found in: Earl of Stanhope, *Notes of conversations with the Duke of Wellington* (London, 1938); John Croker, *The Croker papers* (London, 1885), 3v and The Seventh Duke of Wellington, *Conversations of the First Duke of Wellington with George William Chad* (1956).

Sir Charles Oman, *A history of the Peninsular war* (Oxford, 1902–30; reissued London, 1995–7), v.7 and Sir John Fortescue, *History of the British army* (London, 1899–1930), v.10 are invaluable sources for the Battle of Toulouse, but perhaps the most detailed examination of the battle is Jean-Paul Escalettes, *10 avril 1814: la bataille de Toulouse* (Poret-sur-Garonne, 1999).

Chapter VI: Hill

The latest biography of Hill is Gordon Teffeteller, *The surpriser: the life of Rowland, Lord Hill* (Newark, 1983). The Reverend Edwin Sidney was Hill's private chaplain and wrote *The life of Lord Hill, G.C.B.* (London, 1845).

For detailed accounts of Arroyo dos Molinos, see: Sir Charles Oman, *A history of the Peninsular war* (Oxford, 1902–30; reissued London, 1995–7), v.4 and Sir John Fortescue, *History of the British army* (London, 1899–1930), v.8.

Chapter VII: Archduke Charles

The outstanding work in English is Gunther Rothenberg, *Napoleon's great adversaries: the Archduke Charles and the Austrian army 1792–1814* (London, 1982; revised edition published in 1995), but official German biographies include: Moriz von Angeli, *Erzherzog Karl von Österreich als Feldherr und Heeresorganisator* (Vienna, 1896–8), 5v. Try also Oskar Criste, *Erzherzog Carl von Österreich* (Vienna, 1912), 3v. Alexander Rodger, *The war of the Second Coalition, 1798–1801* (London, 1964) illuminates the background to some of Charles's actions during the Revolutionary wars, while Francis Loraine Petre, *Napoleon and the Archduke Charles* (1976) is a detailed but dull account of the 1809 campaign.

For the battle of Aspern–Essling, see Ian Castle, *Aspern & Wagram 1809: mighty clash of empires* (London, 1994; reissued 1998) and Harold Parker, *Three Napoleonic battles* (Durham, NC, 1983).

Chapter VIII: Blücher and Gneisenau

The best biography of Blücher in English is Roger Parkinson, *Hussar general: the life of Blücher, man of Waterloo* (London, 1975). See also: August von Gneisenau, ed., *The life and campaigns of Field Marshal Blücher* (London, 1815; reissued 1996); Paul Vermeil de Conchard, *Marshal Prince Blücher as portrayed in his correspondence* (London, 1896); and E. Henderson, *Blücher and the uprising of Prussia against Napoleon 1806–1815* (London, 1911). A leading German account of his life is: Wolfgang von Unger, *Blücher* (Berlin, 1907–8), 2v. Unger's *Blüchers Briefe* (Berlin, 1913) is also useful.

For Gneisenau, try Georg Pertz and Hans Delbrück, *Das Leben des Feldmarschalls Grafen Neithardt von Gneisenau* (Berlin, 1864–94), 5v, and Hans Otto, *Gneisenau: Preussens unbequemer Patriot* (Bonn, 1979). Carl von Müffling served on Blücher's staff throughout the campaigns of 1813–14 and as the Prussian liaison officer with Wellington's army in 1815. His reminiscences, *The memoirs of Baron von Müffling* (reissued, London, 1997), are interesting but sometimes unreliable, given his tendency to exaggerate his own role.

A good account of the 1813 campaign is: Antony Brett-James, *Europe against Napoleon: the Leipzig campaign of 1813 from eyewitness accounts* (London, 1970); for the 1814 campaign, see: Henry Houssaye, *Napoleon and the campaign of 1814* (London, 1914), trans. R. McClintock. Houssaye is particularly interesting on the Battle of Laon. See also Joseph Tyran, *Laon, ville militaire* (Cambrai, 1999). For Blücher's role in the 1815 campaign, see Andrew Uffindell, *The eagle's last triumph: Napoleon's victory at Ligny, June 1815* (London, 1994).

Of related interest are the memoirs of Blücher's great-great-grandson: see Evelyn, Princess Blücher and Major Desmond Chapman-Huston, ed., *Memoirs of Prince Blücher* (London, 1932).

Chapter IX: Bagration and Barclay de Tolly

For an excellent biography of Barclay de Tolly, see Michael and Diana Josselson, *The commander* (Oxford, 1980). A similar English-language account of Bagration's life and career is badly needed, for at present his only biographies are in Russian.

Accounts of the epic 1812 campaign include George Nafziger's *Napoleon's invasion of Russia* (Novato, 1988; reissued 1998); Eugene Tarlé, *Napoleon's invasion of Russia 1812* (London, 1942); Antony Brett-James, *1812: eyewitness accounts of Napoleon's defeat in Russia* (London, 1967) and Paul Britten Austin's magnificent trilogy based on memoirs by soldiers of the Grand Army: *1812: the march on Moscow; Napoleon in Moscow; The great retreat* (London, 1993–6). All these authors give details of the bitter fighting at Smolensk.

Chapter X: Kutusov

Leo Tolstoy's unforgettable *War and peace* (1863–9; reissued 1993) paints a subjective picture of Kutusov. The standard Soviet accounts contain useful information but are also biased. See, for example, M. Bragin, *Field Marshal Kutuzov* (Moscow, 1944), trans. J. Fineberg. Roger Parkinson's *The fox of the north* (London, 1976) is the best biography in English, but plays down Kutusov's flaws. For a refreshingly hostile view, see A. Brett-James, ed., *General Wilson's journal* (London, 1964). Alexander Mikhailovsky-Danilevsky, *Vie du feld-maréchal Koutouzoff* (St Petersburg, 1850), trans A. Fizelier, is also useful.

Christopher Duffy, *Borodino: Napoleon against Russia* (London, 1972) and Digby Smith, *Borodino* (Moreton-in-Marsh, 1998) are the best English-language accounts of the epic battle. Digby Smith speculates on how the Russians could have won Borodino in 'The Russians at Borodino', part of a collection of essays edited by Jonathan North, *The Napoleon options: alternate decisions of the Napoleonic wars* (London, 2000).

Index